D0096417

The Tour to End All Tours

The Story of Major League Baseball's 1913–1914 World Tour

James E. Elfers

University of Nebraska Press
Lincoln and London

Unless otherwise credited, photos are reprinted from
World Tour National and American League Base Ball Teams
October 1913 March 1914: The Triumph of Organized Base Ball.
Photographs by Frank Farrell, M. Dick Bunnell, and Lee Magee.
Chicago: S. Blake Willsden, 1914.
Library of Congress Cataloging-in-Publication Data
Elfers, James E., 1963–
The Tour to End All Tours : The story of Major League
Baseball's 1913–1914 world tour / James E. Elfers.
p. cm.
Includes bibliographical references and index.
ISBN 0-8032-6748-7 (paper : alk. paper)
1. Tour to End All Tours (1913–1914).
2. Baseball–History–20th century.
I. Title.
GV862.5 .E54 2003
797.357'09041–dc21
2002074220

"N"

To my family
To my wife, Eileen
And to my sons,
Zachary and Jonathan

Contents

List of Illustrations, ix
Preface, xi
Acknowledgments, xiii
Dramatis Personae, xvii
Schedule, xxi
1. A Tour Is Born, 1
2. Filling Out the Lineup, 10
3. Base Paths a Continent Wide, 34
4. Pacific Dreams, 73
5. Across a Restless Sea, 94
6. The Land of the Rising Sun, 108
7. China and Points East, 122
8. Uncle Sam's Tropical Playground, 135
9. Baseball Down Under, 145
10. Sir Thomas Lipton and the Shadow of the Pyramids, 171
11. Across a Storm-Tossed Europe, 197
12. Baseball Fit for a King, 227
Afterword, 245
Coda, 251
Notes, 253
Bibliographic Essay, 265
Index, 269

Illustrations

Following page 114

Pitching great Christy Mathewson in Blue Rapids, Kansas

The Giants and White Sox stride into Blue Rapids, Kansas

Wally Mattick Evans squares around to bunt

An advertisement for the world tour

White Sox manager Jimmy Callahan

White Sox owner and president Charles Comiskey

The New York Giants world tour roster

New York Giants manager John McGraw

The White Sox welcome-home banquet, 10 March 1914

Filipinos attending the first game in Manila

Attempting to sweep the water off the
diamond prior to the final ballgame in Manila

A snake charmer

Josephine Callahan gets a camel's-eye view of ancient Egypt

Tourists examine the plane of Mark Poupre

Comiskey, McGraw, and Callahan just
moments after their audience with the pope

Buck Weaver inspects the equipment box

London's Chelsea Football Grounds decked out for baseball

Umpire Bill Klem gets a ride in a Tokyo ricksha

King George V observes the game with interest

The White Sox world tour roster

Political cartoon about the new Federal League

Preface

Ninety years ago, some of the most colorful men ever to play the game of baseball performed a remarkable feat. During the world's last golden winter of promise, when there was no such term as "world war," Charles A. Comiskey and John J. McGraw took their baseball teams around the world. More amazingly, after an odyssey of thirty thousand miles through thirteen nations, their tour was promptly forgotten about.

This story has fascinated me ever since I came across the tale by accident more than ten years ago. While engaged in some research for Kevin Kerrane, an English professor at the University of Delaware and author of several wonderful baseball books, I stumbled across some moldering accounts of this baseball adventure in the stacks and files of the Baseball Hall of Fame Library in Cooperstown, New York. I had heard of the tour before, but I had no idea that their adventures had been so robust. Delighted with the discovery, I was amazed that almost nothing had been written about this tour since 1914. It was almost as though the tour had never occurred.

I knew then that this was a story that had to be told. This tour was, after all, Jim Thorpe's first exposure on the international stage after the loss of his Olympic medals in 1912. This is a tour that involved two of the first five inductees to Cooperstown. How could men such as these gallop across the nation and around the world only to have their adventure be almost completely forgotten?

Plunging through piles of microfilm, I discovered a tour far more lively than I had even imagined. An almost shipwreck, a broiled ox head, a midnight party on the roof of the Manila Hotel, unexplained doings by baseball players in Shanghai; it was a boys' adventure writ large by men who played a child's game for a living.

In telling this story, I relied entirely on firsthand accounts. Newspapers from towns large and small gave me insights into how this tour was perceived by the inhabitants of so many different towns with so many different tastes. What was a boon for Blue Rapids, Kansas, was looked askance at in Los Angeles. In sports page after sports page, I found gems—stories and turns of phrase that were just too good to ignore. The Chicago newspapers provided the best coverage of the world tour and proved most invaluable. Especially useful were the writings of G. W. Axelson for the *Chicago Record-Herald*. One of two journalists to accompany the teams around the world, Axelson's accounts are full of details and gossip that the columns of H. P. Burchell of the *New York Times* lack. Burchell, who also served as John McGraw's ghostwriter for the tour, provides useful information, but when he writes as John McGraw, we encounter a John McGraw who is nothing like the genuine article. Burchell placed his subjects upon a much higher pedestal than did Axelson, resulting in a more stilted, less memorable style.

I think it only fair to the reader that I make it clear that I am a fan of neither the Giants nor the White Sox. As a lifelong Phillies fan, I have no ax to grind with either team. Whatever biases or viewpoints the reader may detect, rest assured that they do not come from the author being a disgruntled Giants fan or a rabid White Sox rooter. In telling the story, I have out of necessity focused on a few principals. McGraw, Comiskey, Thorpe, and Herman Schaefer feature prominently, but other players like Mike Donlin and Fred Merkle get their just due as well. *The Tour to End All Tours* tells a story from a lost era, a single season's worth of adventure crammed into one winter, the last winter when the world would ever know peace.

At some points in the text the reader will discover "baseball" rendered as one word while in other places as two words. I have tried to stay consistent with the usage of the original sources. In the teens, the word "baseball" itself was in flux. *Sporting Life*, based in Philadelphia, usually wrote "base ball" as two words, while the *Sporting News*, based out of St. Louis, usually wrote the word as "baseball." In Chicago and New York, papers used either spelling, and across the country it was whatever the local editor decided. By the 1920s "baseball" became one word the world over, even as the world became more divided and more inconsistent.

Acknowledgments

Without the help and support of a lot of wonderful people, this book would not have been possible. Kevin Kerrane, professor of English at the University of Delaware and gifted baseball writer, believed in this project from the beginning. He has been exceedingly generous with his time and his wisdom. His insights and knowledge about the publishing business were greatly appreciated and indispensable.

I am truly indebted to Don Musil of Blue Rapids, Kansas. Don provided the George Hewitt photographs, taken in 1913, that are included in this book. Other photographs were provided by the good people of Blue Rapids through the Office of the Mayor. Don was also nice enough to interview Ben Mall, the last living witness to the tour, for me. Additionally, Don loaned me his copy of *World Tour National and American League Base Ball Teams October 1913 March 1914: The Triumph of Organized Base Ball*, for electronic scanning. Working from an original copy, with Frank Farrell's wonderful photographs, certainly beat my dog-eared photocopy. I really cannot thank Don enough for his help. Lynn Turner, librarian of the Blue Rapids Public Library, put me in touch with Don, for which I am extremely grateful.

I am deeply grateful to Jim Thorpe's relatives. His daughters, Gail and Grace Thorpe, and his grandson Mike Kholer were all wonderful to me. Each shared invaluable stories, reminiscences, and information about Jim Thorpe. Gail and Grace were nice enough to provide me with a photocopy of their mother's world tour diary, an absolutely priceless resource.

Jack Dougherty of the Society of American Baseball Researchers has provided me over the years with literally a shelfful of books. Time and again, when looking something up, I discover that the book consulted was one of the many that Jack has given me. Thank you, Jack, for your friendship and for making all of this so much easier.

Rob Edelman, also of the Society of American Baseball Researchers, provided information about Victor Miller, the tour's cameraman.

William Hoffman of Durham, North Carolina, was very encouraging about this project from the very beginning. He made it clear to me that this idea was a winner. His insights into the publishing and writing businesses were most enlightening.

I want to thank my friend Chris Wolfe of the University of Delaware's English Language Institute. Chris found a Japanese student, Hisashi Ito, who was willing to try his hand at translating some very antiquated Japanese kanji from 1913. Thanks to both of you.

Kate Buford from New York City provided some great advice. We also shared some wonderful gab sessions. I just hope I was as great a help to her as she was to me.

Dave Thomas of the New York Academy of Natural Sciences provided me with some excellent information on Jim Thorpe's minor league baseball career of the 1920s.

Richard C. Lindberg, author of *The White Sox Encyclopedia* and other books about the White Sox, was giving of his time and provided me with some good leads.

I want to thank the staff of the interlibrary loan department of the University of Delaware. They were able to obtain just about everything I requested, including microfilm of some pretty obscure newspapers.

Rich Campbell provided early proofreading help and was always willing to listen to me prattle on about and pray about this book. He's a wiz at operating microfilm readers, too.

I want to thank Keith Crabbs for the prayers, lunches, and encouraging words.

My wife, Eileen, whom my coworkers refer to simply as "the saint," deserves thanks in abundance for tolerating her husband's obsession with baseball in general and this book in particular. She has put up with much over the years, and there is no way that I could ever thank her enough. No man ever had a better friend, confidant, or helpmate.

If I have left anyone out from this list, please accept my sincere apologies.

I'd like to close by thanking Dave Saadeh for his encouragement. Dave and I spent many happy hours together, attending ball games and being friends. I did things with him I never even did with my own brothers. David's wonderful life of faith was cut short by cancer on 13 April 1997. A juggler and clown of the first rank, Dave could sometimes be spied doing his thing atop the Phillies' dugout in Veterans Stadium. A few weeks before he returned to the Lord, I was granted a wonderful afternoon, where we talked for hours. We talked about everything, including baseball. I told him once of my dreams of a book about the tour. Dave, like he did for everyone he met, encouraged me. I knew that I had to write this book—I could never stand disappointing Dave. As it says on your headstone, Dave, "Beloved Son, Husband, Father, and Friend." I was blessed to be called your friend. Opening Day will never be the same without you.

Dramatis Personae

The World Girdlers

Charles A. Comiskey – Owner and president of the Chicago White Sox, Comiskey supplied the main bankroll for the tour.

Nancy Comiskey – Charles Comiskey's wife.

J. Louis Comiskey – Charles Comiskey's son and heir.

Grace Comiskey – Wife of Lou Comiskey, a honeymooner.

John J. McGraw – Manager of the New York Giants, greatest manager in the history of the National League.

Blanche McGraw – Wife of John McGraw.

Jimmy Callahan – Manager of the Chicago White Sox. One of the original White Sox of 1901, Callahan was on his second go-round as manager of the Sox.

Josephine Callahan – Wife of Jimmy Callahan and mother of Margaret and Danny.

G. W. "Gus" Axelson – Reporter for the *Chicago Record-Herald*.

Joe "Blitzen" Benz – Wildly popular but erratic right-handed White Sox pitcher.

John Joseph "Jack" Bliss – Former big league catcher. Recruited off of the roster of the Pacific Coast League's Sacramento Senators for the tour.

William Buhl – Chicago businessman and White Sox fan who paid his own passage to accompany his favorite team around the world.

H. P. Burchell – Reporter for the *New York Times*.

"Wahoo" Sam Crawford – Detroit Tiger and Hall of Fame inductee. Played next to Ty Cobb for years while genially despising him.

Tom Daly – Canadian catcher who was constantly having his name misspelled in the papers. Hit the game-winning home run in London.

"Turkey" Mike Donlin – Hard-drinking actor/baseball player with a vicious,

violent temper. Toured vaudeville with his wife, Mabel Hite. Recruited from Newark, New Jersey, team of the International League.

Mickey Doolan – Phillies shortstop during the 1913 season. Phenomenally gifted at guessing how many knots the various ships on which the tourists sailed covered each day.

"Laughing Larry" Doyle – Team captain and second baseman of the New York Giants. Won Chalmers Award as the best hitter in the National League for 1912. Newly married, he and his wife, Edith, had an around-the-world honeymoon.

Dick Egan – Utility player, primarily a shortstop with the Cincinnati Reds who ended up with the White Sox for the world tour.

Steve Evans – Comedian and outfielder from the St. Louis Cardinals who donned American League colors for the duration of the tour.

Urban "Red" Faber – The White Sox's top minor league pitching prospect. When the Giants found themselves a pitcher short, Red Faber was loaned to the Giants for the duration of the tour. Eventual Hall of Famer.

Frank Farrell – Owner of the New York Yankees. One of the most obsessive photographers on the tour.

Joe Farrell – Active member of the Woodland Bards Association, a group that existed to celebrate all things having to do with Charles Comiskey. No relation to Frank Farrell.

Dr. Frank Finlay – John McGraw's doctor.

John Gleason – Owner of the rights to the motion picture of the tour.

Mrs. D. Hardin – A widow, James J. Callahan's mother-in law.

J. Hill – Chicago tourist off for adventure with the Sox.

Mrs. Frank Isbell and infant daughter – Frank Isbell's old body became too worn out to play baseball, so he abandoned the tour in Seattle. While his wife and daughter went off to see the world, Frank went off to Washington State for six months of hunting and fishing.

Bunn "Bunny" Hearn – Giants left-handed relief pitcher. Bunny had a pronounced drawl and a love for maritime adventure stories. He spent most of the tour reading cheap sea novels.

Mrs. Hugh Keough – Widow of Hugh Keough, the first great baseball photographer. During the sea cruises, Mike Donlin would put the moves on her.

Arthur T. Kinney – Signed John McGraw to his first professional baseball contract. Offering him a spot on the tour was one of the many ways that McGraw said thank-you to the man who saved his life.

Bill Klem – Home plate umpire for the world tour and John McGraw's constant irritant.

Walter Leverenz – Left-handed pitcher from the American League's St. Louis Browns who toured the world as a member of the White Sox.

Hans Lobert – Lightning-fast Phillies second baseman who raced a horse around the bases. During the Pacific crossing, he raced surging waves to prevent his wife, Rea, from being pulled out to sea.

Thomas Lynch – Rotund Chicago businessman and Sox fan on the world tour at his own expense.

Lee Magee – Giants left fielder, borrowed from the St. Louis Cardinals.

James A. McAleer – The recently forced out president of the Boston Red Sox. On tour in part to chaperone Tris Speaker, the BoSox's biggest box office draw.

N. E. McBride – Member of the Illinois state legislature and a lifelong Comiskey confidant.

Frank McGlynn – Movie director of the film *Giants–White Sox World Tour*, the world's first full-length sports documentary.

Rev. John McNamara – John McGraw's personal priest. Rev. McNamara befriended McGraw during his days in Baltimore with the Orioles of the National League. McGraw paid the priest's way around the world.

Fred Merkle – Much maligned first baseman of the New York Giants.

Victor Miller – The cameraman working under Frank McGlynn's direction.

John Mullen – Owner of a Chicago brewery, he was also a White Sox fan and a member of the Woodland Bards Association.

N. L. O'Neil – Treasurer of the White Sox world tour, he was in charge of paying the bills.

William Ryan – White Sox fan touring on his own change.

Herman "Germany" Schaefer – Member of the White Sox and the tour's comedian.

James "Death Valley Jim" Scott – White Sox pitcher married to one of Joe Benz's cousins.

Jack Sheridan – Walruslike base umpire for the tour.

Andy Slight – Minor leaguer assigned to the Sox for some seasoning.

Harry Sparrow – Comiskey's secretary, responsible for scheduling games and lining up transportation.

Tristam "Tris" Speaker – Possibly the greatest fielding outfielder in history and one of the game's great pure hitters. Hall of Famer but not a good sailor.

Timothy Paul "Ted" Sullivan – Held the purse strings for the tour. Comiskey's best friend.

James and Iva Thorpe – Honeymooning couple. The world's greatest athlete would be one of the sensations of the tour both at home and abroad.

George "Buck" Weaver – White Sox shortstop. Later an all-time great at third base.

George "Hooks" Wiltse – Giants curveball specialist.

Ivy Wingo – Giants catcher and general whiner.

Schedule of Games and Results

1.	18 October 1913	Cincinnati	Giants 11, White Sox 2
2.	19 October 1913	Chicago	Giants 3, White Sox 1
3.	20 October 1913	Springfield, Illinois	Giants 6, White Sox 4
4.	21 October 1913	Peoria, Illinois	White Sox 6, Giants 4
5.	22 October 1913	Ottumwa, Iowa	White Sox 7, Giants 2
6.	23 October 1913	Sioux City, Iowa	Giants 6, White Sox 3
7.	24 October 1913	Blue Rapids, Kansas	White Sox 8, Giants 5
8.	25 October 1913	St. Joseph, Missouri	White Sox 4, Giants 3
9.	26 October 1913	Kansas City, Missouri	Giants 6, White Sox 2
10.	27 October 1913	Joplin, Missouri	Giants 13, White Sox 12
11.	28 October 1913	Tulsa, Oklahoma	White Sox 6, Giants 0
12.	29 October 1913	Muskogee, Oklahoma	White Sox 7, Giants 1
13.	30 October 1913	Bonham, Texas	Giants 4, White Sox 1
14.	31 October 1913	Dallas	White Sox 10, Giants 3
15.	1 November 1913	Beaumont, Texas	Giants 3, White Sox 2
16.	2 November 1913	Houston	White Sox 9, Giants 4
17.	3 November 1913	Marlin, Texas	Giants 11, White Sox 1
	4 November 1913	Abilene, Texas	RAIN
18.	5 November 1913	El Paso, Texas	White Sox 10, Giants 7
19.	6 November 1913	Douglas, Arizona	Giants 14, White Sox 5
20.	7 November 1913	Bisbee, Arizona	Giants 9, White Sox 1
21.	8 November 1913	Los Angeles	White Sox 5, Giants 3
22.	9 November 1913	Los Angeles	White Sox 7, Giants 7
			(called on account of darkness)
23.	10 November 1913	San Diego, California	Giants 4, White Sox 3
24.	11 November 1913	Oxnard, California	Giants 3, White Sox 2
	12 November 1913	Sacramento, California	RAIN
25.	13 November 1913	Oakland, California	White Sox 5, Giants 2

26. 14 November 1913 San Francisco   White Sox 3, Giants 2
27. 15 November 1913 San Francisco   Giants 6, White Sox 3
28. 16 November 1913 (A.M.)Oakland, California White Sox 12, Giants 8
29. 16 November 1913 (P.M.)San Francisco   White Sox 4, Giants 2
30. 17 November 1913 Medford, Oregon   Giants 3, White Sox 0
                                               (6 innings)
31. 18 November 1913 Portland, Oregon   White Sox 2, Giants 0
     19 November 1913 (A.M.) Tacoma, Washington RAIN
     19 November 1913 (P.M.) Seattle   RAIN

On the evening of 19 November 1913 the Giants and White Sox left from
Victoria, British Columbia, for Japan aboard the R.M.S. *Empress of Japan*.

32. 6 December 1913 Tokyo   White Sox 9, Giants 4
33. 7 December 1913 Tokyo   White Sox 12, Giants 9

On 9 December 1913 the tourists departed Japan via Kobe and Nagasaki.
They arrived in Shanghai, China, on 11 December 1913.

     11 December 1913 Shanghai   RAIN

On the night of 11 December 1913 the *Empress of Japan* set sail for
Hong Kong.

34. 14 December 1913 Hong Kong   Giants 7, White Sox 4
                                               (5 innings)

The tourists departed Hong Kong for the Philippines on board the
S.S. *St. Albans* on 14 December 1913.

35. 17 December 1913 Manila   White Sox 2, Giants 1
36. 18 December 1913 Manila   White Sox 7, Giants 4
                                               (7 innings)

The *St. Albans* set sail from Manila on 18 December 1913 bound for
Australia.

37. 1 January 1914   Brisbane   Giants 2, White Sox 1
38. 3 January 1914   Sydney   White Sox 5, Giants 4
39. 5 January 1914   Sydney   White Sox 10, Giants 5
40. 7 January 1914   Melbourne   Giants 12, White Sox 8
41. 8 January 1914   Melbourne   Giants 4, White Sox 3
                                               (11 innings)

On 8 January 1914 the tourists departed by train for Adelaide, Australia,
where they boarded the R.M.S. *Orontes* bound for Ceylon. The long
crossing included a brief stopover in Fremantle on 13 January 1914.
They recrossed the equator on 20 January 1914.

42. 23 January 1914   Colombo   White Sox 4, Giants 1
                                               (5 innings)

On 23 January 1914 the *Orontes* left Ceylon bound for Egypt.

43. 1 February 1914   Cairo   Giants 3, White Sox 3
                               (called on account of darkness after 10 innings)
44. 2 February 1914   Cairo   Giants 6, White Sox 3
    After arriving by train at Alexandria, Egypt, the tourists boarded a
    German liner, the S.S. *Prinz Heinrich*, for the trip to Naples, Italy. The
    group arrived in Naples on 7 February 1914. Two days later the group
    arrived in Rome.

    11 February 1914   Rome   RAIN
    12 February 1914   Rome   RAIN
    13 February 1914   Rome   RAIN

    On 14 February 1914 the teams arrived in Nice, France. The next day the
    players donned their uniforms and mingled with the crowds at Mardi Gras.
45. 16 February 1914   Nice   White Sox 10, Giants 9
    The players arrived in Paris on the *Riviera Express* train on 17 February 1914.

    18 February 1914   Paris   RAIN
    19 February 1914   Paris   RAIN
    20 February 1914   Paris   RAIN
    21 February 1914   Paris   RAIN

    The White Sox and Giants departed France for England on 22 February
    1914. The next three days were spent sightseeing and shopping.
46. 26 February 1914   London   White Sox 5, Giants 4
                                                (11 innings)
    On 28 February 1914 the tourists boarded the *Lusitania* in Liverpool for the
    return trip to the United States. Upon arrival in New York on 7 March
    1914, the Tour to End All Tours came to an end. Comiskey and McGraw
    would hold two self-congratulatory banquets. The first was held in
    New York on 7 March 1914. The final banquet was celebrated in
    Chicago on 10 March 1914.
    The Giants and White Sox took on local nines several times while touring
    the world. The results of those games:

    7 December 1913   Tokyo   Giants–White Sox 16,
                                                Keiō University, 3
    (the Giants and White Sox combined their squads to play Keiō University.)

    3 January 1914   Sydney, Australia   White Sox 10,
                                                New South Wales 1
    5 January 1914   Sydney, Australia   Giants 15,
                                                New South Wales 2
    7 January 1914   Melbourne, Australia   Giants 18, Victoria, 0
    8 January 1914   Melbourne, Australia   White Sox 16, Victoria 3

THE TOUR TO END ALL TOURS

ONE

A Tour Is Born

Last Spring the world tourists brought back from across the sea a wealth of pleasant recollection and the assurance that their excursion has done much to cement the friendly sport interest of the leading nations of the earth. The tremendous European war has no doubt postponed the effects of this friendly journey but they are not lost. They are at worst merely delayed, and some day this record journey will take its place as one of the most conspicuous single events in the history of athletic sport. – *Base Ball Magazine*, December 1914

America in 1913 was remarkably similar to today. It was a smaller nation but not by much—with the admission of Arizona and New Mexico in 1912, there were forty-eight states in the Union. No new stars would be added to the flag for another forty-seven years. The population stood at 97,028,497, almost a third of whom had been born on foreign soil. The recent presidential election had been a bitter three-party affair, and immigration had been one of the major issues.

The American population was generally of two classes, either very rich or very poor. It was the age of robber barons and industrialists, a time when men such as Rockefeller, Carnegie, and Ford had become household names. American industry ran on political machines, monopolies, and graft. A brand new consumer class arose in this industrial era, fueling the age of "consumption." Disposable shirt collars, Colgate toothpaste, Kellogg's Corn Flakes, innumerable brands of cigarettes, and Ford automobiles were among the products everyone owned or aspired to own.

For the first time, America began raising revenue directly from its citizens; 1913 marked the introduction of the federal income tax. Married couples with no dependents earning the luxurious salary of $5,000 a year and claiming the usual deductions paid $6.25. If you were even more fortunate and earned $10,000, you owed Uncle Sam $45.83.

It was an age of wonders of every sort. The Panama Canal was at last nearing completion after more than a decade of toil through malaria-laden jungle. A worldwide symbol of "Yankee ingenuity," "the Big Ditch" stood as the engineering marvel of the day. In the field of exploration, the South Pole had at last been reached. In England, the Piltdown Man was the sensation of the century. Scientists, explorers, and engineers were public heroes, with Thomas Edison perhaps the most revered man on the planet.

For entertainment, every town of any size at all had a marching band or symphony orchestra. Harry Houdini, without rival as the most popular entertainer of the day, made all manner of escapes before huge throngs of spectators in every corner of the globe. Hollywood and its motion picture industry were in their infancy yet were already producing stars with worldwide appeal. Mary Pickford, Lillian Gish, and Douglas Fairbanks were as well known in Paris as they were in Detroit.

Americans of all stripes were also drawn to the sports arena. Boxing and college football were enormously popular. Golf's popularity was exploding, and even polo matches drew respectable crowds. Yet in all of America only one sport was followed with equal passion by poor and rich and black and white alike, the game Americans had invented and the one game that virtually every American believed was superior to all other games on the face of the globe—baseball. These times and these circumstances birthed baseball's greatest adventure, the Tour to End All Tours.

This most ambitious of sports enterprises was hatched over drinks in "Smiley" Mike Corbett's bar at Twelfth and Lyttle on Chicago's East Side. One bitterly cold December night in 1912, huddled in the warmth of Mike's back room, a domain open only to athletes, sportswriters, and their close associates, the two most powerful men in baseball—John J. McGraw and Charles A. Comiskey—discussed the boldest scenario either could ever conceive of, namely, taking two baseball teams around the world.

The meeting offered a study in contrasts. John McGraw, president and part owner of the New York Giants and the greatest manager in the history of the National League, stood just five feet six inches tall. He was balding, pudgy, and acerbic. Behind his close-set beady eyes operated a keen, almost criminal, managerial mind. McGraw had been dubbed "the Little Napoleon" in recognition of not only his stature but also his tactical brilliance on the diamond. Behind his back, McGraw's foes risked incurring his wrath by calling him "Mugsy," a nickname he detested.

Charles Comiskey, owner of the Chicago White Sox and the richest man in baseball, stood an even six feet tall. He was overweight, florid faced, and sanctimonious. Behind his large, watery eyes dwelled the miserly mind of one of the game's greatest benefactors and one of its cruelest tightwads. Because his countenance so closely resembled that of a contented senator of ancient Rome, Comiskey had been dubbed "the Old Roman." Most everyone, however, called him "Commy."

Among the men sharing their table that evening was the man responsible for brokering the meeting, Ted Sullivan, baseball pioneer and Comiskey's best friend. Sullivan had known Comiskey longer than any other man alive. Although largely forgotten today, Timothy Paul "Ted" Sullivan was one of the most important figures in nineteenth-century baseball. As founder of both the Texas and Northwestern Leagues, he helped spread professional baseball beyond the Northeast, hastening its transformation into the national game. As multifaceted as anyone ever connected with baseball, Sullivan was, at various intervals, player, manager, scout, journalist, promoter, team executive, team owner, and league founder. The Northwestern League later spawned the American League. Sullivan was the first person to coin the phrase "fan" to describe baseball enthusiasts. Even the most casual follower of the sport owes a debt of gratitude to Ted Sullivan.

The Comiskey-Sullivan friendship began when they were roommates at St. Mary's College in Kansas in 1877. In addition to rooming with Commy, Sullivan also managed the college baseball team. Forever onward their lives would be enmeshed. On and off the field, the two worked together whenever possible. Their friendship became familial when Comiskey married Sullivan's sister.

Ted Sullivan also held the respect of John McGraw. Almost two decades earlier Sullivan had gone to Europe at McGraw's behest as an advance man for the Baltimore Orioles. In 1896 the Orioles, then the powerhouse dynasty of the National League, wanted to tour the Old World to showcase America's pastime.

This tour never came to pass. As Sullivan wrote, "In 1896 the writer [Sullivan] went to Europe for the Baltimore club, but as that club could not leave America until late in the Fall, the tour was abandoned."[1]

Now, seventeen years later, McGraw could envision a much broader landscape. While in Chicago, McGraw paid a call to Sullivan. He hoped that Sullivan would be willing to promote a postseason tour, which the Giants were planning.

The New York skipper had been in the Windy City performing in vaudeville. McGraw's "shows" required minimal acting ability. A natural

raconteur, the Little Napoleon merely stood upon the stage and answered
questions about the game and related tales of his adventures before rapt
audiences. Great theater it wasn't, but it was lucrative. For a brief time
the Giants manager was the highest paid entertainer in vaudeville, pulling
down an enviable $3,000 a week for sixteen weeks.

From Ted Sullivan's own hand comes the following account of how the
Tour to End All Tours was conceived.

> McGraw spoke to me in January, 1913, while he was filling a theatrical
> engagement in Chicago, about going ahead of the New York teams
> should they go around the world. I told him that Mr. Comiskey
> was thinking the same thing. And why not make it a joint affair, as it
> would be bigger in the eyes of the world in having the two great teams
> from the two largest cities in America! With that characteristic of this
> leader of leaders, he said, "All right Ted, you arraing [sic] for me to
> meet Mr. Comiskey." When I told Mr. Comiskey what Mr. McGraw
> said, he was delighted and they both met and the result was that the
> machinery of the world's tour was at once put into operation.[2]

The unlikely pairing of Comiskey and McGraw was a marriage of
necessity; it would not have evolved naturally. The Little Napoleon and
the Old Roman differed on virtually everything—disposition, approach to
the game, and attitude toward players. There was some commonality, of
course. Both were Catholics of Irish descent and immigrant backgrounds.
Both were driven to success and popular acceptance. As players, both men
initiated revolutions in how the game was played, and both of their fathers
frowned on their sons' interest in baseball.

John McGraw survived an impossibly nightmarish childhood. When he
was just eleven years old a diphtheria epidemic ravaged his family. Killed
in a span of a week were his mother; two of his sisters, aged thirteen and
eight; his four-year-old brother; and his infant brother. His father, John
J. McGraw Sr., was never the same man again. His alcohol-fueled grief
transformed into a violent rage, which he loosed upon his eldest son and
namesake. John McGraw Jr. was beaten regularly and mercilessly by his
father. Baseball saved John McGraw's life; by the time he had reached his
sixteenth birthday, he had left home and was playing professional baseball
in the minor leagues.

Charles Comiskey, in contrast, had never suffered want. His father,
"Honest John" Comiskey, an alderman in Chicago's Seventh Ward, man-
ufactured bricks. Chicago's city hall had, in fact, been rebuilt after the
great fire of 1871 with bricks made by "Honest John" Comiskey. The senior

Comiskey's most ardent wish was that his son would follow in his political footsteps. Although sorely disappointed in his son's choice of vocation, the senior Comiskey continued to support his son.

Charles Comiskey, like McGraw, had also lost an opportunity to go on a world tour. He had actually been offered a place on A. G. Spalding's world tour of 1889–1890. Commy, then the greatest first baseman alive, would have made a natural complement to the All-Star squad. Commy, however, could not accept the invitation.

Two reasons have been put forward to explain why Comiskey did not accept the invitation. Ted Sullivan claims that Chris Von Der Ahe, owner of the St. Louis Browns of the American Association and Comiskey's boss, would not give him permission to go. Rumors at the time, however, claimed that Comiskey turned down Spalding because the fee offered for touring the world was insufficient.

By 1913, now sedentary and portly, Comiskey held sway as the richest man in baseball. As owner of both the Chicago White Sox and the ballpark that bore his name, Commy had at last reached a position where he could fulfill this dream, which had long eluded him.

Comiskey had officially been thirsting for a world stage as early as 1906. That year a pitching-rich, hitting-poor edition of the White Sox known as "the Hitless Wonders" won the World Series. Comiskey had announced plans for a world tour, but he needed a partner. Seven years later he had one.

Before long the alcohol-stoked conversation around the table in Mike's back room centered on Spalding's world tour. During the winter of 1889–1890, Albert Goodwill Spalding led his own Chicago White Stockings and a team of All-Stars across the United States and then around the world. In six months the teams visited Hawaii, New Zealand, Australia, Ceylon, Egypt, Italy, France, and England.

With the twenty-fifth anniversary of Spalding's tour fast approaching, both McGraw and Comiskey realized that they had an opportunity to present the world a much better exhibition. Spalding's achievement in leading two baseball teams in a circumnavigation of the globe had been the envy of most in the game. It had also left a sour taste in the mouths of baseball men everywhere. Spalding had ostensibly launched his tour to promote baseball in foreign lands; it quickly became little more than a marketing tool for Spalding Brothers, Incorporated.

To the further dismay of baseball purists, Spalding allowed a carnival-like atmosphere to permeate the tour. Not secure enough to let the game stand on its own, he brought along additional entertainment, including a balloonist and Clarence Duval, the "mascot" of Spalding's Chicago White Stockings. Duval, an African American, was hired by Spalding to dance on the dugout roof in Chicago and degrade himself for the entertainment of his employers. Around the world, Duval "entertained" the crowds assembled to watch baseball. The indignities he endured climaxed with his being dragged by a rope through the streets of Cairo, Egypt, by the American All-Stars while wearing a catcher's mask.

McGraw, and especially Comiskey, had enough run-ins with Spalding to despise him. Comiskey had lost a string of Temple Cup Series (the nineteenth-century version of the World Series) to Spalding when he was manager of the American Association's St. Louis Browns. McGraw simply chafed at Spalding's audacity.

Spalding served as president of the National League for a quarter of a century. During his tenure, he abused his position to build his sporting goods company into a multimillion dollar empire. His firm held exclusive rights to sell the league its baseballs, equipment, and uniforms. The league's official publications were *Spalding Guides*. Spalding was among the first to place advertisements on outfield walls. He catered to wealthy baseball cranks (fans), creating baseball's first "luxury boxes."

An ardent practitioner of theosophy, Madame Blavatsky's occult religion, Spalding had no trouble viewing himself as baseball's grand deity. His paternalism was so strong that he took upon himself the task of creating American origins for the game he loved. To Spalding, who viewed himself as not only a sportsman but also a patriot, foreign origins for baseball were anathema. Spalding rejected out of hand even considering the truth; British games such as rounders and cricket were the antecedents of baseball. In their place, Spalding supplied the legend of Abner Doubleday, a myth he created out of whole cloth.

Unlike most propagandists, Spalding had the power to subsume all detractors and have his version of the truth prevail. His preferred myth of baseball's creation at the hands of Civil War general Abner Doubleday has no basis in reality, yet because the story was presented as authentic in such official baseball publications as *Spalding Guides*, the improbable tale was rendered "genuine." The Doubleday myth was cited as authentic in textbooks and encyclopedias and became nearly impossible to eradicate.

The result has made Cooperstown, New York, home to three of the greatest frauds ever perpetuated against the American public—James Fenimore Cooper, the Cardiff Giant, and Doubleday Field. The history of this town demonstrates, perhaps better than any other place in North America, the truth of the axiom that a lie repeated often enough becomes the truth.

James Fenimore Cooper, whose grandfather founded and named Cooperstown, had never seen or heard of baseball. Spalding placed his myth in Cooper's hometown in part to honor America's first great novelist. Just as Cooper had proven to Europe that America could produce its own literature, Spalding through the Doubleday myth "proved" that the United States could produce its own team sports.

Cooper's brooding "noble savages" and rugged outdoorsmen were already considered passé in Spalding's day. Whatever reputation Cooper had left was savaged by Mark Twain, an authentic genius of American letters, in his pithy essay "Fenimore Cooper's Literary Offenses."

By happy coincidence, Cooperstown is also the final resting place of the Cardiff Giant, a most brazen and unscientific hoax. Carved out of a single block of gypsum and passed off as literal proof of the statement in Genesis that "there were giants in the earth in those days," the "find" electrified the nation. Deemed authentic by more than one scientist and derided by others, the fraud netted its "discoverers" somewhere between $33,000 and $110,000.

Despite their differences, Comiskey and McGraw emerged from Mike's back room and staggered off into the cold night united on two principles. They wanted to bring baseball to the world, and they wanted to do it with more panache than Spalding had shown. For the Old Roman and the Little Napoleon, it would be first class or nothing. Comiskey went so far as to pledge on bringing his entire team en masse if they won the World Series of 1913.

Needless to say, McGraw would have loved nothing better than another National League pennant for the 1913 season as well. Imagine the interest and the revenue of a world tour featuring the champions of both leagues. One could easily imagine an "exhibition World Series" extending over the continent and around the globe.

Before adjourning for the evening, Comiskey and McGraw finalized some of the major details of the tour. The two appointed Dick Bunnell, president of the Western League, as the tour's treasurer. The title was mostly symbolic, however, as Ted Sullivan would hold the purse strings for the tour. Sullivan was appointed to the position of managing director of the tour.

Sullivan's importance to the project is impossible to underestimate. It was, arguably, the key point of agreement between McGraw and Comiskey. Without some sort of a mutual blind trust, it is unlikely that any tour could have taken place. Neither man would have revealed their financial situation to one another, yet without such cooperation, a tour would have been impossible. Both Comiskey and McGraw entrusted Sullivan with their portion of the capital for the tour. Sullivan, perpetually circumspect, made an excellent friend and blind trust, one unlikely to betray either man's confidence. Such confidence was essential, for unlike the previous world tour, which had been personally financed and under the control of one man, two contrasting and dominant personalities would attempt to share the spotlight—and the glory.

Commy and McGraw agreed to meet whenever they could during the 1913 season. Through such meetings the two would plan the tour's route, select accommodations, and give each other input on roster selections.

Responsibility for selecting umpires to accompany the teams around the world was turned over to the National Commission, a decision McGraw would rue. The National Commission, baseball's governing body before the inception of the Office of Commissioner, consisted of Ban Johnson, president of the American League; Thomas Lynch, president of the National League; John E. Bruce, secretary; and August Hermann, chairman. All four had at various times borne the brunt of McGraw's ire. The New York manager mocked, taunted, and harassed each one on a regular basis. Not surprisingly, none of the quartet much liked John McGraw.

Johnson, easily the most powerful member of the commission, had been feuding with McGraw since the turn of the century. The Johnson-McGraw feud became so intense that it led to the first World Series cancellation in 1904. Johnson saw to it that McGraw's arch-nemesis, umpire Bill Klem, was selected to represent the National League. Comiskey, long-time friend of Ban Johnson, got off easily; umpire Jack Sheridan was chosen as the American League arbiter.

McGraw, who honestly believed his own often-quoted maxim that "the only good umpire is a dead umpire," detested Klem's umpiring most of all.[3] William Klem was the all-time terror of National League umpires. Behind his back, the future Hall of Famer was called "Catfish" by fans and players alike because of his long face and sour demeanor. The dour Klem thrived on confrontation while remaining a figure of unquestioned integrity. He once refused a $10,000 bribe offered him by gamblers.

McGraw fought with Klem more than he fought with all other umpires combined. From Klem's debut in 1904 through the final game of the 1932 season, when John McGraw at last hung up his manager's spikes, there were few times, it seemed, when the two were not at each other's throat. Their rivalry began with Klem's very first big league game. The New York manager challenged one of the rookie ump's calls, but Klem stood his ground. Incensed, McGraw vowed to break Klem and drive him out of baseball. This proved to be one of the few boasts that John McGraw was unable to deliver on during his long career. True to form and, no doubt, the National Commission's expectations, the two squabbled incessantly during the tour.

The American League's Jack Sheridan was an old acquaintance of Comiskey. The two had even umpired in the same league. Sheridan and Comiskey were among the field arbiters for the Players League during its one and only season of 1890. The Players League, product of a players' revolt, possessed all of the stars in the game. The owners whom the players had revolted against, however, possessed the trump card, a steady cash flow. Young Comiskey learned much from the failure of the Players League.

Sheridan umpired the American League's very first game in 1901. A large man with an equally large mustache, the walruslike Sheridan spent his off-seasons as an undertaker. "I call 'em out in the summer, and carry 'em out in the winter" is his own description of his divergent careers. A competent umpire, he nonetheless had borne the brunt of McGraw's wrath in the past. Sheridan had been involved with Spalding's tour twenty-five years before. In 1889 Sheridan served as base umpire for the games the White Stockings and All-Stars played between Chicago and San Francisco. When Spalding and company sailed off for Hawaii, Sheridan stayed home. This time he would go the distance.

To ensure that the umpires remained impartial, the National Commission would pay all of their tour expenses. Sheridan and Klem were empowered to run games in accordance with the commission's rules and standards. Baseball's ruling powers wanted these games, whether played in Chicago or Cairo, to be run like any game during the regular season, meaning that the games would be played as anything but exhibitions, thus guaranteeing that an air of confrontation would hang over the tour.

During their conversations, Comiskey and McGraw had decided their own tour, like Spalding's, would be divided into sections. The first phase of the tour would barnstorm across the United States. The second part of the tour would bring baseball to Japan, China, and points east. McGraw and Comiskey hoped that the revenues generated from the domestic phase of the tour would offset the expenses incurred overseas.

Even though the 1913 baseball season had not yet begun, the postseason had already colored it. John J. McGraw and Charles A. Comiskey realized that no matter how exciting or how disappointing the upcoming season proved to be, afterward would come the adventure of their lives, the Tour to End All Tours.

TWO

Filling Out the Lineup

The purpose of the trip was twofold—to prove to the foreign element that baseball is better than cricket, roulette, hopscotch, baccarat, Parcheesi or any of the other sports in vogue abroad, and to convince Herman Schaefer and the rest of the heathen included on the roster of the two clubs that Ireland, one of the stopping points, is the greatest country in the atlas. – *Ring Lardner*

Comiskey and McGraw announced their plans for a world tour to the greater baseball world immediately after their all-night bender in Chicago. An article, reprinted endlessly, even as late as the February 1914 issue of the *Base Ball Magazine*, entitled simply "The World Tour of the Chicago White Sox and New York Giants," fired the first salvo in a season-long publicity campaign. With no byline but bearing all of the pompous stylistic earmarks of Ted Sullivan, the article laid out in black and white all of Comiskey's and McGraw's hopes for the tour of their dreams.

The highest and greater object of this trip of the world is to try and transplant America's game in athletic and sport-loving countries— who desire to adopt some game that has both the athletic and mental attributes conducive to the physical development of the youth of their country.

Baseball has all of those qualities, which has led to its great popularity in America. This circuit of the globe by those two major league clubs, led by the game's two greatest leaders and sportsmen, namely, Charles Comiskey, president of the Chicago White Sox, and John McGraw, leader of the New York Giants, is a tour that is not a money making affair. The outlay of this circle of the world by the two ball teams and their necessary attendants will exceed by thousands of dollars any revenue collected at the gates for the exhibition games.[1]

To the world, this tour would wear the dual faces of missionary zeal and philanthropic largesse. Of course, McGraw and Comiskey were ardent capitalists, but by publicly distancing themselves from the foul stain of money, Commy and Mugsy allowed themselves a not-so-subtle dig at A. G. Spalding and his lucre lust. The article listed the following itinerary: "The foreign countries that will be visited by these two great Major League clubs are Japan, China, Philippines, Australia, India, Egypt, Italy, Austria, Belgium, France, Germany, Ireland, England, and Scotland."[2]

This grandiose schedule would undergo some pruning; Germany and Austria-Hungry became far too volatile to even consider visits. Yet for the most part it remained intact. Throughout the 1913 season McGraw and Comiskey generated reams of publicity to realize their shared dream. "Long before the season was over the obligations assumed approached the $100,000 mark."[3] Needless to say, Comiskey and McGraw had no desire to lose money. Like most entreprenuers, they used other people's money to build their dream. The *Sporting Life* of 1 November 1913 listed some of the ways that the organizers attempted to recoup their losses. "It is said that $40,000 in cash has already been subscribed to defray expenses. It is said that two sporting goods houses have contributed $10,000 and it is known that the National Commission has donated $1,000, besides guaranteeing the expenses of Umpires Klem and Sheridan. Comiskey it is said, posted $25,000 sometime ago to care for the White Sox. In Japan three games will be played for a $10,000 guarantee with the promoters."[4]

Further reducing costs to the organizers was a fee for appearance system that guaranteed that the teams would make money. Any city or town wishing to host the Giants and White Sox would be required to put up either $1,000 or 80 percent of the gate and grandstand receipts, depending upon which was larger. Not only did this system ensure Comiskey and McGraw that no money would be lost in cities where attendance was low, it encouraged the locals to promote the game in their own city to maximize their profits. Promotion of games in every city outside of Chicago and New York was paid for locally. Comiskey and McGraw exploited civic pride for personal gain. Instead of funding an enormous national advertising campaign, Comiskey and McGraw received free coverage from print outlets such as *Sporting News*, *Base Ball Magazine*, *Sporting Life*, and an uncounted number of local papers.

The true cost of the Tour to End All Tours will never be known, but the tab was sizable enough to put a crimp in Commy's coffers. Millionaire Comiskey spared no expense to ensure the tour's success. Never having a problem spending money on himself, Comiskey bore the lion's share of the costs, laying out $90,000 in steamship fares alone. For expenses overseas, Comiskey brought along "a letter of credit for 25,000 pounds sterling, approximately $121,000."[5] Ostentatious display was the order of the day as far as Comiskey and his wife were concerned. Nancy Comiskey lugged along all of her finest jewelry. Just one diamond necklace with a matching set of earrings that she took with her around the world was valued at $12,000 in 1913. No reason could be imagined for bringing such baubles along other than to impress the celebrities, royals, and other dignitaries whose paths the tourists would cross.

To make the trip even more palatable financially, Comiskey brought team manager Jimmy "Nixey" Callahan on board as a third bankroll for the tour. Callahan had in his years of managing for Comiskey grown accustomed to spending his own money for the benefit of his ballplayers. A classic example of this occurred during the 1912 season. Comiskey had sold advertising space to a tobacco company on the outfield fence in dead center. The huge advertisement was very large, very white, and a murderous distraction for White Sox batters. The Sox players urged Callahan to speak to Comiskey about removing the advertisement. Comiskey would not allow the ad to be painted over unless Callahan agreed to pay Commy the remainder due from the tobacco company's contract.

McGraw, while comfortable financially, was not in Comiskey's league. McGraw drew baseball's highest salary as manager of the Giants. His other sources of income were the aforementioned earnings from vaudeville lecture tours and quite a bit of green from ghostwritten articles in newspapers and magazines. All of it added together made McGraw fairly well off for the times. However, the Giants manager assumed a greater financial risk in comparison to Comiskey to fund his half of the tour.

While McGraw sincerely believed in the tour, his business partners, especially the heirs of John Brush, the late Giants owner, did not share his enthusiasm. The group gave their blessings to McGraw and the world tour but did not risk a dime out of their own pocketbooks. Consequently, the Little Napoleon spent nearly his entire personal fortune to bring off his part of the tour. At times like this, McGraw missed John Brush more than ever. Brush, an Indianapolis haberdasher who dabbled in baseball, had lured McGraw to New York, appointed him manager of the Giants, and later even allowed him to purchase part of the team. Brush's death in November 1912 not only cost McGraw a close friend but also his strongest financial backer.

McGraw himself was personally very close with his finances. Never very far from the poor boy he had been in Truxton, New York, McGraw was most assuredly not about the trappings of wealth. He lived modestly, even frugally, in a New York apartment. He frowned on gaudiness, discouraging his wife from wearing makeup. John McGraw himself dressed fashionably, tastefully, and modestly. His only apparent personal extravagance was the diamond ring he wore. While on the world tour a reporter from the *Kansas City Star* wrote that off the field he looked more like a lay delegate to a Congregational Church assembly than the most successful manager in the history of the National League. For the Little Napoleon, money was a tool for building security and lessening the crushing load of life; it was not a "recreational drug."

There can be no doubt, however, that McGraw's investment in the tour would pay off handsomely. Exactly how well he, Comiskey, and Callahan made out is impossible to determine. The tour made a good deal of money, but the only thing approaching an official assessment came from the pen of Ted Sullivan, who, of course, had a vested interest in making it appear as though the Sox and Giants were not-for-profit enterprises. Sullivan's suspect account of the tour's revenues appears in his self-published book, *History of World's Tour, Chicago White Sox and New York Giants*:

> The trip across the continent as far as the Pacific Coast was directed by myself and Mr. O'Neil, and the ending of the trip at Portland, Oregon, placed Mr. McGraw and Mr. Comiskey in a position to care very little whether they got any revenue in foreign countries or not, but at that I will say for the sportsmanship of Comiskey and McGraw, they put the exhibition of America's game in foreign countries far above the dollar mark, and at that the amount of money got in foreign countries would not make five per cent. [*sic*] of the total outlay of the tour. The teams traveled in the highest style, both on shipboard and in hotels at home and abroad, and if the enterprise broke even in a financial way it would be wonderful, but if there was any loss, those two gentlemen never spoke of it, but I am positive that there was no gain.[6]

While Sullivan repeated the ruse that the tour made no money, sources outside the reach of Commy's parsimonious talons were under no such constraints. In fact, most of their costs had been recovered even before the teams had left the United States. The returning ballplayers would be bombarded by rumors that the tour had cleared as much as $75,000. To quell these whisperings, McGraw went public and declared that the tour had only made about $30,000. Whatever the true figure, both men made out quite well. The published public financial record that is available tends to favor the $75,000 figure. Take the case of Blue Rapids, Kansas. The smallest town to host the tourists, this town boasted an official population of 1,850, a figure that more than quadrupled for the ball game. Afterward the *Blue Rapids Times* ran the numbers. "The settlement was made on the basis of the number of tickets taken up at the gates which were as follows:

1278	General Admissions at $1	$1,278
323	General Admissions at $1.50	$492
386	Grandstand Admissions at $1.50	$579
34	Children's Tickets at 50¢	$17
2026		Total $2,366

The Tourists received $1,892.80 and the boosters $473.20. In addition the Boosters received $43.50 for automobile tickets and 25¢ or bleacher tickets. The Boosters will have total receipts of between $800 and $900. The bills are not all in, but probably will not exceed $300, so the Boosters have come out in fine shape financially."[7]

The reporter for the *Blue Rapids Times* clearly knew that the published numbers did not jibe with either the announced attendance or the box office receipts. More than the paper's own bad math was at work. The *Times* explained: "From the above, it will be seen that the total paid admissions were a little over 2,000, but we think it is a conservative estimate, after counting the Boosters, the band, the ball teams, workers who were passed in, etc. to say that not less than 2,500 people witnessed the game. Next to Bryan day at Chautauqua, it was the largest 'pay' crowd ever in town."[8]

Remember that this is the haul from the smallest town visited. San Francisco would see more than ten thousand fans crammed into its stadium for just one of the three games played in that city. If the tourists averaged a take of $3,000 in the thirty-five games they played, the $100,000 mark was reached long before the domestic phase of the tour closed in Seattle.

If anyone could make a tent-full of money on a world tour, it was Comiskey. The most single-mindedly profit-driven owner in baseball understood the bottom line like few others. While other owners of the day were notoriously tight with their money, Commy was truly in a class by himself. Despite the fact that the White Sox were the greatest box office attraction of the era, Comiskey scrimped and scammed on just about everything.

In 1913 Comiskey was better off financially than any other owner in the game. Unlike Connie Mack, the Philadelphia A's owner, Comiskey had no major partners or co-owners. John McGraw had to deal with an ownership board. Clark Griffith's Washington Senators were mortgaged to the hilt and would ever remain so. Commy had no equal. Willing to spend lavishly on himself and his friends or to donate use of his stadium to some charity if it meant he received good publicity from the event, he saw no need to direct money to his players or his ballpark.

While McGraw funneled his monies back into the Giants, Comiskey lined his pockets. When he did spend money on talent, more often than not it would go for some worthless rookie or washed-up veteran. Commy tended to have a brass touch when it came to assessing talent. Stories about his pettiness are legendary. He gouged everyone he could. Under the direction of his son (and fellow tourist), Louis, the team brewed its own soda, which was then sold at greatly inflated prices to the Sox fans. Comiskey treated his employees like serfs. White Sox salaries were the lowest in the Majors; still, Comiskey siphoned off as much of their salaries as he could. The Old Roman charged his players for the broken bats and torn uniforms that accumulated over the course of the season. Last-place teams in far worse financial shape gave their players a meal allowance of $4 a day, while the White Sox made do on $3.

Although often arbitrary and contradictory when dealing with his players, Commy entertained reporters as though he were hosting royalty. He curried sportswriters' favor, setting lavish buffets and bottomless troughs of alcohol before them. Influential Chicago sportswriters like Ring Lardner, Gus Axelson, and Bill Bailey were among those Comiskey would invite along when he visited his wooded retreat in Eagle River, Wisconsin. The group that accompanied Commy on these excursions and "hung" with him at the ballpark and various Chicago saloons called itself the "Woodland Bards Association" or the "Royal Rooters." With so much largesse coming their way, it is not a surprise to discover that the Chicago media lionized Commy and never pried into his business affairs.

Tellingly, none of Comiskey's players ever became a member of the Woodland Bards. The idea of Comiskey forming the kind of friendships with his players that John McGraw or even Connie Mack had is simply not fathomable. Commy threw his lot in with the establishment of Chicago. He viewed himself primarily as a businessman, not a ballplayer. By 1913 virtually no trace remained of the innovative first baseman who had jumped contract in 1890. That year, when the players revolted against ownership, Commy pledged his loyalties to the Players Brotherhood and joined the Players League. In middle age he had become everything that he had despised in his youth.

For the actual planning of the tour, McGraw could not have found a duo more suited to the task than Comiskey and Sullivan. Comiskey was the first owner in baseball to make extensive use of trains. The White Sox traveled in the comfort of a private train of Pullman cars, the forerunners to today's private airplanes and buses. The trains made sense economically and also met Comiskey's personal needs for luxury. Commy may have gotten the idea from his team secretary, Harry Sparrow. Sparrow was previously employed by a circus and had learned every corner-cutting, travel expense–saving tactic known. The White Sox were the single most experienced baseball team in chartering trains across the continent, each year journeying from Chicago to Texas or California for spring training.

Ted Sullivan had "revolutionized" minor league travel. A term now extinct from the lexicon of baseball is the "Sullivan Sleeper." Sullivan Sleepers were railroad cars with short day couches instead of berths. Cramped, hot, and uncomfortable, they were, however, extremely economical. Cramming all of the players onto one car meant Sullivan did not have to rent a Pullman car for the team to sleep in. This money-saving "innovation" soon became the standard mode of transportation for virtually every minor league team. For a generation of ballplayers, a promotion to the Majors also meant a promotion from Sullivans to Pullmans.

John McGraw was himself an experienced baseball traveler, having worked the game in the smallest American hamlets. He also possessed international experience from playing winters in Cuba. In addition, McGraw had taken a trip to Europe on his own late in 1896. He and Comiskey would draw upon their varied experiences to shape their tour.

From the outset, McGraw understood that it was impossible to outspend Comiskey, so he instead focused on winning the publicity war. The Little Napoleon possessed more media savvy than either Sullivan or Comiskey. He realized that if the names McGraw and Giants were kept foremost in people's minds, then he and his team would be perceived as the "winners" of the tour no matter what the box scores said. Fortunately for McGraw, the publicity engine of the age had just become available. Almost as soon as the meeting in "Smiley" Corbett's bar had concluded, McGraw began the process of wooing the greatest athlete of the twentieth century, James Francis Thorpe.

Already famous for his athletic achievements at Carlisle Indian School, where he had been a five-letter man, Jim Thorpe returned to America as *the* hero of the 1912 Olympic games. Thorpe achieved the unprecedented, winning both the Olympic decathlon and pentathlon. In the pentathlon, Thorpe won three of the five contests. His point total for the two events would not be exceeded for twenty-five years. So dominating was his performance that his closest challenger finished almost seven hundred points behind him. The closest American in the trailing field was Avery Brundage, who placed fifth in the decathlon and worse in the pentathlon. Brundage, scion of a Chicago construction firm, later became president of the International Olympic Committee (IOC) and remained Thorpe's eternal rival.

In Stockholm, Sweden, Thorpe's legend was permanently secured. On the Olympic podium, Sweden's King Gustav V declared Thorpe "the greatest athlete in the world." A heady return to the States followed. The *New York Times* plastered his face on the front page. President William Howard Taft was among the scores who sent congratulatory telegrams. Thorpe ate dinner with former president Teddy Roosevelt at his mansion in Oyster Bay, Long Island, and Thorpe enjoyed his nation's ultimate tribute, a ticker-tape parade down Broadway. For the proud Native American, the future appeared unbelievably bright. Thorpe was the living personification of his Sac tribal name, Wa-tho-huck, which means "Bright Path." Then the bottom fell out.

Thorpe's story has become such an ingrained part of American sports lore that even the most casual sports fan is familiar with it. The United States Olympic Committee (USOC) discovered that he had played minor league baseball for $30 a month during the summers of 1909 and 1910. For this infraction, this "professionalism," the USOC decreed that Thorpe had forfeited his amateur status. Thorpe's name was expunged from the record book, and he was ordered to return his Olympic medals and awards. Thorpe played baseball for the Rocky Mount, North Carolina, Railroaders of the Eastern Carolina League because he needed the money, typical behavior for countless numbers of college athletes of the day.

Lou Gehrig, for example, while still a student at Columbia University, spent a summer playing minor league baseball in Hartford, Connecticut. Mickey Cochrane, when not in the classroom, toiled in Delaware for the Dover Senators of the Eastern Shore Baseball League. Thorpe was no different from them, save one respect. If one were to scan the box scores of the *Hartford Courant* or the *Delmarva Star*, the names Gehrig or Cochrane would not appear. Gehrig and Cochrane, to preserve their college athletic eligibility, played under aliases.

Thorpe, either out of ignorance or a simple lack of foresight, played under his own name, and it cost him his medals. No failed drug test, no under-the-table payoffs, no fouls during competition, only a past that included Louisville Sluggers and base paths. Thorpe's "indiscretion" was, essentially, being too decent to lie. Had he played under an alias, in all likelihood he would never have had his medals taken away. Creating an alias allowed college athletes to accept money for their services while simultaneously permitting them to deny that they were "really" being paid. This charade was especially helpful to college athletes short of cash. So widespread was the practice that even a future president of the United States, Dwight Eisenhower, had no qualms about using it.

Eisenhower, while a cadet at West Point, had faced Thorpe on the gridiron when Carlisle defeated Army; he also, like Thorpe, had played professional baseball. While still at West Point, Eisenhower played a few games in the Kansas State League under the name "Wilson."[9] Engaging in professional athletics clearly violated the West Point honor code. Had "Ike" been discovered, he would have been expelled, and our world might be drastically different.

The USOC's decision to strip Thorpe of his medals galled Americans of all stripes. Thorpe had violated the rules, but nearly everyone thought that the USOC was being arbitrary in its handling of his case, especially in light of the widespread use of professional aliases among "amateur" athletes.

The decision to strip Thorpe of his medals was based as much upon classism and racism as upon strict interpretation of the rules. European, British, and American men of leisure controlled the IOC at the time. This group did not even like mixing with blue-collar workers or laborers; that Thorpe should be the best athlete in the world shattered every conceit the IOC held. The committee preferred athletes like Avery Brundage, a snobbish, high-living millionaire whose primary "occupation" was training for the Olympics.

The greatest and most galling irony, however, is the almost unreported fact that Jim Thorpe *played baseball* as part of the 1912 Olympic games under the auspices of the IOC. Baseball was a demonstration sport in Stockholm that year. On 15 July the United States beat host Sweden 13–3. "The following day, an all-U.S. exhibition was held as the U.S. delegation members from the western part of the country bowed to their eastern counterparts by a score of 6–3. Jim Thorpe, the celebrated U.S. amateur athlete and future Major leaguer, played right field for the eastern team."[10]

A fascinating footnote to this game was the two coaches for the U.S. squad, A. G. Spalding and George Wright. George Wright, with his brother, Harry, led baseball's first international tour. In 1874 the Wrights took teams from Philadelphia and Boston on a tour of England to show off the American game. One of the players the Wright brothers brought overseas was a young A. G. Spalding, then the sport's greatest pitcher. Fifteen years later, in 1889, Spalding surpassed his mentors by leading two teams of his own around the world. The two were reunited for the last time in the shadow of the Arctic Circle, rubbing elbows with Thorpe, future star of the third great international baseball tour.

In an age when most white Americans closed their eyes to the plight of virtually every other Native American, those who maintained a marginal existence on reservations, Jim Thorpe was adored. The public sympathy generated by his plight paradoxically afforded him even greater access to white society and forums than otherwise might have been accessible. Certainly if not for the controversy, Jim Thorpe would never have become a New York Giant and toured the world playing baseball.

The IOC's act of stripping his medals made Thorpe a de facto professional. Continuing in college athletics was out of the question. The only option left Thorpe was how to profit most from his situation.

Only two sports had significant professional leagues in 1913, the National Hockey Association (forerunner to the National Hockey League) and baseball. Football, while popular, remained the sole domain of college men. The new sport of basketball had not yet spawned any league that could truly be classed "professional." Thorpe did receive offers from prize fighting, but boxing, then as now, was perceived by the public as somewhat corrupt and tawdry. Baseball reigned as undisputed king of North American sports. Organized down to Class D and semipro levels, the Major and minor leagues brought the game to every part of the continent. In addition, the game was played with enthusiasm by children and adults everywhere. The local nine, whether amateur or professional, was a point of civic pride in even the most remote hamlet. No other sport attracted as many fans or made as much money.

Baseball teams drooled over Thorpe's box office potential. Eight of the sixteen Major League teams offered him contracts. Unique as a free agent in the age of the reserve clause, Thorpe was able to choose the best offer from among the eight clubs. John McGraw waved the most cash and landed the prize for his Giants.

Thorpe's contract with New York's National League team was huge. The Giants paid him $6,000 a year for three years, a salary comparable to that of some of the game's superstars. While not as lucrative as Ty Cobb's $11,333 a year, it was not that far behind Tris Speaker's $9,000. Eddie Plank, star pitcher of Connie Mack's Philadelphia A's, received $5,000 for his services in 1914. Urban "Red" Faber makes an interesting comparison case. Faber, a fellow member of the tour, was one of the best pitching prospects in the White Sox farm system; despite this, Comiskey paid the future Hall of Fame inductee only $1,200 for his rookie season of 1914.

Only one other team, the American League's St. Louis Browns, remained in the running before Thorpe signed his contract with New York. The Giants offered prestige and financial security. The Browns, however, probably made the offer Jim Thorpe should have accepted, a spot in the starting lineup.

Thorpe and McGraw both knew that, as a Giant, he was destined to be a bench warmer. The utility role would erode his considerable athletic gifts. In signing with New York, Thorpe limited his own potential. Thorpe explained his rationale for signing with the Giants during a 1 February 1913 press conference.

> I could have gone to St. Louis and, according to what the scout told me I could have been a regular. But it occurred to me that I have never seen any startling stories about what the St. Louis team had done. That is what decided me in favor of the Giants. If the St. Louis club were willing to put an untrained man like me on the regular team they would likely put other untrained men on it, and it wouldn't be much of a team. I think I would rather sit on the bench with a good team than be on the field with a bad one. After seeing what good players do I might be able to do it myself. I have never heard of a ball-player who sat on the bench with the Giants turning out badly. A lot of good coaching I figure is worth more to a young player than a little bad playing.[11]

For his part, McGraw was delighted with his new acquisition. At the same press conference he said, "Thorpe has the ideal build for a ballplayer. He is broad shouldered, clean limbed, and weighs 176 pounds. His mind is quick and his record is ample evidence of his gameness. I like the way he has of studying things out. Of course, I realize that he will be a big novelty for the public, but I also expect to turn him into a good player."[12]

Despite McGraw's public pronouncement that he hoped to turn Thorpe into a good ballplayer, there is no doubt that signing him ranked primarily as a publicity stunt. Al Schacht, who pitched for the Giants during Thorpe's tenure with the team, is quoted as having heard McGraw say, "If he can only hit in batting practice, the fans who pay to see him will more than offset his salary."[13]

McGraw's investment in the Olympic hero paid off handsomely. Thorpe became the tour's greatest attraction, drawing standing ovations all over the United States. When the tourists left America, Thorpe's fame preceded them. In places where baseball had not been heard of, Thorpe and his accomplishments enticed large and curious crowds to games that otherwise might have seen sparse attendance. Next to McGraw and Comiskey, Thorpe's name got mentioned most often in the press.

Jim Thorpe was the first of the many players recruited for the tour. McGraw and Comiskey made deliberate attempts to recruit star players for their squads. Not only would this increase gate receipts, but it would also provide one more "dig" at Spalding. The teams that Spalding took around the world consisted mostly of mediocre players, whom he nonetheless dubbed "All-Stars." Commy and McGraw wanted to show the world the genuine article.

Surprisingly, the player-friendly Giants manager proved less adept at coaxing his players to sign up than did the restrained Comiskey. Both men encountered understandable resistance from rival managers and owners who were unwilling to loan their valuable players for a six-month, danger-laden glory ride. The greats they did approach often shied away from the tour, sometimes with good reason.

Ty Cobb, a terror on the base paths who regularly hit close to .400, was asked to go, but the Georgia Peach turned the offer down. As *Sporting Life* put it, "The Peach intends to make a lot of money this Winter writing signed base ball stories and selling them all over the country."[14]

Cobb's devotion to the dollar may have been a blessing to everyone else involved with the tour. The prospect of spending six months with this meanest and most intolerant of baseball personalities would be too horrific to contemplate. Paranoid, bigoted, and belligerent, Cobb made enemies of teammates and fans alike. The Georgia Peach was a southern Protestant who hated northerners, Catholics, blacks, and apparently anybody else who was different from him. Most of the participants of the world tour were northern and midwestern Catholics.

Cobb's temper was as legendary as his batting average or base stealing. The warped and deluded Cobb in 1912 actually strode into the stands and beat up a fan who was heckling him. This particular fan had lost his hands in an accident, but that did not prevent Cobb from beating him senseless. Had Cobb been part of the tour, he might either have been thrown overboard in midocean by his teammates or perhaps lynched in some foreign clime by a mob of enraged locals.

Napoleon Lajoie, Cleveland's player-manager, also turned down a place on the tour. Lajoie, the first man to reach three thousand hits, was one of the finest second basemen ever. Such were his talents that, to honor him, the Cleveland team changed its name from Spiders to Naps. Lajoie would have made a wonderful catch for the tour, but this fish wasn't biting.

At the behest of Comiskey, Sox manager Jimmy Callahan broached the subject. Gus Axelson, who accompanied the tourists as columnist for the *Chicago Record-Herald*, relates the story in *"Commy,"* his fawning biography of the White Sox owner.

Napoleon Lajoie . . . had originally been slated to round out the Sox infield. Callahan approached him on the subject during the summer.
"Clear around the world, did you say?" queried Nap.
"Sure. And you will be back in time for the regular season," added Callahan by way of convincing argument.
"Fine! I am with you, but I suppose it will all be by land," cautiously inquired the Cleveland star.
Callahan, knowing Lajoie's aversion to the vast deep, explained that the bridge builders had been slow in linking up the continents, but the water trips would be only a hop, skip and jump.
"Too damp a prospect," was Lajoie's laconic rejoinder.[15]

Lajoie avoided all sea travel. Even crossing the Great Lakes was too daunting a task. When his team traveled to Detroit to face the Tigers, Lajoie would not take the boat with the rest of his squad, taking the long way round by train on his own instead.

The great Pirates shortstop Honus Wagner also begged off. "The Flying Dutchman" had endured a series of leg injuries during the 1913 season and needed rest. More important, he needed to tend to his dying father.

Comiskey's successful recruiting errands resulted in landing some prominent star players to the world-touring version of the White Sox. Newly married "Wahoo" Sam Crawford of the Tigers and his wife saw the tour as an opportunity to see the world on one long honeymoon, with the decided benefit of having all expenses paid by Comiskey and McGraw.

Stationed next to Cobb in Detroit's right field, Crawford rarely spoke to the Georgia Peach. Sam Crawford was as beloved as Ty Cobb was hated. The two were a sort of Janus incarnate. The perpetually cheerful Crawford and the eternally dour Cobb could have served as models for the masks on a drama guild poster.

As a hitter, Crawford, much like Cobb, was a lethal combination of power and speed. He set one career record some believe will stand forever, 312 triples. Since Crawford's retirement in 1917, no other player has even managed to reach the 300 triples mark.

Comiskey also talked Tristam "Tris" Speaker of the Boston Red Sox into coming along. The second highest paid player in baseball, Speaker produced box office magic. Comiskey, no doubt, hoped Speaker's drawing power would repeat itself around the globe. Despite the prematurely gray hair that gave him his nickname, the Gray Eagle, Speaker was as dashing as any matinee idol. An authentic Texas cowboy, Speaker was at home on the back of horse and could rope and ride with the best. One of the first Major Leaguers to learn how to fly an airplane, the new technical marvel that was only ten years removed from Kitty Hawk, North Carolina, Speaker played baseball like he lived his life, with swagger and panache. Clark Griffith, owner and manager of the Washington Senators, said simply, "Speaker is the most remarkable fielder that ever lived."[16] He still holds the record for the most unassisted double plays turned by a center fielder.

Playing an amazingly shallow centerfield, Speaker would leap high into the air, snag the ball on the fly, and outrace the base runner to second for the tag, an unassisted double play. He accomplished this feat nine times over his long career and is the only man to have pulled it off in World Series play. Ironically, the team he turned it against was McGraw's own Giants in the 1912 Series. Speaker's bachelor status, combined with his noted zest for adventure, probably gave James McAleer, the former president of the Red Sox, and his wife good cause to chaperone the Red Sox's biggest star and most valuable asset.

While certainly not a star, Herman "Germany" Schaefer of the Senators also signed up with the barnstorming White Sox. A decent fielder, Germany had virtually no power: his lifetime batting average registered a lowly .257 with only nine home runs. He was certainly versatile, however. During his seventeen years in the Majors, Schaefer played every position on the diamond, including two stints as emergency relief pitcher. His main contribution to any team that he played on, apparently, was that of team comedian.

Years later one of his teammates, Hall of Famer Davy Jones, remembered Germany Schaefer as "far and away the funniest man I ever saw. He beat Charlie Chaplin any day of the week."[17] Schaefer did stints in vaudeville during the off-season, and routines he created on and off the field later served as part of the inspiration for the Busby Berkeley movie *Take Me Out to the Ball Game*. Comiskey or, more likely, Jimmy Callahan understood the need for a comedian to keep everybody loose on such a grueling road trip. For Germany, the tour represented an opportunity no clown could resist, the chance to make the world his stage.

Schaefer caused the baseball rulebook to be rewritten especially because of one of his stunts. The "Schaefer rule" exists because one day Germany

Schaefer stole first base. Davy Jones recounted the story in Lawrence Ritter's *The Glory of Their Times*:

> We were playing Cleveland and the score was tied in a late inning. I was on third base, Schaefer on first, and Crawford was at bat. Before the pitcher wound up, Schaefer flashed me the sign for the double steal—meaning he'd take off for second on the next pitch, and when the catcher threw the ball to second I'd take off for home. Well, the pitcher wound up and pitched, and sure enough Schaefer stole second. But I had to stay where I was, on third, because Nig Clarke, the Cleveland catcher, just held on to the ball. He refused to throw to second, knowing I'd probably make it home if he did.
>
> So now we had men on second and third. Well, on the next pitch Schaefer yelled, "Let's do it again!" And with a blood-curdling shout he took off like a wild Indian *back to first base*, and dove headfirst in a cloud of dust. He figured the catcher might throw to first— since evidently he wouldn't throw to second—and then I could come home as before. But nothing happened. Nothing at all. Everybody just stood there and watched Schaefer, with their mouths open, not knowing the devil what was going on. Me too. Even if the catcher *had* thrown to first, I was too stunned to move, I'll tell you that. But the catcher didn't throw. He just stared! In fact, George Stovall, the Cleveland first base man, was playing way back and didn't even cover the bag. He just watched this madman running the wrong way on the base path and didn't know *what* to do.
>
> The umpires were just as confused as everybody else. However, it turned out that there wasn't any rule against a guy going from second to back to first, if that's the way he wanted to play baseball, so they let it stand.
>
> So there we were, back where we started, with Schaefer on first and me on third. And on the next pitch darned if he didn't let out another war whoop and take off *again* for second base. By this time the Cleveland catcher evidently had enough, because he finally threw to second to get Schaefer, and when he did I took off for home and *both* of us were safe.[18]

After the game, a rule change make Schaefer's stunt illegal, no matter that it had actually helped his team win the game. Baseball's powers believed Schaefer's play made a mockery of the sport. At least one other player had performed this stunt before Schaefer, but no one had made as much of a production number out of it. Likely, Schaefer's antics factored in the Rules Committee's opinion. As a tourist, Schaefer clowned the world round, inspiring laughs everywhere—most important, perhaps, from his teammates.

The bulk of the team that Comiskey sent around the world ended up looking pretty much like the team that played all season long at Comiskey Park. Eight White Sox, including some of the team's finest players, agreed to make the trip.

George "Buck" Weaver was easily the most talented of the White Sox to go around the world. In only his second Major League season, Weaver, at twenty-three years old, was already an elite shortstop. In later years the Sox moved him to third. So effective was he at the hot corner that Ty Cobb refused to bunt against him. In all of baseball, no other third baseman ever received such an honor from Cobb.

Baseball was Weaver's adrenalin; from the playgrounds of his hometown, the smoky steel and coal city of Pottstown, Pennsylvania, to the Majors, Buck Weaver loved to play. After permanently breaking into the Sox lineup in the second game of the 1913 season, he played in every one of the next 150 games. Weaver was an iron man on tour as well, playing in all but one game.

New groom Hal Chase of the White Sox also signed on for the tour. A brilliant-fielding first baseman, "Prince" Hal was quite possibly the most crooked athlete in history. With equal parts larceny and skill, Chase began throwing ball games almost as soon as his big league career began. Chase honed his skills at tanking games so well that, eventually, no confederates were necessary; he could throw ball games all by himself.

Had Hal Chase never strayed from the straight and narrow, there is no doubt that he would be in the Hall of Fame today. He stood six feet even and weighed 175 pounds in his prime. Originally a pitcher but converted to the first sack in college, Chase was a true oddity in the batter's box. Chase remains the only right-handed-batting, left-handed-throwing player to ever win a batting title. A strong leader, he served as player-manager of the New York Yankees for part of the 1910 season and for all of the 1911 season. Although some in baseball were suspicious of him from the beginning, Chase was beloved by most of his teammates and coaches. John McGraw was a big fan of the Prince and became the last man to manage him in the Major Leagues. For his part, Chase had no qualms about betraying friends to line his pockets.

Six years later, when gamblers needed an inside man to help them fix the World Series, they approached Hal Chase. Chase served as the principal instigator and corrupter of his former teammates, becoming the "blackest" of the "Black Sox." A nickname Chase was given early in his career, "the Man with the Corkscrew Brain," developed an irony no one could have foreseen.

Ray Schalk, Chicago's notoriously straitlaced redheaded catcher, enjoyed his second big league season in 1913. Once promoted to the job of the Sox's everyday catcher, he began to put up numbers that would eventually lead him to baseball's Hall of Fame. Like Chase, Schalk would only commit to tour as far as Seattle.

The remainder of the White Sox tour squad were, for the most part, average or journeyman players. As we will see, recruiting continued even as the tour barnstormed across the continent. Comiskey truly wanted to put on the best show he could. It was, after all, *his* show.

Curiously, the Sox team cobbled together for the tour tilted top-heavy with catchers. In addition to Schalk, Commy brought along Tom Daly, Andy Slight, and Jack Bliss. Canadian Tom Daly had been on the Sox roster, but his big league experience consisted of just a single game with three at bats in 1913. Slight and Bliss signed on to the tour from the Sox's minor league affiliates. Slight, a young but promising catcher and Chicago native, signed on to the tour for some seasoning. John Joseph "Jack" Bliss had been the St. Louis Cardinals backup catcher from 1908 to 1912. A weak hitter with an anemic Major League batting average of .219, he could be described as a basic second-string catcher. He spent 1913 in Sacramento, California, of the Pacific Coast League, attempting to resurrect his Major League career, finishing with an average of .205 and nowhere to go but down.

Two of the White Sox reserve second basemen, Morris Rath and Joe "Fats" Berger, and outfielder Wally Mattick made minor contributions to the tour. Maurice Charles Rath, a Texan out of the town of Mobeetie, stood five feet eight and a half inches tall, weighed 160 pounds, and would never be considered a star, bouncing back and forth between the Majors and the minors throughout his brief career. Usually at second, Rath could play short and third. He had no power to speak of, but he was fast. Oddly, Rath owned more lifetime triples than home runs. Joe Berger, reserve second baseman, stood five feet ten and a half inches tall. His nickname, "Fats," was clearly meant as a gag; he tipped the scales at 170 pounds, a veritable beanpole. In 1913, his rookie season in the Majors, he appeared in seventy-seven games, mostly at second, platooning with Morris Rath. Like Rath, Berger had virtually no power. Before the arrival of "Shoeless" Joe Jackson, the Sox never could seem to land an authentic power hitter. Walter "Wally" Mattick could only be considered a marginal Major Leaguer at best. Appearing in sixty-eight games for the Pale Hose in 1913, Mattick mustered only a .188 batting average. Perhaps more significant than his playing career is the fact that his son, Bobby, would become a Major League player and manager.

From the roster of the St. Louis Cardinals, Comiskey and Callahan recruited outfielder Steve Evans. A southpaw, Evans provided the Sox with additional power from the left side of the plate. He also distinguished himself as a comedian. Evans started out with the New York Giants in 1908, but McGraw traded him after only eight games. Evans's comedic antics did not ingratiate him to his manager. There was no room for comedians on the Giants. To the pugnacious McGraw, baseball was so akin to war that it precluded comic relief.

The Cards had no such prejudices, and from 1909 on Evans became their regular center fielder. Owning some power, he was a lifetime .287 hitter. Evans leaped at the chance to choose to go around the world with the White Sox. On the tour, he and Germany Schaefer would exercise their comedic gifts in a good-natured "duel." Together, the duo kept everyone loose.

Utility man Dick Egan, the Cincinnati Reds' lone contribution to the tour, could play third, short, and second. The right-handed Egan hit .282 in 1913, his lifetime best. Egan shared the distinction with Steve Evans of being the only active National Leaguers to tour the world as members of the White Sox.

Pitching for the barnstorming Sox was an assortment of solid starters and shabby castoffs. Guy Harris "Doc" White still remained as one of the sturdiest starters on Jimmy Callahan's staff. White led the American League in wins with twenty-seven in 1907, but in 1913 he was thirty-four years old, his arm and career fading fast.

From the other team in St. Louis, the American League's Browns, Comiskey signed Walter Leverenz. Typical of the sort of starters the perennially sad-sack Browns sent to the mound, Leverenz's record in 1913 was a most unspectacular six wins and seventeen losses. Born in Chicago, Leverenz leaped at the chance to represent his hometown in exotic locales in the States and around the world.

Genial James "Death Valley Jim" Scott accompanied the Sox around the globe. Known for his wide smile and jokey manner, Scott had been with the Sox since 1909, but the right-hander turned in his finest season thus far in 1913, winning twenty games. He also led the American League in losses with twenty-one. His prosaic moniker was a play upon the name of his hometown of Deadwood, South Dakota. Not only was death in the name of the town, but as every card player knows, Deadwood is the town where "Wild Bill" Hickok was shot to death while holding two aces and two eights, the "dead man's hand."

Joe "Blitzen" Benz, a versatile fireballing right-handed pitcher, toured the world. Alternately used as starter and reliever, he appeared in thirty-three games in 1913, posting a 7-10 record with three saves. Joe enjoyed enormous popularity with White Sox fans, more because of his stylish manner and brilliant smile than for his athletic prowess. Benz was destined to be just another pitcher with a lifetime .500 record. His fame and reputation as a speed pitcher did result in Benz having a race car named after him.

Special mention must be made of Urban "Red" Faber. Perhaps the Sox's hottest minor league prospect, he, like Andy Slight, was assigned to the tour for some seasoning. Faber became the tour's oddity when McGraw realized that his barnstorming Giants were short one pitcher. Comiskey loaned Faber's services to the Giants for the duration of the tour. So splendidly did the redheaded, switch-hitting, right-handed pitcher perform that when the tour concluded, McGraw sought unsuccessfully to purchase his contract from the White Sox.

These are the principal players recruited by Callahan, Comiskey, and their agents. Other players appeared on the White Sox roster, some for a game or two, others who barnstormed as far as Seattle. These players ranged in ability from living relic Frank Isbell to Hall of Fame pitcher Walter "the Big Train" Johnson. Their exploits will be told in the next chapter.

McGraw, in contrast to Comiskey, involved himself in every area of his players' lives. This may explain, at least in part, the difficulties he had in recruiting players for the tour. To Comiskey, baseball and every other aspect of life were a business. The Little Napoleon, on the other hand, saw baseball as being larger than business and something far more than a game. To McGraw, baseball *was* life.

A pine tar addict who took third base with his spikes slashing and who delighted in pushing rules and umpires to their limits, this was John McGraw. His professional and social network consisted almost solely of baseball. Camaraderie became the key component of any team McGraw managed. Never was this truer than when he assembled his team of tourists. McGraw certainly did not want to spend his time circling the globe with players he didn't like. It was hardly an accident, then, that most of the players he recruited for the barnstorming version of the Giants were players who not only possessed impressive baseball skills but whose personalities were compatible with his own.

To be a Giant, one had to like and be liked by John McGraw. Although the New York manager was genuinely fond of many of his players, none held a place in his heart larger than the space reserved for Christy Mathewson. One of McGraw's favorite players as well as one of his closest friends, "Matty" was everything his short, balding, and pugnacious manager was not. Tall and as handsome as any Broadway star, the gentlemanly Mathewson was the most dominating pitcher of the dead-ball era.

Matty possessed pinpoint accuracy and a graceful, seemingly effortless delivery. The 1913 season typified the brilliance on which his fame rested. That season he won twenty-five games while losing eleven; he also pitched sixty-eight consecutive innings without a walk. Matty went through the entire 1913 season without hitting a single batter.

Matty was adored and idolized as no player before him had ever been. His combination of charm, good looks, and athletic ability, combined with his college background, resulted in his becoming the first ballplayer held up as a role model for America's youth. Prior to Mathewson's ascendancy, the national pastime had difficulty shedding its image as a haven for ruffians and drunkards. The man from Factoryville, Pennsylvania, changed everything. His visage adorned just about every product imaginable: books, games, pipe tobacco, and sporting goods.

As a sideline, Matty dabbled on Broadway as an actor and playwright. He was the one man in America that every man wanted for a brother and every woman wanted for a husband. And he had no greater fan than his own manager, who treated him like the son he never had.

Aside from Mathewson and the internationally famous rookie Jim Thorpe, McGraw signed on fellow Giants second baseman Larry Doyle, catcher John "Chief" Meyers, first baseman Fred "Bonehead" Merkle, outfielder Fred Snodgrass, and pitchers Bunn "Bunny" Hearn, George "Hooks" Wiltse, Arthur Fromme, Al Demaree, and Jeff Tesreau.

Team captain "Laughing Larry" Doyle had been with the Giants since 1907. A solid hitter with strong defensive skills around the keystone, Doyle won the National League's Most Valuable Player Award for 1912. He possessed the combination of talent and confidence that McGraw loved. As team captain, Doyle managed the Giants whenever McGraw got himself tossed out of a game, which was often.

Studious John "Chief" Meyers was as quiet as Doyle was loud. Perhaps the best catcher of the era, Meyers was a full-blooded member of the Cahuilla tribe from the San Diego foothills in California. Introspective and cerebral, Meyers's one lifelong regret was his failure to graduate with his class at Dartmouth. He and Jim Thorpe made natural roommates. Meyers

came to know Thorpe better than any one else in baseball and remained
Thorpe's friend for life.

McGraw invited Fred Merkle and Fred Snodgrass along not only because
they were talented athletes but also because the two deserved vacations more
than any other ballplayers in North America. Both had spent the 1913 season
as targets of abuse from baseball fans in every big league city. The torrent of
abuse these two men endured is truly incredible. Even the repellent epithets
hurled at today's players by the most drunken of louts pale in comparison
to what Snodgrass and Merkle endured.

Center fielder Snodgrass and first baseman Merkle both made crucial
errors in the tenth and final inning of game seven of the 1912 World Series.
Their errors helped the Red Sox to erase a one-run deficit to tie and then
win the game and the Series.

The throngs that filled the Polo Grounds had a large, unforgiving
memory and spent the entire 1913 season doing their collective best to
make the lives of Merkle and Snodgrass living hells. Snodgrass's error, a
misjudged fly ball, was dubbed the "$30,000 muff," implying that his error
had cost the Giants the winner's purse of the World Series. At first base,
where he dropped a throw, Fred Merkle's ears were assaulted anew with
calls of "Bonehead." For Merkle, it was "déjà vu all over again." Merkle had
been tagged "Bonehead" during his rookie season of 1908 when he failed to
touch second base in a crucial game. The play, which remains controversial
to this day, occurred late in the season in a game against the Chicago Cubs.

With the score tied 1–1 in the ninth inning, Merkle's pinch-hit single
drove "Moose" McCormick to third with the potential winning run. With
two out, Al Bridwell hit a single to drive in what should have been the
winning run. However, once Merkle saw McCormick touch home, he
thought the game was over and did not continue running to second. Instead,
Merkle ran directly to the Giants clubhouse.

Pandemonium ensued in every part of the Polo Grounds. A jubilant
overflow crowd swarmed onto the playing field; the game was over. Or
so everyone in the park believed, except canny Cubs second baseman
Johnny Evers. Evers, immortalized as part of the legendary Cubs infield
of Joe Tinker, Frank Chance, and Harry Steinfeldt, owned one of the
keenest baseball minds around. He called for the ball, intending to touch
second base and force out Merkle. Giants pitcher Joe "Ironman" McGinnity
perceived what Evers was up to and tried to break up the play.

McGinnity rushed to the ball and hurled it deep into a crowd of fans
celebrating in the outfield. Nevertheless, a baseball was produced from
somewhere and relayed to Evers, who touched the bag. When Evers touched

second, umpire Hank O'Day ruled Merkle out and nullified McCormick's run. Instead of a win, the game remained tied 1–1 after nine. The joyous crowd instantly turned into something akin to a mass exodus from Bellevue. The Cubs braved a gauntlet through the incensed mob of New York fans and dashed for their lives into the sanctuary of their clubhouse. The ravaged condition of the turf and the swirling knot of irate fans made resuming the game an impossibility. Instead, the controversy was allowed to fester for three days before National League president Harry Pulliam rendered his decision. In a verdict that satisfied no one, Pulliam nullified the game, deciding that it should be replayed at the end of the season if necessary to determine the pennant. As luck, or some cruel baseball gods, would have it, the Giants went into a late season swoon that left them tied with the Cubs and necessitated the rematch, which the Cubs won. Chicago went on to the World Series and their only World Championship, while New York fans fingered Merkle as the scapegoat for their frustrations.

Even the staid *New York Times* poured it on, referring to the "censurable stupidity on the part of player Merkle."[19] Only nineteen and fresh from Toledo, Ohio, Merkle was completely unprepared for the ensuing public onslaught. He seriously considered giving up the game, but McGraw talked him out of it. The Giants manager never blamed Merkle, saving his wrath for O'Day and Pulliam. In fact, McGraw gave Merkle a $1,000 bonus at the season's conclusion.

Forgotten amid this background is the irony that Merkle was one of the most intelligent players in baseball. A top-notch chess player, algebra whiz, and bridge player, he was the farthest thing from a "bonehead," yet he was never allowed to forget his "errors." "When I die," he once said bitterly, "I guess they'll put on my tombstone: 'Here lies Bonehead Merkle.'"[20]

"Turkey" Mike Donlin, in contrast, was forgiven his every excess by the bleacher denizens at Coogan's Bluff. Always a fan favorite, Donlin's nickname was a description of his running style, darting and strutting about the bases like a turkey. A hard-drinking Irishman with a penchant for violence, Donlin had once served jail time for assaulting a woman in broad daylight in the middle of a city street. Donlin was one of the best pure hitters baseball has ever seen. He was also John McGraw's favorite player and perhaps the closest friend the Giants manager ever had. A talented vaudevillian, Donlin had exited baseball for a few years to tour with his wife, actress Mabel Hite. After her death in 1912, Donlin returned to baseball via the Newark, New Jersey, team in the International League, a AAA circuit. McGraw asked Donlin to join the tour not only as a kind of therapy but also to be his drinking buddy.

Arthur Fromme and Jeff Tesreau were solid fixtures in the Giants' firmament of pitching stars. A midseason acquisition from the Reds in 1913, Fromme went 10-6 for the Giants in twenty-six games, principally in relief. Tesreau was an underrated right-hander who led the National League in complete games in 1913 with thirty-eight, winning twenty-two games while losing thirteen. He would be remembered today as a great pitcher had he played anywhere but New York, where he was continually outshone by more brilliant stars.

George "Hooks" Wiltse had been a member of the Giants since 1904. Early in his career he had been a fine pitcher, but now at age thirty-three his arm was nearly gone. Wiltse's record for 1913 was 0-0 in seventeen games, only two of which were starts. Bunny Hearn appeared in only two games during the 1913 season, winning one game and losing the other. Hearn, like Wiltse, was a southpaw. Generally, the superstitious McGraw hated lefties, so their inclusion on the tour is something of a mystery. Hearn spent just this one year with the Giants before returning to the minors. By joining the tour, Hearn certainly made the most of his brief time in Gotham.

From elsewhere in the National League McGraw recruited Lee Magee and Ivy Wingo from the St. Louis Cardinals. Magee, born Leopold Christopher Hoernschemeyer, could play every position except the battery. A solid athlete in his third big league season, Magee was a talented switch hitter who stood five feet eleven inches tall. An ardent shutterbug, Magee left a legacy of wonderful photographs from all parts of the world. Owning more of an artistic bent than most ballplayers, Magee dabbled as a cartoonist. A few of Magee's sports cartoons were even published in some New York newspapers.

Ivy Wingo enjoyed his third big league season in 1913. Christened Ivey Brown Wingo in Gainesville, Georgia, the sturdy catcher hit .260 lifetime. Wingo possessed a keen baseball mind and would become a big league manager in 1916.

The Philadelphia Phillies' tour contributions were Mickey Doolan, a durable but weak-hitting shortstop, and Hans Lobert. Born Michael Doolittle, Doolan had quite a canny baseball mind; in 1906, a few years before Germany Schaefer made the stunt famous, Doolan had also stolen first base.[21] The ironman of the Giants' world-touring team, Hans Lobert played in every one of the Phillies' 151 games of 1913. John Bernard Lobert had been dubbed "Honus" in his rookie season of 1903 by the great Honus Wagner himself. Wagner, the all-time greatest shortstop, was struck by how Lobert physically resembled him. "From then on he always called me Hans number two," Lobert recalled with pride.[22] Lobert's nose and speed were as great as Wagner's. Like his namesake, Lobert appeared gawky yet moved with an easy, rapid grace. No one, not even Jim Thorpe, could fly around the bases with greater speed than Lobert. Lobert's birthday corresponded with the opening date of the tour, 18 October 1913. A newlywed, he, like fellow "benedict" Giants Thorpe and Tesreau, and his wife spent a unique honeymoon circling the globe.[23] These couples enjoyed some of the most unforgettable moments of their lives.

For the opening game of the series, McGraw and Comiskey selected Redland field in Cincinnati, the city where professional baseball began in 1869. The Giants and White Sox would begin their around-the-world lark one week after the conclusion of the World Series. Dramas of every sort awaited the two teams. They would encounter rapturous crowds and indifferent masses. They would meet governors and diplomats, the king of England, the last khedive of Egypt, and the pope in Rome. The teams would play through blizzards in the American Midwest, broiling heat on the deserts of Arizona and Egypt, and rain just about everywhere else. The Tour to End All Tours was one colossal blast, especially for the players. It was a wonderful time to be young and to be a ballplayer.

THREE

Base Paths a Continent Wide

By an oversight Ted Sullivan failed to schedule a game in Lahassa, which is unfortunate, as he may want to scout the Himalaya League some day. – *Portland Oregonian*, 5 November 1913

The 1913 baseball season ended in frustration for John McGraw and his Giants. Once again his team lost the World Series, this time in five games to Connie Mack's Philadelphia A's. Matty pitched brilliantly in the Giants' only victory of the Series. But the Giants' bats went to sleep in October, and without support, the Giants pitchers could not win the Series on their own. Losses, especially World Series losses, had a way of making John McGraw unpleasant. This year, however, he had something to take his mind off of the Series loss, a baseball tour like no other. Already, the winter extravaganza was the main topic of hot stove league conversations.

No one in baseball gave much thought to an event that occurred the same day that the Philadelphia A's were dividing their shares of World Series receipts. In Indianapolis, the independent Federal League was holding its fall meetings. Edward Steininger, president of the St. Louis franchise, gave a war talk, declaring, "We are going to invade the majors and we will take some of their players too."[1]

The Feds were ignored while sportswriters focused on McGraw and Comiskey and their audacious quest. For weeks leading up to the tour, newspapers had kept track of who was in and who was out of the tour line-ups. Retellings of Spalding's around-the-world adventures were common, often printed side-by-side with exaggerated claims of baseball's popularity in various countries around the globe.

Early on, the papers noted a glaring difference between McGraw and Comiskey. Each held very different views on how they should participate in the domestic barnstorming phase of the tour. McGraw, who practically bled pine tar, committed himself to touring with his team through every city, every game, and every inning. Comiskey would be there for the opening games in Cincinnati and Chicago, then he would be off to his retreat in the Wisconsin woods until the tour steamed into San Francisco.

Contrasts in the two men's personalities were obvious long before their simultaneous departures for Cincinnati. The Giants gathered at New York's Grand Central Terminal at 10:30 A.M. on 17 October 1913 to meet the train the team had chartered for the journey. With so few athletes, the train seemed enormous. The three sets of newlywed Giants, the Tesreaus, the Thorpes, and the Doyles, were among the first to arrive at the station. Jeff Tesreau and the former Helena Elizabeth Blake were the most recently married couple, having tied the knot only two days before on 15 October.

The unusual opulence of the train caused one of the hundreds of fans gathered at the terminal to see the players off to remark, "Pretty soft for you fellows."[2] Arthur Fromme took the bait and replied, "In one way perhaps, but don't forget that while you're asleep in your nice comfortable bed at home we'll be bumping along on the rails huddled in narrow berth while heading for the next one night stand. But we're going to see the world that's true, and it's a chance we may never get again. So long! See you next March."[3]

John McGraw made sure the following bold-faced lie was the last words he left with the New York reporters on the platform. "We do not expect to make any money on the trip," said McGraw as he boarded the train. "Our trip is solely to exhibit the national game in foreign lands. It's a treat for the boys."[4]

In Chicago, the White Sox were coming off their own incredibly busy couple of weeks. The City Series had gone the full seven games, with the Sox taking bragging rights for the year. With the Giants and A's engaged in an East Coast Series, the Second City newspapers covered the Cubs-Sox series with a passionate, almost comical intensity. The *Chicago American* even issued an extra edition on 14 October 1913 with a banner front-page headline two inches high reading: "SOX ARE CHAMPIONS OF THE CITY!" The final box score shared the front page.

The City Series was once the much anticipated finale to Chicago's baseball season. Often, the city flag served as a nice consolation prize to tide a team or its owner over through long, cold, Lake Michigan winters. No expense was spared in staging the event, including paying four umpires for their services. At the time, four umpires appeared only in World Series games; every other time of the year, two men worked the games. One of the four men in blue for the City Series was Jack Sheridan. Sheridan's working vacation as one of the world tour umpires brought him to Chicago early for a refresher course.

Even after all this baseball, Chicago was gearing up for two more games. The world tour would be passing through Comiskey Park, of course, but before that there was to be held in the same park a benefit game on 16 October for the family of Jimmy Doyle. Doyle played for the Chicago Cubs for two years through the 1911 season before being felled by illness. After enduring a botched appendectomy, he passed away late in 1912, leaving a widow, a young son, and a mountain of debts, which the benefit hoped to ease. The exhibition game between the Sox and Cubs was viewed by some in Chicago as a continuation of the City Series, one last chance for the Cubs to get even. This was the angle the media harped on. "Johnny Evers Urges Men to Maul Sox in Doyle Benefit Game" read one headline in the *Inter-Ocean*.[5] Detroit's Sam Crawford, who had signed up for the world tour, came to Chicago early on 15 October so that he could participate in the exhibition game.

Unfortunately, at the last minute an October thunderstorm rumbled through the Midwest, making play impossible. Mrs. Doyle would have to wait a few months to get her benefit game. The following February, while the tourists were reveling in Paris, an indoor baseball game was staged for the Doyle family at the Chicago armory.

In the wake of the benefit game's cancellation, the White Sox grabbed their overnight bags and headed for Cincinnati for the kickoff of the world tour. The tourists would do their serious packing when their special train returned them to Chicago on 19 October. The trek to Ohio would mark the first and last time that the tourists would travel in separate trains to the same city. The Sox left Chicago on a quiet note; no White Sox bon voyage party was scheduled until the evening of the nineteenth, when the team would be getting out of town for good.

The Sox made their way to Cincinnati on the train that all of the tourists would call home for the next month. Three sleeping cars, a combination buffet and luggage car, and an observation car made up the train. The White Sox would travel in one car, the Giants in another car, and the third car would be set aside for the honeymooning couples of both teams. The newly married Sox included Joe Benz, Reb Russell, Hal Chase, and Charles Comiskey's son, Lou. The most recently married of the White Sox, Reb Russell shared the same anniversary date as Jeff Tesreau. Reb Russell wed Charlotte Benz, a cousin of teammate Joe Benz, on 15 October. The presence of so many newlyweds on board the train at one time caused some members of the press to dub the train "the Honeymoon Express" or "the Honeymoon Special"; both labels stuck.

Arriving in Cincinnati early on Saturday morning, 18 October 1913, the two teams had their day scheduled to the minute. The pattern for the teams' visit to every subsequent city was set in Cincinnati—arrive, greet well-wishers, tour the city, eat lunch at one of the city's finest restaurants or hotels, play a baseball game, enjoy the postgame spread, head to the train station for the trip to the next burg.

McGraw and Comiskey chose to open their tour in the Ohio city for several reasons. It honored professional baseball, which had been born in the city in 1869 with the famous Reds. Playing game one in the Ohio city served as a thank-you to Cincinnati for enduring what had been a very hard year.

Spring floods tore through the Midwest in March and April of 1913. The Reds' ballpark, Redland Field, flooded, as did Cincinnati's downtown. After the waters receded, the remains of hundreds of horses, businesses, and homes littered the city. The Reds were forced to open their season on the road. Even after the floodwaters dried, the turf and the ballpark were wet all season long. Trying to inject a bit of levity into the situation, *Sporting Life* referred to the team as the "Red Marines."

An enthusiastic welcoming committee greeted the tourists at the station, then led them to a fleet of waiting automobiles for a tour of the Queen City. Their first stop, the site of the 1869 Reds' ballpark. After paying homage to the birth of professional baseball, the cars headed for the zoo. Zoological gardens would be popular destinations for the two teams at all points around the world. Among the exhibits at the Cincinnati Zoo was the last surviving passenger pigeon. When Comiskey and McGraw had been youths, the birds darkened the sky. Now every tourist took a somber pass by the cage where the last passenger pigeon, a female, mutely awaited the extinction of her species. In less than a year's time she would breathe her last, becoming both a taxidermist's memento and a warning to coming generations.

After departing the zoo, August Herrmann, president of the Reds, hosted the tourists at a local eatery, Smearcase John's, for some prime German cuisine. America's most German city, Cincinnati offered food on a par with anything found in Bavaria. The players feasted on sausages, sauerkraut, pigs' knuckles, and other German delicacies, then chased it all down with some great German pilsners. Everyone had such a good time devouring the savory meal that both teams lost track of time and ended up arriving half an hour late at Redland Field.

The game was supposed to start at 2:30 in the afternoon, but at that hour, the ballplayers were still chowing down. Thoroughly chilled and damp, 2,499 fans waited patiently in the stands. Finally, at 3:17 P.M. the Giants and White Sox took the field.

Both teams unveiled new uniforms for the tour. In the sartorial contest, at least, the Giants came out the winners. McGraw had an eye for style. The all-black uniforms he decked the Giants out in for the 1905 World Series garnered high praise from players and fans, even if they did not result in a World Championship. For the around-the-world venture, the Giants donned blue pinstripes and caps adorned with a patriotic shield. The shield was a copy of that worn by the U.S. Olympic team the previous July. To keep his Giants warm, McGraw had smart-looking navy blue sweaters knitted. Each sweater was emblazoned with the patriotic shield of thirteen stripes and thirteen stars, matching the shield on their caps.

Comiskey clad his men in dark blue with the traditional white socks adorned with a blue stripe. Emblazoned on the sleeves were stylized American flags flapping in the breeze. The White Sox wore blue caps with white piping. For warm-up jackets, Comiskey went with a double-breasted look. The jackets required two rows of buttons to close, and every one hung to at least the middle of the thigh. Like their uniforms, two flags adorned the sleeves. Wearing them, the Sox looked very much like a cadre of businessmen waiting for a train. Jimmy Callahan had a miniature outfit made up for his son, Danny, who would be serving as White Sox mascot and batboy once the tour entered foreign lands.

It did not take long for the teams to disappoint the chilled crowd, as a much ballyhooed pregame event was summarily canceled. For weeks the promoters had advertised that prior to the game, Jim Thorpe and Hans Lobert would engage in a match race around the bases.

Before the World Series, Lobert had garnered newspaper headlines across the country for beating Thorpe in just such a contest. While Thorpe was up for the venture, Lobert backed out at the last minute. According to Jack Ryder of the *Cincinnati Enquirer*, "He said that if he started running here he would have to do it everywhere the team shows on its way to the west. He did not care to set a precedent in a game in this city."[6]

The appearance of Joe Benz on the mound for the Sox appeased the crowd somewhat. To boost local box office receipts, whenever possible both teams strove to make sure that players with a local connection took the field. Benz, who had grown up nearby in Batesville, Indiana, and worked as a butcher's apprentice until baseball intervened, had a trainload of fans in the crowd. Opposing him would be Christy Mathewson. Such was Matty's popularity that in every city along the tour route Matty was prevailed upon to pitch. Aside from Mathewson and Benz, most of the fan interest focused on Jim Thorpe. Only Benz and Thorpe had their photographs in the next day's *Enquirer*. There seemed to be as much fascination with Iva Thorpe as there was with her husband. Iva's picture appeared in the *Enquirer* as well, wedged between that of Joe Benz and her husband. This was the first game Jim Thorpe had ever played in Cincinnati, and the fans were duly impressed. "He hit well and showed a vast amount of speed on the bases."[7]

After Benz's scoreless turn on the mound in the first inning, the game was stopped so that the fans from Batesville could present him with a gold loving cup. William Phelon, the *Inter-Ocean*'s acerbic sportswriter, described the event this way: "Between innings they gave Mr. Benz a handsome loving cup, easily holding 20 cents worth, if you knew the barkeeper, and afterwards, they made a tear jug out of it."[8]

The butcher's boy immediately made the hometown crowd question whether he was truly worthy of their appreciation. In the second inning he surrendered six runs. Benz gave up two more runs in the fourth and was then unceremoniously yanked in favor of Walter Leverenz. The final score of 11–2 favored the Giants. The morose Batesville booster club members were not the only unhappy customers to file out of Redland Field later that afternoon. The *Enquirer* described the last game of the year in Cincinnati as "worse than terrible."[9]

Earlier in the day, Buck Weaver of the White Sox set the tone for this game and the series. Buck ensured that the games would be intensely competitive almost single-handedly. Prior to the contest, both teams were taken to the Hanlin Hotel to stretch their legs and dress for the game, where Buck Weaver was introduced to Christy Mathewson. Reporter Bill Bailey tells the tale:

> Mathewson was in the lobby so was Weaver and they were not far apart when manager McGraw came along.
>
> "Matty this is Buck Weaver, the famous Sox shortstop," said the Giant boss.
>
> "Glad to meet you," said Mathewson.
>
> "And I'm glad to meet you," answered Weaver. "I've heard lots about you," continued Buck, and the great pitcher began to show signs of being bored. You know that's what they all say when they meet Mathewson. But this bored expression didn't last long. They never do when Buck's in the neighborhood.
>
> "And I'm willing to make a little bet with you," continued Buck.

"How's that?" queried Mathewson, and there was a flicker of interest.

"I've got a hundred that you don't get the first pitch by me," said Buck.

Matty was interested, vitally interested. He looked over Weaver very carefully. That was a new experience, even for the great Matty.

"Your all right," he answered with a laugh. "I'm beginning to believe that I won't."[10]

Fortunately for his wallet, Mathewson declined the bet. The first pitch Matty tossed Weaver was a ball. Weaver belted the second pitch deep into the corner of Redland Field for a triple. From his perch on third base, Weaver just smiled at the great Matty. The Giants did not appreciate anyone showing up Christy Mathewson. For the rest of the tour competition between the teams would be fierce, with neither side conceding anything to the other. These games would be exhibitions in name only.

Despite their shellacking on the field, the White Sox returned to the Hamlin Hotel with the Giants for dinner. Unexpectedly, Ban Johnson showed up to confab with Comiskey and August Herrmann. Johnson and McGraw made it a point to avoid each other whenever possible. McGraw's absence from Comiskey's separate dining room and its repast of wild pheasant was no accident. McGraw dined along with his players, shepherding everyone off to their special train on a Cincinnati railroad siding.

The Sox's return and farewell to Chicago occurred the next morning, 19 October 1913. The Royal Rooters pulled out all the stops, ensuring that five thousand thoroughly chilled White Sox fans paid their way into Comiskey Park to see their heroes one last time. The Sox unveiled their second set of road tour uniforms. Whenever the Sox were to be the "home" team on the tour, they would wear blue pinstripes adorned with flags on the sleeves and blue stars on the collar. Though much more attractive than their dark blue "road" uniforms, the Sox rarely wore them because from a distance they could easily be confused with the Giants' togs.

The change of attire did not help the Sox obtain a win, and they fell to the Giants 3–1 in a game that was superbly played. Despite the bone-chilling cold and the damp field conditions, both Reb Russell for the Sox and Al Demaree for the Giants went the distance, with Russell losing the game in the ninth inning when the Giants bundled four hits for two runs.

That evening Chicago said farewell to their Sox in style. Amid pomp and ceremony, the special train pulled out of LaSalle Station on the Rock Island Line at precisely 11:00 P.M. Getting away had not been an easy task for the teams. The fans had a hard time letting their heroes go. Nearly as many fans as had attended the ball game came to the station to see the teams off. White Sox fans were everywhere and were into everything. Twenty-five fans even took a train from Chicago to Cincinnati to attend the world tour's opening game and also celebrated at the bon voyage party in LaSalle Station. More than fifty well-wishers managed to sneak on board the train to shake hands and party with the players. These folks had to be shooed off the Honeymoon Express so that the tourists could be on their way.

Among the stories in the next day's coverage of events, much attention was paid to an agreement signed that same day between Walter Johnson and the White Sox. The contract had the Senators' ace agree to pitch for the White Sox against Christy Mathewson. The single most fantasized pitching matchup of the decade was finally becoming a reality. Baseball fans had been dreaming of just such a meeting for years. All eyes would be on Joplin, Missouri, come 26 October.

The bad weather of Cincinnati and Chicago was nothing compared to what awaited the tourists the next morning. When they arrived at 6:00 A.M. in Springfield, Illinois, snow was falling. Winter had come early to the Midwest—a winter that promised to be especially cruel at that. The schedule for the day underwent an immediate revision. The marching band and parade through town were scrapped. Rumor central had it that the game itself had been canceled, not just the parade. Amid a Christmas postcard landscape, the players huddled in the St. Nicholas Hotel and tried to stay warm. On ordinary days there was much of interest to see in Springfield, Abraham Lincoln's mausoleum for one. Today, however, everyone stayed close by to try and figure out what was going on. Light snow fell as the players boarded automobiles for the trek to League Park. It continued to snow even as the players took their warm-ups. At game time, not one of the players was sure whether a game would be played that day. At 2:15 in the afternoon McGraw and Callahan held a conference on the mound and decided to play ball.

Most of Springfield was convinced that there would be no game that day. Only five hundred frozen die-hards turned out at the ballpark to watch Illinois governor Edward F. Dunne, a Cook County Democrat, throw out the first pitch and shake hands with Callahan and McGraw. Art Fromme, the Giants' starting pitcher, and Larry Doyle, both of whom had passed through Springfield during their sojourns in the minor leagues, were put into the game for the benefit of the frigid locals. Jim Scott towed the rubber for the Sox. It was so cold that more than half of the players on both teams played wearing their warm-up jackets. Despite the brutal weather, the five hundred frozen faithful witnessed a pretty good ball game. The highlight of the Giants' 6–4 win had to be Jim Thorpe hitting the very first home run of the tour. In the bottom of the first inning, Thorpe sent Scott's first offering over the fence for a solo home run. In the fourth inning Mickey Doolan clouted the first grand slam of the tour.

The players could not wait to get back to the warmth of their train for a ride in comfort to their next stop, Peoria, Illinois. Arriving in Peoria, the tourists discovered weather that made the city, if anything, even colder and more inhospitable than was Springfield. The day dawned raw and cold. What had been a stiff breeze in the morning became a strong wind at noon. From there the weather took a turn for the nasty. Although the cold and wind were tolerable enough when the players arrived at the ballpark, by game time they were tapping out hits in a blizzard. Wiltse and Leverenz took the mound, but both had trouble gripping the ball with numb, blue hands. Despite the cold, both pitchers went the distance.

In Peoria, the tourists came under the scrutiny of movie cameras for the first time. A local man attempted to capture the game on film. Whether the man could capture images of anything other than driving snow is a big question mark. If he wanted to add some color to his narrative, he could have turned the camera on the stands and recorded the activities of the thoroughly miserable fans. From a fan's perspective, this very well may have been the single worst game of the entire tour. The driving snow obscured any view of game action, and the cold and wind were simply unbearable. So bad were conditions that some enterprising fans broke up seats in the old wooden stadium and used them as firewood. The crowd huddled around these small fires seeking warmth while the players tried hard to avoid frostbite on the field.

The White Sox took advantage of the chill to grab their first win of the tour, beating New York by a score of 6–4. "Wahoo" Sam Crawford was the most impressive offensively, clouting two triples. The postgame lunch at the Hotel Jefferson provided warmth and shelter for what was a miserable day all around.

Even Comiskey was having a bad day. Commy, accompanied by Walter Johnson, was traveling to his retreat in Eagle River, Wisconsin, when he made a stop in Milwaukee and attempted to sign the Senators' George McBride to a world tour contract. The premier fielding shortstop in the American League, McBride would have made a fine addition to the tour; unfortunately, McBride was nowhere to be found.

Rumors in Milwaukee explained McBride's absence as the result of meddling by Clark Griffith. Griffith, like many Major League owners, wanted his players to have no part of the world tour. Allowing Walter Johnson to pitch one or two games with the tourists was one thing, but there was no way he was going to allow Comiskey to take McBride on a dangerous six-month jaunt that only benefited Comiskey and McGraw. All year he had consistently advised McBride not to sign on. This *Chicago Daily Tribune* headline says it all: "Think 'Grif' Warned M'Bride, Milwaukee Fans Believe 'Old Fox' Told His Star to Hide and Escape World's Tour."[11]

If McBride's sudden "hunting trip" made Comiskey irritable, the news coming out of Chicago's municipal court was guaranteed to make him feel even worse; he had just been sued. Contractor John S. Murphy filed suit against Comiskey and the American League Baseball Association to recover his unpaid bill for the box seats he had installed for the start of the 1913 season as well as for the general repairs Murphy had made to the stadium throughout the year. After waiting all season for payment, Murphy filed for the $2,811 he was owed.

The White Sox's boss performed one more duty that day, sending a telegram to Fort Smith, Arkansas, informing them that their city had been dropped from the tour. The city leaders of Fort Smith had let it be known that they intended to present Comiskey and McGraw with watch fobs fashioned out of hangman's nooses and gallows. This act of bad taste spooked Comiskey, who wanted his tour to have nothing to do with death. Superstitious McGraw was cool to the macabre gift idea, too.

A bit farther north, in South Bend, Indiana, the day's bitter weather was enough to cause the Cubs to quit baseball altogether. The Sox's crosstown rivals left for their own tour on 18 October. Much less ambitious in scope, the Cubs were out barnstorming industrial and league teams throughout the Midwest. The winter weather of 21 October 1913 caused the Cubs to cancel all of the remaining games on their barnstorming schedule. The decision delighted the Cub barnstormers' manager, Ward Miller of Dixon, Indiana. A farmer, he promptly grabbed a train home to try and get his corn crop harvested ahead of the blizzard the tourists had played through.

On that same day, 21 October 1913, A. G. Spalding decided to foist himself upon the world tour. Retired and living in California, the reclusive millionaire chose this day to sail to Europe from Hoboken, New Jersey, aboard the *Kaiser Wilhelm II*. The *New York Telegraph* reported on his first European trip since 1889. "It is his attention while abroad, to meet the baseball players now touring the world and travel with them on the Continent."[12] Such an arrangement was the very last thing either Comiskey or McGraw wanted.

Comiskey had met face to face with Spalding earlier in the year, ostensibly to talk about the tour. This was, in fact, the only time the two met socially. The meeting was primarily a staged event for the benefit of news photographers rather than a meeting for holding any sort of qualitative discussion about touring the world. Comiskey met with Spalding because he was expected to, not because he had any interest in what the old man had to say. It was the same sort of distasteful "political" job Comiskey had seen his own father do time and again as a Chicago alderman. McGraw, who refused to rise to occasions such as this, never met with Spalding at all.

Wednesday, 23 October 1913, found the tourists in Ottumwa, Iowa. Iowa had the distinction of putting in more requests for a stop by the tourists than any other state. Twenty-five cities vied for the right to host the Giants and Sox. In the end, Comiskey and McGraw accepted bids only from Ottumwa and Sioux City.

In towns such as Ottumwa, the tourists' visit was financed by consortiums of sometimes very odd business alliances. Hoping for a windfall from folks coming into town to see games, some of whom would travel long distances to witness the Giants and White Sox, various local companies would combine their wealth to put up the $500 guarantee to cover the gate. Not surprising, most of these business alliances were comprised of stores that catered to men. In Ottumwa, Iowa, the coalition consisted of Hutchinson's Palace Cigar Store, Younkin's Cigar Store, the Colonial Billiard Parlor, and Sargent's Drugstore.

To promote the game, Hutchinson's Palace Cigar Store distributed large lithographs of the players from both teams. Small investments by local shopkeepers often netted smart returns for the dollar. More than three hundred people came to Ottumwa from the nearby town of Centerville, Iowa, alone. Whole families made holiday to see baseball. The White Sox would be the "home" team for this contest and accordingly became the town's sentimental favorite.

In a schedule that was already routine, the tourists' day in Ottumwa was arranged to give the local citizens as much of the tourists as possible. The Honeymoon Special arrived at 5:00 in the morning. Nearly every tourist slept through the train's arrival. To help local worshippers pay homage to the stars that morning, the train was parked on a prominent siding. At 10:00 A.M. Germany Schaefer, Jimmy Callahan, and Mike Donlin were seen strolling about the downtown business district. As visitors came into Ottumwa for the game, they were escorted through the town by the Fifty-fourth Regiment Band. Fairly early in the day, groups of fans began clustering around the tourists' train, cheering and demanding an appearance from one of their heroes. In Ottumwa and most other cities, Germany Schaefer was sent out to entertain the crowd.

Germany Schaefer was not who the inhabitants had been clamoring to see. In town after town, the cheers and calls were for "Matty, Matty, Matty." Christy Mathewson was a private man, however, who really did not cater to the celebrity culture he inhabited. Sometimes McGraw would send out Schaefer, who would impersonate Mathewson. The two men looked nothing at all alike, but in an age when even the best newspaper photographs were grainy images and newsreels were little better, few in the crowd could really say that they knew what Matty looked like, especially at a distance and in a mad mob of fans knotted around a railroad car.

McGraw, Matty, Schaefer, and the rest of the players on tour enjoyed Germany's impersonations enormously. While Schaefer delivered platitudes about some town's scenery, its beautiful landscapes, and its friendly people with the aplomb of the most adept politician on a whistle-stop tour, the players inside the train pulled down the shades and laughed their heads off.

More than thirty-five hundred fans from across Iowa turned out at the Myrtle Street Grounds in Ottumwa to take in the game. Jimmy Callahan, who had passed through Iowa several times during his minor league career, received the biggest hand from the crowd. To the audience's delight, the White Sox dominated the Giants with a 7–2 win. In a battle of the bridegrooms, Reb Russell defeated Jeff Tesreau, with both going the distance.

It may surprise modern readers, but by 1913 every "modern" facet of baseball already existed, including rabid fans and autograph seekers. One Ottumwa story involved a wizened farmer from Fairfield, Iowa, named Samuel Salts. The *Ottumwa Daily Courier* wrote of Salt's day in the big city.

> Mr. Salts came to Ottumwa to see the game because he is an ardent fan, and proved it to a number of those near him in the grandstand yesterday afternoon. He was not at all bashful. In fact he was an enthusiastic fan and so much so that when the opportunity offered itself he searched out the famous "Muggsy" [sic] John McGraw, manager of the New York Giants and discussed the national pastime with his genial "Jawn" at length. Those nearby thought for a time that they were old friends or possibly "townies" from the same country. At any rate the spectators who could not resist peeping were surprised to see the Giants manager present Mr. Salts with a ball. Nor was that all. This Mr. Salts is not only a fan but a curio or autograph collector

and finding someone in the crowd with an indelible pencil asked Mr. McGraw to write his name upon the horsehide sphere, which with the date of the game and the place thereof, made a souvenir of the game that could not be bought from this Salts person for love or money. He was heard to say upon placing the ball in his pocket after having fondled it for some time, that he would probably will it to some of his male posterity who showed sufficient love for the national sport to prize such a gift. Mr. Salts is 69 years old and a resident of Jefferson county for the past forty-five years. He admits that he is a baseball fan.[13]

After the game the tourists congregated at the Ballingall Hotel to wash up, feast on dinner, and prepare for the next day's adventures. Their special left in the evening for their next destination, Sioux City, Iowa, where at last they caught some nice weather as autumn reappeared.

The day was a beautiful, humidity-free seventy degrees. Christy Mathewson's mind, however, certainly was not in Sioux City that day. The famous Giants pitcher's day was one of distractions. An ardent golfer, the Big Six was prescient enough to bring along his golf clubs. On the morning of 23 October 1913 he and Mike Donlin hit the local links. It is unlikely that even a morning of tooling around the links, a pleasure that Matty especially enjoyed, completely eased his thoughts this day. More than likely Matty's mind was back in New York, on Broadway to be precise.

That afternoon, while the Giants and White Sox were entertaining the crowds in Sioux City, *The Girl and the Pennant*, a play Mathewson had cowritten with Rida Johnson Young, opened at the Lyric Theater on Broadway. The play is a conventional tale of romance between a young woman who owns the fictional Eagles baseball team and her star pitcher. The hurler is menaced by gamblers, who want him to throw the championship game. At the same time, he struggles with his feelings for the woman who owns the Eagles and also valiantly strives to overcome his own battle with the bottle. While this sort of melodrama may be a tad out of fashion today, the play received rave reviews and had an impressive run in New York. The play's popularity was such that it was even turned into a novel and serialized in newspapers all around the country.

It is difficult to know how much of the plot was contrived by Mathewson. More than likely he provided Young (who also starred as the female lead) with insights into baseball between the lines. Mathewson may also very well have supplied the names of the characters, the most obvious collection of roman à clefs in history. The names ballplayers are given in the cast include Harry Doyle, Cy Dobb, Fed Terkle, Otto Knafe, Cosy Jolan, and Tom MacNish.

This day was a day for the Giants. Mathewson won raves on Broadway, and the crowd raved for their favorite team in Sioux City, the Giants. Just across the Missouri River in Nebraska were reservations housing the Winnebago and Omaha tribes. Members of both nations were out in force to cheer on the Giants, especially John "Chief" Meyers and Jim Thorpe. In a time when Native Americans were not even citizens, finding something to root for was a rare pleasure. Native American participation in baseball was at its zenith in the first two decades of the twentieth century. Native Americans were accepted on the athletic field in a way they simply were not accepted anywhere else. Albert "Chief" Bender of the Philadelphia A's and Meyers were not only prominent as Native Americans, they also stood among the very best at their positions in the game. Jim Thorpe, almost alone among his peers, was never called "chief," the racist appellation hung regularly on Native American players.

Nearly all of the Native Americans in baseball in the 1910s tended to be private, almost shy, men. The fans in Sioux City were simply too much for the studious Meyers. The baseball player's every action was greeted with cheers and reported about in the press the same way that today's pop stars are. Here is how the *Sioux City Tribune* described the tourists' reception and the colorful impression that the athletes made on middle America.

> The lobby of the Martin Hotel was as crowded as political headquarters at convention time while the Giants and White Sox were taking luncheon. The curious in the hundreds snaked around the entrance to take a peek at the most advertised athletes in the world. The inconveniences undergone by those anxious to view the ballplayers was more than repaid when the big leaguers returned to the lobby and mingled with the throng. Judging them as mere men, they are splendid specimens.
>
> Take as an average they are tall, well developed, with well-tanned and tightly drawn skin, the sure sign of an athlete in training. They carry no surplus flesh, although the generous manner in which they fill their coats about the neck and shoulders indicates a hardened supply of muscle. They are a clean-cut lot of athletes who pay little or no attention to the tributes of the curious.
>
> As to clothes—well a body of tailors in convention would expire with joy to have such models to display their handiwork. The heroes of the diamond appear dressed in the latest and finest offerings of the

haberdasher. Well-tailored suits, elaborate cravats, "nifty" hats and the most English of English shoes are earnestly professed by the touring athletes.

Mathewson and Big Chief Meyers were the chief objects of curiosity. Mathewson had a hard time pushing his way through the lobby. He was gracious, of course, in shaking hands with those who advanced to meet the "Big Six," and was all smiles during the brief conversations, but he was also anxious to get away from the crowd.

The "Big Chief" did not enjoy the homage, as could be seen by his facial expression. He shifted his gaze rapidly around the lobby until he saw a side door leading to Pierce street. He bolted for the exit, leaving his admirers in the hotel except two or three of the more persistent hero worshippers who followed in the immediate vicinity of his greatness.[14]

The largest crowd to see a ball game in the history of Sioux City went home well satisfied. If there were any disappointed customers, it would have been the assembled Native Americans, as McGraw did not even bother to insert Meyers into the lineup, and Jim Thorpe went hitless. The audience, however, was pleased to witness a Giants' 6–3 win, the big hit being Sam Crawford's mammoth home run. After the game and dinner at the Martin Hotel, it was back onto the train for transit to Blue Rapids, Kansas.

Blue Rapids made more of an impact on the tourists than did any other city on the tour. The smallest town to sponsor a game, Blue Rapids had a population of just eighteen hundred souls, but for one brilliant Friday afternoon in October 1913 it became host to more than four thousand people (by some estimates five thousand) turning out to watch the White Sox beat the Giants 8–5. Like something out of W. P. Kinsella's novel *Shoeless Joe* or the movie it inspired, *Field of Dreams*, this town, described by Gus Axelson "as a speck on the Prairie," swelled to almost triple its population for an exhibition baseball game.[15] Folks came across the plains from as far away as a hundred miles. The afternoon was pure American magic.

Still viewed by its inhabitants as one of Blue Rapids's finest hours, the little town put on a show that wowed even the jaded media of New York and Chicago. As the *Minneapolis Messenger* newspaper aptly stated, "The New York Giants and Chicago White Sox will play in Blue Rapids on the 24th of this month. On that day president Wilson would not attract much attention in Blue Rapids."[16]

Blue Rapids was and remains a gypsum-mining town, but Blue Rapids has never been a typical prairie town. Settled mostly by upstate New Yorkers who had come to make their fortune in the mines, Blue Rapids retained its sophisticated roots. Chautauqua regularly stopped by; Blue Rapids was the smallest town to ever host Chautauqua. A planned community with a public square, acres of parkland, a baseball grounds, and a library, which in 1913 was already thirty-nine years old, Blue Rapids was far more urbane than most of the farmer settlements elsewhere in the state.

Gus Axelson, reporting in the *Chicago Daily Tribune*, was simply amazed at the turnout in the tiny town.

Warm weather and tremendous enthusiasm greeted the White Sox and Giants today when they arrived for the seventh game of the trip around the world. Most of the people in three counties assembled for the noteworthy event, about 3,500 being present. They crowded the little ballpark, hung on the fences like fringe, and peeked through all the knotholes. The Sox won the game 8 to 5.

From early in the morning when the tourists' special pulled in, until it departed tonight, the town was a moving mass of baseball fans. At noon all the stores closed their doors and the schools dismissed their pupils. Everyone congregated in the city square and it was declared the biggest day the town of Blue Rapids ever had.

The special train arrived a little ahead of schedule time, but the reception committee was not caught unawares. Twenty-five motorcars were at the depot, and all the tourists were driven around the town and out into the country while the natives looked on in admiring wonder. Thorpe, Russell, and Mathewson were the athletes most sought by the townsmen as they had been especially advertised.

The country folk swarmed into the town early in the morning. They came in automobiles, top buggies, milk wagons, and lumber wagons. It is estimated that 500 automobiles were in town, and Main street "resembled" State street in Chicago.[17]

The *New York Herald* said simply, "This town is on the map."[18] Even bustling San Francisco was impressed by the turnout. George E. Phair of the *Examiner* remarked, "Those 4,000 rooters who gathered to watch the world tourists in Blue Rapids must have caused the constable a hard day's work."[19]

The reception the two teams received in Blue Rapids was seen in some quarters as a referendum on the popularity of the game of baseball itself. The *New York Herald* extolled the tourists and their tour.

Baseball has almost ceased to be a sport. It is greater than that. It is now a national institution.

The most illuminating insight into the character of the American people was afforded in the smallest town in the entire itinerary, unless Bisbee and Douglas have shrunk of late. This is Blue Rapids, Kan. This town in the gypsum belt has at least one thing in common with the metropolitan cities, in that the inhabitants are certain that Uncle Sam cheated them while taking the census.

This Blue Rapids is a staid town and it has grown out of its swaddling clothes. The hotel in which the tourists hung their clothes was built about 1858, so you might expect considerable conservatism from the inhabitants, who have seen the village grow from a frontier camp to a place where two railroads are almost in sight of the outlying residences.

This is only meant as a preliminary to the question again proposed. "Why is baseball?" For with such people it might be expected that life would mean more than sport. The day of the "great game," however gave a lie to that conjecture. In parenthesis it might be stated that when the Sox and Giants promised to come here the town went absolutely "nutty."

The tourists found practically every house decorated. Every automobile, and there were plenty of them, carried flags of every description in honor of the occasion. The most prominent minister in the town opened his house for the accommodation of the players, as he boasted one of the few bathtubs, and his family was proud to have them as guests.

Judges, lawyers, and politicians crowded the athletes off the sidewalks for a chance to shake hands with them, and thus the miracle of the loaves and fishes was repeated in that a town of 1,800 furnished more than 3,000 paid admissions to the game.

Were there some doubling at the gate? Assuredly not, but the problem in figures was solved by the fact that it was the neighbors of Blue Rapids who helped out. These neighbors came from considerable distance. One brought his family of four to the game in his new automobile, and the distance he traveled there and back was 260 miles. Considerable enthusiasm for the national game all right. Towns within a radius of fifty miles poured in several hundred and the majority came in their own machines, as the trains, run for the occasion, were not overcrowded.

In the motley crowd which pushed through the canvas walls were scores of pioneers who used to sleep on their rifles at night to ward off Indian raids. One farmer who went by the name of "Uncle Ben" and whose hair had been bleached to a snowy white under the Kansas sun, was asked why he traveled forty miles to see a couple of strange ball teams play.

"I may not look so young as I once was, but I keep track of the scores and I had to come in and get a peek at 'Christy' Mathewson" was the rejoinder from the octogenarian. Two-thirds of the spectators called the players by their first, second, and third nicknames immediately. "Bill" Klem, umpire, had introduced each player by his given and surname. These natives were readers of the daily newspapers. Rural delivery has indeed made baseball a national institution.[20]

Other towns scheduled to host the tour were as awed by the attendance figures from the Kansas prairie town as were New York and Chicago. In Missouri, the *Joplin Daily Globe* tabulated this amazing statistic. "Blue Rapids is in Marshall County, Northwest of Kansas City, which has a population of 23,000. More than one person to every six in the county saw the game. At this ratio there would be more than 15,000 persons at Miners Park Monday when the teams play here."[21]

Spectacular weather and the astounding turnout certainly put the athletes in a genial mood. Christy Mathewson, usually humble and unassuming before crowds, engaged in a rare feat of machismo in Blue Rapids. Before the game, the Big Six had one of the locals procure a plank, which Matty then split with a fastball thrown from forty paces. Supposedly, the board was six feet long and a quarter of an inch thick, yet Matty's ball passed through the board with ease.

Over time this tale has, no doubt, been embellished. Surely the dimensions of the board and the distance the ball traveled have grown over the years. Yet without question the origins of the tale are authentic. We know this because there remains in Blue Rapids an eyewitness, one-hundred-year-old Ben Mall, who, as far as this author can determine, is the last living witness to the Tour to End All Tours.

As a twelve-year-old, Ben rode a motorcycle with his uncle David Huffman to the game in Blue Rapids from his home in Clay Center, Kansas. The distance between the two towns is roughly forty miles, a difficult, dusty ride on the primitive motorcycles of the time. Ben's cousin James Scott was one of ten local businessmen who put up $100 each to lure the tourists to Blue Rapids. This relationship garnered Ben a great seat along the first base line.

Before the game, Ben mixed with the massive crowd swelling Blue Rapids. From the town square, he watched the band march into town followed by the athletes, all decked out in their uniforms. Part of the route the players took, ironically, had them pass before a massive billboard advertising their game.

Like most of the town, Ben shook hands with the Giants' Jeff Tesreau. Another resident, George Hewitt, spent the day photographing the baseball heroes. Hewitt took photographs of Tesreau, the teams marching into town, and some game action shots; he even got Christy Mathewson to tip his hat for the camera. The town went all out for the strangers, swelling the grandstand of the local ballpark. The folks coming to the game whether from far away or close by were in for a real treat this game day. Kansas's dry laws magically vanished, and beer was sold openly at the game.

The Blue Rapids baseball field (without a name) is one of just three stadiums still remaining from the tour. It looks much the same today as it did back in 1913, save that the grandstand roof was torn off in a windstorm in 1977. Site of sandlot and Little League ball today, in 1913 the stadium was filled to overflowing with fans occupying every corner and every crag. An impromptu outfield wall was created by lining up an armada of Model T's in an arc stretching from foul pole to foul pole. The town's boosters did not miss a trick, charging these cars fifty cents for the privilege of being part of the game.

Schools and businesses dismissed at noon, giving the inhabitants an early start to the weekend and allowing all the locals to get good seats at the game. The perfect weather and the great crowd brought out the best in the athletes, who played their most exciting game of the tour thus far. The White Sox slugged four home runs off of Hooks Wiltse in an 8–5 victory. Nearly ninety years later, Ben Mall could still recall how angry Wiltse became at surrendering so many gopher balls. The greatest day in Blue Rapids went off without a hitch. After departing Kansas, their ears still ringing from the cheers of five thousand grateful fans, the tourists headed for Missouri, where the teams would play their next three games.

Blanche McGraw, most assuredly not a baseball fan, skipped the early part of the tour. She would reunite with her husband in El Paso, Texas, on 5 November. Until then, she amused herself by visiting friends throughout the Midwest. In Milwaukee, a reporter for the *New York Morning Telegraph* tracked her down at the home of Mrs. Joe O'Brien, the Giants' former office manager. On the same day that the Giants and White Sox were making an indelible impact on the town of Blue Rapids, the reporter asked Blanche McGraw how she felt about the game of baseball. "Me a fan? No hardly that. You see, I like baseball, but I like it because it is my husband's business, and every wife should know her husband's business, so she can be his confidant when he wants to get his troubles out of his system. A wife, if she knows conditions, is the one person to tell troubles to. I'm not a suffragette. Women should be wives and help their husbands, not try to be too independent."[22]

The Missouri phase of the tour began for Blanche's husband and his charges on 25 October 1913. First up would be St. Joseph. Like every town in which the tourists would play in the state, St. Joseph sits on the Missouri River, in the western part of the state. The tourists were met at Union Station and paraded through town in a fleet of automobiles close behind a marching band. After touring the city, it was off for lunch to the Robidoux Hotel. In the evening everyone ate dinner with the St. Joseph Boosters Club.

Five thousand people turned out on a beautiful fall afternoon to see Christy Mathewson pitch and to welcome Tris Speaker into the White Sox fold. Boston's magnificent outfielder had taken a rather roundabout route from Texas to join the tour. The Sox were, of course, glad to see him, but they had expected him at least a few days earlier in Sioux City.

The game itself was a classic pitchers' duel. Christy Mathewson and Walter Leverenz squared off for a 4–3 White Sox victory. Matty was on top of his game, utilizing all of his legendary pinpoint control; he did not surrender a walk. The White Sox defense spelled the difference in the game. The trio of Schaefer at second, Weaver at short, and Chase at first turned two double plays. The second of the twin killings was a costly one for the Sox, however. Buck Weaver speared a line drive and sped the ball to Hal Chase, who recorded the out but in the process awkwardly turned his ankle. Instantly, Chase crumbled to the turf in pain. Doc White relieved Chase, whose injury, at first glance, appeared so severe it seemed unlikely that he would be able to continue with the tour.

Next it was downriver to Kansas City, largest city in the state and future home of Major League Baseball. Kansas City had teams for brief periods in both the American Association and the National League in the final two decades of the nineteenth century. From 1914 to 1915, the city would house the Federal League's Packers. Almost a hatchling, the incubating Federal League was beginning to make noises. The very day the tourists visited Kansas City, the Feds announced that George Stovall, former manager of the American League's St. Louis Browns, would be managing the Kansas City Feds come springtime. That team would play across town at Gordon and Koppel Field, one of six new "Fed" ballparks.

More than four thousand fans ignored atrocious weather and entered Association Park to get a glimpse of the Sox and Giants. Rain mixed with snow fell all day long, turning the field into a sloppy mess. The Giants won easily by the score of 6–2. Helping the Giants greatly was the Sox's Doc White, filling in at first for the ailing Hal Chase. Normally a pitcher or outfielder, White had trouble making the transition to the first corner of the diamond. Red Faber made his first appearance in this game. He gave up several walks and no runs; the damage had already been done, but because of the scoring methods used in 1913, Faber nonetheless was charged with the loss.

Joplin, Missouri, site of the contest for the next day, 27 October, heralded the long-awaited arrival of Walter Johnson. Walter "the Big Train" Johnson, the Senators' star pitcher, was Christy Mathewson's only serious rival for the title of the greatest pitcher in baseball. The pride of Coffeyville, Kansas, arrived in town alone late in the evening of Sunday, 26 October. If all went according to plan, the two would face off on Monday afternoon at 2:30 at Miners Park.

Joplin had actually gotten its first glimpse of Johnson a fortnight before when he scouted the town as a guest of Jimmy Bronson, one of the local promoters. The arrival of the man whom the local paper dubbed "Human Shrapnel" set all of Joplin on its ear.[23]

> Joplin got its first look at Walter Johnson yesterday. And Joplin wasn't disappointed.
>
> Six feet of Athletic stature hove in when King Walter dropped off a Frisco train yesterday morning. Bespangled in the latest toggery, neat as the dapper chap who piloted him, and squaring his broad shoulders till he looked the part of the athlete he is, he began a hike to the Connor Hotel.[24]

A bit farther down the same page we read, "Before the hotel was reached, however, Bronson stopped an acquaintance and presented Mr. Johnson. 'I'd rather shake that hand than the mitt of the president,' came from the Joplin man. He's known for his membership in a club that knows nothing but baseball."[25]

Johnson was only too happy to give his opinion about the upcoming face-off with Matty.

> Johnson talked enthusiastically when his engagement to pitch against Christy Mathewson in Joplin next Monday was mentioned. He wants to meet the "Old Master" just as much as the thousands who will be here are desirous of witnessing their meeting.
>
> "You tell them," he said, "that I am for this game. Nothing ever pleased me more. I'm a great admirer of Mathewson, for he is a wonder in the box." And he grinned a satisfied grin when he said it.[26]

As the tourists progressed steadily west and southward, primarily following the trail that one day would become Route 66, they found a more rustic America. Certainly the *Joplin Daily Globe* was the most unsophisticated paper to cover the teams thus far. Mickey Doolan, for example, was billed as being a member of the Philadelphia Athletics instead of the crosstown Phillies. Arthur Fletcher, Giants shortstop, never left New York, was never considered for the tour, yet for some reason was advertised as being a part of the world tour. The proprietor of Baum's Mercantile Company devised his own novel ad copy to draw attention to the game. His advertisement, published the day before the game, read in part, "Tomorrow there will be more than 57 varieties of fans and fanesses out at Miners Park, looking at the classiest article of the National Game that this section of the United States has ever seen."[27]

While the writing may have been firmly entrenched in the Missouri vernacular, in other ways Joplin was as advanced as Chicago. Its theater showed first-run films. If any of the tourists had some spare time they could have stopped in at the Ideal Theater to see filmed highlights of the 1913 World Series between the Athletics and the Giants. Admission to the two-reeler cost just five cents, but it is likely that McGraw had seen enough of the A's at the beginning of the month.

As in Ottumwa, an enterprising man filmed the proceedings with a movie camera. The local man, Laurence Simmons, actually invented the camera he wielded to capture the athletes in action. In those days, most inventors, tinkerers, and crackpots could find at least one rich person in town to act as their personal philanthropist. Small town moneybags were always hot on the trail of the next Thomas Edison. Simmons's device had been embraced by A. B. Reese, one of the game's promoters. Reese followed a simple rationale: make money promoting the game and then make money promoting movies of the game.

If Simmons arrived at the ball yard early, he would have captured shots of fans still filing into the grounds. Bad weather wreaked havoc with many folks' travel plans. For more than a few of the thousands who turned up in Joplin, just getting to the game was an adventure. The *Joplin Daily Globe* documented the misadventures of a quartet of baseball fans from a nearby town who braved the day's nasty weather.

Death might have stopped four Fairview, Mo., men from watching Walter Johnson pitch yesterday, but under the circumstances it is doubtful.

They were Colonel Al Hudson, T. Perry, F. H. Forsythe, and W. W.

Goosetree. They started on the Missouri & North Railway Company train. Near Neosho the train was delayed by a wreck. Walking back to Fairview the men climbed in Forsythe's car and pulled the throttle back. Between Diamond and Granby the motor car skidded into a ditch three and one half feet deep, and turned over. Goosetree received a sprained ankle. Hudson was pulled from under the machine. They righted the car and started again. This time they reached Joplin safely. Arriving at Miners Park they saw Walter Johnson pitch part of the third inning. They were glad to get there.[28]

These four adventurers, and everyone else attending the game, had to put up with snowy, soggy, treacherous roads. What Joplin did not have was baseball weather. Three inches of snow covered the town when the tourists arrived. The early morning sunshine burned most of this off but left the field at Miners Park a swollen, soggy mess. Christy Mathewson took one look at the deplorable field conditions and refused to play. The tourists gave serious thought to canceling the game, and if it had been left to the managers and teams it would have been.

However, the local boosters, led by Reese, who had made his money in the Tulsa, Oklahoma, oil fields, would not hear of it. There were four thousand fans in the seats, expecting a match between Mathewson and Johnson, and the boosters were in no mood to start issuing refunds. Rather than forfeit their share of the gate, Callahan and McGraw had their men take the field. The match between Matty and the Big Train was postponed until the next day in Tulsa. Walter Johnson, still fresh and eager to please the "fans and fanesses," took the mound. He would only pitch three innings, however, on the sloppy field before making way for Joe Benz. McGraw sent Bunny Hearn to the mound, who promptly started pitching like a frightened rabbit.

The appallingly bad conditions made play a nightmare for both teams, a fact reflected in the final score of 13–12 in favor of the Giants. The muddy conditions made fielding difficult, and the muddy, sopping-wet baseball sailed up to the plate like an oversized softball, making an inviting target for the hitters. That evening, the players and their wives enjoyed an all-night buffet in the Connor Hotel. Along with A. B. Reese and a few of his friends, the teams partied until almost 1:15 A.M. when their train left Missouri for Oklahoma.

Tulsa, Oklahoma, should have been the greatest single day of the tour. The meeting in Tulsa on 28 October should have been more than a forgotten footnote linking the careers of Walter Johnson and Christy Mathewson.

Whatever one imagines as to how this particular Oklahoma day should have played out, events as they actually transpired are assuredly not part of that vision.

The day started well. The stadium filled to overflowing. Governor Lee Cruse, in town for the International Dry Farming Conference, threw out the first pitch under an aluminum October sky. The air was raw and cold, but otherwise it was a fine day for baseball. The South Main Street Park had not seen a game in over two years; all of Tulsa fandom seethed with anticipation. Then, half an hour before game time, "without even a warning crack, the frail wooden stands crashed, hurling 500 men, women and children into a struggling, screaming mass of humanity."[29]

The overloaded right-field bleachers collapsed just as a contingent of soldiers from Company L Ninth Infantry out of Fort Root, Arkansas, was passing underneath them. The soldiers were buried beneath broken planking, twisted metal, and scores of distraught and injured baseball fans. One soldier, Private Chester Taylor, had his skull fractured in several places by the jagged edge of a wooden support beam. He died on the way to the hospital. In all, fifty people were injured, some severely. Every available ambulance, automobile, and policeman was pressed into service to ferry the injured to the hospital. Twenty-five people had injuries that necessitated hospitalization. Injuries ranged from a wrenched back to multiple and compound fractures of limbs.

These very same collapsed stands had been used only moments before as an entrance to the stadium by the wives of a trio of Giants, Rea Lobert, Anna Meyers, and Edith Doyle. The women had been forced to use this entrance to avoid the massive crowding at the main gate.

Only a generation before, Oklahoma had been Indian Territory. Now a state run by whites, it still boasted the largest population of Native Americans in the United States. Hundreds of Native Americans came to this game, just as they had in Sioux City, and for the very same purpose, to cheer on Chief Meyers and Jim Thorpe. Their turnout helped fill the stadium to overflowing.

Oklahoma governor Cruse and his staff were seated only a few feet away from the collapse and witnessed the entire spectacle. Instead of insisting on a postponement, the governor shared the opinion of the crowd that the game should go on. After clearing the area surrounding the collapse and tending to the wounded, that is exactly what happened. Astoundingly, after a thirty-minute delay, the game went on as scheduled in the rickety old wooden ballpark.

The two pitching rivals shook hands on the mound before tearing into each other. Walter Johnson was in fine form. He mowed through the Giants, turning in a complete-game shutout, scattering nine hits and recording eight strikeouts. An obviously tired Mathewson did not fare so well. Matty left the game after four innings behind by a score of 2–0. In his four innings Mathewson surrendered seven hits and only managed two strikeouts. Hooks Wiltse relieved Matty, who exited to a standing ovation and the cheers of Tulsa. The final score of 6–0 aptly demonstrated Johnson's domination and control over the Giants. The tragedy more than likely had an impact on the pace of the game. All nine innings were played in a brisk one hour and ten minutes, only fourteen minutes off the Major League record.

Sadly, the Tulsa grandstand collapse was a foreseeable disaster. The stands that gave way had been blown over by high winds back in 1911. They had been hastily repaired, but even at the time there were suspicions about the quality of the work. The ensuing two years of weathering did nothing to improve the situation.

After a night of heavy partying and banqueting and trying to put the collapse out of mind, the Honeymoon Special wound its way along the Arkansas River. The tourists arrived in Muskogee, Oklahoma, which had replaced Fort Smith, Arkansas, on the schedule, at around 6:00 on the morning of 29 October 1913. Most of the athletes slept until late in the morning before stirring and milling about town. The game was to be played at the brand new diamond at the fairgrounds.

Although the Muskogee game was organized late (Ted Sullivan came into town ahead of the players on Tuesday evening to finalize the details), attendance was surprisingly robust. No doubt the attendance was boosted by the good weather. More than three thousand people made their way to the diamond to see the Sox pummel the Giants 7–1. Jim Scott defeated Arthur Fromme, knotting the transcontinental series at six games apiece. Several hundred authentic Oklahoma cowboys filled the stands in Musko-gee. All day long the athletes' ears rang with the sound of cowboy yells and cheers. The rowdy cowboys' ecstatic, almost sing-song cheering was like nothing the athletes had ever heard before. After a banquet at the Hotel Severs, it was off to the Lone Star State.

Texas, land of the open prairie, hosted games in more of its cities than any other state. Seven cities from every part of Texas were scheduled to host games. Many of the tourists had strong links with Texas, either from their minor league careers in Texas's many leagues or, as in the case of Reb Russell and Tris Speaker, from being homegrown heroes. Even some of the northerners had deep roots in the state. Ted Sullivan learned how to be a baseball magnate during his early years in Texas. Sullivan's skills at organizing led to the formation of the Texas League. His hands-on approach to league building left him with a comprehensive knowledge of Texas. He had probably visited or had knowledge of every town of any size in the state. The founder of the Texas League had friends scattered about every corner of Texas and was as well connected in the state as any Longhorn politician.

The star attraction in Bonham was Reb Russell, who had been born and raised there. Bonham lies just a few miles south of the Red River, which forms the border between Oklahoma and Texas. On this cold Thursday morning, Bonham went all out to welcome home its native son. The day dawned with a chill, like a New England autumn; you could easily see your breath out-of-doors. Though they had been progressing steadily southward, the tourists just could not seem to find much warmth.

The temperature did not phase Bonham's residents, who were busily engaged in providing a Texas-sized welcome to Russell. At 9:00 A.M. when the tourists' train pulled into the station, everyone knocked off work for an hour to greet it. A band playing Texas standards, the mayor, and every dignitary worth his or her salt turned out at the station that morning and shadowed the teams all day long.

The White Sox hurler was ready for his audience and determined to impress the home folks. Aboard the train, "a suspicion was abroad that Russell had not gone to bed, as he was decked out in his finest regalia hours before Bonham was reached."[30] Russell and his new bride were the first persons off the train and were immediately escorted to the lead automobile for the de rigueur motor tour of the city. Russell wished to take his bride home to meet his parents, so he sped ahead on the route, veered away from the motorcade, and, taking the back roads, spirited his wife home. Russell's decision frustrated the excited clusters of fans surrounding the Alexandria Hotel who had hoped to meet him. However, all was forgiven by the time game time rolled around at 2:30 P.M.

Baseball shut down Bonham, Texas, on 30 October 1913. The factories let out, the schools and courts closed, and even the post office dismissed its employees early. A sellout crowd of four thousand filled the stadium to cheer for Reb Russell. The afternoon sun had taken some of the chill off, making the day more comfortable all around. The southpaw strode to the mound and pitched a dandy of a game. The fact that he lost it had more to do with the Sox's numerous fielding errors, which accounted for all four of the Giants' runs, than from any flaw in his delivery. His opponent, the Giants' Jeff Tesreau, didn't make things any easier. Tesreau threw spitballs all day long, surrendering only a single run to claim the victory. The final score of 4–1 was the only blot on Russell's day.

After the game concluded, Russell received permission to take a brief leave from the tour so he could spend some more time at home. No doubt the honeymooners wanted more privacy than a shared railroad car could provide. Russell headed home even before his teammates had consumed the fine postgame banquet provided by the Bonham Board of Trade.

Halloween would be spent in Dallas. With the Texas State Fair going full tilt, exhibition baseball became just one more exhibit at the fairgrounds. The night before, the tourists got to know what being a sideshow freak feels like; they were hijacked and displayed like a troop of geeks. Their train was supposed to be parked for one hour in Denison, Texas. More than a thousand locals turned out to cheer a parked train. The Denison Elks Club set out a massive feast before the already-stuffed athletes, then bribed railway officials into keeping the train well past its scheduled time. Finally, at 3:30 A.M. the trainload of calorie-laden baseball players sped off to Dallas.

Texas rail transit was perhaps the quirkiest in the country in 1913; freight and stock transport took priority over human passengers. Passenger routes often strayed far from straight lines, looping from city to city in great arcs, while cattle took the express lines. Denison is actually north of Bonham; it is, however, located on one of Dallas's main railroad spurs. To get to Dallas, the players steamed north and west before they could turn south. There was no direct route (at least for passenger trains) between Texas's agricultural capital and its corporate capital.

At 6:40 A.M. the tourists, bleary-eyed and bedraggled, arrived in the big D. The day dawned bright and warm. It would be a great day for baseball. The sparkling weather made the golf courses attractive as well, which is where Fred Merkle and Christy Mathewson spent their morning. Even better, the duo got to extend their green time courtesy of Dallas's hardworking office drones.

A day before the game, four hundred bank clerks had successfully petitioned the city to push the starting time back a half hour from 3:00 to 3:30 P.M. Starting the game after bankers' hours would boost attendance; it would also mean that toward the end of the game the players would be battling the setting sun. Both teams would have to keep things moving along quickly if they wanted to avoid tangling in the twilight.

At the appointed hour, five thousand fans made their way into Gaston Park to watch Christy Mathewson and Walter Leverenz. For the first three innings it was a contest. In the top of the fourth, however, Matty had one of the worst innings of his life. The inning started innocently with Hans Lobert allowing a dribbler through his legs for an error; then the deluge began. The Sox sent eleven batters to the plate, slugging four doubles and three singles, scoring seven runs off Mathewson. The final score read 10–3 in favor of the White Sox. Both Mathewson and Leverenz went the distance. Played in a brisk one hour and thirty-three minutes, the tourists finished just as the sun crept below the horizon and the Texas sky began to chill.

At the conclusion of the game, Tris Speaker excused himself from the tour for a few days to visit his mother in Hubbard, Texas. As "Spoke" departed, ancient Frank Isbell arrived to join the tour. Isbell's participation in the tour was strictly a favor offered him as a benefit for being a White Sox alumnus. In 1913 he was thirty-eight years old and had not pitched at the Major League level since 1907. Isbell would contribute little more to the tour than to serve as an extra body on Callahan's bench.

The following day, Friday, the first day of November 1913, found the tourists in Beaumont, Texas. Oil country in the midst of a boom, Beaumont's landscape was littered with the conical spiderwebs of oil wells and echoed with the incessant drone of machinery. All about the town, millions of dollars were being won or lost in the Texas oil fields. Ordinarily, such an environment fascinated the players, but this day the tourists were in a foul mood.

Not only was it still cold, now there was nothing to eat. A slew of mechanical problems had made the train ride to Beaumont a nightmare. The journey had been unrelentingly dark and eerie, since no one could get the train's interior lighting to work. Morning relieved that gloom, but another quickly replaced it when breakfast time rolled around. There was no breakfast. In fact, there was not a scrap of food to be found anywhere on the train. The very hungry tourists did not get a bite to eat until they arrived in Beaumont in the afternoon. McGraw and Callahan laid into the railroad company with their full wrath. Invective after invective was spat at railroad officials. You really didn't want to be cursed at by John McGraw. The two managers even phoned the railroad company's headquarters and cussed a blue streak through the corporate offices. Their Irish anger must have been something to see. According to Gus Axelson, "The managers meant business this time and kept the wires to Chicago hot all day."[31]

Surprisingly, starving the players produced an exciting game. Red Faber impressed his bosses with this outing, holding the Giants scoreless through five innings. Faber surrendered just one earned run, a homer to Sam Crawford, and an unearned run before being lifted in the eighth inning in favor of Joe Benz. Unfortunately for Faber, he would not get the win, as

Benz promptly tossed the game-winning home run to Larry Doyle for a
3–2 Giants' win.

The same day, 1 November 1913, the Federals fired the first shot over
the bow of the Major Leagues. Meeting in Indianapolis, league officials
admitted teams from Buffalo, Baltimore, and New York. The Feds were
moving east, taking on both the Majors and their principal minor league
cities in the International League. The league also offered a justification for
its action of ignoring the reserve clause.

> The directors in their decision to try to sign players of the two major
> leagues voted not to ask any man in organized baseball already under
> contract to join their organization. They held that any player under a
> reserve clause would be tendered a contract if he wished to play in the
> new organization. This, it was said, was done because the directors
> felt that the contract of any player would be upheld in the courts, but
> that the reserve clause was illegal, and would not be sustained in the
> courts.
>
> The Federal League will take no further steps toward carrying out
> the war upon organized baseball unless the major leagues attempt to
> retaliate, but if they do, the directors declared, their organization is
> well equipped with money and will fight any attempt to disrupt its
> ranks.[32]

Sunday, 2 November 1913, heralded the return of Reb Russell to the
White Sox lineup. The day's game was scheduled for Houston. This day
would be the first since the tour began that the tourists slept in real beds.
Their special arrived in Houston at 1:00 A.M. Since most of the tourists were
still awake, they opted to go to the Rice Hotel for some restful sleeping in
beds made for sprawling.

Travel wore on all of the tourists. Road weariness often manifested
itself in the form of short tempers and irritation. The bachelor ballplayers
resented the married couples and their honeymoon glow. The sometimes
indiscreet romantic shenanigans of the honeymooners, not to mention
their roomier private car, only served to exacerbate tensions. Some of the
bachelors retaliated by loudly bemoaning the condition of matrimony,
taunting the grooms as "benedicts," and reveling in their stag status and
flaunting it like a badge of honor.

Illness was also starting to take a toll. Harry Sparrow, traveling secretary
for the tour, and Giants catcher Ivy Wingo were both sick with bad colds.
The two spent the entire day in their beds in the hotel, and Frank Isbell's
age had caught up with him fast. Isbell awoke on 2 November so stiff from

playing the day before in Beaumont that he could barely move. Aside from the illnesses, however, the day was typical for the tour.

John McGraw held court with the media and used the time to vent an unflattering opinion of Ban Johnson. The American League president, in one of his more egregious moments of meddling, suggested that a prohibition against imbibing alcohol be inserted in all player contracts. As one can imagine, the hard-drinking, ardently Irish firebrand was none too impressed with Johnson's posturing. From the *Houston Chronicle* of 3 November 1913:

> When John J. McGraw, who was here with the Giants–White Sox baseball troupe on Sunday was told that ministers all over this town were praising Ban Johnson on his reported statement that a "no booze" clause would be inserted into next season's contracts, he smiled and let out his opinion on the relation of booze to ball playing.
>
> "Like the Scotchman, 'I has me doubts' about that clause," replied John J. "In the first place, I don't believe that such a contract would have much effect, and in the second place I don't believe that the men would make them. Men in baseball today are as big as those in other lines of business. With the big advance in salaries to those engaged, the morals of the men have increased in like proportions. I believe they would regard such a contract as an attempt to interfere with their personal liberty. Some men might sign such an agreement, but if they wanted a drink they would get it anyway. And I know others who never touch intoxicants at all who would refuse to sign it."[33]

The game in Houston featured warm weather at last and great attendance; forty-seven hundred people paid admission to the ballpark. To the crowd's supreme disappointment, however, Christy Mathewson was a no-show. So many fans turned out that West End Park's outfield had to be roped off to accommodate spectators. Their presence in the outfield meant some new ground rules for the game. Any fair balls hit into the crowd would count as doubles.

Arthur Fromme was hard hit by the Sox, who took advantage of the "living fence" in the outfield for six doubles, two of them by Sam Crawford. Reb Russell pounded out one of the cheap doubles and pitched well enough to get the win. Russell surrendered eight singles, but the Giants had only two extra-base hits in the 9–4 White Sox win.

Bill Klem exercised the authority given him by the National Commission to eject players for the first time in this game. Mike Donlin got himself tossed out in the sixth inning. The incident had it origins in the fourth inning when Klem had forgotten the count with Mickey Doolan batting. Aware that Klem had forgotten the count, Doolan stood his ground in the box after the third strike. Sox pitcher Reb Russell pointed out to Klem that he had already struck the batter out. The home plate umpire promptly came out of his fog and told Doolan to take his seat. Mike Donlin, on the Giants bench, let Klem have it. According to the *Houston Chronicle*, "Among other things, Mike said that Klem was colorblind and had lost his sense of proportion." As his parting shot, "He called Bill a 'Bonehead' in a voice that carried to all parts of the stands."[34]

Donlin got a chance to deliver his taunts up close and personal two innings later. Russell plunked Jim Thorpe on the left arm when Thorpe batted in the fourth inning. In the sixth, his arm still hurting, Thorpe was taken out of the game to rest his limb. McGraw sent Donlin in to bat for Thorpe, and fireworks ensued. The *Chronicle* again, "Klem called Mike out on strikes in the sixth, whereupon Donlin formed the opinion that Bill had it 'in for him.' More blunt words were passed, one of which shocked the female patronage because of its torrid relations."[35]

After the game the tourists headed for Marlin, Texas, the Giants' spring training home. Henry Sparrow, too ill to leave Houston, remained at the Rice Hotel. He would catch up with the teams on the coast. The Giants did take along the less ailing Ivy Wingo. Christy Mathewson left Houston with his reputation there in tatters. Matty's absence from Sunday's game was not simply a matter of his pious refusal to play baseball on the Sabbath. Matty chose to spend the day away from the park on a duck-hunting expedition. The Giants pitcher, accompanied by two local businessmen, went after waterfowl at the very hour that the Giants and White Sox were hitting the field. Mathewson would not pitch on Sunday, honoring a promise he made his mother. Because of this well-known and much-celebrated stand, Houston fandom did not expect to see him pitch. They did, however, expect a chance at least to *see* him.

Once word leaked out regarding Matty's activities on Sunday, Houston was enraged. Many residents took Mathewson's action as a personal affront. The *Chronicle* noted the mendacity inherent in the situation with a sports section editorial:

> In the language of the mighty Christy Mathewson baseball is a business and not a sport and hunting is a sport and not a business. Moreover, it is written in Matty's own personal code of morals that a man should not transact business on Sunday, but that he might indulge in sports to his hearts content.

This preamble ought to explain why Mathewson went hunting last Sunday instead of appearing at West End Park in the uniform of a New York Giant. While the two clubs were fighting it out tooth and nail upon the diamond, Christy was banging away at the hard flying duck.[36]

Marlin, Texas, brought Steve Evans of the St. Louis Cardinals to the tour. Long anticipated as the foil to Germany Schaefer, Evans made one of his typical grand comedic entrances. Arriving in Marlin early in the morning before any of the other tourists were up and about, Evans wasted no time in making mischief. A dining car had been attached to the Honeymoon Special to provide dinner for the tourists after their game in Marlin. However, Evans passed word around that the railroad company had decided to provide a free breakfast for the tourists. Naturally, the dining car was immediately swamped with athletes pigging out as only athletes can. Once the huge bills arrived and were set before them, the players realized that they had been duped. That everyone cheerfully paid up and that Steve Evans did not promptly receive a fat lip indicates how well liked Evans was.

The game in Marlin should have been John McGraw's day. The Texas city served as New York's springtime home, and the entire city revolved around the Giants. McGraw liked Marlin's mineral water spring and its isolation, just the tonic for randy young ballplayers. McGraw's Giants tolerated Marlin's mineral water and resented its isolation. In Marlin, John McGraw *became* Napoleon, running his players through drills and exercises, whipping them into disciples of the John McGraw style of baseball— aggressive, cunning, and subtle as a sledgehammer.

This November homecoming was to be McGraw's triumphant show, a reward to Marlin for having embraced the Giants with so much fervor. Marlin's citizens swelled the ballpark to overflowing. The Giants had put their town on the map, and a grateful populace turned out in full force. Unfortunately for McGraw, this would be a day of sad duties; he would do no managing this day.

Just before game time a messenger delivered a telegram to McGraw informing him that his mother-in-law, Joan W. Sindall, had died suddenly while on vacation in Atlantic City, New Jersey. While strolling the board-walk, she felt a sudden pain in her chest and signaled a policeman, who came to her aid. He could do little. By the time an ambulance arrived, Blanche's mother had passed away.

John McGraw took the news hard. He loved everything about his wife, Blanche, even her mother. The loss of anyone's mother was apt to make John

McGraw misty-eyed, but the loss of someone so close to him evaporated his facade of machismo. McGraw could not coach; instead, he went to the local telegraph office and attempted to contact Blanche.

Blanche McGraw had been in Chicago but was currently somewhere between Illinois and El Paso, Texas. The plan had been for her to reunite with John in El Paso, go with him to the Pacific coast, and then join the tour around the world. These plans obviously had to be changed. McGraw sent his wife a telegram ahead of her arrival in El Paso, then went out to meet the media.

His first act was to deny the rumor that sprang up immediately after the news hit, which claimed that the tour would be abandoned. The schedule would not be altered in the least, McGraw reassured the press. Forgetting the soldier's death in Oklahoma, McGraw said, "This is the first sad incident of the trip."[37] But said sadness would not impel him to depart immediately and comfort his grieving wife. McGraw said, "It would be no good for me to go east as I could be of no assistance. I hope that Mrs. McGraw will be able to join us at Vancouver. I don't know anything about funeral arrangements."[38]

For Blanche McGraw, the days ahead would be ones of sadness, arduous travel, and distance. Dick Kinsella, a Giants scout doing some low-level duties with the tour, was dispatched to Houston to intercept Blanche there. He would accompany her back east. Because of the peculiarities of Texas's train system, Blanche would have to go south for hundreds of miles before she could go north. From Houston, she would have to travel to New Orleans. Only in New Orleans could she catch a northbound express. Blanche McGraw would have a mere fifteen days to get to Atlantic City, claim her mother's body, have the remains shipped to Baltimore for burial, organize and hold a service, then rush across the country to reunite with her husband. She surely did not want John to sail away without her.

The same vagaries of the Texas railroads put a pall over the game in Marlin. Everything had to be rushed. The late starting time caused by Joan Sindall's heart attack and her son-in-law's impromptu press conference meant that the players would barely have time to change their uniforms before the train pulled out for Abilene. Once the game started, the Giants whaled away on Joe Benz and Red Faber. Big Jeff Tesreau gave up just four hits while getting three of his own. The Giants pasting of the Sox by a score of 11–1 was savored with delight by the hometown crowd.

The biggest casualty of the day from the players' point of view might well have been the loss of Tris Speaker's ducks and quail. The big Texan returned from Hubbard with a sack full of the game birds. Intended for the huge postgame spread, they were instead left steaming on the table while the players hustled for their train.

Their next scheduled game in Abilene was a washout, the first rainout of the tour. The tourists never even thought about playing once they got a glimpse of the torrential rains greeting their train. The tired athletes spent the day sleeping or lolling about town. The reactions they received here were the same as elsewhere in the country. The *Abilene Daily Record* for 5 November 1913 stated, "Hero worship was a fetish in Abilene Wednesday. Lads hardly out of their kilts envied the big husky players, planned interminably for their own rise in the baseball world." A bit farther down the page we read, "Wherever there was a player there was a crowd. A ballplayer for the time was figuratively turned into a lump of sugar, all about which were flies of fans."[39]

With no ball game, the "highlight" of the day was a genuine badger fight. All of the men on the tour and a large number of locals gathered in secret in a barn on the outskirts of town and placed their bets on a fight to the death between a badger and a dog. The way it worked was simple yet repulsive. A dog and a badger were released at the same time into a ring. Whoever placed bets on the surviving animal would collect. A few days before reaching Abilene, McGraw phoned ahead to make sure that the badger was suitably starved and tormented in preparation for its match. The *Abilene Daily Record* detailed the scene:

> The difficulty of staging the badger fight is in finding a disinterested, non-betting individual who had never before seen a badger fight and who had never had the signal honor of pulling him out of his cage. McGraw was emphatic in his belief that the man who took the honor should be eulogized and his name flashed wherever wires permeate. The names of bill [sic] Sheridan and Billy Klem, umpires were suggested, and it seemed at times that one of them might be induced to do the act. After much parlaying, assurance was given that some one would be obtained for the very important work. It was decided to stage the fight in the arena of Wall's livery barn. This decision of place caused hundreds to brave the rain and a scamper over the mud to the chosen arena. In the rafters of the barn more than a score of players and local fans stood, while more than a hundred others stood on the ground floor. Much time was consumed in finding a man to liberate the badger.
>
> Umpire Bill Klem was nominated, but he stood upon a rafter above the scene and said in a stentorian voice with a guttural twang: "No,

you ain't going to get Mr. Klem to pull no badger, either." The crowd that was "on" laughed.[40]

At last a local innocent was summoned to the ring to draw out the badger. In a matter of seconds it was over, the dog being no match for the angry badger. McGraw, always working the angles, had put his money on the badger. After returning from the blood sport at the livery stable the tourists steamed out of Abilene, headed for El Paso, at 5:30 P.M.

By the time they reached El Paso on 5 November, every player was healthy. Hal Chase's ankle felt well enough for him to play on it again. Even "Old Baldy" Frank Isbell was feeling better, though he would sit this game out. Some of the healthy players were the happiest they had been so far on the tour. On a separate morning train several of the men's mates arrived. Maria Klem, Della Wiltse, and Jane Mathewson, along with her son, Matty Jr., arrived to join their husbands.

The El Paso game was held at the old fairgrounds some five miles out of town. While the weather was beautiful, the ballpark's playing surface was a mess. This area of Texas, the westernmost border region, had been enduring a drought for the last fourteen months. The drought caused the soil on the diamond at the fairgrounds to react in bizarre ways.

The sandlot portion of the diamond crumbled underfoot, creating clouds of dust and hazardous conditions for running and fielding. So much of the grass had died that the field was essentially all sand. The outfield sand became intolerably bright in the midday sun. Its glare, combined with high, erratic winds, made catching flies well nigh impossible. Both Fred Merkle and Jim Thorpe got "cheap" triples this way. The huge crowd of close to five thousand often had their vision obscured by the dust the players raised.

Everyone in El Paso wanted to see this game. Jim Scott would pitch for the Sox against Christy Mathewson. This could not have delighted the locals more. A few years earlier Scott had been paid $1,000 just to pitch one game in this city. All of the locals wanted to see how well the rough Texan would do against the sophisticated Pennsylvanian.

But Christy Mathewson was tired from the constant touring, and it showed; he gave up four hits and three runs in the first inning. Bunny Hearn came in as relief and was even worse, surrendering seven runs. Jim Scott may also have disappointed the local hero worshippers; like Hearn, he gave up seven runs but managed to get the win.

The game itself came to a total stop in the third inning when an aviator from Milwaukee named Earl Wagner decided to land his airplane in centerfield. Gus Axelson described the incident as follows, "The game broke up for a time, every small boy and Germany Schaefer making a bee line for the machine. Schaefer was given a ride to first base."[41]

Bill Klem at last restored order, exiling the pilot and his flying machine so that the game could continue. The crowd attending this game was the most international of the tour so far; a fair number of Mexicans crossed the border to watch Major League baseball (the sport already had made inroads into their country). Also present in the stands were several hundred African American soldiers from nearby Fort Bliss. With El Paso, the tour closed its Texas campaign and headed for the year-old state of Arizona.

The tourists would play two games in Arizona copper-mining towns. Their first stop, the city of Douglas. Founded in 1901 and named after an executive of the Phillips Dodge Corporation, Douglas was the main rail center for smelting and exporting the company's copper ore. Just twenty-five miles away, at the end of the rail line, lay Bisbee, where hard-muscled, hard-living men blasted rocks in the desert sun and lugged tons of ore out of the ground. Bisbee, site of one the world's largest copper mines, would host the tourists' second and final Arizona ball game.

The railroad climbed steadily upward as it headed west. The towns of Douglas and Bisbee are nearly a mile high. This high desert was America's last frontier. With Arizona's admission to the Union in 1912, the continent was at last filled, coast to coast and border to border.

The Honeymoon Special caused more than the normal amount of excitement when it pulled into Douglas. The arrival of a train, the Ninth Cavalry Band's bursting into sound, the banners flying, and the cheers of the crowd led some across the border in Mexico to conclude briefly that an invasion force of U.S. Army soldiers had arrived. Relations between Mexico and the United States had not been this low since the Mexican War of 1846–1848. General Victoriano Huerta's coup rendered the Mexican government impotent and corrupt. No one in Mexico City could deal with Pancho Villa and other bandits raiding with impunity on either side of the border. Anger from affected American interests was growing louder every day. President Wilson had several proposals for dealing with the "Mexican Problem" on his desk, most of which involved military intervention.

The Phillips Dodge Company had carte blanche in the two Arizona cities. The firm employed, either directly or indirectly, virtually everyone residing in both communities. For the two-game desert series, the copper works and the mines would shut down. The two-day layoff with pay would cost the executives at Dodge a bundle of money but would do wonders for morale.

The athletes received a tour of the copper works and the town of Douglas itself. Afterward, they were treated to the usual banquet. Douglas, home to most of the Phillips Dodge corporate executives, was a meticulously planned community, a sedate, almost East Coast suburban town stranded in the desert. The copper smelter was located here rather than in Bisbee because Douglas had adequate water for the task and a better approach for railroad tracks. From Douglas, the El Paso and Southern Railroad carried copper ingots both east and west. Unlike today's automated steel mills, in 1913 the ore was worked by hand. Whole mountains of coal, shoveled by an army of poorly paid workers, disappeared into the maw of the furnaces. Limestone and unwanted materials were heated until the copper precipitated out, then the molten metal was guided into great troughs for cooling and shipping. The ever-present aroma of burning sulfur and coal dust brought visions of the *Inferno* to mind unbidden.

While touring Douglas before the game, the tourists beat General John "Blackjack" Pershing to Mexico by more than a year. The tourists made their first international foray from Arizona, visiting the town of Agua Prieta, Mexico. The Mexican village bore the scars of its nation's troubles in the form of bullet-ridden doorways, vandalized buildings, and tales of marauding border bandits.

Both of the Arizona baseball fields where the tourists played, Douglas Field and Warren Ball Park, remain standing. Douglas Field was site of game one; the players found a well-watered grounds surrounded by a beautiful ballpark. The Southwestern League played there, and Dodge money made sure that the teams did well. Jim Scott had spent time there in the minors several years before, and he still had friends in town. To the disappointment of those locals, Walter Leverenz would do the pitching for the Sox. Hooks Wiltse took the hill for the Giants. The game was not even close, as the Giants crushed the Sox by a score of 14–5. The thin desert air and the pitchers' tired arms resulted in five home runs. According to one report, "The hits pounded off Leverenz were something scandalous."[42] In reality, it was worse than scandalous, as Leverenz did not even *try* to pitch. On the way to Arizona, Jim Scott regaled the pitchers on both teams with horror stories of pitching in the thin desert mountain air. In the high Arizona desert, curve balls did not curve, at least not for a few days, by which time the pitcher could grow accustomed to the atmospheric conditions and finally figure out how to make a curve break.

McGraw and Comiskey did well financially in Douglas. A rare account of how much money was made on the game appeared in the *Bisbee Daily Review*. From it, one gets a sense of just how skewed the books were in favor of the tourists. "The total receipts for the smelter city game were

$1,960 of which the teams received $1,578. After the expenses of the game which amount to about $200, the committee will divided the balance equally between the Y.M.C.A. and Chamber of Commerce. It is estimated a balance of about $70 will be left for each organization."[43]

The players spent some time in the fabulous Gadsen Hotel. The finest hotel in the Southwest, the Gadsen was first class all the way, even importing a chef from New York to cater to its guests, and the banquets at the Gadsen were always superb. The players' train was kept in Douglas all night Thursday; it would not be safe to send the teams to Bisbee before Friday.

In 1913 if you went looking for the wildest, most open, most lawless frontier town in all of America, you might very well end up in Bisbee, Arizona. Inhabited by vast numbers of copper miners, most of whom were young single men who liked to get liquored up and belligerent at night, Bisbee was a notorious haven of crime, filth, and disease. Why any self-respecting newlywed groom would even allow his bride to enter Bisbee, with its drunken miners, disease, and flagrant brothels, is a question that this author cannot answer. Nonetheless, on Friday morning the ballplayers and their wives made their way to Bisbee. For a blessed change from the train, most of the tourists took advantage of the line of automobiles that arrived to ferry them the twenty-five miles through the desert. The fascinating view included cacti, sagebrush, emptiness, and sand for miles as the cars wound their way up to the five thousand–foot elevation of Bisbee.

The tourists would play at 10:30 A.M., not only to beat the desert heat but to comply with the train schedule. The train to Los Angeles would be leaving at 2:00 P.M. The mines closed in Bisbee that day, and lots of folks who had been at the game in Douglas attended this one as well. The athletes toured the town, promenading about in their cars down the streets of Bisbee. They viewed the mines and had lunch at the Copper Queen Hotel.

While today Bisbee is a town of eighty-five hundred people, in 1913 the copper boomtown boasted the largest population between St. Louis and San Francisco. It was not your typical city, however. To give one an idea of the hazards of Bisbee, the Copper Queen Hotel was closed for much of 1913 because of spinal meningitis and smallpox outbreaks in the community. It was a normal occurrence to find several dead bodies on the streets every morning, disease or violence taking victims in equal measure.

In the midst of all this chaos lay one of the prettiest baseball fields in the West, Warren Ball Park. Situated between two mountains, the cozy ballpark offered beautiful vistas for batters and fans alike. Refurbished especially for this game, its short fences made an inviting target, and the Giants teed off with vigor. On a day picture-perfect for baseball, Bisbee turned out in full force for the tourists. A local reporter noted, "From the heights in Warren, the pilgrimage to the park could be observed to an advantage. The pilgrims came from the northward, some on foot, others on horseback, still others on motorcycles, on the trolley cars, in the special trains, and lastly, in automobiles. It was a kaleidoscopic scene with the gray of the hills for a background and the sunlight furnishing the calcium effects."[44]

The Giants crushed the Sox as they had done the day before, winning the final Arizona game by a score of 9–1. The Giants clouted five home runs, three of which were inside-the-parkers. Larry Doyle and Jim Thorpe, two of the most powerful men on the field, were the only batters to clear the fences. Sam Crawford and Tris Speaker swung for the fences with all of their might but came up short. Unscathed by the hazards of Bisbee, the tourists' train rolled into the state of California.

FOUR

Pacific Dreams

"My arm is sore," said Mathewson . . .
"Why, what's the trouble?" asked McGraw . . .
"Since we left eastern climes, I figure that I've shaken hands about
five million times." – Ring Lardner on Matty's lament, *Chicago Daily
Tribune*, 14 November 1913

Unlike most everywhere else the tourists had been, fans on the Pacific
coast were used to witnessing some pretty good baseball. Even at this early
stage the Pacific Coast League was only a rung or two below the Majors in
terms of talent and quality. Many California teams had better attendance
than the St. Louis Browns, Pittsburgh Pirates, and other weak members
of the Major Leagues. If you wanted as much baseball as possible, the
Pacific Coast League was for you. The Pacific Coast League actually had
the longest regular season baseball schedule ever devised. Taking advantage
of the region's fair weather, the league played two hundred games a season.
It was not without some justification that West Coast residents believed
that they had a product superior to that of the East. Despite such boasts,
however, most of California's fans were as anxious to see the Giants and the
Sox as were the folks in Ottumwa, Iowa. And everyone, no matter where
they lived, wanted to get a glimpse of Matty and the rest. The tourists arrived
in the Golden State with a great weight of expectations to live up to.

The first stop was Los Angeles, where the tourists would play games on
8 and 9 November. Los Angeles, already an amorphous, sprawling city, had
its sedate sections as well; the sleepy neighborhood known as Hollywood
had fewer than five hundred residents in 1913, but already its products had
global impact.

The tourists arrived in Los Angeles around noon on 8 November 1913 and
were taken out to lunch at the quaint Alexandria's Hotel. The proprietor,

Mrs. Alexandria, fed the players some of the best cuisine in the city, then it was off to Washington Park for the game. Outside the ballpark, pandemonium reigned. So many folks turned out that the game had to be delayed until all who wanted tickets could purchase them. In the words of Harry A. Williams of the *Los Angeles Times*, "A vast number of persons were found lined up fighting desperately to separate themselves from their money. The game was held until all of them succeed in doing this that none might be disappointed."[1]

Among the faces in the park, John McGraw was pleasantly surprised to find that of Frank Chance, manager of the New York Yankees. McGraw extended a hand to his crosstown rival, an event dutifully recorded by press photographers. Chance's trip to California was an annual pilgrimage, as he owned a ranch in suburban Glendora. When not herding cattle, his free time was taken up scouting talent in the winter leagues. Today it is Florida, but in 1913 the place to take in off-season baseball was in the nation's second largest state.

To entertain the multitudes already in their seats, the players broke into a game of shadow ball. An East Coast invention, shadow ball proved enormously popular with Pacific coast audiences. The Los Angeles crowd reveled in the pantomime show and laughed hysterically, as the men on the field pretended to play the game with an imaginary baseball.

When the actual game started at 3:45 P.M., Bill Klem theatrically introduced each player as they approached the batter's box. As far as Los Angeles was concerned, Bill Klem *was* the star of the world tour. Whereas the tired players with spent arms and legs were nothing special, the man behind the plate was a novelty supreme. As Harry Williams wrote,

> The voice of Bill Klem was then heard crying in the wilderness. And, believe me, nature endowed Bill Klem with some trumpet. When he opens his pipes the earth trembles on its axis, the stars fall, and the Panama Canal springs a leak.
>
> Klem first brought his vocal batteries into action by introducing the firm of Callahan and McGraw. He then proceeded to deliver a lecture on each batter as he—the player not Klem—came to bat. He dealt with each case individually and never seemed at a loss for a satisfactory explanation of how the player came to be here.
>
> Klem's remarks never ceased to interest, and he was given a tremendous ovation every time he introduced a player. When he introduced Mathewson he was given one of the greatest ovations ever accorded an umpire.[2]

Frank McGlynn joined the tour in Los Angeles, having arrived from New York on 7 November. An actor who drifted into the fledgling motion picture industry by directing movies at the behest of Thomas Edison, McGlynn prepared to film his single most ambitious movie thus far. Financed mostly by businessman Jack Gleason, who would also tour the world, as well as by a pittance from Pathè, McGlynn, accompanied by his cameraman, Victor Miller, would film history's first full-length sports documentary. No prior movie about athletics had ever conceived of such a grand scale for a backdrop. Part documentary, part travelogue, part sports action adventure, with some fictional bits of melodrama and comedy thrown in for good measure, McGlynn's movie, *The World Tour Giants and White Sox*, would have to be filmed on the fly and edited into a cohesive whole once the tourists were safely home. The technical problems in regards to filming would be enormous, keeping track of film cans, preventing accidental exposures, preserving film in tropical climates, protecting the camera from damage or loss, all the while trying to maintain some sense of artistry.

From Los Angeles onward McGlynn would shadow the Giants and White Sox. Whenever they turned around, there would be McGlynn directing Miller and yelling "action" at the players. Long before the tour concluded the tourists began to refer to Miller simply as "the spotlight man." McGlynn had known just one tourist socially before he began his film adventure. His own vaudeville path had crossed with that of Mike Donlin's.

Christy Mathewson arrived in Los Angeles with absolutely nothing left in his arm. A solid month of pitching, shaking hands, banquets, night-owl train departures, and cramped sleeping accommodations left him with a poor show for the Angelinos. Whoever that man was on the mound, he certainly did not look like the legend who went through almost the entire 1913 season without walking a man. Matty pitched poorly, surrendering five runs and managing only a single strikeout. Reb Russell, Matty's opposite in every way, pitched spectacularly for the Sox. The semiliterate, barely educated Texan gave up two earned runs and recorded six strikeouts. On this day, chalk up a win for Dixie.

In the eighth inning of this game, Hal Chase reinjured his knee and was replaced by Tom Daly. Standing out from the lackadaisical play were Buck Weaver's spectacular catches. Otherwise, the Los Angeles press could not have cared less. Harry Williams wrote what he found the most singularly memorable thing about the teams. "The thing that impressed me the most about either team was the number of lefthanders in the White Sox lineup. Never before have I seen so many deformed people on one team."[3]

Sunday, 9 November 1913, the White Sox and Giants played another game at Los Angeles's Washington Park. Neither team won, neither team lost; the fiasco of a game played before eight thousand fans ended in a 7–7 tie, the first no-decision of the tour. Harry Williams summed the game up nicely, "If this be major league baseball, then friends, let us remain a minor league for the rest of our lives."[4]

This was such a comedy of errors that at one point Lee Magee caught what he thought was the third out and tossed it into the stands as a souvenir, only to realize that there were only two outs in the inning as the base runner came in to score. Everyone had a bad game. Ray Schalk suffered three passed balls, Jim Thorpe dropped a fly allowing a run to score, and Buck Weaver crossed paths with Bill Klem during his second at bat and got himself tossed out of the game. Weaver's argument with the umpire may have cost the Sox the game; it definitely left his manager in a bind. Sam Crawford had been given the day off, confined to bed with a charley horse, and Frank Isbell's old body just could not handle playing anymore. Isbell injured himself at first, leaving the Sox shorthanded. Jimmy Callahan ran out of substitutions in the fourth inning and ended up having to activate himself into the lineup. The old man surely could teach the youngsters he managed a thing or two. Callahan legged out a triple and a single, stole second, scored two runs, and capped it all off by driving in the tying run. The Sox erased a seventh-inning six-run deficit, but there was nothing stylish about how they did it. After two hours and seven minutes of thoroughly sloppy ball and with deep twilight already cloaking the field, Bill Klem called the game on account of darkness. The crowd of six thousand listlessly filed out of the stadium trying to puzzle out what exactly they had just witnessed.

After the game Frank Isbell took Callahan aside and resigned from the tour. "Izzy" did not know when he would heal and saw little reason for continuing with the tour if he could not make a useful contribution. Callahan tried to get Isbell to reconsider, but he would only agree to continue traveling with the Sox. That night the players ate a tremendous beefsteak dinner with guests Frank Chance and Barney Oldfield, the champion race car driver. At midnight their train slid out of its siding in the Los Angeles train yards and rolled south for San Diego, Chief Meyers's hometown.

San Diego's Athletic Park had twenty-six hundred seats, but for the game at least forty-four hundred fans shoehorned themselves into the ballpark. Will Palmer, president of the San Diego team, made a special effort to beautify the ballpark for the big leaguers. Not as fancy as Los Angeles's beautiful all-grass Washington Park, the all-dirt Athletic Park had seen better days. Palmer's men filled all the divots, rolled the field, and leveled it as smooth as a dance floor. Temporary stands were thrown up along the third base line and the outfield parking lot. The game of Monday, 10 November 1913, would provide San Diego with a chance to welcome home Chief Meyers and revel in the glory of Major League baseball.

So many fans turned out that much of the outfield was roped off. Not even the outfield could hold all of the fans who wished to attend, and pockets of them were disbursed about the grounds. So densely packed was the playing surface that one player, while legging out a double, collided with four fans crowding the baselines.

It is only fitting that this game belonged to Meyers. Born in a Cahuilla village, John Meyers had grown up in and around San Diego. A full-blooded Cahuilla, one of California's Native American tribes, Meyers attended public school and, briefly, Dartmouth College before family duties called him back to California. Large numbers of members of the Cahuilla and other mission tribes came out to cheer on Chief Meyers and Jim Thorpe. The crowd could not have more delighted in how this game turned out.

Meyers's heroics came about largely because Bill Klem committed an unpardonable error for an umpire, forgetting which half inning the game was in. With the score tied 3–3, Klem announced that the bottom of the ninth had just been completed. In reality, it was only the top of the ninth. With darkness rolling in, Klem declared the game a tie. Meyers and his wife were already out of the stadium sitting next to Will Palmer in his automobile, preparing to drive off for the U.S. Grand Hotel, when Klem realized his mistake and called everyone back to their places. The Giants would get one more chance to bat.

Chief Meyers, the scheduled lead-off hitter, was nowhere to be found. McGraw had to dispatch a messenger to the parking lot to get Meyers back into the stadium. The *San Diego Sun* described what happened next. "Meyers came back grudgingly and told Klem what he thought of umpires in general and Bill Klem in particular. Then after Scott had him 'in the hole' with two strikes and a ball 'Chief' Meyers picked one and broke up the party."[5] The home run capped a most satisfying night at home.

The first question Meyers asked reporters when they interviewed him after the game was whether a local haberdasher still awarded hats for home runs. A tradition in San Diego several years old had local merchants award a hat to anyone hitting a home run. Meyers owned several of these from playing in local semipro games and for an exhibition home run the previous winter. He had a special fondness for this particular haberdasher's hats and had, in fact, been wearing one when he arrived in San Diego for the game.

The next morning Chief Meyers strode about the U.S. Grand Hotel proudly sporting a brand new blister abalone tie pin, a present for hitting his big home run. An admirer, W. S. Eldredge, a local businessman, had wired Meyers several days before, promising him a tie pin in exchange for a home run. On Monday morning he delivered on his promise, just as happy to present the pin as Meyers was to receive it. Meyers reflected on the happiest homecoming of his career as the Honeymoon Special rolled back up the California coast.

Oxnard, California, their next stop, would be the last small town in which the tourists would play. It would also be perhaps the most fondly recalled individual game of any on the tour. This game featured everything, a Christy Mathewson win, an ox roast, and Hans Lobert racing a horse around the bases.

To reach Oxnard, north of Los Angeles in the heart of Ventura County, the tourists' train backtracked north through the California foothills and into the state's "cattle ranch" belt. Not that far from Frank Chance's Glendora ranch, this region would see several Major Leaguers purchase land to become gentleman farmers. The Golden State had many inducements for players to invest their extra cash. A booming economy, great weather, and a growing demand for quality meats made ranching quite an attractive profession. In the 1920s Jim Thorpe endeavored to purchase just such a ranch. He believed that it would provide a haven for his family and serve as a place to rekindle the love between himself and Iva.

Like every small town the tourists passed through, Oxnard, the hometown of Fred Snodgrass, the main hero fussed over in this town, went all-out to welcome the tourists. More than a hundred automobiles and a booming brass band greeted the tourists at the station. The players filed into cars and after a brief tour of the town arrived at the ranch of Charles Rowe, where the oddest breakfast feast the tourists would ever encounter awaited them.

Hans Lobert famously recalled the day in Lawrence Ritter's *The Glory of Their Times*: "We arrived in Oxnard at about seven in the morning and we were met at the train by about ten stagecoaches, in which they took all of us out to this big ranch for a barbecue. That was great cattle and lima bean country around there then. They had a tremendous ox roasting, been roasting for a couple of days, and lima beans with onions, and beer. That was our breakfast! Did you ever try roasted ox and beer for breakfast? Not bad. Puts hair on your chest, to say the least."[6]

Lobert may have misremembered the detail about the stagecoaches. All of the other sources state that the players were driven in cars to the ranch, but Lobert was interviewed more than forty years after the event, so a memory lapse is not surprising. Frank McGlynn described the actual operation of the feast:

> It was an ideal California day. Spread under sheltering palm branches were long tables about which the tourists were seated with their hosts, and an assemblage of Snodgrass' immediate friends. Great steel frames were spread over charcoal fires holding up hundreds of choice cuts of beef, which sizzled in an appealing way. Everything that accompanied a beefsteak dinner was on hand. Mrs. Rowe and other ladies of the receiving party waited upon the tables. After the first course of grilled steaks came the *piece de resistance*—the bull's head, which had been roasted in the hot ground overnight.[7]

The mayor of Oxnard took advantage of the moment and asked Hans Lobert if he would race a horse around the bases. For some reason, the locals had discussed whether a cattle horse specially trained in turning could beat a man around the bases. At first Lobert declined, " 'Lord,' I said, 'I'm not here to run horses around the bases. I'm here to play baseball.' "[8] Eventually Lobert was persuaded, and it was agreed that the race would be run at the conclusion of the game.

Interest in seeing Matty pitch and in welcoming home Fred Snodgrass swelled attendance to more than five thousand. Snodgrass, the first man up to bat for the Giants in the bottom of the first, received a gold watch from the citizens of Oxnard. The game ceased, and the mayor strode to the plate and made the presentation. After a few words from the hometown hero, it was back to baseball.

The Sox had been whacking Mathewson around on the tour, mostly because of what they perceived of as his bad attitude. Harry Williams of the *Los Angeles Times* got the dope from an anonymous member of the White Sox.

> It was apparent that the Sox always turned loose their heavy hitters while Mathewson was on the mound. One of the players offered up an explanation of this when the teams were here.
>
> "We all intended to be good fellows when the trip started, but Matty didn't have much to do with the rest of us," said the player. "When he met us on the street he couldn't see us."
>
> "I am not saying that he was swelled up. It may have just been his way. But if he couldn't see us on the street we decided to impress

him with the fact that we could see him on the ball field and the box
scores tell the things we have done to him."

"We are giving him a sample of some of the stuff he would have
to face if he was in the American League."

"He speaks to us now, all right."[9]

The Big Six would exact a little revenge this time, but his arm was so
worn out that Matty had to resort to trickery. For the only time in his
career, Christy Mathewson resorted to throwing the spitball. Mathewson
prided himself on never having to resort to such vulgar stunts as daubing
the horsehide with saliva, so his desperation to put on a good show for the
people of Ventura County must have been tremendous indeed. As Harry
Williams put it, "The next thing we know, Matty will be chewing line cut
or horse plug."[10]

After seven innings the game stood 2–1 in favor of the Giants. While
having trouble with his curve, Mathewson the spitballer was masterful.
He surrendered a homer to Sam Crawford but otherwise got out of most
trouble. Matty did not walk a man and even managed to steal a base. Joe
Benz pitched hard as well. Perhaps barbecued oxen and beer is really the
breakfast of champions.

The cowboy ranchers on their rickety grandstands demanded that the
man versus horse race be run *now*. More and more bets had changed hands
in the crowd as the game progressed, and things were close to boiling over.
Rather than risk a flare-up of cowboy emotions, John McGraw made Hans
Lobert the seventh-inning stretch entertainment. McGraw approached
Lobert and told him, "John we can't finish this game. You might as well get
ready to run the horse around the bases."[11]

Frank McGlynn, who filmed the moment for posterity, described what
he witnessed as Hans Lobert raced the fastest cattle horse in the county:

Lobert smiling and confident, advanced to the plate. The horse's
jockey was a Mexican vaquero. After discussing their line of progress,
Lobert and the rider moved to the scratch. Klem gave the word "Go,"
and both horse and man were off in a flash. Lobert got into his stride
quicker than the horse, rounding first, well in the lead. At second he
was still a yard ahead and lengthened the lead on the turn to about
twenty-five feet. When the spectators saw this great athlete actually
leading the flying horse to third base, they rose en masse and their
cheers could be heard for miles. It was a thrilling moment, one never
to be forgotten. "Honus" reached third first but only by a shade.
Wheeling like a thunderbolt; the horse forced to his utmost, came

abreast of Lobert and flashed past him about two yards from the plate, winner by half a length in 14 seconds (Lobert's record time for the distance).[12]

The cowboys cheered heartily in salute to Lobert and the horse. One can assume that most of the betting action ran against the Philadelphia Phillie. Both Lobert and McGlynn concluded that the race was lost for the human racer when Lobert turned his head at second base to get a fix on the horse. Never again would Lobert ever try to race a horse, it was simply too dangerous.

After cheering, saluting, and drinking a toast to both man and horse, the ranchers settled down to watch the conclusion of the game. Christy Mathewson pitched out of trouble in the final two innings to capture the win. The final score read 3–2. After the game the players rushed off to catch the train to Sacramento, some twelve hours away by rail. Barely having time to change out of their uniforms, the White Sox and Giants steamed out of Oxnard for the very different atmosphere of the California state capital.

The Honeymoon Special pulled into Sacramento, only to find the city awash in a downpour. With heavy clouds hovering over the city and no end in sight to the rain, the tourists were forced to cancel the game. The two teams hung around just long enough to pick up Jack Bliss, the last world circler to join the tour, before catching the first train for Oakland. McGraw spent some time talking to Jack Atkin, owner of the Pacific Coast League's Sacramento Senators, between trains. A local scribe caught McGraw bragging to Atkin, "The world's tour of the Sox and Giants so far has been a big financial success."[13]

The barnstorming teams had thought there was a chance that Comiskey would rejoin them in Sacramento. Since that did not pan out, they knew to expect him in San Francisco. The Old Roman and his wife were on the way and would catch at least some of the five-game series scheduled for the Oakland Bay area. At 8:30 P.M. the tourists' train arrived in San Francisco. The teams checked into two hotels, splitting their accommodations for the first time. Callahan, McGraw, Mathewson, Merkle, Donlin, Schaefer, Evans, and a few favored others lodged at the St. Francis; most everyone else stayed at the Palace. The St. Francis was a bastion of free-flowing liquor; one of the hotel's bartenders had been busted for selling alcohol under the table on election day. Just the place for McGraw and his cronies to unwind.

San Francisco's media sought interviews with as many of the tourists as they could. Rampant rumors had it that a number of the tourists were going to drop out of the tour, so many, the scuttlebutt had it, that there would not be enough players to fill out two full squads. Harry B. Smith, a reporter for the *San Francisco Chronicle*, attempted to discern fact from fiction, cornering one player after another as they made their way to their hotels.

> Of the Giants it is settled that Chief Meyers, Snodgrass, Tesreau, and Fromme will leave the tourists at Seattle, after the last game on American soil is played. Whether Mathewson is to make the trip or not is definitely not decided as yet, and the "Big Six" when questioned last night pleaded that he was tired out and would prefer to answer questions in the morning.
>
> "Really," said McGraw on that point, "I don't know what Christy is going to do, and I don't believe that his wife does. He would like to make the trip but he is a little bit afraid of the water. I am hoping at the last moment that he will decide to continue around the world with us."
>
> Jimmy Callahan will leave behind him Hal Chase, Tris Speaker, Schalk and Russell and Faber, both pitchers, which will leave him with three twirlers, an ample supply for across the water.[14]

Fromme's announced departure came as a surprise. He had been among the first to brag about his participation in the tour, greatly anticipating the trip around the world. In the end, the hardships of touring had simply been too much.

After a night of rest between two sheets in real beds, the tourists arose early on Thursday, 13 November 1913, toured San Francisco, and caught the ferry for Oakland. At 2:30 in the afternoon the tourists were guests of the Oakland Oaks. The Oaks played in aging Oaks Park, but team owner Jack Ewing would soon start construction on a new baseball palace. The new ballpark, Ewing Field, would open in 1914. When Jimmy Callahan got a glimpse of the Oaks' new home he pronounced it "the finest major league park west of Chicago."[15]

The day opened with nature providing an inauspicious backdrop of mist and fog. By noon, however, the sun had dried out the dampness, and four thousand fans wedged themselves into Oaks Park. Players who had put in turns in the Pacific Coast League received big hands from the crowd. Buck Weaver led off and was rewarded with cheers, as fans acknowledged his tour of duty with the San Francisco Seals.

Reb Russell won the game, primarily on an error by Jim Thorpe in the seventh inning. Thorpe's dropped fly allowed two runs to score and permitted Hal Chase to come to the plate where he tripled, then scored on an error by Mickey Doolan. Just before Thorpe's miscue had come the game's real fireworks. For the first time on the tour, Bill Klem tossed John McGraw out of a game, then, for good measure, exiled Mike Donlin as well. According to Gus Axelson, "McGraw did not have anything in particular to kick about, but the accumulation of rain and train service yesterday worked on his nerves and he took it out on the ump."[16]

Douglas Erskine of the *San Francisco Examiner* gives us a fuller picture, even if he does get Bill Klem's league wrong.

> It was in the seventh inning with Morris Rath on third, two out, and Tris Speaker at the bat. Two balls and two strikes had been called on the Red Sox slugger when Wiltse wafted a nice slow one right over the middle of the plate.
>
> Umpire Klem said "ball," the next pitch hit Mr. Speaker in the short ribs and he went to first base. Mr. McGraw was very angry. He walked up to Umpire Klem and told him a number of things which the American League [*sic*] umpire had not even suspected. Klem could only retort, "Out of the game you go Mr. McGraw."
>
> Then McGraw turned loose. If it had been a world's series he could not have been more vehement. Everything he didn't say about Klem is not included in the McGraw vocabulary. All Klem could do was point toward the clubhouse in centerfield.
>
> While McGraw was arguing the point Mike Donlin jumped in to help his chief. One remark from Mike was all Klem needed to send him across the grass and muggsy and mike made a dual exit through the club house doors.[17]

While the two angry Irishmen were making their way off the field, Bill Klem in his best announcer's voice deadpanned for all parts of the stadium to hear: "Christy Mathewson is now coaching third base, Jeff Tesreau is now coaching at first and Muggsy McGraw is about to leave the field."[18] The final score, Chicago 5, New York 2, put only two games between the Giants and Sox. The Giants had won fourteen versus twelve wins for the Sox.

At the same time that the barnstorming teams were battling in Oakland, Charles Comiskey, accompanied by an entourage fourteen-persons strong, had at last arrived in California. Pulling into the sleepy agrarian village of Oroville, Comiskey and company were presented with fruit-bearing boughs of plum and orange trees. The local orchard farmers' friendly greeting impressed the White Sox's boss. He would be in a very good mood when he rejoined his team.

San Francisco was essentially a brand new city in 1913. The great earth-quake and fire of 1906 had leveled the city. Virtually nothing that the tourists set eyes upon was more than seven years old. The newness, prosperity, and bustle of San Francisco gave it the same reputation for excitement and adventure in 1913 that it has today. The Giants and White Sox would play three games there. No other city received the honor of as many games; indeed, the San Francisco Bay brought out the best in both teams.

Then as now, San Francisco abounded in culture. The players spent most of Thursday night at the Gaiety Theater on O'Farrell Street. The theater's stage became one huge dance floor with continuous "rag dances" playing all night. Not far from the stage, an overflowing buffet table beckoned. Later, the last act of *Candy Shop*, then the city's most popular play, was performed, and Callahan and McGraw were called up onstage to receive cheers from the crowd. Seemingly every theatrical person in the city turned out to wish the two teams well. After the actors cleared the stage, the tangos and rags continued until the wee small hours of the morning.

The game of Friday, 14 November 1913, gave Charles Comiskey some-thing to crow about, a 3–2 win for the Sox in a dandy game. Cool weather and the absence of Matty on the mound prevented a sellout. The Giants and White Sox were enthusiastic about the game anyway, putting their hearts into their play. The teams opened with their shadow ball antics, sending the crowd into hysterics. One sportswriter thought the act so good that it would find success in vaudeville. The players were always delighted at how crowds reacted to baseball without the ball. With each performance the improvisation and the humor became broader and more comical.

Andy Slight arrived with Comiskey from Chicago, but the farmhand from the Logan Square section of Chicago did not suit up for the game. John McGraw did not appear at all in this game, either in the stadium or on the field. Still miffed at being thrown out of the game the day before, the Little Napoleon was sulking. At first the enraged McGraw claimed that he would prevent Klem from going around the world, but when it was pointed out that Klem's authority came from the National Commission and that only the commission could make such a decision, the Giants manager boycotted the game at Recreation Park in protest.

McGraw missed a brilliant game, an old-fashioned pitching duel be-tween Arthur Fromme and Walter Leverenz. Down by two runs in the bottom of the ninth, the White Sox staged a three-run rally to win the game. Ray Schalk's game-ending double brought in the winning run, sending the six thousand fans present for the stirring contest home happy.

The tourists had a wonderful time on the morning of Saturday, 15

November 1913. The men received a tour of the grounds for the Panama-Pacific Exposition of 1915, which were still under construction. Arriving at Filmore Street, they were given a behind-the-scenes tour of the exposition's lighting system, toured the already completed Palace of Machinery, and viewed models of buildings yet to be constructed. The teams were presented with a banner to carry around the world bearing the inscription "Panama-Pacific Universal Exposition, San Francisco 1915." The exposition, like today's convention centers and amusement parks, was expected to bring a financial windfall to the city. Already people were arriving in San Francisco seeking employment at the huge fair. Such jobs were no sure thing, however, and ministers, suffragettes, and editorial writers across the West were encouraging young women, especially, to stay home rather than journey to San Francisco in quest of exposition gold.

Saturday's contest was the game everyone in San Francisco wanted to see. Matty would be pitching. Ten thousand fans made their way to the Seals' park to pay homage to Mathewson. Despite not having his best stuff, the Big Six did not disappoint the standing-room-only crowd. Leon Wing of the *San Francisco Examiner*, after witnessing this performance wrote, "Matty is all that he has been pictured. He is an artist. Deliberate, cool under fire, the guiding genius of the machine behind him, Matty pitched as he always does. It was a distinctive Mathewson victory."[19]

The appreciative California fans gave Matty a big hand when he came to bat in the first inning. The loud ovation lasted for several minutes, but Matty did not acknowledge the crowd. Rather than being seen as snobbery, the press viewed Matty's aloofness as a logical reaction of a man who heard such cheering often.

Mike Donlin's misplay of a fly ball in the fifth allowed one Sox run to score. In the eighth, the game safely in hand, Mathewson eased up a bit and allowed the Sox to score two runs. The final tally read 6–3 in favor of the Giants, who dismantled Jim Scott with relish. The Sox were never in this game, and they took their frustrations out on Bill Klem in the sixth inning after the Giants plated their sixth run. Bill Klem had to put down a White Sox mutiny against his authority.

The call appeared easy enough to make, but Klem blew it. With Jim Thorpe on third, Chief Meyers at first, and one out, Fred Snodgrass came up to bat for the Giants. Snodgrass struck out, Meyers broke for second, and Thorpe came charging home. Snodgrass, however, did not vacate the batter's box, screening the onrushing Thorpe from Sox catcher Ray Schalk's view and simultaneously blocking the catcher's throw to second. Thorpe came in to score, tagging the plate under the immobile Snodgrass. Instead of charging Snodgrass with interference and sending Thorpe back to third, Klem allowed the run to stand.

The White Sox exploded angrily at the home plate umpire, with Buck Weaver being especially vociferous. Weaver became so obnoxious that he was cited for censure by the local press. The *Examiner* wrote, "Buck Weaver was the most persistent of the trouble-makers, and Weaver went a bit too far. Some of the language he used would hardly be complimentary to him if it was heard as plainly as it was in the press box."[20]

Frank McGlynn filmed some of his movie in San Francisco before and during the game. Pathos was the order of the day for the filmmaker. A synopsis of the day's filming reads like something out of the films of Harold Lloyd or Charlie Chaplin and comes courtesy of the *San Francisco Chronicle*:

> Through all the pictures is being told the story of a daffy New York fan, who first reads in the papers that the tour will be made. He makes up his mind to accompany the ball teams, and as he has no money for traveling, is caught in all sorts of stunts. Pictures were taken yesterday in the San Francisco bleachers showing this same "fan" making a fuss over imaginary stunts and finally being compelled to seek the assistance of Germany Schaefer to prevent his being thrown off the grounds all together.[21]

After a Saturday night on the town the Giants and White Sox geared up for a most unusual doubleheader. The tourists would close out their California sojourn by playing a doubleheader in two different cities. At 10:30 A.M. the Giants and White Sox would put on an exhibition in Oakland, then the teams would hightail it to the ferry for the trip to San Francisco, where the start time was scheduled for 2:30 P.M.

People in the Bay area responded by buying thirteen thousand tickets to the games. Andy Slight would get his first chance to play, as would Dick Egan, who arrived late on Saturday afternoon. Ring Larder's favorite player, Ping Bodie, would also put in an appearance. The two games were not equal value entertainment packages, however; the Oakland game featured youth, poor play, and a ton of runs from sloppy baseball. The afternoon affair featured first-rate pitching, tremendous fielding, and ten thousand satisfied fans. Many of the athletes starred in both games, including Jim Thorpe, Tris Speaker, Sam Crawford, Mike Donlin, Fred Merkle, and Fred Snodgrass.

Game one drew three thousand fans despite the early hour. No doubt there was a substantial dip in attendance because of late Sunday morning church services. Perhaps attending this game qualified as penance though.

The Sox and Giants combined for twenty-six hits, eleven walks, four doubles, and two wild pitches. The Sox's Red Faber opposed the Giants' Bunny Hearn. Neither pitcher turned in a performance that was even halfway adequate. Leon Wing of the *Examiner* pithily dismissed the game, "After the first three innings the play was so bad that they [the fans] would have been happy with the Oaks."[22] The final score of 12–8 in favor of the White Sox demonstrates just how much of a mess this game was. Even Jimmy Callahan got into the act, inserting himself in as a pinch runner in the seventh inning.

The afternoon game in San Francisco set Reb Russell against Jeff Tesreau. The contrast of junk pitcher versus control freak entertained the crowd of ten thousand enormously. Russell used the spitball, or as one scribe had it, the "diphtheria ball," exclusively, winning the game 4–2. Tesreau got better and better as the game progressed, but wildness in the early innings gave the Sox an insurmountable lead. The White Sox's win gave Chicago four of the Golden Gate games and nearly knotted the overall series. After twenty-nine games, the Giants had won fifteen while the Sox owned fourteen.

At the conclusion of this game, several of the White Sox and Giants departed the tour, Chief Meyers and Ping Bodie being two. Both natives of California wanted to continue with the tour but could not. Chief Meyers had a great many business ventures to attend to. Ping Bodie honestly wanted to go around the world but joined the tour too late to make the necessary arrangements.

Bodie was beset with a host of problems, both personal and legal, that prevented his joining the global phase of the tour. For Bodie, this autumn could best have been termed "The Misadventures of 'Ping' Bodie." Long before the age of aluminum bats, Frank Bodie was nicknamed "Ping" because of the sound made when he hit the ball. One of the first Italian Americans to play big league baseball, Bodie's name at birth was Francesco S. Pezzolo. The San Francisco native caught the eye of Ring Lardner, who mentioned Ping often in his columns. Lardner may very well have drawn from Bodie some of the characteristics of his great fictional creation Jack Keefe, with whom Ping shared many traits.

Adored by White Sox fans of all stripes, the malaprop-spouting right fielder had enough of a following that vaudeville promoters sought out his services. On 14 October 1913 Bodie inked a contract with R. L. Jacobi, manager of the Alhambra Theater in Chicago. For eleven weeks Bodie was to lecture audiences throughout the Midwest on the topic of "scientific baseball." Most of the material was actually penned by his booking agent, Morris Silver. For Ping, however, performing before the crowds at Comiskey

Field was something quite different from appearing in the limelight before a crowd in the close confines of a theater. On the morning of 15 October 1913 Bodie lost his battle with stage fright. Early that morning he and his family checked out of their Chicago hotel and boarded a train for San Francisco. Bodie hoped to avoid forfeiting his $500 guarantee, which was due the theater owner if he failed to show. Jimmy Valentine he wasn't. As Handy Andy succinctly put it in his column in the *Chicago Tribune* of 16 October 1913:

> Another peculiar incident of the affair is the disappearance of one of the signed contracts. The manager of the theater had the signed paper on exhibition in a glass case in front of the show house and says that the glass has been broken and the contract stolen. Mr. Silver of the agency, however, still possesses one of the three papers signed, so says the loss of the one held by the theater will not stop the suit against the "artist."
>
> Manager Callahan of the White Sox had the promise of Bodie to travel to the coast with the team and take part in the exhibition games and knew nothing of this disappearance. Callahan, however, had no contract holding Bodie to play with the team.[23]

The one game Bodie did play with the Sox in San Francisco was a glorious homecoming. Bodie's absence from the global phase of the tour was lamented by some sportswriters. Grantland Rice was particularly disappointed that Bodie did not get a chance to see the world. As he wrote in his column "Playing the Game" in the *Chicago Evening Post* of 7 March 1914, "We are sorry that Ping Bodie did not make the trip, as we would esteem it much bliss to see a signed story by Mr. Bodie upon 'The Decadence of the Roman Empire' or 'The Importance of Asiatic Archaeology as Related to the More Acute Pragmatism of Japan.' "[24]

After a stint with the 1917 Philadelphia A's, one of the worst teams of all time, Bodie ended his Major League career with the New York Yankees. His Yankee roommate was Babe Ruth, or as Ping once accurately stated, "I don't room with him. I room with his suitcase."[25]

A very sad Blanche McGraw arrived in San Francisco just in time to join her husband on the team train. Though he had not gone east with his wife, John McGraw went out of his way to comfort her in her grief now that she had returned. McGraw would rarely leave his wife's side from now until the end of the tour. McGraw, who had seen more death then most men, including the loss of his first wife, Minnie, during his days with the Orioles, understood grief and how to overcome it. The McGraws were a perfectly matched couple. Times like these made their marriage even stronger.

Everyone else hustled aboard the Honeymoon Special for the long trek through the California interior to Oregon. As the train drove up the spine of California and passed into the wilds of Oregon, the skies returned to their familiar foreboding gray. Medford, the tourists' first stop in the sparsely populated state, would be overcast and misty.

Medford had been filling up since Sunday with out-of-town visitors for the game, folks from all over southern Oregon and the northern California forest regions. The noontime arrival in Medford stirred up the usual pomp and circumstance. After getting off the train, the tourists were segregated by gender and sent separate ways. The men were hustled off into a waiting fleet of automobiles and driven to the nearby town of Ashland to view some of the state's finest apple orchards along the Rogue River valley. The women were taken to the Medford Hotel to be entertained by a committee of Medford-area women.

A state "holiday," 18 November 1913 was Apple Day in Oregon, promoted by the Oregon State Chamber of Commerce. The aggressive marketing campaign had started a day early, with every hotel in the state pushing apples. Apple fritters, applesauce, apple dumplings—the tourists soon grew accustomed to spotting apples in the most unlikely of places. Up in Portland, "the Northern Pacific sent forth a great motor truck fitted up like a dining car, from which colored waiters tossed thousands of apples to the populace."[26]

By the 2:30 P.M. start time the Oregon mist became a steady downpour. Twenty-five hundred folks were in the stands demanding baseball. They wanted their two dollars' worth. For a few moments the rain ceased, and the Medford organizing committee insisted that the game be played. Touched by the dedication of so many people to sit patiently in a downpour, the Giants and White Sox played a surreal game of baseball in the rain. Tris Speaker said of the scene, "But when you see a bunch of people ready to stand out in the rain just to see their National game played by big leaguers, a man would be willing to go out and court rheumatism just to gratify them."[27]

Also pleasing the locals was seeing one of their own, Don Rader, on the field at second base. Rader, an emergency substitute for Germany Schaefer, who was nursing a sore shoulder, played briefly with the White Sox early in the 1913 campaign before being returned to the minors.

Some of the drenched fans had really gone out of their way to see this game. W. H. Kilgore, a sixty-eight-year-old homesteader from rustic Evans

Creek, had to start his day well before the crack of dawn to attend the game. Arising at 2:00 A.M., Kilgore hiked fourteen miles through the backwoods and forded two creeks just to catch the train for Medford.

For the next six innings Medford witnessed one of the most bizarre baseball games ever played. If Monty Python's "Ministry of Silly Walks" ever ran a sporting event, it would resemble this game. Bill Klem, hunkered behind the catcher in an overcoat, and the players went about their business as though it were a normal occurrence to play baseball in a driving rain. Athleticism quickly morphed into farce. It was almost as if the day had a theme, that theme being umbrellas. There were umbrellas everywhere. The stadium housed a sea of umbrellas. Virtually every occupant of the stands held an umbrella. Umbrellas even migrated to the field. The coaches patrolled the foul lines, signaling with one hand while manipulating umbrellas with the other. Even some of the players wielded a bumper shoot. Lee Magee played the outfield while toting an umbrella in his right hand and a baseball glove in his left, and sure enough, he made a spectacular one-handed grab on a screaming liner without ever losing control of his umbrella. Once the game became "official" (can an exhibition game ever really be official?), Bill Klem ended the farce, giving the Giants a 3–0 victory in the rain-shortened contest. After the game, the players rushed over to the Medford Hotel for a scrumptious turkey dinner, and by 5:00 P.M. they were on their way to Portland.

Anticipation among everyone aboard the train—players, managers, officials, wives, and regular tourists—about Wednesday's departure for Japan and points east had reached a fever pitch. Tuesday would be the last day that the tourists would be concentrating solely on baseball. Potential foreign adventures became the main conversation topic.

Traveling under consistently dour skies, the tourists arrived in Oregon's largest city at 7:30 A.M. Tuesday morning. For the only time during the cross-continental trek, no brass band awaited to serenade the barnstormers' train, a novelty that all of the tourists appreciated. Dawn brought sweet weather, temporarily blowing the cloud cover off and allowing the sun to shine with autumn brilliance. John McGraw slept until well past 9:00 A.M. The welcoming committee swelled in size while McGraw sawed logs. Lifting the shade and peering out the train window, McGraw addressed the crowd.

> "Folks out on this side of the Rockies are jealous—know that?" The crowd, given this unexpected greeting simply responded by asking "How so?"

"Well down in California, the home guard talked in a way that made me think we would have to put on bathing suits and swim out of the cars. I was almost afraid this train would take on so much rain that we would float in. And there—by gosh, right on this platform—is the sun, shining just as if it had never heard of rain. I only hope she keeps peeking through until we've played. That isn't entirely a selfish statement. There's something more behind it than a mere respect for gate receipts.

"You see, my boy, it's this way. We play here, in Seattle and in Tacoma. Then we leave American soil. Think of all of the strange places we'll play our game in after we leave Seattle. As the time draws near for leaving the old U.S. a funny sort of feeling comes over a man."

And John J. McGraw had one of those far away looks in his eyes.

"Been playing this game for years and years in this land, and it seems kind of strange to be going away now, leaving this the country where baseball is the National pastime, to play in places where they have never seen the game before."[28]

From the train station, the teams departed for their hotels. For the second time on the tour the teams were housed in two different hotels. The White Sox were dispatched to the Multnomah Hotel; the Giants would spend the day at the Oregon Hotel. Neither team spent much time there. Some players like Hal Chase and Sam Crawford looked up old friends. A strong friendship had already been forged between the newlywed Doyles and Thorpes. A reporter found the four strolling about Portland and tried to get some good copy, but he was only partly successful.

"One thing I've noticed," remarked the Giant captain. "This thing they say about 'all the world loves a lover' is true. Folks seem to greet you in a different sort of a manner after you're married. What do you think? A minister came up to congratulate me and shake hands soon after I arrived in Portland. Makes a fellow feel sort of good, and it's a good thing for the game, too, when people of all classes look upon the players that way."[29]

The anonymous reporter found Jim Thorpe a less forthcoming interviewee. Thorpe, loquacious in the locker room and around the guys, was a virtual clam in public. When pressed for a quote, Thorpe offered only, "Guess I'm a better listener than a talker."[30]

The tourists discovered everyone had fans on the U.S. tour, even the umpires. Bill Klem ran into an old friend and longtime fan, Jack Crows, in Portland. Crows, manager of the Marion Hotel in Salem, Oregon, had played sandlot ball with Klem back in Lakewood, New Jersey, when both were youths. The two had not seen each other for more than fifteen years before being reunited by the tour. The two reminisced all morning before the game, and when the game concluded Klem gave Crows a most valuable heirloom. Taking Crows up to his room in the Oregon Hotel, Klem presented his old teammate with a baseball signed by every member of the Giants and White Sox to which he added the following note, "World's Tour—Giants—White Sox from Billy Klem, to my old friend Jack Crows." Crows proudly showed the ball off all over town and declared, "They can call Klem 'Catfish' all they want to, but he's my pal."[31]

By the 2:30 start time, the game had attracted six thousand fans to Recreation Park. The morning sunshine had given way to raw, damp, and overcast weather. The preceding day's rain left the field slick and soft. Despite the poor field conditions, both teams put on a nifty display of baseball. Arthur Fromme faced off against Jim Scott, who turned in one of the gems of the U.S. tour, a complete-game shutout. The difference in this game was the Sox's sparkling defense, which repeatedly got Scott out of trouble, and Sam Crawford's bases-loaded single. The final score was White Sox 2, Giants 0. After thirty-one games the series stood even at fifteen games apiece, with one tie. Weather permitting, bragging rights for the American phase of the tour would be won in Washington State. Both teams desperately wanted to be leading the series before it left the country.

That evening Portland's boosters held a mammoth shindig at the Multnomah Hotel. The planning for this event had taken months. One of the biggest debates concerned how the banquet tables should be arranged. After much debate, the boosters decided that a diamond shape was best. The boosters were quite proud of their work, even submitting a diagram of the plans to the *Morning Oregonian* for publication. The *Portland Evening Telegram* described the layout: "The tables in the banquet room were arranged in the form of a diamond, with a pitcher's box in the center and players benched on the outside, with the tablecloth representing the baseline with green edges imitating grass."[32] To the long rows of tables in geometric shapes the boosters added a great entertainment package. The Ad Club Quartet and the Hawaiian Quintet were among the featured acts. Fielder Jones, a local Major Leaguer and a notoriously great checkers player, served as greeter. Portland mayor Harry Russell Albee said a few words. Ted Sullivan delivered one of his pompous oratories, and a good time was had by all present. Charles Comiskey felt so good that he actually shook Ray Schalk's hand. Incredibly, even though Schalk had been catching games for the Sox for two years and had seen Comiskey on numerous occasions, this was the first time that the boss extended his hand in friendship.

Since the banquet was held in the same hotel where the White Sox were staying, the Chicagoans turned out in large numbers for the free food. Most of the Giants, however, did not show up. The absence of so many Giants caused some ill feelings among the boosters. McGraw's absence especially was noted, and before long rumors were flying around Portland that the manager had snubbed all of Portland by ducking the banquet.

In reality, John McGraw had spent the night comforting his wife. Blanche was simply in no mood for a party. She and John went out for a quiet dinner with the Doyles and the Loberts. After dinner the two spent the night in their hotel room until the 12:30 A.M. departure time for Tacoma and Seattle, Washington. To smooth over any hard feelings, McGraw sent a telegram to the boosters, apologizing if anyone had taken offense.

As a Northern Pacific locomotive steamed out of Oregon, the cold, moisture-laden air reminded everyone that it was still autumn in North America. Wind stirred up whitecaps on the Columbia River as the tourists made their crossing. Within an hour most everyone on the train was asleep to the sound of steel rolling on steel, and a mass of stratus clouds began to gather above the state of Washington.

FIVE

Across a Restless Sea

All well except the passengers. – Joe Farrell's telegram to Chicago, transmitted from somewhere in the middle of the Pacific Ocean

It was a weary group that arrived in Seattle, Washington, on 19 November 1913. The White Sox and Giants had just completed playing thirty-one games in thirty-four days in twenty-seven different cities before a minimum estimate of one hundred thousand fans. The players' only respite as they barnstormed across the United States had been the rainouts in Abilene, Texas, and Sacramento, California.

Bad weather, which had dogged the tour across virtually every foot of the continent, preceded the tourists to Puget Sound. The storm front, which had drenched the game in Medford, Oregon, now hovered above Tacoma, Washington. While weakening, the storm retained its antibaseball disposition. Driving rain and wind made any game scheduled for that city an impossibility.

Some of the tourists no doubt viewed the Puget Sound downpour as a gift from above. The grueling plans for the day had called for a morning-afternoon doubleheader—a morning game in Tacoma, then an afternoon game in Seattle, followed by the immediate departure of the tourists for Victoria, British Columbia, by way of Vancouver, to board the ship that would carry them to Japan.

The *Seattle Post-Intelligencer* for 19 November 1913 published this body-numbing itinerary for the day.

The two clubs will arrive in Tacoma early this morning on their special train which will be held in readiness to hustle them over to Seattle on a special "run wild" order.

The moment they arrive in Seattle they will be taken to another special which will be standing on the Jefferson street spur of the

Seattle, Renton, & Southern line on Jefferson street between Third and Fourth Avenues. This train will run through to the ball park in Rainier Valley without a stop. President Dugdale said last evening that it was planned to have the ball teams working out on the field a few minutes before 1:30 o'clock so that the game could be underway at 2 o'clock. At first it was thought best to start the battle at 2:30 o'clock but on account of the quickness with which it darkens these days and the necessity of getting the big party on its way to Victoria to connect with the Canadian Pacific Steamship for the Orient, the time was moved back a half hour.[1]

With the Tacoma game canceled and believing that the rain would continue all day, the players voted at their headquarters, Seattle's new Washington Hotel, to cancel the second game of the doubleheader. Desperate for a rest, the players sacrificed the game in their host city. While the players welcomed the rest, they were denied an opportunity to play in brand new Dugdale Park. Home field of the Northwestern League Seattle Giants, Dugdale Park offered one of the most breathtaking vistas of any stadium in North America. Snowcapped Mount Rainer dominated the horizon beyond the left-field fences, a spectacular backdrop that made Dugdale a favorite of fans and players alike.

The cancellation of the second game was especially irritating to the residents of Seattle because of its suddenness. Word of the cancellation "was spread broadcast as soon as possible, all the newspapers and cigar stores being especially notified. Conductors on the Seattle, Renton & Southern line took pains to inform all the passengers that the game had been called off, but the fans would not believe it, and hundreds went out to the park to see for themselves."[2]

The disappointment cut across the forty-ninth parallel, as more than two hundred Canadians had ventured south from Vancouver to take in the game. The decision to cancel the game proved embarrassing for the tourists. While the cloud cover remained, by noon the rain had ceased. Dugdale Park had been especially designed for Seattle's rainy weather. It possessed perhaps the best-designed drainage system of any ballpark in North America. Even after a two-day soak the field was dry within a few hours.

Daniel Dugdale, president of the Seattle Giants, had been an undistinguished Major League catcher in 1886 and 1894. He found his true calling as a minor league baseball entrepreneur, establishing the first professional baseball team in the Pacific Northwest. Dugdale Park was the culmination of its namesake's foresight and perseverance.

Dugdale was incensed at the cancellation, which caused him to lose over $500 in preliminary expenses alone. Denied a chance to recoup his investment and also his share of the expected sizable gate, he minced few words about the cancellation. "The grounds were all right," said President Dugdale, "and if this had been a Northwestern League game, there is no question but what it would have been played."[3]

Despite the players "ducking" the game, Seattle still opened its arms to the tourists. Lee Magee, who in 1909 had been the ace of the Seattle Giants staff, found that he had lost none of his popularity in the ensuing four years. Magee spent so much time answering phone calls from old acquaintances that he had to be pulled away from the phone by his teammates in order to catch the taxi for the pier in time.

To this point the players had seen just about everything there was to see of the nation and had received every imaginable sort of gift and honor that the cities, towns, and corporations of America could bestow. The Northern Pacific Railroad, however, would present the most unusual gift. At a 3:00 P.M. reception at the train station, the railroad company wheeled in a 125-pound fruitcake festooned with icing portraits of Comiskey, McGraw, and White Sox manager Jimmy Callahan, as well as reproductions of Comiskey Park and the Polo Grounds. As an added bonus, baked into the cake was a hidden $20 gold piece.

The touring party, despite the weariness and strain of the transcontinental trek clearly evident on their faces, remained gracious as they posed for pictures with the gargantuan brick-shaped cake. Unsure of what to do with the unusual gift, the tourists had it hauled down to the docks, where it joined the baggage being loaded for the trip around the world.

Two hours later the tourists bid farewell to the United States and began the second phase of their round-the-world endeavor. It was also time to bid good-bye to the players who were not journeying any farther. Scattering to the four winds were Ray Schalk and Morris Rath, who returned to Chicago; Jeff Tesreau and his wife, who boarded a train for Los Angeles; Hal Chase, returning to his home in San Jose; and Reb Russell and his wife, destined for San Diego.

John McGraw's most heartfelt farewell had already been said. Three days earlier in San Francisco, Christy Mathewson took leave of the tour. While Matty would have loved to see the world with his mentor, he begged off, citing a desire to spend the winter in Pasadena, California, with his wife and young son. The real reason was not so prosaic; America's greatest sports idol suffered from seasickness. "He might have gone to please McGraw and his friends," Jane Mathewson once said. "But on our honeymoon we took the boat to Savannah, where the Giants were training, and Christy became terribly ill. He never forgot that, and people had a hard time getting him on a boat again."[4] Rather than admit this failing to McGraw, Mathewson hoped that the explanation offered for his absence would be acceptable.

At 5:00 P.M. on 19 November the entourage, now pared to sixty-seven people, nineteen of whom were ballplayers, gathered at Seattle's waterfront to catch the ship that would carry them to Canada. A pocket transport, the S.S. *Prince Rupert*, would bring the tourists to Victoria, where a luxury liner, the R.M.S. *Empress of Japan*, waited to take the teams to Japan, Shanghai, Hong Kong, and points west.

Never one to allow an audience to forget his "talents," Germany Schaefer wasted no time in launching his first nautical comedy routine. As the *Prince Rupert* steamed away from the pier, Schaefer stood at the rail leading a group of Chinese deckhands in a farewell song. The tuneful nonsense sing-along serenaded the gathering of well-wishers and reporters on the dock. An hour later Schaefer was seen sporting the purser's cap. The *San Francisco Chronicle* opined, "It is predicted that ere the ocean voyage is over he will be wearing the captain's whole outfit."[5]

As the *Prince Rupert* steamed northward through the twilight, the heavy clouds, at long last, lifted. The tourists first viewed the *Empress of Japan* by moonlight. It was beautiful, 298 feet long with yachtlike lines. Its white hull with red trim gleamed in the moonlight. Lights from the portholes shone like suns. Its twin stacks were painted buff, and the deck was polished teak. Above its stern the *Empress* flew the red-and-white checkerboard flag of the Canadian Pacific Railroad. At the bow, its figurehead, an intricately carved Asian dragon, glowered menacingly at the horizon.

The *Empress of Japan* was one of the crown jewels of the Canadian Pacific Railroad's shipping line; its name described the route it plied. The railroad's other ships bore names such as *Empress of Ireland*, *Empress of Australia*, and *Empress of Wales*.

A year after this cruise the *Empress* would make a cameo appearance in Ring Lardner's short story "The Busher Beats It Hence." Jack Keefe, the semiliterate malaprop-spouting hero of Lardner's classic "Busher" stories, nearly declines a chance to go around the world once he gets a glimpse of the ship, which he calls "The Umpires of Japan."[6]

Once the tourists boarded the *Empress*, they awaited completion of the time-consuming process of having their baggage stowed (Charles Comiskey alone traveled with seven huge steamer trunks). Just after 11:30 P.M. the journey to the Land of the Rising Sun began. As the ship left the dock, McGraw and Comiskey distributed pay envelopes to their teams. Each contained the $300 deposit the players had put up to hold their spot on the tour as well as an additional $250 bonus.

While the players no doubt considered the tour a reward in itself, the size of the bonus was truly insulting, particularly when one considers the fact that the tour to this point had earned "$100,000 at the gate."[7] In fact, the White Sox players had made better money from the City Series against the Cubs. In that October contest, each of the Sox player's winning shares had been $807.22.[8] For comparison, the Washington Senators had planned an exhibition tour of Cuba after the close of the 1913 season. Every player who participated was slated to receive $500. Additionally, the Sox and Giants players would not receive any salary while on tour.

Measly bonus in hand, the players settled into life aboard the *Empress*. Many emulated the Thorpes in cabin 218 and went straight to bed. The first twelve hours of the journey, a cruise through the Strait of Juan de Fuca, provided the smoothest and most uneventful sailing of the entire voyage. It would also be about the last hours conducive for sleeping.

The tourists had the great ship largely to themselves, as only a handful of other passengers were making the Pacific crossing. Including the tourists, there were a scant ninety-five souls on board. The Canadian Pacific Railroad pulled out all the stops for its celebrity guests. Separate bridal suites were set aside for all of the honeymooning couples. The cavernous Imperial Suite was turned over to Charles Comiskey and his wife, his son and daughter-in-law, and John McGraw and his wife. The scheduled route of the *Empress* was the inside passage, a simple arc along the Alaskan panhandle and Aleutian Islands, then across the northern Pacific Ocean to the coastline of Japan. This route offered spectacular views of the forbidding, primordial, and barely inhabited territory of Alaska. Among the natural wonders on view were glaciers and an active volcano. The weather this time of year was generally uneventful. For the tourists, however, this trek would be anything but ordinary.

The first storm hit one day out while the *Empress* was cruising past the Alaskan panhandle. Rough seas promptly made nearly everyone aboard seasick. Ted Sullivan euphemistically dubbed it offering tribute to Neptune. Jack Sheridan offered the most expensive tribute to the watery king, losing his "store-bought teeth" over the side. The crew of the *Empress* could not recall when they had had so many sick passengers on board at once.

Ironically, the most severely affected were some of the best athletes on board: Tris Speaker, Sam Crawford, and Hans Lobert. In addition,

Charles Comiskey soon developed a nasty case of either intestinal flu or food poisoning. Whatever the ailment was, it tenaciously clung to Commy, making him miserable for much of the rest of the tour. The Old Roman did not even enter the luxurious dining room of the *Empress* for the first five days of the journey.

Commy's predicament amused many. Charles C. Spink, editor of the *Sporting News*, memorialized the Old Roman's condition in "Commy Relates His Experience," a parody of Poe's "The Raven."

> Ah distinctly I remember
> 'Twas the nineteenth of November,
> While our party, every member,
> Sadly watched the fading shore.
> As we noted each maneuver
> As the vessel left Vancouver;
> Watched the turbines slowly move her
> From the fast receding shore.
> In my mind there rose a question:
> Would I ever see it more?
> Echo answered, "Never more."
> And the undulating motion
> Of that vessel on the ocean
> In me started a commotion
> I had never felt before;
> Suddenly there came a retching
> And a straining and a stretching
> From my commissary fetching
> Things I'd eaten years before;
> Many quaint and curious tid-bits
> I had eaten many years before,
> Many years before.[9]

Summing up the situation for the entire party, John O. Seys of the *Chicago Daily News* penned a poem entitled "Aboard the Good Ship Empress of Japan."

> We were crowded in the cabin.
> Not a player was asleep.
> There was breakfast on the waters,
> There was luncheon on the deep.
> 'Tis a fearful thing in winter

To be shattered by the blast
And be forced to give up dinner—
Or whatever went down last.
So we shuddered there in silence.
Even Schaefer held his breath;
(It was all the Dutchman could hold)
As he lay there still as Death.
As we sat there in the darkness,
Each one busy with his prayers.
"Have a drink!" Comiskey shouted,
"It will drive away your cares."
It was Germany who whispered.
As he tried in vain to stand,
"That's the noblest thing you've said, sir
Since we left our native land."
Then we all went in and had one,
And the dear Old Roman paid:
And we felt much better for it;
Commy surely knows "First Aid."[10]

Actually, Germany Schaefer was one of the few athletes immune from seasickness. He, the Phillies' Mickey Doolan, and, naturally enough, Jim Thorpe were the only ballplayers to remain completely free of seasickness throughout the entire voyage. The Callahan children, Margaret, ten, and Danny, eight, who doubled as the White Sox mascot, were apparently born with sea legs. The two gamboled spiritedly down the long, deserted hallways and ornate rooms of the *Empress*, enjoying the grandest adventure of their young lives. Comiskey spoke for virtually everyone else when he said of the crossing, "It was awful, simply awful."[11]

Of all the players, however, probably none suffered more than Tris Speaker. Originally scheduled to be with the White Sox for only the transcontinental phase of the tour, he decided a scant two hours before the *Prince Rupert* weighed anchor go around the world. This decision was no doubt partly influenced by a pep talk from his boss, outgoing Boston Red Sox president James McAleer, who had himself only joined the tour in Seattle. Continually seasick during the Pacific crossing, Speaker took no food at all for days. He would regret his impulsiveness every inch of the six thousand–mile voyage. The Pacific Ocean was one of the few challenges to ever get the better of the mighty Gray Eagle.

Close on his heels, or perhaps ahead of Speaker, for the title of sickest passenger was twenty-five-year-old Red Faber. Not yet a Major Leaguer, the former Iowa farm boy and future Hall of Famer coughed up so much fluid that he spent most of the trip in the sick bay under the care of the ship's doctors. When the teams finally reached Japan, Faber was still so weak and unsteady that he was scratched from the opening game in Tokyo.

Although the *Empress* was a Canadian vessel, its crew was entirely British. The captain, the delightfully named W. Dixon-Hopcraft, was the only member of the crew familiar with the game of baseball. Somehow, during his travels Captain Dixon-Hopcraft had become a baseball fan.

When the weather and the players' stomachs permitted, McGraw and Sox manager Jimmy Callahan gathered their charges on deck for practice sessions. Curve balls amazed the English crew, who were familiar with the straight sidearm delivery of cricket bowlers. Most surprisingly, despite the presence of Red Faber and twenty-game winner Jim Scott, the sharpest curves were tossed by infielder Germany Schaefer.

High, often treacherous seas became the hallmarks of this voyage, usually preventing the players from practicing on deck. Captain Dixon-Hopcraft's log entries for the Pacific crossing were alarmingly similar: "November 20th: Fresh breeze, rough seas, hard squalls, pitching, shipping very heavy seas. . . . November 21st: Fresh gale, rough seas, and swells. Heavy rain. Squalls. Watertight doors worked. . . . November 22nd: Strong head winds. Rough seas, high swell, frequent hail and squalls. Watertight doors worked."[12]

The dreadful weather did have a positive side benefit. The togetherness of shared misery erased the intense, sometimes bitter rivalry between the teams. Before boarding the *Empress*, some of the tourists barely spoke to others. The games had been played with an intensity that belied their "exhibition" status.

With above-deck amusements eliminated, activity shifted below deck. Reading, singing, and dancing were available diversions, but since these were ballplayers, card playing became the principal occupation. After a few days of cards, cigars, and jokes, almost every one of the tourists became close friends.

John McGraw's preference was whist, and he wasted no time in organizing game after game. McGraw's table quickly established itself as one of the more popular spots on the *Empress*. Captain Dixon-Hopcraft, when he could get away from the bridge, was one of its regulars.

Terminally sullen umpire Bill Klem played loud pinochle games with Fred Merkle and Mike Donlin in one corner of the game room. Elsewhere, one would find ensconced a group dubbed "the seven-up friends," in honor of their preferred card game, a variation of poker. This collection of Royal

Rooters was comprised of Jim Mullin, Tom Lynch, Joe Farrell, and Billy Buhl, Chicago businessmen and White Sox fans who had booked and paid for their own passage, perhaps the earliest example of fans going on the "ultimate fantasy camp." The group neatly encapsulated the world in which Comiskey moved. Mullin and Lynch were in the construction business, Farrel sold sheet music, and Buhl brewed beer.

Tom Lynch, six feet tall, rotund, and weighing at least three hundred pounds, was another of the tourists completely free of motion sickness. During the hellish Pacific crossing, Lynch could often be observed in the otherwise desolate dining room, consuming prodigious amounts of food.

Of the four, Joe Farrell was closest to the Sox players and management. Ring Lardner, himself a member of Comiskey's inner circle, remembered Farrell this way: "There was a White Sox fan named Joe Farrell who was more or less ubiquitous and omnipresent, and who was a greater natural comic than I have ever seen on the stage."[13] Farrell became the instigator or the straight man for many of the stunts and gags that the tourists pulled on their jaunt around the globe. He also served as a correspondent for the *Sporting News*.

A shipboard singing group, seven men who humorously dubbed themselves the "Sextette," was assembled in short order. The product of a bygone era, when every home had a parlor with a piano and singing was a primary means of family entertainment, the choral group contained a most eclectic group of tourists. Buck Weaver, James Scott, Joe Benz, Andy Slight, Steve Evans, Fred Merkle, and Germany Schaefer made up the "Sextette." The group sang a variety of songs, from ragtime to somber ballads. Irving Berlin's current hit songs were popular choices. Their repertoire also included "Garten House," an original composition by Germany Schaefer.

Musical ability set the standard for joining the "Sextette," not team, league, or experience. The seven were Giants and White Sox, grizzled veterans and green bush leaguers. Andy Slight, who without a doubt had the best singing voice, was not even a Major Leaguer. Slight had spent the 1913 season in Des Moines, Iowa, playing for the local Sox affiliate. Although destined never to make a Major League roster, as a tourist Slight was a star.

Buck Weaver and James "Death Valley Jim" Scott had been close friends for years. The two had been roommates during the 1913 regular season. Their close friendship eventually became familial; the two married sisters and became brothers-in-law. Their experience with the shipboard septet led to a vaudeville career in 1914. As part of those shows, Scott and Weaver sang while wearing their world tour uniforms.

The most interesting dynamic among the seven, however, was the (usually) good-natured rivalry between Schaefer and Steve Evans. The Cardinals' Evans was the comic equal of Schaefer. During the tour each tried to prove himself the funnier man. Schaefer preferred the broad gag. He orchestrated stunts such as the "horse" races down the long corridors of the *Empress*. The "horses" were large players like Tris Speaker and Jim Thorpe gamboling about on all fours with smaller players on their backs.

An inveterate prankster, Evans specialized in the practical joke. His favorite target for mischief was umpires, with Jack Sheridan being a frequent victim. So well could he dupe Sheridan that a month later, as the tourists were crossing the equator, Evans had convinced Sheridan that this imaginary line was actually carved into the surface of the planet. To Evans's delight, the umpire peered over the side of the ship to catch a glimpse of it as their ship passed from one hemisphere to the other.

Evans's humor expanded over the course of the tour. By the time the tourists were on their way to Australia, he was successfully passing himself off to other travelers as an English duke. The antics of Schaefer and Evans would provide much-needed laughter during the stress-filled trek across five continents.

Maintaining what traditions they could while away from home, the tourists were the first Americans in the world to celebrate Thanksgiving in 1913. When the *Empress* crossed the international date line, Tuesday, 25 November, became Thursday, 27 November. Many jokes ensued about the missing Wednesday. Most of those jokes ran along the lines of, "Did you see what I did on Wednesday?"

Rough seas made for a unique Thanksgiving. Sometime during the day someone, possibly H. P. Burchell of the *New York Times*, wired the following greeting to the Associated Press. "Baseball party all well owing to special attention of Captain Hopcraft and crew of the Empress. Wish friends at home happy Thanksgiving. (signed) Giants–White Sox."

This would be one of the last messages received from the *Empress*. Communication became sporadic after Thanksgiving. Press speculation for its silence centered on the wireless. Still new technology, the Marconi wireless was, even under the best broadcasting conditions of the day, hardly an ideal communications medium. The first wireless message across the Pacific occurred only in 1910, and that one was land based, having originated in Hawaii. Messages at sea were especially difficult to pluck from the "ether." Broadcasting and receiving equipment sets were themselves cumbersome and subject to short circuits, atmospheric disturbances, moisture, and power failures.

The Canadian Pacific Railroad haphazardly distributed the Marconi wireless among its ships. None of its ships had even been equipped with a wireless until 1910. By 1913, while all of its passenger liners had been issued a wireless, much of the rest of the Canadian Pacific fleet sailed in silence. If an emergency were to strike any of these ships, the crew had flares, flags, and their lungs.

By Thanksgiving the party had also decided what to do with the giant fruitcake from Seattle. Originally, the tourists had planned to serve it up with the Thanksgiving feast, but mass seasickness made this a most unappetizing prospect. Rather than eat the thing themselves, the players decided to save the cake for the welcome-home banquets back in the States. They would cut one half in New York and send the other half to Chicago, the first round-the-world fruitcake.

The change in dates had also heralded a change in the severity of the weather. That afternoon a rogue wave crashed into the *Empress*, knocking down many who were on board. Giants pitcher George "Hooks" Wiltse had a steamer trunk slam into his right hand as he went down. The trunk opened a sizable gash on his hand; fortunately for Wiltse, he was a southpaw. Harry Sparrow, the tourists' overseas business manager, suffered a sprained right arm, and H. P. Burchell received a cut on his head and a sprained shoulder when the wave sent him sprawling.

Despite these and other minor injuries, the tourists strived to ignore the storm and churning seas to enjoy the holiday. They feasted, as best they could, in the dining room, with Captain Dixon-Hopcraft presiding. The great ship pitched like one of the bulls that cowboy Tris Speaker used to break in his prebaseball days. Still, the tourists persevered, the "Sextette" sang, and everyone exchanged stories and pleasantries, with the revelries continuing until the early morning hours.

The next evening, Friday, 28 November, the ship was entertained in a completely different manner. The Mulligan band, led by Mr. Willets, boatswain's mate, serenaded the tourists. The band's bizarre instruments were all handmade from whatever was available, "old scrap iron, broken buckets, sheet tin, tarred yarn, sail cloth and other fabrics," yet the band played in perfect harmony.[14]

Willets, a bear of a man who stood at least six feet three inches tall, dressed in a garish parody of John Philip Sousa's signature white suit. Playing the part to the hilt, Willets had even trimmed his white beard to match that of the American impresario. Wielding his baton, Willets conducted several rousing marches.

A few days before this dinner, the Mulligan band had made its first appearance. During a lull in the storm, Willets and the band led a march around the decks of the *Empress* in celebration of what was naively believed to be the end of the stormy skies.

The Mulligan band stood in sharp contrast to the ship's regular band, a full complement of versatile musicians led by Jerry Murphy, a six-foot six-inch relic of Victorian-era militarism. Murphy wore his beard in a Vandyke and sported gold-rimmed glasses. His red satin jacket bore a bedazzling array of medals, testaments of his heroic service to England in the Boer War.

The following morning, 29 November 1913, the bad weather turned positively nightmarish, as a late-season typhoon ripped open the heavens. This storm, easily the worst the Northern Pacific had seen in at least twenty years, turned the sea into a hellish cauldron. Winds of hurricane force, heavy snow, and mountainous seas battered the *Empress*.

Frank McGlynn, the movie director who had joined the tour in California, and his cameraman, Victor Miller, sprang into action. Disregarding their personal safety, the two made their way to the bridge. From this vantage point forty feet above the deck, they shot footage of the angry seas breaking over the forward deck. Both were quickly drenched to the bone, despite the fact that they wore sailors' oilskins.

Taking only as much time as necessary to complete filming, the duo returned below deck to dry off themselves and their equipment. No one realized that they had recorded only the beginning of the storm. The next sixteen hours would be the worst hours the tourists would ever endure.

By four o'clock in the morning the ship's first officer, Mr. Holland, declared an emergency. The darkness was so absolute and the waves so high that neither he nor anyone else on board could guess which way the ship was headed. The waves, estimated by Captain Dixon-Hopcraft at sixty feet high, completely obliterated the horizon. So loudly did the waves batter the *Empress* that it sounded, according to McGlynn, "like artillery." Three boat booms were snapped, and a lifeboat was shattered by the force of the waves. One mammoth wave slammed into the bridge, nearly tearing it from the ship. Holland and the crew on duty barely escaped the bridge just ahead of the surging waters. Captain Dixon-Hopcraft's ominous log entry reads: "Nov. 29, 1913 Overcast weather and blowing a storm of Hurricane force. Mountainous sea running. Steamer straining heavily and shipping much water, 4:30 A.M.—Increased speed three revolutions. Falling off from sea becoming unmanageable. Emergency boats' crews mustered. Overcast, gloomy, heavy snowfall. Rain, hail."[15]

The *Empress* began shipping water both fore and aft. Water streamed into its coal bunkers, while below deck the stokers, in water up to their knees, worked feverishly to keep the turbines humming. Frank McGlynn's gripping account gives the best sense of terror and dread that was life on the *Empress of Japan*:

> As she mounted a wave and dipped toward the yawning gulf of gray below, her twin screws would be in the air, then, taking the sea, as she slipped down the incline, they would send a shudder through the frame; down, down, down, it seemed an interminable distance the stout old craft would go; then like a thing of life, she would seem to pause and judge the oncoming mountain of water that threatened to completely submerge her. How she ever kept her head up is a mystery that can only be answered by the brave men who stuck to their work through cold and wet and impending disaster; but she rose on each occasion and gradually up, up, up till near the top when, crash! The last crest would strike her slightly off the port bow and hundreds of tons of roaring brine would cover her forecastle. Like a giant animal she seemed to strain and stagger and finally come through the seas as the water rushed along her decks seeking an outlet over the sides through the scuppers and oft times into the coal bunkers, causing her to shudder and apparently lift in a spasmodic way as if she righted herself for the next plunge down into the seething gulf.[16]

One can easily imagine the fate of the passengers and crew if Captain Dixon-Hopcraft *had* issued the order to abandon ship. Fortunately for all on board, the storm blew itself out on 1 December. In the wake of the typhoon, the crew discovered that even though the *Empress* had been traveling at full throttle, they had actually been blown backward nearly two hundred miles by the force of storm, costing them valuable cruise time. Soon a great cloud of storm-bedraggled birds appeared above the ship's stern. The birds, having been blown many miles out to sea by the storm, followed the *Empress* back to land. So much of the coal in the bunkers was saturated that only three of the ship's seven boilers were able to operate at full capacity, causing further delays. There was open speculation among the crew and passengers that the ship would have to pull into port in northern Japan, well short of the scheduled destination of Yokohama harbor. In all, three days were lost to the storm and damp coal. Not in ten years of crossing the Pacific had the *Empress* been more than a few hours behind schedule.

The tourists did not get their first view of the Japanese coastline until 5 December. All were euphoric at the sight. Land, any land, looked heavenly after the pounding the *Empress* had endured. With great relief the touring party made ready to enter Japan. On 6 December 1913, having survived the worst that the Pacific could throw at them, the Giants and White Sox sailed past Mount Fuji into Yokohama Harbor and were greeted by the storm of the greatest heroes' welcome Japan had ever seen.

SIX

The Land of the Rising Sun

They are all athletes, fast on the bases, good hitters, always alert, and, with a pitching staff of equal excellence to their general playing, would give any major league nine a hard tussle. – John McGraw, commenting on Japan's baseball players

Nothing, absolutely nothing, prepared the tourists for the reception they received in Japan. More like a homecoming than greetings from a foreign nation, at the docks were a riot of color, teeming with droves of fans and sportswriters. Japan was every bit as mad about baseball as was the United States. Under gray, raw skies, amid the crowd of rabid baseball fans, U.S. consul general Thomas Sammons ferried out in a tug to be the first to greet the tourists. Accompanying Sammons were several Japanese officials and sportswriters who served as the welcoming committee. While the Japanese needed interpreters to converse with the players, many of them knew at least one American phrase, greeting the players with a big "Howdy!"

The ballplayers found the local press corps every bit as savvy as their U.S. counterparts. In an impromptu press conference, they asked penetrating questions and made pithy observations. "The great manager McGraw's pin made of diamond on his necktie was shining with the rising sun," wrote a reporter for the *Jiji Shimpo*, a Tokyo daily.[1] One of reporters for the *Keihin Press* asked about game strategy: "What strategy would the managers employ against each other and against Keiō University?"[2]

The Americans were more candid with the Japanese press corps than they had been with their own. When disappointed reporters asked the reason why Mathewson had not come, the tourists replied, "He was a bad sailor and also he didn't like the ship. We tried to bring him but he declined."[3] In the United States, virtually the only reporter who had dared state the truth about Matty had been Bill Bailey of the *Chicago American*. Bailey, actually the pen name for Bill Veeck Sr., wrote on 20 November 1913, in his typical "take no prisoners" style, of Matty's gradual transformation as the tour progressed.

When Christy Mathewson joined the world's tourists in Cincinnati and pitched the first game there was no question in his head about going. He was talking enthusiastically about China, about Japan, about Australia. He was even worried because there was a chance the Mathewson cash could dwindle until there might not be a great deal of it left for the shops of Paris and London.

As they neared the western coast Matty underwent a change of heart.

"I'm not going," said Matty one fine day.

"Why not?" was the demand.

"I can't stand the water. Why do you know I have been almost sick on a ferry from New York to Brooklyn?"

Of course if the fellow sent to cause Matty to engage his heart again and make the trip had represented that it wasn't the water but the place he was going to that made him sick on those short excursions the great pitcher might have consented to continue the journey.[4]

Nearly every other reporter mentioned Matty's seasickness as gossip or rumor.

The Japanese press was also disappointed not to find Jeff Tesreau and Fred Snodgrass among the players disembarking from the *Kogo* (Japanese for empress). Nonetheless, they dutifully listed the names of every player and other tourists in the party. The Japanese media were particularly taken with Comiskey. Witness this quote from the *Keihin Press*: "Callahan, the manager of the Chicago team and Comiskey were in high spirits. He is a dauntless looking man who also looked the gentleman."[5]

After making their way through the crush of well-wishers and reporters, some of whom had even boarded the ship to get interviews, the party made its way to customs and examinations by doctors. Some members of the party, especially the women, were a bit apprehensive at what to expect, but everyone sailed through. The processing completed, the tourists boarded rickshas to take them to the consul general's residence. Germany Schaefer immediately dubbed them "gin rickeys" (a pun based on the then-current pronunciation of the word for the vehicles, "jinrickshas").

Comiskey, Callahan, and McGraw chose a different mode of transport. Accompanied by their families, they rode in automobiles to the consulate. Just as in the United States, every luxury materialized for the tourists' use. The only tourist not enjoying himself was Red Faber, still languishing on board the *Empress*. The ship's surgeons would not allow the former Iowa farm boy out of the sickbay until he was strong enough to rejoin his teammates.

After a brief meeting with Sammons at his residence, it was back into rickshas and cars for the trip to the Grand Hotel. Throngs of Japanese tagged along behind the cars and rickshas to the consul's residence. This same throng shadowed the tourists to the Grand Hotel. Rest was not on the agenda, however. About all the players would have time for would be to check in and change; a game was scheduled for that afternoon at the baseball stadium at Keiō University. The players would be forced to play even before they had lost their sea legs.

Owing to the lateness of the arrival of the *Empress*, the tourists' schedule in Japan had to be trimmed by two games. Cut were the games scheduled for Kōbe and Osaka. Three contests remained, all of them in Tokyo.

For the players, just being in Japan was an accomplishment in itself. Joe Farrell noted, "The fans can now understand why base ball world tours are 25 years apart. It takes that long to forget the initiation on the Pacific."[6]

Arrival at the Grand Hotel precipitated a flurry of activity. Joe Farrell sets the scene, "Arriving at the Grand, the lobby bore a resemblance to a Chicago department store in a bargain rush. The main floor was thronged with vendors of kimonos and mandarin coats. All the ladies were busy bargainers at once. The male members rushed to the nearest silk shirt stores to select material and get measured for the lightest kind of stuff, for it is only a week before the party will be sweltering near the equator."[7]

Those who had owned cameras deposited their film for processing. Some photographs of the era were actually designed to double as a postcard, complete with a little box on back for the stamp. The *Chicago Record-Herald* of 28 December described one such card sent to White Sox player John Burns in Chicago. "John Burns yesterday received a postal from the world tourists. It was a photo card, the picture having been snapped on board the Empress of Japan. It showed Buhl, Callahan, Evans, Farrell and Mullen in a slightly emaciated condition. On the correspondence side of the card was this touching verse:

> If we ever get back to the loop again.
> We'll never sail a day;
> Tho' we had fun the world around
> We   all the way."[8]

The newspaper censored the final line of the doggerel verse, but readers could easily supply their own substitute.

After a very hasty lunch, the tourists dashed back to the rickshas and were delivered to the train station. Arriving a little after noon, the tourists were once again ferried by the human-powered craft to the stadium at Keiō University. Along the way, a wheel came off the ricksha carrying the Thorpes, tumbling the newlyweds into a Tokyo street. Fortunately, no one was injured. After dusting themselves off, the adventurous Iva and Jim climbed into another ricksha and continued their trek.

Keiō University was and remains the most prestigious collegiate baseball power in Japan. Baseball on the college level in Japan was itself only little more than a decade old; the game itself had been played in Japan since before 1870. One of the early popularizers of the sport was American college teacher Horace Wilson, who taught at Kaisei Gakkō University (now Tokyo University). It did not become part of high school athletic programs until 1900. By 1903 an intense rivalry between Keiō and Waseda Universities had become one of the most eagerly followed sporting events in all of Japan. Waseda proved its international mettle in 1908 by beating the visiting University of Washington team four times. In 1912 Keiō sent its team to barnstorm against college teams in the western United States. Now, a year later, they got a chance to play host.

Keiō was at first embarrassed about the condition of its field. Thinking that it did not compare to the fields they had seen in the States, either in size or amenities, T. Kimishima of the Keiō Base Ball Association offered these words, "I hereby wish to make an apology to you, the greatest of all exponents of the game. It is in an embarrassed state of mind that the Association invites teams to have the use of this midget field, but at all events your welcome is not belittled."[9]

After reassuring Kimishima that the field was better than 30 percent of the fields in the United States, the game began. The proceedings were so rushed that the ballplayers didn't even get to work out beforehand. McGraw did treat the crowd to a game of shadow ball, which put the crowd into hysterics. This was the very first game of shadow ball the Japanese had ever seen, and it was the perfect icebreaker. The tourists found one element of conforming to local custom most amusing. The Japanese tradition of removing one's shoes when entering a house meant that before and after the game, each player had to doff his spikes before entering the clubhouse. Wooden cloglike slippers were provided for navigating the clubhouse.

Intensely covered by the Japanese media, every Tokyo paper had at least one reporter at the game, and some papers sent as many as five. This game, like the others played, would feature no fewer than four future members of the Japanese Baseball Hall of Fame. The guest of honor was Jiro Murao. Known as "The Father of Japanese Baseball," Murao was a cross between Alexander Cartwright and A. G. Spalding. As a youth, he fell in love with baseball at a time when it was viewed as either a foreign curiosity or a dangerous Western influence. Murao almost single-handedly made Japanese baseball the obsession it became. Largely due to his influence, every high school and college in Japan added baseball to their physical fitness curriculum. By 1913 he had been zealously promoting baseball for thirty-five years.

Murao understood that the Japanese game could not excel in isolation. He encouraged U.S. college teams to tour Japan, and in 1912 he led Keiō University's team on a barnstorming tour of U.S. West Coast colleges. One of Murao's lifelong dreams, however, had been to see U.S. Major Leaguers play in Japan. This tour was everything he had ever hoped for.

Also present was Isoo Abe, the founder of university baseball in Japan. Abe established the first college program in Japan at Waseda University. This day he was one of the guests of honor. Kazuma Sugase, who acted as interpreter and pitched, had been part of the Keiō barnstormers of 1912. He stuck close to President Kamada of Keiō University, another guest of honor. To everyone's delight, the sun chose this moment to break through the clouds. The early December day became almost springlike and far more tolerable for both fans and players. After lots of picture-taking by the assembled news outlets, umpires Klem and Sheridan were introduced, and the ceremonial first pitch was thrown from the mound by President Kamada to Consul General Sammons half crouching at home plate.

Five thousand citizens wedged themselves into Keiō's baseball grounds and cheered themselves hoarse. Space was at such a premium that many of the fans sat on bamboo mats crammed into any open plot of land. To the Americans, it was all very heady and overpowering. The intensity of the Japanese fans and their knowledge of the game impressed the Americans. Veteran sportswriter Gus Axelson claimed that they were every bit as loud as any group of Giants fans under Coogan's Bluff.

The Giants and White Sox played fair baseball considering how seasick everyone had been for so long, with the Sox winning 9–4. The seasick Texan Tris Speaker had a great game, two home runs and a couple of hard liners. The very short right- and left-field fences and the exotic atmosphere probably made everyone play much better than they felt.

Just as he had done in the States, Bill Klem, in his most windows-rattling bass voice, elaborately introduced each player as he strode up to the batter's box. Klem's mammoth vocal power, elaborate style, and pugnacious attitude were unlike anything the Japanese had encountered before in an umpire. Klem quickly became a favorite of both the crowd and the sports reporters. Just how much of an impact Klem made could be seen in the next day's *Jiji Shimpo*. The paper had sent a caricaturist to the game to capture the day's activities. Klem's caricature was rendered larger than anyone else's.

For Japanese fandom, the tour was nirvana. Although their nation had adopted baseball as its national pastime (second only to sumo wrestling), no games of Major League caliber had ever been played there.

Racist anglophile A. G. Spalding had completely bypassed Japan twenty-five years earlier during his tour. Preferring to journey to nations under British or American rule, Spalding's trail was considerably more southern. From Hawaii, Spalding's All-Stars sailed to New Zealand and Australia before dodging north to Ceylon, Egypt, Italy, France, and Great Britain. Only in Italy and France had Spalding been out of the British sphere of influence.

In 1908 Japan had been visited by the Reach All-Americans, funded by the Reach Sporting Goods Company. The All-Americans visited the Philippines and Hawaii after playing seventeen games in Japan. The 1908 tourists consisted of only one team, none of whom could even remotely be considered star players. They specialized in steamrollering local nines. The Reach All-Americans drubbed their Japanese opponents 17–0. The only positive aspect of the 1908 tour as far as the Japanese were concerned was that the humiliation fueled their desire to excel at the sport and to one day beat the Americans at their own game.

Fortunately, the tour by Comiskey and McGraw promised to bode far more goodwill for everyone. In the intervening years, players who had visited Japan on their own had smoothed over some of the hard feelings remaining from the Reach All-Americans. During the winter of 1910, Arthur "Tillie" Shafer, utility outfielder and second baseman, along with Tommy Thompson, a pitcher, both of McGraw's Giants, visited Japan and dispensed a great deal of good coaching on the finer points of the game to this very same Keiō University. Curiously, although Shafer was still on the Giants roster in 1913, he expressed no interest in going on the tour.

The abilities of the American Major Leaguers, even after enduring the strength-sapping Pacific Ocean, were far above what everyone in Japan was familiar with. It was like knowing a few dance steps and then having Vernon and Irene Castle show up to give you a tutorial. They watched each play carefully, studying and learning. Of the various baseball skills, the art of pitching was the area where the Japanese lagged farthest behind the Americans. To the American sportswriters present, it seemed as if the Giants and Sox had left their arms on the *Empress*, yet their pitchers still packed more heat than the locals had ever seen. The Japanese were also impressed with the prodigious home run power of the tourists. Though the year 1913 is considered a part of the dead-ball era in the United States, it was a far livelier version of the game than the one in Japan.

After this game the tourists returned to the Grand Hotel for some hurried sight-seeing and a feast that they could finally keep down. The banquet entertainment included geishas. Iva Thorpe was awed by the geishas' gracefulness. Like all the banquets of the tour, this one included speeches and toasts and lasted until late in the evening.

The next morning, Sunday, 7 December 1913, was the date for what was perhaps the most eagerly anticipated baseball game in Japan's history. A team composed of both the White Sox and Giants was scheduled to challenge the Keiō University team. For this event, seven thousand people crammed into Keiō's stadium. This was to be the first game of a doubleheader. The Sox and Giants would play each other in the afternoon, the last contest in Japan. The morning game marked the first time that the teams would challenge a local nine on their global sojourn. For the first time the two teams would play as one. The starting lineup of American big leaguers that day consisted of Lee Magee, Larry Doyle, Fred Merkle, Hans Lobert, Mickey Doolan, and Ivy Wingo of the Giants, with Tris Speaker, Sam Crawford, and Buck Weaver of the White Sox. "Death Valley Jim" Scott of the Sox pitched, and the Giants' Mike Donlin replaced Crawford in right field after six innings. The early morning hour of play meant that right field would be bathed in glare, leading Sam Crawford to remark, "And to think I came 7,000 miles to play the sun field."[10]

Klem and Sheridan umpired this game, as they had all the others. Klem crouched behind the squatting catchers while Sheridan worked the bases. Klem's booming voice and mannerisms were soon being imitated by the crowd, which ordinarily did not endear itself to umpires. Paralleling their U.S. counterparts, the Japanese loved to ride the umps. Mike Donlin drew applause his first time at bat because the Japanese fans appreciated the way he had argued with Klem in the previous day's game.

If anything, the Japanese fans were harsher to the "men in blue" than were Americans, as the sad case of C. T. Mayes proves. Mayes, an expatriate American, had worked the 1905 game between Keiō and Waseda Universities. Tensions from the bitter rivalry boiled over into an on-field riot. In the leap of his life, Mayes hurdled the left-field wall to escape a mob of enraged fans. Mayes hid in a house near the ballpark for several hours,

Pitching great Christy Mathewson in Blue Rapids, Kansas. (Photographed by George Hewitt. Courtesy of Don Musil, Theodore Musil, and the Office of the Mayor, Blue Rapids, Kansas.)

The Giants and White Sox stride into Blue Rapids, Kansas. (Photographed by George Hewitt. Courtesy of Don Musil, Theodore Musil, and the Office of the Mayor, Blue Rapids, Kansas.)

On a perfect afternoon for baseball, Wally Mattick squares around to bunt while Sam Crawford makes his way back to the bench. (Photographed by George Hewitt. Courtesy of Don Musil, Theodore Musil, and the Office of the Mayor, Blue Rapids, Kansas.)

An advertisement for the world baseball tour. (*Times Democrat.* Muskogee, Oklahoma)

White Sox manager
Jimmy Callahan.

White Sox owner
and president
Charles Comiskey.

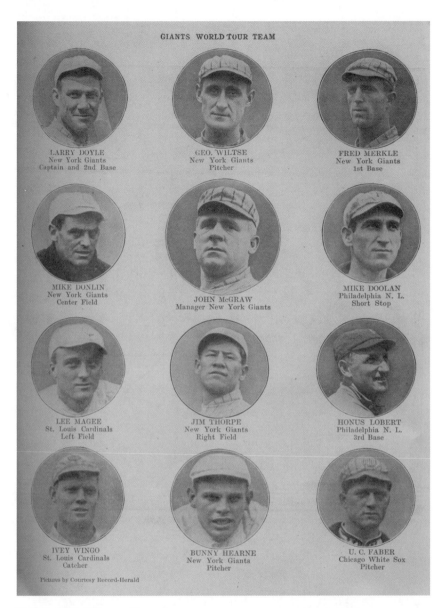

GIANTS WORLD TOUR TEAM

LARRY DOYLE
New York Giants
Captain and 2nd Base

GEO. WILTSE
New York Giants
Pitcher

FRED MERKLE
New York Giants
1st Base

MIKE DONLIN
New York Giants
Center Field

JOHN McGRAW
Manager New York Giants

MIKE DOOLAN
Philadelphia N. L.
Short Stop

LEE MAGEE
St. Louis Cardinals
Left Field

JIM THORPE
New York Giants
Right Field

HONUS LOBERT
Philadelphia N. L.
3rd Base

IVEY WINGO
St. Louis Cardinals
Catcher

BUNNY HEARNE
New York Giants
Pitcher

U. C. FABER
Chicago White Sox
Pitcher

Pictures by Courtesy Record-Herald

The New York Giants world tour roster.

New York Giants
manager John McGraw.

The White Sox welcome-home banquet at Chicago's Congress Hotel, 10 March 1914.

Filipinos, attired in their Sunday best, attending the first game in Manila.

Filipino natives attempting to sweep the water off the diamond prior to the final ball game in Manila.

Sir Thomas Lipton provided a snake charmer as part of the entertainment for his lavish tea party at the Galle Face Hotel.

Josephine Callahan gets a camel's-eye view of ancient Egypt.

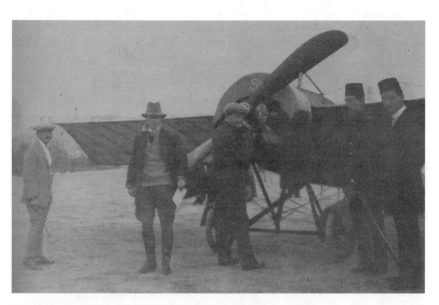

The tourists examine the plane of French aviator Mark Poupre, "the Birdman from Khartoum."

Awestruck Comiskey,
McGraw, and Callahan
just moments after their
audience with the pope.

Buck Weaver inspects the equipment box just before game time in Nice, France.

London's Chelsea Football Grounds decked out for baseball.

Umpire Bill Klem
gets a ride in a Tokyo ricksha.

King George V observes the game with interest.

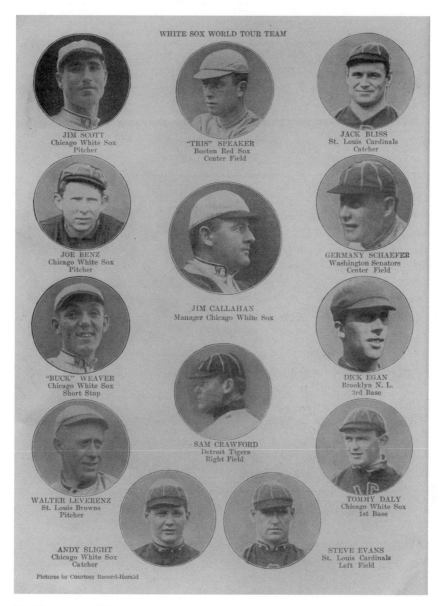

The White Sox world tour roster.

This political cartoon sums up the problem created by the new Federal League. (*Inter Ocean*, 17 February 1914.)

then swore off umpiring forever. The game he was forced to vacate never was completed. The Japanese government, after quelling the riot at the Keiō baseball grounds, thought it better that the game remain unfinished. For the next twenty years baseball games between Waseda and Keiō were banned by law.

Keiō University's baseball team was the best collegiate team and therefore the best team in all of Japan. There was no question that much Japanese pride rested on this contest. Keiō batted first and played full bore. Shigeki Mori, Keiō's center fielder, led off with a triple. A play later he scored on Daisuke Miyake's single. The crowd exploded with joy. By good fortune, Frank McGlynn and Victor Miller had the movie camera rolling. As Mori crossed the plate, Miller used the panoramic lens to get a wide shot of the seven thousand screaming fans in full ecstasy.

Moments later the Japanese were retired without further scoring. The Americans now got a chance to silence the crowd. Lee Magee, playing left field, matched Shigeki Mori by leading off with a triple. He scored immediately on Larry Doyle's single. After shutting the Americans down in the second inning, the floodgates opened. The Sox-Giants plated sixteen runs, scoring in every inning. Keiō scored only two more runs, for a final score of 16–3.

The game was not such a blowout as the score might indicate. The Americans found the Japanese to be very good ballplayers. Gus Axelson said of their playing that it was a "revelation to the major leaguers." While their fielding, work on the bases, and ability to think on their feet were nearly as adept as the pros, the Japanese had one glaring weakness, pitching. Keiō could not hit much American pitching, and their pitcher could not serve up much that the Americans could not hit.

The Japanese pitcher, Kazuma Sugase, also served as team captain. Nearly as tall as Jim Scott, he looked quite professorial in his owlish glasses. His arm, while mastering Japanese players, was no match for the Sox and Giants. Every member of the Sox-Giants except Doolan and the still sea-woozy Weaver touched home at least once. Sugase did go the distance, however, and did not surrender any home runs. He actually gave up fewer bases on balls than did Scott, and he recorded three strikeouts. On the negative side, Magee tripled twice, Merkle was hit by a pitch, and Sugase had to endure three passed balls by his stone-gloved catcher, Takahama. The defensive highlight of the game for the Japanese had to be turning an exotic 5–3–5 (third to first to third) double play that sent an awed Tris Speaker back to the bench.

Jim Scott started poorly but just kept getting better as the game progressed. After shaking off the cobwebs of idleness and seasickness, his pitching completely mastered the university students. Scott surrendered single runs in the first, third, and fifth innings, then shut Keiō down. In the ninth inning Scott was humming along so well that he struck out the side, ending the game with an awesome flourish. The game took a brisk one hour and forty-eight minutes from start to finish. What had started as a sporting event became a delightful encounter between cultures. Politeness ruled the day. The Americans were applauded by their hosts every time they made a good play. McGraw and the American pros were sincerely impressed with the Japanese's abilities. Had a Major League–quality pitcher been on the mound for the Japanese, the results of the game could easily have been very different.

Great shouts of appreciation from the seven thousand fans erupted at the conclusion of the game, with lengthy ovations that poured over the Americans like a wall of sound. After the game there was just enough time for a quick lunch while the field was prepared for the afternoon contest. For the second time, the tourists would play a morning/afternoon doubleheader. The first one had been on 16 November in Oakland and San Francisco, California, when everyone, even after a month of nonstop touring, had been in better shape.

The afternoon show, the last game played by the tourists in Japan, saw six thousand fans retain their seats from the first game. The Japanese continued to revel in the tourists' skillful ball playing. The Giants and White Sox used their regular lineups against each other, with most of those who had played in the morning back in action for the "nightcap." The White Sox swept the "series" in Japan, winning the second game 12–9.

This game ended with one of the most thrilling plays of the entire tour. Tris Speaker threw Mike Donlin out at the plate from the deepest part of centerfield. From a distance of nearly 483 feet, as far as the centerfield bleachers in the Polo Grounds, Tris Speaker pegged "Turkey" Mike Donlin at the plate with an absolutely perfect throw to Ivy Wingo. An amazed John McGraw called it one of the greatest plays he had ever seen. The awed Japanese fans cheered the play in a riotous cacophony of sound. No dramatist could have come up with a more appropriate ending to the game or the series in Japan.

The women of the party were not in attendance for either of the day's games. Rather than sit through more baseball, all of the wives were on the *Empress*, sailing ahead of their mates to Osaka, 250 miles east. The men would join them many hours later; after the second game the athletes were to catch the first train out of Tokyo for Osaka, known as the "Chicago of Japan."

It is fair to say that the Giants and White Sox sent every one of the eighteen thousand fans who attended the three games home happy. Whatever differences existed between the U.S. government and the empire of Japan over issues such as the Japanese Exclusion Act were for the moment forgotten.

The Japanese press ran out of superlatives and hyperbole in describing what they had witnessed. The *Yokohama Gazette* stated: "The Games have been a revelation to those of us who had not witnessed anything of the sort before."[11] Alluding perhaps to the Mayes incident of the past, the *Japan Advertiser* of Tokyo said: "The teams seem to move like clockwork. Each signal is exactly followed and the umpire's decision is obeyed silently. It is this system of arbitration that the ball player of this country must note and develop so that further friction in international baseball games may be averted. The speed and alacrity of the base stealing, too was a revelation to the Japanese."[12] The *Tokyo Times* reported:

> Like a cyclone the big men of America came and went causing a whirlwind of sensation. What did they do? Well ask the fans; they know it. And also ask those people living down in the Mita Road, and they will give you complete statistics of windows smashed, houses damaged, and dogs in the street hit by flying balls. They worked more wonders and showed more true ball playing than the Japanese fans could see. The cyclonic visit of the American stars has left its memory in the sporting history of Japan—besides those mementos on some houses in the neighborhood of the Keiō grounds. And fortunate was the Keiō team, which was able to get practical suggestions and advice from such base ball brains as John McGraw and Jim Callahan.[13]

After the game some of the party returned to the Grand Hotel. Most of the players, however, checked into the Imperial Hotel in Tokyo, which was much closer to the ballpark. Everyone tried to squeeze in some sightseeing and banqueting before reporting to the train station for a journey by rail to Osaka. Adjacent to Kōbe, Osaka sits on the west coast of Japan's main island of Honshu.

Joe Benz, who could always laugh at himself, had an amusing incident occur while the teams were housed at the Imperial Hotel. Around dinnertime Joe decided to take a walk. Almost immediately he managed to get himself lost. Desperately chasing about the city, he spied a trolley car coming down the street. Benz chased it down, breathlessly climbed aboard, and asked the conductor if he knew the Imperial Hotel.

" 'Yes sir,' replied the man in good English, to Joe's surprise. 'Well let me off at the right street.' 'Excuse, please, mister. Imperial Hotel, two blocks back. Same way you run,' said the conductor."[14]

Upon boarding the 7:00 P.M. train at the station for the fourteen-hour train ride, the players had one more culture shock. The size of the train's berths was a most depressing discovery. Built for the smaller stature of the Japanese, the berths measured only five feet eight inches long and two feet wide. Ivy Wingo in particular was especially perturbed. Wingo caught both ends of the doubleheader and wanted nothing more than to lie down and rest his aching bones. That would, however, be impossible for the five-feet ten-inch, 160-pound catcher to do comfortably. Wingo whined that he would probably be crippled for life if he got into his berth. Sleep is a powerful force, though, and before long all of the men, including six-foot Tris Speaker, were crammed into their berths speeding through the night-shrouded Japanese landscape. The only sound, snores mixed with the steady hum of steel upon steel.

Arrival in Kōbe was at 9:00 A.M. on 9 December 1913. The wives had already spent a most enjoyable day in Kōbe shopping, sightseeing, and socializing. The distaff members of the party had traveled to Kōbe ahead of their husbands on board the *Empress*. For them all, this passage on the *Empress* marked the longest period apart from their husbands since the tour's opening game in Cincinnati. This was the first separation for some of the newlyweds. For these women especially, the reunion in Kōbe was most emotional and deeply satisfying.

The ballplayers' train pulled into the Osaka terminal at 7:30 A.M. Await-ing the train was the city's large, loud, and enthusiastic welcoming com-mittee. Cheers went up, along with calls for Thorpe, Comiskey, McGraw, and Doyle. All of the players emerged stiff-limbed and bleary-eyed to a thunderous ovation. McGraw and Callahan were presented with two elaborate floral wreaths, each carried by young Japanese girls. Elsewhere, men hoisted banners with welcoming messages in English high above the milling crowd.

The committee and the citizens of Osaka were greatly disappointed that the game scheduled for their city had been canceled. The chairman of the welcoming committee, an English-speaking editor of the *Osaka Daily News*, while understanding the reason for the cancellation, could not hide his sadness. Callahan and McGraw made brief speeches. Then it was on to Kōbe to the thunderous shouts and cheers of the Japanese.

The *Empress*, with the players' wives, would not return to Kōbe until 10:30 A.M. For the next three hours the men went on a buying spree. Kimonos, silk, summer clothing, souvenirs, jewelry, gifts for spouses and girlfriends—in short, everything that could be bought. McGraw, while strolling down the streets of Kōbe, came across a vendor with wares he most assuredly had no interest in. The earnest Japanese man was proffering recently slaughtered rats for human consumption. Politely, McGraw declined the man's sales pitch and moved off in the opposite direction. The Giants manager nonetheless took great delight in telling fellow travelers of this encounter, regaling his audience with all of the grisly details and elaborating the story with each retelling.

The *Empress* steamed off toward the rising sun and dropped anchor in Kōbe at 10:30 A.M. The women boarded a launch to greet their husbands waiting on the shore. For the next two hours the wives joined their husbands in sightseeing, spending, and spooning.

At 12:30 in the afternoon everyone returned to the *Empress*. As a reunion present, the Canadian Pacific line presented each woman with a large basket of flowers as they reboarded the *Empress*. At 2:00 P.M. the ship sailed out of the harbor, making for Nagasaki at full speed.

The approach to Nagasaki took the tourists past Japan's famous Arch Rock and the island of Pappenburg, a sight that must have stirred up many emotions in the predominantly Catholic group. In the sixteenth century, believing that Christianity was a dangerous foreign influence, Toyotomi Hideyoshi, Shogun emperor, sought to put an end to the faith in his nation. Christianity was outlawed and its followers sentenced to death. From these cliffs in 1579 seven Catholic missionaries, along with seventeen Japanese converts, were bound hand and foot and thrown into the sea. Afterward, Rome elevated the martyrs to sainthood, and Japan turned inward. For more than two hundred years the Land of the Cherry Blossom would be a closed society.

Arrival at the port of Nagasaki proved that the Japanese could still be leery of outsiders. A fortified port vital to Japan's security, the city prohibited by law photography and the taking of motion pictures, so naturally Lee Magee and the other shutterbugs took pictures on the sly. The ban on photography helped Nagasaki keep its secrets from outsiders and, more important, from the rest of Japan.

Nagasaki was like no other city in Japan. The fastest coaling station on the planet, the city moved at a quicker pace than the rest of the country. Unlike elsewhere in Japan where women played a subservient role, in Nagasaki they were an essential part of the coaling operations, the city's prime source of revenue.

Women dressed in white performed most of the work. As soon as a ship dropped anchor in the harbor, coal barges surrounded it, and coaling operations commenced. Men threw ropes woven out of rice plants over the side of the vessel. These were then lashed to the deck, a process that took only a matter of seconds. Once the ladders were in place, an army of women, each standing above the other on the rungs of the rice ladder, passed a twenty-eight-pound basket of coal up from the barge to the ship's bunkers. Once emptied, the basket was tossed back to the coaling barge to be refilled for another journey up the ladder. There were about twenty-five crews working on each side of the *Empress* from noon until 10:30 P.M. The women toiled like ants moving earth. When they were finished, fifteen hundred tons of coal had been transported into the ship's cavernous bunkers. For their labors, the women received the equivalent of twenty U.S. cents.

Witnessing this toil was too much for some tourists. As Frank McGlynn put it, "The liberal hearted members of the world touring party threw coins to the patient laborers, and no doubt a great majority of them were happier at their day's pay than on many a similar occasion."[15]

When recounting this episode, one is especially frustrated that McGlynn's film has been lost to time. After bribing the local constabulary, McGlynn was permitted to film the coaling of the *Empress*. McGlynn must have been quite generous with his cash. Despite the ban on photography and motion pictures within six miles of the city, McGlynn was also allowed to set up his tripod in the streets of Nagasaki.

Unlike Kōbe and Osaka, no game had been planned for Nagasaki; 9 December had been a scheduled treat for the players, an open date. To the players' delight, Nagasaki offered more diversions and attractions than did even Tokyo. For the first time since they had sailed out of Seattle, the players got a chance to relax and enjoy themselves.

The Thorpes did some Christmas shopping, toured around town in rickshas, then, like most visitors to Nagasaki, ascended the thousands of steps to the top of the temple. Here as well they got to see how the ordinary Japanese citizen lived. Iva took note of the local custom of attaching a piece of rice paper to the door to ward off evil spirits. Away from the more urban and industrial centers of Kōbe and Tokyo, the tourists encountered a Japan more ancient, mysterious, and delightful than they imagined.

Unfortunately, like just about everywhere the tourists appeared, trouble followed. Fred Merkle, Mike Donlin, Germany Schaefer, and a few other of the tour's bachelors went out for drinks with the officers from an American liner whom they had befriended. In some dive near the waterfront, the sailors and the ballplayers stumbled across a pool table. Like delighted children encountering a favorite toy or delinquents finding their favorite vice, the group proceeded to play round after round.

Billiard balls and alcohol shots chased each other for hours. Finally, close to 10:30 P.M., the players realized that the launch for the *Empress* would soon be leaving and that if they didn't catch it, there was a chance all of them might get left in Nagasaki. If nothing else, they had to get back on time to avoid a tongue-lashing from McGraw. One of the hard-partying athletes chose to take one last shot for the road and, in his drunken state, sent the cue ball careening off the table and onto the floor before it disappeared under a couch. Too drunk to bend over, the players left the ball where it was and beat a hasty return to the *Empress*.

The players' actions, however, did not escape the notice of the harbor police. Unable to find his valuable cue ball, which, after all, was made out of solid ivory, the owner of the bar reported it stolen and named the American ballplayers as the prime suspects. (Perhaps the players didn't tip the barkeep well enough, or maybe they skipped out on their tab.) To the athletes' chagrin and the steamship line's supreme displeasure, Nagasaki's harbor police boarded the *Empress*, demanding the missing cue ball and an explanation from the plastered Americans.

Germany Schaefer approached the police, turned on the charm, and confessed to his misadventure. While Schaefer was trying to charm his way out of arrest, word came to the police that the location of the "missing" cue ball had been discovered, and the *Empress* was now free to sail.

Immediately inflated by the American press, the cue ball story became fodder for U.S. tabloids and scandal sheets. Burchell, Axelson, and Farrell, the writers on the tour, protected the athletes they covered; they did their best to sweep the story under the rug. After all, it just would not do to have reports of drunken ballplayers in the newspaper.

Under the cold light of a waning moon, hours past the scheduled departure time of midnight, the *Empress* slipped out of Nagasaki for Shanghai.

SEVEN

China and Points East

It was impossible to give a very good exhibition of the game. – Joe Farrell in the *Sporting News*, 22 January 1914

With the recovery of the missing cue ball, the *Empress* was free to set sail, finally departing at 2:00 A.M. Its course ran almost directly southwest to the mainland of China and the mouth of the Yangtze. Whatever problems the *Empress* may have had with her Marconi wireless on the voyage from Seattle were apparently repaired. As the *Empress* sailed across the serene Yellow Sea, Comiskey exchanged dozens of Marconigrams with the game organizers in Shanghai. There was much anticipation in the Chinese city for the ball game.

Accessible by water to all parts of China, Shanghai served as China's shipping port to the world and its center of domestic commerce. First opened to British trade in 1842, Shanghai was essentially a foreign city in the midst of a dying Chinese empire. Home to a vast number of expatriates from every part of the world, Shanghai was an oasis of sin and piety, wealth and poverty. The foreigners were attracted to the city through equal combinations of industry, military intervention, criminal enterprise, and missionary endeavors. Smuggling, trade, narcotics traffic, and prostitution made some of its inhabitants wealthy beyond comprehension. Shanghai was a city where one could buy or arrange anything if you were a Westerner. If you happened to be one of the 1.5 million Chinese residents (excluding the few of great wealth), Shanghai was a land of drudgery and servitude.

Apartheid favoring Westerners was part of the very fabric of the city. Even the criminal justice system was divided, one court for the fifteen thousand Westerners and another, much harsher system for dispensing punishment to the Chinese majority. So mistrusted were the native residents by the

Westerners that they were confined to their own neighborhoods, and all city parks were deemed off-limits to the Chinese.

Shanghai was a warren of diverse nationalities; some sixty-four languages were spoken within the city. Power, however, resided in the hands of a few. The British effectively controlled the city government. Having smaller hands in the pie were the Americans and the even weaker French. Shanghai's foreign population supported a Catholic church, several Protestant congregations, a synagogue, and a mosque. Always the focus of much Western attention, the city was in many ways still reeling from the effects of the Boxer Rebellion of 1900. The bloody revolt had been even more bloodily repressed by the British. Although the Boxer Rebellion had occurred primarily in Beijing, the British acted fast to secure Shanghai. England had won the right to control the world's opium trade in the aptly named and hard-fought Opium War of 1839–1842. They had no intention of seeing some other nation gain control of the lucrative market.

Adding to the usual simmering tensions in Shanghai, Beijing, and other cities in China toiling under Britain's thumb were the aftereffects of a tax revolt. Sun Yat-sen's growing Republican movement had organized a series of tax protests against the British. These revolts were in turn suppressed by the Crown in August of 1913, leaving troops in the affected cities on high alert.

Following Great Britain's example, in 1845 the United States forced China to sign a treaty giving it the right to protect American industry and nationals in Shanghai and four other cities. Over half a century later, it seemed as though both the Royal Navy and the U.S. Navy and Marine Corps would reside there forever.

Shanghai's elite were on edge with excitement about the game scheduled to be played there on 11 January. As usual, however, the weather was not cooperative. As the *Empress* entered the Yangtze River, gray skies and rain returned. The *Empress* anchored a dozen miles south of Shanghai at the juncture of the Whangpoo and Yangtze Rivers. Heavy silting here meant no ships as large as the *Empress* could progress any farther north, so the tourists transferred to a fast, shallow-draft steam tender named *Alexandra* for the journey to Shanghai. At this transfer point, all the tourists underwent cursory physical examinations to verify that they were healthy enough to enter the city. Few ports in the world could match the atmosphere of this part of the globe. The most advanced fighting ships from the British and American navies, decrepit Chinese sampans, Chinese junks in every state of order and disrepair, aging sailing vessels from the scattered corners of the globe, along with canoes and rafts crowded the shipping lanes.

Here also the tourists witnessed the bitter poverty of the disenfranchised Chinese. The tourists did not react to the hardships they encountered as we might. Joe Farrell reports, "They were entertained by half a hundred beggars, with their entire families in rowboats. They surrounded the boat in a rainfall and beseeched with hands upraised for alms. An American dollar tossed into one of the boats by Speaker nearly caused the capsizing of all."[1]

One tugboat captain confided to the tourists, "Times are not as they used to be. When I first came here it was the proper thing to kick a Chinaman if he got near enough to you, but now it is different. Why, you are likely to go to jail if you kill one."[2]

As the *Alexandra* steamed the final twelve miles to Shanghai, the tourists heard whistles, bells, horns, and cheers of welcome from seemingly every inch of the riverbank. When their tender passed the American gunboats *Quiros* and *Helena*, the tourists were treated to the sight of hundreds of men lined up on the decks. Then, like a graduation ceremony, the sailors and marines cheered and hurled their caps into the air in salute of the arriving American baseball expeditionary force.

A few miles from Shanghai, mist and heavy fog mingled with a steady rain, making the morning seem gloomy and surreal. Upon arrival at the wharf at 9:00 A.M., the tourists found their welcoming committee gathered at the customhouse jetty. Greeting the tourists were a thousand cheering baseball fans, a collection of local nines, and a smattering of Shanghai politicos, all with an accompanying brass band blaring out John Phillip Sousa's "The Liberty Bell March." The entire assembly stood, withering under the steady downpour.

Since Shanghai was an open city, no passport was necessary. Visitors were treated to a cursory pass through customs and left alone. The tourists simply got off the ship at the wharf and journeyed down the Bund (Shanghai's main business district) a short distance to the Astor House Hotel for lunch and to prepare for the game.

Their exuberant welcoming committee made progress toward that goal difficult, however. Despite the rain, the crowd surged forward to shake hands with the athletes, especially Jim Thorpe, whose fame in Shanghai was greater than that of the rest of the players combined. Here also came the queries asking, "Where is Mathewson?" "Which one of you is Mathewson?" After forcing their way through the throng, the tourists discovered the same modes of transportation that they had grown accustomed to in Japan. The tourists had their choice of automobiles or rickshas. (The latter vehicles were invented in Japan and later made their way to China.) Reportedly, every automobile in Shanghai was placed at their disposal.

No hotel in Shanghai, and few in the world, surpassed the Astor House Hotel. A handsome and impressive stone edifice of arched windows and balconies, the hotel stood six stories high and sprawled over three acres of land near the heart of the city. As elsewhere, the tourists received red carpet treatment.

For the tourists' benefit, the Astor House's Grand Ball Room had been set aside and elaborately decorated in a baseball motif, where a gourmet lunch was served. Despite the luxurious surroundings, no one especially enjoyed their time there. Disappointment about the weather cast a gloom over the festivities. Everyone was concerned that the game scheduled for 2:00 P.M. would not be able to be played. No doubt some of the tourists prayed for an instantaneous dry spell.

No one was more keen to see the game played than Comiskey and McGraw. A crowd estimated at twenty-five thousand was gathering at the city's beautiful racetrack, easily the largest potential single payday of any city in the world. Two solid months of steady promotion had swelled the crowd to beyond expectations. The backers' promotion efforts even resulted in the banks and schools declaring a half holiday so all could partake in the spectacle of American baseball.

In addition to the American civilian and military population, the tour had attracted interest from the British and the local wealthy Chinese. American missionaries and military men had introduced baseball to the local citizenry with limited success. While there was a Shanghai Amateur Base Ball League, the far larger and more influential British population was having greater success importing cricket and soccer. Gus Axelson bluntly stated the prime reason for baseball's limited popularity in China, "It would probably have a better chance to sprout were the celestials allowed to mingle with the elect but such is not the case at present."[3]

Indeed, Thomas F. Cobbs, president of the Shanghai Amateur Base Ball League, made little effort to educate the local Chinese about the game. When asked why the Chinese were excluded from local sports he replied, "The same as in California. There are too many of them. The Chinese sometimes get excited just like occidentals, and were we to let them in to our games there is no telling when a riot might break out and if it were to start, there would be no finish."[4]

After their elegant hotel lunch the players made their way to the Shanghai Race Club, a country club with a horse-racing facility. Membership in this club established one as having arrived in Shanghai society. It was also the headquarters for the Amateur Base Ball League. A proud landmark with its soaring clock tower, the club stood prominently in the center of town amid offices and hotels.

The local backers of the game were trying their utmost to keep the grounds ready should the weather clear. An army of Chinese swept the grounds; from somewhere a tarp had been procured to cover the infield.

The players would have played in a drizzle or even a moderate rainstorm. Back in Medford, Oregon, they had played in miserable conditions, but at one o'clock in the afternoon a deluge began. Sheets upon sheets of driving, stinging, blinding rain rolled down out of the heavens. Had the rain relented even a bit, there very probably would have been a game, but the torrent refused to cease. Comiskey and McGraw had no choice but to cancel the game.

There was no end to the disappointment on the part of the audience, especially the expatriate community of Americans. Thousands of miles from home, their only chance to see big leaguers was ruined by rain and mud. The disappointment was universal, with the players just as upset as the fans. The American-themed welcome and the overwhelming enthusiasm of Shanghai's fans had impressed all the players and made everyone anxious to play. So great was the prevailing frustration with the weather that a few fans actually made plans to travel to Hong Kong, the tourists' next stop, so they could take in a game. One fan, as a hedge against that game being washed out as well, bought a ticket for the Philippines. So distraught was the Shanghai audience and so great the potential payday that McGraw and Comiskey toyed with the idea of extending their stay in the city.

But the weather did not promise to get any better, and the tourists were still making up time from their encounter with the typhoon on the Pacific. Also, adding a game in Shanghai meant that one would probably have to be dropped somewhere else, an unpalatable solution. Really having no alternative, Comiskey and McGraw told the teams to be ready to play in Hong Kong.

Without a game to play the tourists whiled away their day sightseeing, shopping, dancing, and banqueting. While most went shopping, some of the men got a glimpse of Shanghai's darker undertones. Joe Farrell, Fred Merkle, and Tris Speaker visited Shanghai's walled-off Chinatown. Here, segregated from Shanghai's ruling Western inhabitants, the city's manual laborers, servants, and impoverished working class dwelled. Joe Farrell described it as follows: "This is a turbulent district, heavily patrolled, and the best influence in Shanghai could not arrange a permit to visit certain parts of it."[5]

Though unmentioned, one wonders which "certain parts" of Chinatown the three bachelors wished to visit while out stag. Were they perhaps hoping for a clandestine visit to one of Shanghai's legendary brothels? Was their goal an opium den? In the end we are forced to leave these questions unanswered. As it turned out, the three spent most of the day in Chinatown, only returning to the hotel at 6:00 P.M., just thirty minutes before the *Alexandra* was scheduled to ship off for its return trip to the *Empress*. H. P. Burchell of the *New York Times* stated that the three, upon returning to the Astor House, claimed to have gotten lost in Chinatown. That may be the truth. It is also possible that the three were just being coy.

While the players on the tour had by now almost resigned themselves to Thorpe's apparently universal fame, the stay in Shanghai led to encounters with the best and worst elements of America's celebrity culture. A group of adoring Phillies fans on business in China enthusiastically greeted Hans Lobert, leaving him feeling like a king. Dick Egan had a very different sort of encounter. Burchell gives the details:

> "Dick" Egan was walking about the streets of Shanghai and doing a little shopping, a party of American sailors off of one of the battle ships met him.
>
> "How are you doing Fred?" said one, friendly enough. "I saw you play when my ship was at the Brooklyn navy yard two years ago."
>
> "I'm not Merkle," replied Egan. "My name is 'Dick' Egan, and I am with the Cincinnati club, or I was when I left the United States."
>
> "Get out," answered the sailor, who was as positive of his identification as a fly cop. "I know you. And say, tell me why you didn't touch second base?"
>
> "I wish I had heard him say that," remarked Merkle when Egan told him of the mistake later. "One member of Uncle Sam's navy would have had a serious war on his hands right there."[6]

Merkle wasn't catching any breaks at home either. When this story was printed in the *Chicago Daily News* for 17 January 1914, it appeared on the same page as a regular feature of blurbs and vignettes entitled "Spotlight on Sporting Men and Incidents." One of the small items abutting Egan's encounter read, "It is suspected Pitcher Willard Melkle, secured by the Boston Braves, changed 'r' to an 'l' in his last name so it would not be Merkle."[7]

Sportswriters and most fans had long ceased looking for the human being who played first base for the New York Giants. Instead, they turned

Merkle into a verb. Not even at the ends of the earth could the man escape the year 1908.

The women had a much happier time shopping. Fast friends Edith Doyle and Iva Thorpe teamed up with a member of the U.S. consulate, who made sure that the women paid fair market value for their purchases. He also no doubt looked after their welfare in this dangerous city.

Not surprisingly, the reporters spent most of their time at the Shanghai Club, home to the longest bar in the world. At 110 feet long with sixty bartenders working simultaneously, it certainly topped anything back home in the States. The reporters enthusiastically put the club's claim that it could "satisfy more thirsts in a given time than any other establishment on earth" to the test.

That afternoon's 4:30 reception at the Astor House was spectacular. The hotel flaunted its wealth by presenting each guest with a most memorable souvenir, a polished mahogany walking stick topped with a silver handle inscribed "Shanghai 1913."

At 6:30 P.M., with heavy rain still falling, the *Alexandra* pulled away from the customhouse jetty, concluding the tourists' one-day stopover in Shanghai. As at their arrival, hundreds stood in the rain to see the baseball adventurers off. As the ship sailed farther downriver, the tourists were once more hailed and cheered by the sailors and marines aboard the U.S. gunboats. This time, the timbre of the salutes was different; melancholy and lament mixed with cheers of adulation and appreciation. The tourists saw how grieved the men were. So profound was the disappointment of the rainout that grown men actually wept as the *Alexandra* slid by. In reply to the salutes and good wishes received, as well as the obvious sadness they were witnessing, the tourists sang a song and returned the cheers of their well-wishers.

Returning to the *Empress of Japan* at 8:00 P.M. was bittersweet. There had been no game in Shanghai; also, this would be their last voyage on the great ship. In Hong Kong the tourists would transfer to another ship for the trek to the Philippines. By now nearly all had considerable affection for their second home, and they would miss it. A series of Marconigrams revealed more bad news. Still behind schedule, the tourists were now due to arrive in Hong Kong on Sunday, 14 December 1913. Under British law, no admission could be charged for athletic contests held on a Sunday. Unwilling to disappoint fans in yet another city, Comiskey and McGraw decided to bite the financial bullet and asked the British authorities if they could stage their exhibition for free. This request was granted. Now all the tourists needed was dry weather.

In the meantime, the touring party prepared to depart the *Empress*, their home of nearly a month. On the evening of 13 December 1913 every member of the party turned out for the "commander's dinner." Thrown to honor Captain Dixon-Hopcraft and the ship's officers, every tourist expressed gratitude to them for preserving their lives during the dangerous crossing and for making the rest of the trip so pleasant. The tourists presented the captain with a diamond pin to the accompaniment of three cheers. He and his men were treated to several choruses of "For he's a jolly good fellow." Germany Schaefer soloed on "Shoenus," one of his original compositions. Captain Dixon-Hopcraft, for his part, expressed his gratitude to the players for their company and regaled all present with sailors' tales of the fierce cannibals and headhunters who roamed the wilds of the island of Formosa.

All through the evening of the thirteenth the sailing was smooth and peaceful. The *Empress* steamed into Hong Kong harbor at 8:00 A.M. on 14 December 1913, a gorgeous morning. But the cloud of misfortune that seemed to hover about the tourists once more revealed its presence.

The tourists awoke to find the *Empress* flying the yellow flag of a quarantined vessel. Smallpox, dreaded scourge of civilized and uncivilized nation alike, had crept aboard the ship. Late in the evening of the thirteenth the ship's surgeons determined that a male passenger who had boarded in Shanghai was afflicted.

Even though the man had been immediately isolated from the rest of the passengers and crew, a sudden panic swept through the vessel. Complicating matters, the British government of Hong Kong refused to let the *Empress* dock unless everyone on board could prove that they had been vaccinated against smallpox.

Joe Farrell compared that announcement by the British authorities to a bomb blast going off on the ship. The players were especially perturbed. Administering inoculations in 1913 was a painful, tedious process using one large-diameter needle. This same needle was then sterilized between uses. Often vaccinations were administered while the needle was still steaming from the autoclave or slick from its sterilizing bath in alcohol. Swelling and inflammation were the norm.

Hooks Wiltse of the Giants at first refused to be vaccinated. When told that he and any others who did not consent to the injections would be forcibly detained and held for deportation, he relented. Retaining as much rebelliousness as he could muster, Wiltse insisted on getting his shot in the leg so as not to risk endangering his pitching arm. When the English doctor was finally satisfied that the Americans in the harbor were not harboring the pox, he permitted the *Empress* to advance to the wharf. The delay for inspections and injections spoiled the tourists' planned good-bye. Each had wanted time with Captain Dixon-Hopcraft to thank him for his expert seamanship and courtesy. Instead, there were rushed handshakes while the Mulligan band played a tune from the forecastle. The players presented a parting gift of cash to Willets and his Mulligan band, which they adored. Each player had kicked money into the generous cash kitty.

Arriving at 10:00 A.M. at the wharf, the tourists and most of their baggage went in two directions. The athletes and their sports equipment passed through customs and were forwarded to the Hong Kong Hotel. The rest of their possessions were transferred to the *St. Albans*, a W. and S. liner out of Hong Kong. Smaller and less ornate than the *Empress*, the *St. Albans* would always be recalled as second best by the tourists.

Shanghai and Hong Kong shared similar histories of English domination. Both cities were under British rule. In the case of Hong Kong, however, British control was official. The empire of China had ceded Hong Kong by treaty to the British in 1842. The prize port and surrounding territory were English booty, taken in the Opium Wars.

With a miniscule American population, the reception for the tourists in Hong Kong was muted, the first city without a brass band greeting since Portland, Oregon. The players made their way to the Hong Kong Hotel unmolested and anonymously.

To promote the game in the city, the players did their own publicity. After checking into the hotel and changing into their uniforms, they set up a couple of bases on the wide lawn of the Hong Kong Hotel and demonstrated the game. This attracted a fairly large crowd to the front gates of the hotel. Only a few citizens had heard about baseball, an unknown sport in Hong Kong, mostly from the crews and passengers of American ships passing through the port.

Among the amenities of Hong Kong, sedan chairs carried by two Chinese coolies were available for those wishing to travel like Cleopatra or a European monarch. Almost every member of the party toured the city this way. The exceptions were rotund Tom Lynch, who apparently did not wish to give the coolies simultaneous hernias, and Louis Comiskey. Commy's only son, Lou was already demonstrating more sensitivity to the lot of the working class than his father would ever have.

McGlynn and Miller discovered a curious phenomenon when they whipped out their movie equipment. Every time the duo tried to film one of the tourists in a sedan chair, the Chinese coolies would drop the chair and hide. Two factors were behind these disappearing acts. First was native superstitions against photography and motion pictures. Later, however, McGlynn learned of a far more compelling reason for the coolies' reticence. Most of them were ex-convicts whose experiences with the British justice system left them with no desire to have their faces photographed. Only Germany Schaefer's chauffeurs could be induced to perform for the camera. McGlynn included these coolies in antics staged for the cameras. Under McGlynn's direction, they dodged up a steep hill while Schaefer, ensconced in the sedan chair, hammed it up.

Upon completion of their sedan chair spins around the city, the players checked into the hotel and dressed for the game. As in Tokyo, the wives and husbands went in different directions. The women, realizing that this would probably be their only chance to visit Hong Kong, chose sight-seeing over attending the ball game. While their husbands would be heading to the Happy Valley Athletic Club, they would be on their way to the top of a promontory known simply as the Peak. Like thousands of tourists before and since, they rode to the top via Hong Kong's famous inclined railway. World famous for its incredible forty-five degree angle of ascent and the breathtaking views it offered, the railroad was like nothing else in the world. From the top of the Peak one can see all of the city of Victoria and Hong Kong harbor. Iva Thorpe, like most of the wives, wished that her husband could have accompanied her. The train ride to the top of the Peak would have been quite romantic had the newlywed wives had their husbands along. A great many spectacular houses terraced their way up the Peak. All of Hong Kong's powerful British aristocracy dwelled on the Peak. Originally, the community sprang up here not because of the spectacular views it offered of the colony but rather because its height offered some relief from the heat of Asia's torrid summers. In 1904 all but those who were of European descent were banned by law from the Peak, causing one to wonder if Iva Thorpe would have been able to ascend the mountain if she *had* been accompanied by her husband. Nowhere else in all of their realm did the British rule from on high so figuratively and literally. For the players, just getting to the game was half the fun. A chartered wooden trolley car arrived in front of the Hong Kong Hotel to transport the players to the Happy Valley Recreation Grounds, site of their contest. Like London's famous buses of our era, the trolley was a double-decker. Nearly all of the players clambered to the trolley's rooftop seats. In full uniform, the players rode to their game through Hong Kong's crowded streets, a sight-seeing adventure they would never forget.

Upon arriving at Happy Valley, the players' mood changed. While a sizeable crowd of about seven thousand, mostly British sailors from the nearby port, had materialized, the field on which the athletes were expected to play was ill-suited for baseball. The vaguely triangular-shaped parcel a short distance from the Royal Naval Yard normally saw action as a soccer grounds. Bounded on the north by Wong Nei Chong Road, the east by Morrison Hill Road, and the west by Leighton Hill Road, abutting the grounds on the south was the Wong Nei Chong Valley Race Course. The tourists could not have picked a better spot in all of Victoria to get attention. Their wives on the Peak, if they were lucky, would have been able to discern the crowd milling about the turf. The perpetual smog rising from the city by midmorning from its factories and innumerable coal fires made that a virtual impossibility, however.

Unlike Shanghai, no preparations had been made to the field prior to the athletes' arrival. Klem and Sheridan, with assistance from the players, laid out the diamond. This would be the very first baseball game ever played in Hong Kong. The setting was certainly spectacular. For a backstop, nature had provided the monolithic, barren, craggy, naked face of Mount Morrison. Unfortunately, the game itself would turn out to be an utter mess. Depending upon one's point of view, the game was either high tragedy or great farce. The field was entirely grass, a novel and unwelcome experience for the players. Furthermore, the ground itself was bumpy and irregular, making fielding of even the most routine grounder an adventure. The Sox's Joe Benz and the Giants' Bunny Hearn, for the first time in their professional careers, pitched without a mound. Reach Sporting Goods had thoughtfully sent along a rubber, so Bill Klem could at least call any balks Hearn and Benz might commit. As he had everywhere else, Klem introduced each player in his renowned carnival barker style.

Worse than the miserable condition of the playing surface was the behavior of the crowd. The audience was the most diverse group so far encountered. Reflecting the worldwide reach of the British Empire, there were Muslims along the first base line, Hindus from India along third base, with a smattering of Chinese dispersed at the outer edges of the grounds, who had to sneak into the grounds because, for the Chinese, the fields were officially off-limits. The largest contingent in the crowd, however, was the almost seven thousand rowdy, extremely vocal British sailors who had never seen a baseball game before.

The sailors' curiosity about the sport led them to abandon their seats and to crowd the diamond, where they peppered the players with questions. The sailors had no appreciation of or respect for the foul lines, occasionally getting between a fielder and the ball. This behavior is partly understandable because in cricket there is no such thing as foul territory; every hit ball is fair. Also in cricket, aside from the bowler, players' positions are not set.

Depending upon the offensive or defensive need of the moment, a player might be a wicket keeper or a midoff. Why wouldn't the sailors crowd the field? To their eyes it was just some Yankee hybrid of cricket and rounders, and they wanted a better view. The sailors understood next to nothing of the American game, rabidly cheering Jim Thorpe's mammoth, soaring foul, which nearly reached the foot of Mount Morrison. In cricket, Thorpe's foul would have been a prodigious hit. The more superstitious players were also uncomfortable with the fact that the athletic field shared the name of the cemetery, which occupied part of the grounds. Worse, some of the white tombstones were clearly visible from the batter's box. Lee Magee was so superstitious that he changed the name of the grounds to "Sleepy Hollow" in his accounts of the game.

There were some Americans present. Every crew member of the USS *Wilmington* who could be spared was sent to the crowded grounds. The crowding got so out of hand that both foul lines were trampled into oblivion. This caused squabbles to break out between Sheridan, Klem, and the players. When Tris Speaker hit a mammoth shot toward the racetrack, the distant part of the grounds, the game stopped dead for a considerable amount of minutes until the ball could be retrieved. Amazingly, chaos was kept at bay long enough for the Giants to snag a 7–4 victory out of the mess. Time constraints forced the players to end the game after only five innings. Then, hurriedly, every bit of equipment disappeared into the canvas duffle bags and wooden bat boxes. All boarded rickshas for the trip back to the *St. Albans*. The crowd of English sailors and other onlookers dispersed, presumably just as befuddled as when the game began.

For the American sailors the brief, messy contest was a heaven-sent slice of home. Gus Axelson caught up with Mr. O'Mally, the *Wilmington's* boatswain's mate, just before the game. "This will have to last me until 1915 when I go home. We play the game ourselves but unless we meet one of our war ships there is no fun in it. You see the boys like to risk a few kopecks on the game when there is one. We are not betting on this one. Not because we do not think it is on the square, but we want to see it finish in a tie, we like both teams."[8]

Because the Sox and Giants were composed of players from all parts of the United States and from various Major League teams, everyone on the *Wilmington* could find someone to root for. Three sailors from Chicago, New York, and Boston's Back Bay were quick to take sides, the sailor from Boston rooting with the youth from Chicago because Beantown's Tris Speaker wore the pale hose. At the conclusion of the game, the American sailors surged forward to cheer the athletes and to shake their hands. The sailors cheered themselves hoarse as the ballplayers mounted rickshas for the return trip to the Bund.

Still in uniform, the players boarded a launch at 4:30 P.M., which ferried them to the *St. Albans*. The total elapsed time spent in Hong Kong, six hours and thirty minutes. Once on board, the tourists disappointedly discovered that Captain Dixon-Hopcraft of the *Empress* was not aboard. They had expected to meet their former captain on their new vessel for the very last good-bye. However, Hong Kong authorities would not permit anyone to break quarantine. Captain Dixon-Hopcraft sent his good wishes and regrets via the wireless.

As the tug tender began towing the *St. Albans* out of the harbor, the tourists heard a mighty cheer. Off to starboard sat the *Wilmington*, a huge American flag fluttering above its stern. The sailors who had taken in the ball game had raced back to their ship so they could offer one last salute to the players. It was a truly touching gesture, and the tourists reciprocated and cheered the *Wilmington*.

After this happy incident, the *St. Albans* passed by the blazing white hull of the *Empress*, which some of the tourists gazed at until it disappeared from sight. The *St. Albans* traversed the Limoon Pass, sailed through a fishing fleet of Chinese junks, and finally turned eastward, away from the slanting rays of the December sun, toward the Philippine Islands, Uncle Sam's own colony in the Pacific.

EIGHT

Uncle Sam's Tropical Playground

Girdlers Are Lionized at Manila – Headline in the *Sporting News*, 5 February 1914

Sailing out of Hong Kong, the tourists began to acclimate themselves to the *St. Albans*. Though less than half the size of the *Empress of Japan*, the *St. Albans* was the largest passenger liner sailing between Japan and Australia. Named after Britain's first martyr, the *St. Albans* was not without charm. It featured large promenade decks, and the tourists had plenty of room for shuffleboard, deck tennis, dancing, and a complete novelty, deck cricket. Best of all, the *St. Albans* had a saltwater swimming pool fifteen feet deep complete with a diving board.

The world touring party comprised virtually all of first class, with only three other passengers sharing their accommodations. The *St. Albans* was, however, a crowded ship. While the *Empress* had been a virtual ghost town, the *St. Albans* was packed to the gills. Every second-class and steerage compartment was occupied. This voyage marked the greatest number of passengers the *St. Albans* had ever transported.

Among the first discoveries aboard their new craft was that the ship's crew was determined to outdo the hospitality of the crew of the *Empress*. As Joe Farrell wrote, "Everybody—everywhere and every minute—seems to be trying to outdo all others in showering attention on the tourists. On board the Empress of Japan six servings a day were thought necessary to revive the starving. Aboard the St. Albans seven helpings are considered little enough."[1]

The service never let up. A typical day's fodder: 6:00 A.M., tea and oranges; 8:30 A.M., breakfast (first-class passengers had eight different meat selections alone from which to choose); 1:00 P.M., lunch; 3:30 P.M., tea and cakes; 7:00 P.M., dinner; 10:00 P.M., sandwiches served on deck. Of course, if anyone was still hungry later in the evening, the pursers or a Chinese cabin boy would be more than happy to get them a bite to eat.

Just how different the *St. Albans* was from the *Empress* was seen in how differently the two ships handled storms. Their first night aboard the *St. Albans*, 15 December, they encountered a typhoon. Much smaller than the record storm the *Empress* had endured on the Pacific, this storm nonetheless prompted a fresh round of tourist seasickness. All had acquired their sea legs; the seasickness was prompted by the unfamiliar motion of the *St. Albans*. The *Empress* in storms maintained a steady, rolling motion; the *St. Albans* had what Frank McGlynn described as a "twisting motion," which surprised and sickened the tourists.

The first morning upon the *St. Albans* was especially enjoyable. Spectacular weather, with warm equatorial breezes wafting over the South China Sea, made the ship's decks *the* place to be—the perfect spot to clear one's head and chat after an evening of motion sickness. While all were gathered here conversing, the *St. Albans* sailed through a school of flying fish. The spectacular sight of hundreds of fish leaping out of the brine and sailing through the ether on all sides of the ship sparked one of the tour's more memorable debates.

Hans Lobert and Buck Weaver could not decide whether the fish, while in the air, should be called "herds" or "flocks." Lobert favored "herds," and Weaver favored "flocks." This conversation became quite animated and spilled over to several other tourists. Joe Benz, overhearing this conversation, decided to take matters into his own hands. On the spot he composed the following doggerel, invoking the name of Germany Schaefer to, good-naturedly, put both men in their place.

WHY?
Here the flying fishes fly.
I wonder why, I wonder why.
"The fishes came out here to fly,
Because there is more room, that's why,"
Said Schaefer, "and a fish will fly
From water when a whale is nigh,
That's why a flying fish is fly"[2]

So delighted was Benz by his ditty that he distributed autographed copies of it to all of the women on the tour.

At some point on the Philippine journey Frank McGlynn overheard McGraw say, "Well, I am sure I will meet at least one old friend in Manila.

I have not received a message from him, but I know that he will be there."[3] McGraw would soon discover how accurate his premonition was.

Aside from a brief storm, the two-day sail to Manila was uneventful. The first sight of Uncle Sam's tropical playground was the island of Luzon 150 miles west of Manila. What struck the tourists most were the resplendent Philippine mountains. Here, unlike the ice-shrouded Aleutians, snow-capped Mount Fuji, or the white-tipped, ragged mountains of Formosa, the peaks of Luzon were jungle clad. This was the tropics, no doubt about that.

A brilliant full moon shown upon placid waters as the *St. Albans* steamed past Corregidor and into Manila harbor. At 1 A.M. it dropped anchor. The tourists grabbed as much sleep as they could. Their colonial Philippine hosts had big plans; virtually every moment of the next two days were scripted on an ironclad schedule.

The Philippines was America's largest and most populous colony. Ceded to the United States by Spain in 1898 after its defeat in the Spanish-American War, the U.S. military presence remained strong on the islands. Short-circuiting a native independence movement led by Emilio Aguinaldo, Spain transferred the islands to the United States as part of the peace treaty negotiated in Paris. Before the ink had even dried, the Philippines native populations took up arms against their American "liberators." The insurrection of 1899–1901 was suppressed in an especially brutal manner. The United States spared no expense and obeyed few of the rules of war in quelling the Filipino's dream of independence.

The three-year struggle against the forces of the first Philippine republic resembled both the concurrent Boer War half a world away and the much later American involvement in Vietnam, including shelling of civilian populations, collateral damage, and relentless guerilla war against a jungle backdrop. In all, from war, disease, and general mayhem, tens of thousands of Filipinos and at least forty-two hundred American soldiers had been killed.

By 1913 the U.S. military maintained control of the islands, propping up the American-backed colonial Philippine government. Despite the animosity the fifteen-year American military presence on the islands stirred up, the native Filipinos had heartily embraced baseball. The game flourished at all levels of Philippine society, from jungle hamlets to recreational and semipro leagues in Manila. As in the Dominican Republic, Cuba, Puerto Rico, Panama, and other nations, baseball arrived in the Philippines with America's soldiers.

The game was seen as one of the great potential unifiers of the islands.

Perhaps that explained the extravagance of the tourists' welcome. Their welcome was easily the most elaborately staged event in the islands up to General Douglas MacArthur's return half a century later. The islands were shut down for the tourists' benefit. Governor-General Francis Burton Harrison closed all colonial offices. Commanding General of the Army of the Philippines J. Franklin Bell and Adjutant General Colonel H. P. McCain shut their offices up tight. The treasurer, General Jeremiah L. Manning, closed all the banks, bringing commerce to a screeching halt for the next two days.

The Manila Reception Committee got an early start on the day, ferrying out to the *St. Albans* at 6:45 in the morning of 17 December 1913. The committee, dressed head to toe in blindingly white tropical outfits, was led by Arlie "Duck" Pond, John McGraw's teammate from the legendary Baltimore Orioles of the 1890s whom McGraw had not seen in fifteen years. McGraw made sure that Pond's hand was the very first one he shook in the Philippines.

The story of Arlie Pond is one of those "only in America" tales that have become the staple of Sunday newspaper filler and television news segments. A graduate of the University of Vermont in 1896, Duck Pond worked his two loves simultaneously, toiling as both a Major League pitcher and as a medical doctor. Recruited to the National League's Orioles largely by McGraw, Pond would seem to be an odd fit with the hard-living, hard-drinking, and rule-bending, -breaking, and -distorting ball club. The Orioles certainly did not hire him for his medical abilities. This was a team, after all, that believed that the best treatment for a spike wound or cut was to spit some tobacco juice into it, rub some dirt on the wound, and keep playing.

Ed Hanlon, Baltimore's innovative manager, was a hard, often infuriating taskmaster, yet he made his players winners. No case describes his method for dealing with players better than the story of his greatest pupil, John McGraw. Upon acquiring the youthful McGraw in 1892, Hanlon thought that McGraw was too quiet, so he rode the man mercilessly until he almost cracked. Hanlon taunted McGraw, insulted McGraw, belittled McGraw, and heaped torrents of abuse on his star rookie. Finally, McGraw threatened to punch Hanlon out, the very response Hanlon had hoped for. "I knew Little Mac was all right then," Hanlon used to laugh, "and I had my hands full with him from that time on. So did the other clubs."[4]

Sadistic as Hanlon's methods may appear to modern sensibilities, there is no doubt that they were effective. Hanlon's players became some of the greatest managers the sport has ever seen. In addition to McGraw, Wilbert

Robinson, Hughey Jennings, Kid Gleason, and Fielder Jones all apprenticed under Hanlon.

Pond had left the Orioles in the midst of the 1898 season. Caught up in the patriotic fervor of the Spanish-American War, Pond walked away from the team and into an army recruiting center. The U.S. Army made him a sergeant assigned to the medical corps. The path of war brought Pond to the Philippines. He fell in love with the islands and would rarely leave them again. Fifteen years after America's invasion of Manila, Arlie Pond was living comfortably on the island of Cebu. He owned two hospitals and a prosperous pineapple plantation. Though worth at least half a million dollars, Pond was not content simply to build wealth for himself. He struggled mightily to bring Philippine medicine into the modern age, for which he was respected and appreciated by the Filipinos.

For the next hour and a quarter the committee shook hands with the tourists and briefed them on the welcome that awaited them on shore. Finally, at 8:30 A.M. on 17 December, the White Sox and Giants hit the beaches of Manila. It was the greatest reception thus far. Under a brilliant sun-baked sky, the tourists set foot on the dock while band music blazed through the tropical air. The award-winning, ninety-piece Filipino Constabulary Band serenaded their arrival, alternating between patriotic pieces and the current ragtime hits.

The next half hour was a blizzard of handshakes, introductions, and greetings. Almost every tourist seemed to know someone in the crowd. Friends who had joined the military, business associates, distant relatives, all were part of the greeting party milling along the Manila waterfront. At 9:00 A.M. a fleet of automobiles pulled up to the docks. The tourists hopped in and received a tour of Manila. Manila in 1913 was pure exotica. The old Spanish settlement was gradually being subsumed by the boomtown of the brand new naval base. In the harbor, the U.S. Navy was busily fortifying Corregidor, vowing to make it impregnable. The Pacific Fleet called often; currently among the ships showing American muscle in the harbor was the USS *Saratoga*.

American military men were everywhere, with sailors and soldiers in the streets, in the shops, in the cafés. The Philippines outpost had become as Americanized as any place on the planet. Yet it retained an aura of the alien. Many of the Filipinos darting about the crowded streets wore their traditional native dress. Pony carts loaded with goods threaded their way down busy, palm-lined streets. Best of all, English abounded. As far as all the tourists were concerned, Manila was the best place they had yet visited.

At noon the tourists were feted to lunch at the brand new Manila

Hotel. Opened in 1912, the Manila Hotel sits on one and a half acres of wooded shoreline and offered Old World charm with modern amenities. A chandelier-bedecked lobby with a hand-carved wood-paneled ceiling, marble floor, and ornate hand-built furniture greeted visitors. The bedrooms had spectacular views of Manila Bay or Rizal Park. For the next several hours the touring party feasted on the gourmet lunch provided by the hotel, then dressed for the game.

Arriving at the ballpark at 2:45 P.M., the tourists found the stadium overflowing. While members of the U.S. military got a free pass, those in the grandstand paid top dollar. At $7.00 a head, the equivalent of $3.50 stateside, the Philippine audience paid more than double what their American cousins did. Not surprisingly, at game time every tree with a view of the ballpark was packed with Filipino youths and adults.

General Bell and Admiral Reginald F. Nicholson, commanding officer of the Asiatic Fleet, had given their troops the day off, so that all the enlisted men and officers could see one of the two games scheduled for Manila. Half of the troops would be sent to the grounds on the seventeenth, the remaining men would be sent on the following day.

The games would turn out to be part sport, part festival, and part military exhibition. Led by the Constabulary Band and teams from the Manila League, the tourists paraded about the baseball grounds. Demonstrating its patriotic repertoire, the band alternated between "Yankee Doodle," "Dixie," "My Maryland," "Illinois," and "Suwanee River." Most notable of the Manila League players promenading around the ballpark was Oscar Charleston.

A future Hall of Famer, Oscar Charleston was just seventeen years old. A former batboy for his hometown Indianapolis ABC's, Charleston had run away from home when he was fifteen years old and joined the army. The military discipline was just what the reckless, violence-prone youth needed. The army changed Charleston for the better, teaching him self-discipline as well as providing him opportunities to run track and play baseball. The lightning-fast, heavy-hitting, left-handed center fielder was so talented that he broke the color line of the Manila League. The only black player in the otherwise all-white league, Charleston's greatest days as a player were ahead of him.

Upon returning to the States after his discharge from the army in 1915, Charleston quickly became one of the most prominent stars of the Negro Leagues. In later years Charleston would be one of the players that John McGraw would covet for his Giants. McGraw had tried to integrate the American League in 1902 and gotten slapped down by Ban Johnson. Later,

Judge Kenesaw Mountain Landis, the first commissioner of baseball, rigidly enforced baseball's color line. Though McGraw was never permitted to sign black players to his teams, throughout his long career he compiled a "wish list" of black players he would have liked to sign. Oscar Charleston was prominent among those names. Charleston's contributions to baseball were not forgotten despite his years of obscurity; in 1976 he was enshrined in Cooperstown.

After the teams completed their circuits around the field, the players and fans had to sit through the bombast of various military and civilian speakers. Perhaps most notable in his blather was General Bell. The large Kentuckian delivered his speech from second base in a starched white uniform. General Bell cut quite a dashing military figure. His white uniform fairly glowed in the Philippine sun. Doffing his hat, Bell's snow-white hair flashed like a halo under the tropical lighting.

The culmination of his extended address follows.

It is unnecessary for me to assure you of the hearty nature of the welcome extended by Manillans, the large number of fans which greeted you at the wharf and the record crowd that has turned out to witness your skill on the field and at the bat are sufficient evidence of how local base ball enthusiasts feel about your visit, which has been awaited with eagerness for months.

We here in Manila do not consider you strangers; for you occupy a position in the hearts of all American citizens in the world over. We consider you representatives of a large body of Americans who have been performing a great patriotic service.[5]

Upon conclusion of his remarks, General Bell got a standing ovation from the restless crowd. This probably had a lot more to do with the fact that he was the commanding officer of all of the military men present than his overwrought prose. Proving that rank does indeed have its privileges, General Bell then got to throw out the first pitch.

At 3:30 p.m. came, finally, the event the fans had massed to witness. The players responded by putting on a humdinger of a show. Like vaudeville, with smaller acts leading up to the grand finale, the tourists teased their audience's anticipation. They led off with a shadow ball game. Germany Schaefer trotted out his comedic bits. He and Steve Evans juggled baseballs.

As for the game itself, the Sox and Giants put on a corker of a game. Jim Scott of the Pale Hose and Bunny Hearn of the Gothams responded to the Philippine air with stellar performances; the final score was 2–1. Scott surrendered only four hits, one more than Hearn. Hearn's game was very probably lost on the Giants' two errors versus the Sox's one.

Throughout the ball game, Duck Pond sat in the dugout on John McGraw's left. He had withstood a hard journey to attend this ball game, a trek of more than five hundred miles from Cebu to Manila, but Pond would not have missed it for the world. For that afternoon at least, time rolled back for the former teammates. Once again it was a Baltimore spring, and the Orioles were kings of the world.

As the game concluded, all of Manila opened its doors to the tourists. "A megaphoned young man announced that the freedom of the Army and Navy Club, the Elks Club and the Y.M.C.A. was extended to all members of the party."[6]

The tourists scattered to these various locales. Most of the single and unaccompanied men enjoyed the hospitality of the Army and Navy Club. The couples and women were provided with chaperones and given personal tours of the Philippine hinterlands, including a twenty-mile drive through the jungle to a native village where Filipino dancing girls performed. The tourists also spent time shopping and haggling for trinkets.

At 9:00 P.M. everyone returned to the Manila Hotel for a lavish reception. Here the unique hospitality of the hotel interacted with glorious Philippine weather for a banquet like no other. Held under starlight in the luxurious rooftop gardens of the hotel, the players and their wives ate, tangoed in time to the band, and inhaled the intoxicating aroma of the tropical flora.

The rooftop revelries continued until midnight. Surprisingly, the tourists did not spend the night at the hotel. They were ferried back to their berths on the *St. Albans*, finally getting to sleep at 1:00 A.M.

Awakening on the following morning, it must have seemed to the tourists that day two in Manila would greatly resemble their only day in Shanghai. Rain, steady and thick, beat down upon the city. The tourists were not at any loss as to how to spend their day; the welcoming committee had already made that decision. Far too early in the morning, the ship's Chinese cabin boys had been dispatched to wake the entourage bearing the following missive, "Thursday, Dec. 18—Forenoon—Individuals of the party will be furnished with automobiles by the party and will be allowed to follow their own inclinations."[7]

While some of the athletes took up the offer, most realized that they had not a clue on navigating the crowded Philippine streets. Neither did they know where any of the sights were, let alone how to drive to them. All was saved, however, when the proprietor of a most unlikely tourist destination stepped forward. M. L. Stewart, the director of prisons, sent word that at

11:00 A.M. the Bilibid Prison would be available for tours. All the tourists chose to visit this "attraction."

If there was one thing that the Philippines led the world in, it was its prison system. Bilibid, the apex of the Philippine prison system, was the largest and most modern prison in the world. It had a reputation for being the best-governed and most efficiently run prison known. The jail truly did have an international reputation for being the next wave in housing convicts. Most notable was Bilibid Prison's lack of overt coercion. The tourists witnessed retreat (the prisoners being returned to their cells) at 11:40 A.M. It was an awesome sight, three thousand prisoners marching somberly back to their cells with complete obedience and in total silence. While the tourists were present, not a single guard wielded a gun or a baton. All of the tourists were impressed by this silent spectacle, but former jailbirds like Mike Donlin were especially awed.

At the conclusion of their prison tour, it was time for another stag lunch. Owners, managers, players, and umpires all convened at the Army and Navy Club, with Colonel McCain presiding over the festivities. It was an Irish confab. Guests of honor were the big three of Philippine power: Governor-General Harrison, Admiral Nicholson, and General Bell. General Bell announced that he was placing two U.S. Army automobiles at the teams' disposal. The Manila League sent all of its officials to the lunch for an "eat and greet" with the pros. At 2:00 P.M. the athletes made their way to the YMCA and the Columbia Club to dress for the game. Outside the Army and Navy Club, the heavy tropical rains were still beating down. As in Shanghai, the tourists did not wish to disappoint their hosts, so the teams began the five-minute journey to the ballpark at 2:45 P.M. At the park, multitudes patiently sat in the rain. The second half of the U.S. military and all those who had bought tickets for this second contest filled the stadium. Despite the atrocious weather, the tourists were determined to play. This proved to be difficult. The tourists could not fulfill all of their promises; a scheduled five-inning preliminary exhibition between stars from the Manila League and a combined squad of Giants and White Sox had to be sacrificed.

The rain turned the stadium sod into mud. A small army of Filipino natives armed with homemade brooms fashioned out of palm fronds continually swept the field. This did little more than push the water around and level out the oozing mud. Still, the tourists were determined to play. After a forty-minute delay, the players took to the field in the pouring rain. The game was one of the most bizarre and unintentionally comical ever played.

To the athletes' horror, the Manila mud had two outstanding qualities.

When you stood on it, it acted like quicksand. When you tried to run on it, it was as slick as an iced sidewalk. In moments the players were caked with mud up to their ankles. Somehow a game that vaguely resembled baseball was played. "Played" would not be the proper word; "parodied" would be a more suitable word choice.

Germany Schaefer coached first base while carrying an umbrella and got away with it. The heavy rains tapered off midway through the game, but that did nothing to improve conditions. Running was well nigh impossible. Sliding into base risked breaking one's neck. And how exactly was one supposed to chase down a fly while waddling through ankle-deep muck? The day's hurlers, Leverenz of the Sox and Wiltse of the Giants, at least had the high ground of the pitcher's mound.

Both teams had eight hits, and both teams scored in the second and seventh innings. The teams combined for five errors over eight innings. The White Sox pulled out the victory, such as it was, by a score of 7–4. As Frank McGlynn succinctly put it, "The outcome was largely a matter of luck."[8]

The game was called after eight innings not out of mercy but because the teams had to return to the *St. Albans*. The farewell reception pulled out all the stops in preparation for the 6:00 P.M. sailing of the *St. Albans*. The Constabulary Band played all the patriotic songs in its catalog as they and thousands of soldiers and Filipinos followed the tourists to the wharf. Duck Pond, who had sat next to McGraw in the Giants dugout for the second game as well, clambered above the crowd to make himself more visible to his former teammate, scaling the wire string piece of the wharf to wave good-bye to McGraw. The two men had been practically inseparable for two days; now they were saying good-bye, as far as either knew for the last time ever.

From the deck of the *St. Albans* the tourists, especially misty-eyed John McGraw, viewed Pond waving farewell until he was a speck on the horizon, suspended above the black mass of the crowded wharf while the final strains of the Constabulary Band were swallowed by the echoing surf.

NINE

Baseball Down Under

To see an American base ball team taking the field is to be vastly impressed at the outset. – *Melbourne Age*, 8 January 1914

With the disappearance of the Philippine coast, the tourists turned their attention to relaxing and enjoying the amenities of the *St. Albans*. Its heading was due south, through the East Indies before turning under New Guinea and eastward to Cairns, Queensland, on Australia's tropical northeast coast. If they had no weather or mechanical delays, the voyage would take seven days. Captain Bakie, his English officers, and his Chinese crew continued to do their best to keep their charges happy.

The swimming pool had been their improvised idea. Sitting on the after main deck, it was made out of sailcloth, timbers, and rope. A pump kept it constantly refilled with sparkling warm tropical seawater. Around the jerry-built pool, a rope latticework·of netting was fastened to prevent any passengers from going over the side for an inadvertent and permanent ocean dip. The pool was just the thing to while away the afternoons. The tourists noted that the water became progressively warmer the closer the *St. Albans* got to the equator.

A shuffleboard league and deck cricket enjoyed ardent participation. At the hands of the athletes, the sedate game of shuffleboard became a blood sport. Every ballplayer was entered into the league, which had an elaborate 144-game schedule. Five games were contested daily by teams of two men each, all drawn by lot. Every man anted up equally into the final prize-money kitty. By the time they reached Australia the season was only half completed. The midseason standings found Evans and Egan in first, followed by Crawford and Leverenz in second, with Buck Weaver and Germany Schaefer in third place. Deck cricket became one of the more enjoyed activities of the tourists. The *St. Albans* provided shin guards, bats, wickets, stumps, and balls. The pitch was the teak floor of a screened-off deck on the port side of the ship. Though the tourists had, of course, heard of the game, this marked their first real opportunity to play cricket. Best of all, it provided a chance to mix and play with the crew and other passengers, many of whom were skilled at the game.

On the other hand, no one really got used to the ship's decidedly Asian-themed menu. In Joe Farrell's words, "This tour will be long remembered because of the serenity of the seas and the underbreath profanity hurled at the food."[1] An unfamiliar dish, bizarrely named "Bubble and Squeak," appeared every day. Though the name enticed in a perverse way, no one had the guts to order the stuff. Another item that appeared with regularity was called "Toad in the hole." Upon encountering this menu offering, Lee Magee said, "That's not a food but simply the announcement of the whereabouts of Mike Donlin."[2] (Donlin had been making himself scarce of late, holed up in his cabin for days at a time.)

Aboard the *St. Albans* the players never lacked for companionship; this was one packed vessel. Down in steerage, Russian farmers, now emigrants on their way to new lives in New Zealand and Australia, had brought along their livestock. Their roosters would begin crowing at 4:00 A.M., awaking the entire ship. During the voyage several of the players, principally Tris Speaker and Steve Evans, spent time among these Russian peasant families. All were quite taken by the small children who were heading to an exotic new land with their parents.

Crates of Chinese pheasants scheduled for release in Australia sat in the ship's hold. Sportsmen coveted the birds as ideal prey, hence their introduction to five continents. The *St. Albans* also carried two thousand canaries destined for the pet shops of New South Wales. The Thorpes purchased one of these sweet-singing birds from the shipment. They fell in love with the bright yellow tunesmith. Jim and Iva named him O Sing and hoped to bring him back to the United States.

There were unforeseen hassles to deal with, of course. For one thing, most of the men started sporting mustaches rather than risk losing their upper lips to the ship's Chinese barber. In an age when few men shaved themselves, the barbershop was a prime center of male society. The daily shave was part of the commute to the office. To ward off a five o'clock shadow, a man would see his barber twice a day. While this particular ship's barber was quite able with the new-fangled safety razor on the chin and neck, he lacked proficiency around the "cookie duster" area. In only a few years' time, the safety razor would find its way into every man's bathroom, and the barbershop would lose much of its role in the world of men.

Worse was another round of the feared inoculations. The compulsory shots really took their toll this time around. Marie Klem, Tris Speaker, Buck Weaver, John McGraw, and Hooks Wiltse all had to be confined to their cabins for a time after they suffered severe reactions to the vaccination drugs. Compounding the misery was a notice posted on the ship's bulletin boards stating that the Sydney health authorities might order yet another round of vaccinations for those on whom the shots proved ineffective.

The most memorable Christmas week the tourists would ever celebrate included a major milestone two days out of Manila when, on 21 December 1913, the *St. Albans* crossed the equator. Earlier in the day they had sailed past the Celebes, with active volcanoes visible on the horizon. Natural wonders abounded. Dolphins leaping and dancing off the bow of the *St. Albans* were a daily occurrence. One simply could not have ordered better weather. Clouds only occasionally obscured the brilliant blue sky, and the seas were never less than flat calm. At the start of this phase of the journey they had passed so close to the coast of the Philippine island of Luzon that from the rails of the ship the tourists could see native huts and villages. Farther along in the journey they passed Bird Island, uninhabited save by members of the avian order. The *St. Albans* crept up to the island, then on order from Captain Bakie, one of the ship's rope cannons was fired. The sound sent millions of birds into the air, a rainbow of plumage from a myriad of species, all crying together in a cacophony of noise.

On 24 December 1913 the *St. Albans* sailed through the Torres Strait between New Guinea and Australia; most of the tourists were depressed and homesick. It was, after all, Christmas, and they were missing homes and family. This emotion persisted until the tour's three matriarchs, Blanche McGraw, Josephine Callahan, and Nancy Comiskey, took charge and ordered everyone on deck to decorate a tree. Josephine Callahan had purchased the tree in Manila and secreted it on board, assuring her children a visit from Santa Claus.

Decorating the tree lifted everyone's spirits and put all in the holiday mood. Josephine Callahan had brought along Christmas decorations from her home. Even though the weather was nothing like Chicago, through the tree, she hoped to manufacture all the warmth of the holiday that she could muster. It looked so beautiful when it was completed that some of the women burst into tears. Sentiment and memories of stateside Christmases brought moisture to many an eye. The entire ship had fun with little Danny and Margaret Callahan's Christmas expectations. Margaret and Danny were convinced that St. Nick would "probably come in an aeroplane and for once they were certain that he would have no trouble getting down the chimney."

Also the engineer assured them that he would have the smokestack swept, which was the finishing touch to the reception of Santa."[3]

Christmas morning came and with it the discovery that Santa had indeed been generous. He had left hundreds of presents under the tree. The players made sure that Santa even visited the immigrant children in steerage. The Callahan children were overwhelmed; every one of the tourists had purchased something for them. The Thorpes bought them silver spoons. Between the two of them, the Callahan children received "two trunk loads of toys."[4]

Everyone else received gifts that were either sentimental or just plain odd. Outgoing Red Sox president James McAleer received a stuffed white tiger. Ted Sullivan was quite stunned with his gift, a large diamond pin. As impressive as the pin was the story behind it. Purchased in Chicago by Sullivan's friends, the pin was sent to Manila ahead of the tourists with orders that it be deposited in Sullivan's Christmas stocking. Comiskey allowed himself to be generous as well, giving each male member of the touring party a box of fine Manila cigars. Comiskey also made sure that his friends in Chicago were taken care of this day. The Old Roman left cash and detailed instructions behind on what to purchase for each of his cronies.

Early on Christmas morning Sam Crawford added lifesaver to his résumé. Before most other folks had gotten out of bed, "Wahoo" Sam stood leaning on the rail of the *St. Albans* scanning the horizon with his trusty binoculars. Far in the distance he spied a three-masted schooner flying a distress flag. Crawford was the first person on board to spot the vessel, and he immediately alerted the crew to his find. Captain Bakie promptly veered off course to aid the ship.

When the *St. Albans* reached the stricken vessel, the crew beheld an ancient German sailing ship with a Malaysian crew. A vessel from another age, it had no wireless or other modern amenities; it was also hopelessly lost. At this point the various narratives diverge. The *Sporting News* report reads, "It was learned after much Malay jargon back and forth through a megaphone that the commander was seriously ill and the crew had lost their bearings."[5] Yet according to Frank McGlynn, writing for the *Base Ball Magazine*, "The skipper of the brig, a German trading boat, shouted through his megaphone that he was lost, that is, he did not know where he was, having been becalmed for several days in weather which prevented him seeing the sun, and was drifting from his course. A breeze was stirring now and his boat was making headway, but not until night time when he could 'take the stars' would he know his location."[6]

Farrell's account seems to be far more genuine than McGlynn's. What weather would prevent a captain from "seeing the sun," especially when for the previous three days the seas were smooth as glass and the nights were crystal clear? Was the movie director suffering from poor memory, or was he simply taking dramatic license? In any event, once Captain Bakie supplied the latitude and longitude coordinates, both ships went their separate ways to shouts of "Merry Christmas!"

Christmas night was spent feasting and toasting absent family members. The entertainment program took on a holiday air, with the "Sextette" adding religious and holiday songs to their repertoire. The women inherited center court, with Josephine Callahan and Della Wiltse taking turns at the piano accompanied by Grace Comiskey on her violin. The women were all talented musicians, especially Grace Comiskey, whose playing drew raves. While the women played below deck, a few of the men enjoyed their performance topside. Someone strolling on the hurricane deck had discovered that one of the ship's ventilators was parked directly above the piano. Before long several men were gathered in deck chairs huddled around the vent. Looking for all the world like a group of audiophiles gathered around the horn of an ancient Victrola, the men sat listening to the music waft through the tropical moonlight while smoking Comiskey's Christmas cigars.

The following day, 26 December 1913, the tourists made their first landfall since Manila at Thursday Island. Part of Australia's northernmost frontier, Thursday Island, a beautiful way station only two and a half miles square, was discovered and named by Captain James Cook during his explorations. Once an essential part of Australia's defenses, the island held a garrison and was also home to an extensive pearl industry. Upon reaching Thursday Island, most vessels would take on experienced pilots to assist in navigating the treacherous Great Barrier Reef.

Since the twenty-sixth is the Boxing Day holiday, most of the island was closed. The day's blisteringly hot weather also tended to inhibit activity on the island. Some of the tourists bribed a local shopkeeper into opening, however, and for about $300 were able to purchase "enough pearls to fill a demitasse cup."[7]

To Comiskey's and McGraw's surprise, they discovered that this sparsely populated corner of Queensland might have made a great place for a game. Gus Axelson explains, "Meeting the tourists on landing was Alexander Corran, editor of *The Torres Straits Pilot* who insisted that a game could be played. In proof of his assertion he led Comiskey, Callahan and McGraw to the cricket and soccer field not far from the dock. It was then too late to arrange for a game, but chances are that Thursday Island will have to wait a long time before it has another opportunity to greet an American baseball team."[8]

Corran claimed that baseball had been played on the island, though his details were vague. In any event, the island's population of eighty soldiers, seven hundred Australian citizens, and an untallied number of aborigines would have provided the smallest audience of the tour. Everyone on the island could have fit many times over into Comiskey Park or the Polo Grounds.

For some of the tourists, the visit to the pearl works resulted in shattered illusions and laments for the scope of progress. Axelson again:

> The natives have not taken much to sport. They are mostly of low order, including a large number of Papuans. Among the latter are to be found some of the best pearl divers in the world. Still the romance is gone. No longer is there an even chance between the diver and the shark. The former is encased in a modern diving outfit and he is paid in the coin of the realm instead of a string of beads or a red undershirt. Here the tourists first saw the giant oyster of the Australian waters. It is about the size of a breakfast plate and the house in which it lives furnishes to America a large share of the mother of pearl of commerce.[9]

After their three-hour visit to Thursday Island, the *St. Albans* steamed south and east to Cairns. Following another one-day cruise, landfall on the mighty continent of Australia proper would finally occur. Anticipation filled the *St. Albans*. The day spent navigating the Great Barrier Reef may have been the most dangerous single-day's passage of the tour. By turns azure blue, turquoise, or emerald green, the beautiful sea was deadly. With its innumerable coral reef ridges that often confounded even the most seasoned of captains, the Coral Sea wrecked ships with alarming regularity.

The tourists were well aware of the treacherous seas through which they were sailing. In 1911 the *Yongala*, a steamship out of Sydney packed with four hundred people, went down on the reef with all hands lost. A year later an identical fate befell the *Koombana* in almost the same spot. In the golden age of tabloid journalism, both wrecks had made headlines around the world. Sensational accounts of the wrecks even appeared in newspapers in towns that were safely landlocked as warnings of the dangers of travel and exploration.

The very relieved tourists arrived at Cairns at dawn on Sunday, 28 December 1913. They were in the town itself at 9:00 A.M. Instead of the usual Sunday services on the ship under John McGraw's personal priest, the tourists visited the local congregations before having lunch and heading off to Barron Falls. Located in the mountains twenty-five miles north of the village of Cairns, they were the most beautiful falls on the Australian continent. Barron Falls make a spectacular drop of over nine hundred feet through a verdant green landscape. While the falls was Cairns's most popular tourist attraction, reaching them was no easy task.

Normally, to visit the falls one had to hike a trail through the mountains and allot oneself plenty of time. The tourists could do neither. But here, on the northeast corner of Australia, just like everywhere else, ways were found to accommodate them. Some palms were greased, and Cairns's rigid blue laws magically disappeared. A narrow-gage steam engine and two open cars appeared out of the green Australian hills, and the tourists climbed aboard. The train was used exclusively for hauling freight and produce for the local farms and plantations. The area around Cairns overflowed with pineapple, banana, papaw, and sugar plantations. For the first time this train would ferry passengers.

Comiskey's red-tape busting nearly came to naught as he almost missed the train to the falls. The Old Roman decided to visit a sugar plantation near Cairns while awaiting the arrival of the train. Budgeting himself an insanely brief thirty minutes, Comiskey traveled by automobile to the sugar plantation. Eight miles out of Cairns the car broke down. Comiskey scoured the countryside for a telephone and was able to get a call through to the village. Immediately, another car was dispatched to retrieve the president of the White Sox, pulling into Cairns with him just as the train loaded with tourists was about to pull out.

Comiskey flagged down the little steam engine, jumped on board, and tried to catch his breath. The train started out once again, inching its way up the foothills and deep into the mountains. The tracks followed a route that looked like something out of *Indiana Jones* or *The Perils of Pauline*. The narrow tracks did not have a proper roadbed; they were simply laid over the landscape and more or less lashed to the side of the mountains. Lots of rickety wooden bridges and trellises helped the train penetrate deeper into the forest. More hair raising than a carnival thrill ride, much of the time one or both tracks were suspended over deep gorges and raging rivers.

While stopped on one of these bridges above mammoth Barron Gorge by the falls, Buck Weaver nearly lost his life. The falls caused a considerable updraft. This updraft collided with Joe Benz's hat, blowing it off. Men wore hats in 1913; they were an equal fashion statement for both genders. As Benz's hat disappeared into the vastness of the gorge, the rest of the men and women made moves to batten down their chapeaus, but not before Louis Comiskey's fifteen-dollar hat became airborne. Lou had just purchased the hat in Manila, and this was his first opportunity to wear the thing in public. As it took to the air, Buck Weaver made an impetuous stab for the headwear, lost his balance, and had to be yanked back into the train car by his teammates, who had just saved him from falling 150 feet.

Despite this near fatal mishap, all of the tourists came away with fond memories of their visit to the falls. The Australian landscape ate one more hat; on the return journey Joe Farrell's lid was blown into a palm tree. The rest of the day was spent in Cairns before returning to the *St. Albans* for the journey to Brisbane. While Cairns today is a veritable hotbed of baseball, in 1913 the sport was not widely known in the city. This was not the case in the rest of Australia.

Although A. G. Spalding had visited the southern continent twenty-five years before, he could not claim credit for introducing the sport there. Baseball had come to Australia through American expatriates. American gold miners and prospectors invaded Australia during the gold rush of 1870. Along with their pans and pickaxes, they packed bats and balls. As in the United States before the Civil War, baseball in Australia was largely regional and urban. Though expatriate Americans introduced the sport, organized baseball grew out of Australian cricket. Brownie Carslake, Australian sports aficionado, described for the *Sporting News* the development of the sport in the antipodes: "The big cricket clubs were the first to introduce it. During the winter months the cricketers wanted some sport to keep them in condition. Somehow or other they selected base ball. You know the winters there are not very cold. Snow is almost unknown. Later base ball games were introduced as preliminaries to football matches."[10] Through such spurts and starts the game had developed to the point where leagues were organized. The quality of play remained far below that of the States, however. As Carslake noted, "Just a few years ago the school authorities in one of our large cities made an arrangement where 20 grammar school [high school] boys from California went to school in Australia. Those grammar school boys formed a base ball team and simply outclassed the best teams we had."[11]

So smooth had been the sailing from Manila that the *St. Albans* actually caught up to the tourists' original schedule. The three days lost on the sail to Japan were erased. The tourists pulled into Brisbane right on time, midnight, 31 December, along with the New Year for 1914.

Baseball was more familiar to the residents of Brisbane than to their cousins in Cairns. The welcome in this Australian city was like the rowdiest welcomes in the United States. Weeks of publicity spiked public anticipation, and Brisbane's large media contingent was anxious to interview the athletes and write profiles about the game. Like the welcome in Japan, there were even reporters aboard the tugboat tender seeking interviews. One enterprising reporter ensured a leg up on his rivals. The wily soul, one F. Z. Eager, waited on the tug, foot resting on a sack of mail, for the tourists from the United States. The burlap sack of parcels and letters contained the very first messages from home the tourists had received since 19 November. A moment earlier everyone had been celebrating the New Year and reminiscing about home. Now they were pressed up against the rail pleading for Eager to toss them an actual memento from home, a letter or parcel. All were desperate for word of home—so desperate, in fact, that they could not even wait for the ship to dock. Tris Speaker bent over the rail of the *St. Albans* while two players held fast to his legs. Eager, on tiptoes, tossed the burlap sack to Speaker, who was then hauled in by his teammates. Familiar handwriting, scented letters, and recognizable postage stamps brought a smile to every face. A few were seen literally dancing for joy.

Brisbane waived the customs requirements for the tourists, the first of many courtesies the city would extend. While Callahan and McGraw busily chatted up the Brisbane scribes, Comiskey, suspicious of any reporters he did not own, avoided the media storm and stayed below deck in his cabin in the *St. Albans*.

The combination of celebrating the New Year, letters from home, and the boisterous Australian newshounds turned the *St. Albans* into a huge openended party. Revelries did not conclude until 4:00 A.M., and even then the reporters did not stay away very long. The ubiquitous and enterprising F. Z. Eager, who doubled as an automobile salesman, was back at 6:00 A.M. with a procession of twenty automobiles, offering the Americans a tour of the city at daybreak. Those tourists who were not completely incapacitated by booze or sleep toured Brisbane. It was a view few have ever had, miles of empty streets, having every tourist destination to yourself, and the silence of a sleeping, hungover city as the sun begins to peek over the horizon.

No one went to bed, at least not for very long, when the tourists returned to the *St. Albans*. The reason was simple. The *St. Albans* was scheduled to leave Brisbane at 1:00 in the afternoon of New Year's Day. This meant that the ball game between the Giants and White Sox would have to begin at 10:30 in the morning. The ballplayers, many of whom had been up for twenty-four hours, sucked it up and made their way to the Brisbane Cricket Grounds.

A large, enthusiastic, but not especially baseball savvy crowd greeted them. The New Year's Day crowd was polite, applauding every putout and every hit, but it soon became clear that the Aussie crowd had only a rudimentary knowledge of the game. Nowhere was this more apparent than in the press box. None of the reporters covering the event had ever even seen a baseball game before. The subtleties of scoring were completely lost on the fourth estate. Some of the reporters, confusing cricket's overs with baseball's runs, wanted to assign the teams tallies for every base hit. Gus Axelson offered them a box score for use in their next day's editions, "but this was looked askance at as the opinion gained ground during the battle that the readers were not yet ready for a serious study of batting and fielding averages."[12]

Despite their near total lack of sleep and considerable alcohol consumption, the Giants and White Sox turned in a dandy game. The Giants, behind the pitching of Hooks Wiltse, defeated Joe Benz and the White Sox 2–1, scoring the winning run in the ninth inning. Defensively, Hans Lobert, Buck Weaver, and Mickey Doolan made outstanding plays. While the athletes thrilled the crowd, Ted Sullivan and Charles Comiskey attempted to explain the game to the various local Australian VIPs with whom they shared seating. At the conclusion of the game (which the Australians kept referring to as a "match"), played in a speedy one hour and forty-five minutes, the players grabbed lunch and headed back to the *St. Albans*. Their hosts had hoped that the players could have more time in Brisbane. Had the tourists' schedule not been so tight, a boxing match would have been presented that evening for the men while the women were escorted to the theater.

A mass of disappointed citizens, including Sir Arthur Morgan, governor-general of Queensland; the province's attorney general, Thomas O'Sullivan; and Australia's Speaker of the House, William Finlayson, led the procession to the waterfront. The trio had just enough time to make brief speeches and wish the tourists bon voyage before the *St. Albans* slipped out of its berth under a brilliant midday sun.

The rest of that first day of 1914 and the second day were spent recovering from Brisbane's endless New Year's party. The tourists spent the day in blissful sleep. The smooth sailing and placid seas were very conducive to rest, which everyone needed. A one-and-a-half-day sail brought the now-recovered athletes to Sydney on 3 January 1914, where another glorious welcome awaited them.

Booking passage from Brisbane to Sydney with the tourists was E. A. Tyler, honorary secretary of the New South Wales Baseball Association. A resident of Sydney, he had come to Brisbane for the expressed purpose of taking in the ball game. Comiskey's contact in Australia, Tyler did much of the required legwork to put the tour together in his country. A total baseball crank, Tyler was awed by the players and their adventure. During the journey to Sydney, Tyler made some of the most insightful and prophetic remarks of anyone the tourists encountered.

"It is my firm opinion," said Mr. Tyler, "that no team or set of teams will ever make such a trip as have the Sox and Giants. This journey is marvelous by us down here. I do not see how it could be done, in the first place is time and money. As far as the time is concerned, you are going too fast, but just the same it is the greatest trip ever conceived, and I don't think that it will ever be duplicated. The very fact that it is unique will do baseball and the United States more good in the long run than if you had tarried longer. It is like the flash of a meteor, here one minute, gone the next.

"There can be no chance for anybody growing tired of the visit, no chance of outliving your welcome. It looks like one grand whirl around the globe only touching the high spots, as one of your men expressed it: I don't think Mr. Comiskey or Mr. McGraw will realize the importance of this trip until they get home. They are not only showing one of the greatest games in the world, but they are advertising their country in a way that is not otherwise possible."[13]

Sydney, aside from perhaps Buenos Aries, is the most cosmopolitan city in the Southern Hemisphere; its harbor is among the world's busiest. So much traffic crowded the harbor that deep-ocean vessels like the *St. Albans* were prohibited from entering until after 9:00 A.M. The *St. Albans* arrived at daybreak. Rather than cool his heels with the rest of the tourists, Frank McGlynn had an inspiration. He hailed Victor Miller, loaded up the movie equipment, and commandeered a small launch.

When the time came for the *St. Albans* to queue her way to the Sydney wharfs, McGlynn and Miller had the camera rolling. Sydney had not seen any reception quite like this. Not even visiting foreign diplomats received this kind of welcome. A huge throng of well-wishers crammed onto the wharf like a knotted stream of ants. As the *St. Albans* dropped anchor, a band began playing "The Star-spangled Banner," and every male tourist doffed his hat and wore a solemn patriotic expression. Miller cranked the handle on his camera while McGlynn, to overcome the din of the crowd, directed him by shouting through a megaphone.

The band of forty-six pieces began playing "Take Me Out to the Ball Game," "Yankee Doodle," and various other American tunes. Interestingly, the band, like the players, was American. The forty-six California schoolboys and their conductor/teacher, one Major Peixotto, were also on a tour of the world, although they were circling the planet in the opposite direction from the players. Because the young musicians were in the same city as the ball teams, they were made the tourists' official band, accompanying the teams to the stadium and serenading the crowd between innings. Every American in Sydney was at the dock. Among those present were middleweight boxer Eddie McGoorty and actor Fred Niblo, accompanied by his wife, Josephine Cohan, sister of George M. Cohan.

Before the players could disembark from the *St. Albans* and onto the turf of New South Wales, they had to endure another medical examination. To everyone's delight, this inspection was a breeze. "The medical inspector felt the pulse and looked into the healthy eyes of all in the party, and unhesitatingly declared it unnecessary to vaccinate such a tanned and brawny bunch."[14]

Waiting at the foot of the gangplank was the lord mayor of Sydney wielding the key to the city. The usual speeches were followed by a parade of automobiles to the Sydney Cricket Grounds. The Sydney Cricket Grounds was, quite possibly, the most beautiful athletic complex in the world. Built for $3 million, the beautiful circular stadium offered unobstructed views of every part of the pitch. The Sydney Cricket Grounds was a study in symmetry. Cricket, unlike baseball, is played on fields of uniform dimensions; there is no such thing as a short fence for a cricketer. The manicured green expanse of lawn shimmered like an emerald in the Sydney sun. Circling the pitch was a bone-smooth bicycling track. A short, whitewashed fence encircled the track and pitch.

Awaiting the players at the cricket grounds was the most distinguished group of dignitaries yet encountered. Australia's prime minister, Joseph Cook; the minister of defense; the home secretary; and the lord mayor of Sydney were all honored guests. Also present was C. N. J. Oliver, head of the board of trustees for the Sydney Cricket Grounds, who served as host, and J. A. Minnett, president of the New South Wales Baseball Association. Two well-known cricketers who had toured the United States also partook in the festivities.

Lunch was a combination of bombast and sanctimony accompanied by excellent food. Oliver stepped to the podium and offered a toast to the "King and President." The following summation of his remarks comes from the *Sydney Morning Herald* of 4 January 1914: "Mr. Oliver referred to the gathering as a British-American one and in subsequently giving the health of the visiting baseball teams, he said that they represented the cream of the game in the latter country. Australians were keen sportsmen, and although they did not play baseball to any extent, they were looking forward to the professional exhibitions."[15]

Australia's prime minister Cook next stepped to the podium. "The Prime Minister remarked that it was a very fitting thing indeed that the first sample of Sydney's hospitality should be tendered in the historic pavilion at the Cricket Ground. He had been told the gathering was a British—American one, and he supposed the distinction was necessary for some reasons, though for others it was entirely superfluous. 'They look almost as British as we ourselves,' said Mr. Cook, 'and for the life of me I cannot see the difference. If there is a difference it must be a mighty long way down below the surface. We greet you today as men of our own race.' "[16]

Joe Farrell was designated to speak for the Americans. He spent his time at the podium dismissing A. G. Spalding's tour of a quarter century earlier. Sydney was the first city since San Francisco where the tourists' path crossed that of Spalding's All-Stars. Farrell went to great lengths to point out that the White Sox–Giants amalgam was better because "the players touring now are the very best selected men and with them were the heads of baseball in America, Messrs Comiskey, McGraw and Callahan who were equal partners in the venture."[17]

Jimmy Callahan closed out the speakers with a winning monologue. His diplomatic waffle went like this: "[Callahan] said he had had the great pleasure to him to meet the Australian cricketers in Chicago last year, when they played on the baseball grounds. He did not care for cricket that first day, but the second day he liked it, and on the third day it would not have been difficult to make him a cricket enthusiast. (Applause.) They wanted to introduce baseball on a proper footing in Australia and would help to introduce cricket in America, hoping that international cricket would be played in both countries. (Applause.)"[18]

Australians and Americans have long had an affinity for one another. Both nations seem equally beguiled by the other. This voyage proved no exception; all of the tourists fell in love with the land Down Under. Even John McGraw shouted, "I love Australia!" The Thorpes were so enamored with the continent that Iva gave more than a passing thought in her diary of she and Jim settling there.

Mike Donlin was certainly up for settling in Australia as well. In Brisbane, Donlin assured E. A. Tyler that in the coming winter of 1914 (Australia's summer) he would lead a delegation of American Major Leaguers to assist the growth of baseball in Australia. The plan called for launching a league in the cities of Brisbane, Adelaide, Ballarat, Perth, and Sydney. Each team was to be stocked with a few Americans, giving the league instant credibility, improving the level of play, and ensuring that the league would get plenty of attention from Australia's media and fans.

Australians were more similar to Americans than they were to their Commonwealth cousins; they even knew how to harass the umpire. Although the sport was relatively new in Australia, the men in blue were pariahs here just as much as they were in the States or Japan. The following comes from *Sporting Life* of 13 September 1913, published just a few months before the tourists' visit.

> Baseball has caught on in the Australia. The early days when the game was a curiosity are past. It isn't the number of games played or the space given in the newspapers that show [*sic*] the American game has found a new home. It is the fact that the bugs now mob the umpire. When the old cry "Kill the umpire" is sounded by the crowd it may not be healthy for the indicator holder, but it shows that the game itself is in a thriving condition. In a recent game in a suburb of Sydney a mob chased the umpire from the grounds till he gained shelter in a street car. To make his escape he had to call on a number of friendly collegians. With this episode base ball may be said to have arrived in Australia.[19]

Lunch finished in time for the players to prepare for the game. By the time of the first pitch at 2:30 P.M., more than ten thousand people had filled the stands. The *Sydney Morning Herald* sets the scene:

> If the appreciation and warmth of the greeting to the visitors by the expectant crowd of over 10,000 persons at the Sydney Cricket Ground counts for anything the visitors need have no fears of success of their colorful adventure. The interest evinced was a pleasant surprise.
>
> Many, no doubt, were attracted merely by curiosity, but there was a large gathering of local votaries, who could appreciate the finesse of the game, and were bubbling with enthusiasm for a sport that not a few think may be in the near future a rival to our own national game of cricket.[20]

A preliminary five-inning contest between the White Sox and New South Wales was first on the bill. When the Australian amateurs saw the Americans warming up, they realized how hopelessly outclassed they were, especially in pitching. In an attempt to give the locals some chance, the White Sox and Giants gave them a battery. Ivy Wingo and Walter Leverenz were loaned to the New South Wales club.

Even with American assistance, New South Wales's efforts were mostly futile. The *Sydney Morning Herald* describes their predicament: "The local players, as was to be expected, were completely outclassed, and in the short game of five innings only crossed the plate once, and then by means of a home run, with the circuit unoccupied, by Wiltse, the borrowed pitcher. Rarely did our men connect with the ball, and in fielding, they fell down, too, although several smart plays were produced, revealing an intimate knowledge of the requirements of the sport."[21]

Australians had already developed their own slang baseball terms, which were peppered all through the article. Innings were "attempts," runners in scoring position were "players in scoring stations," second base was the "intermediate cushion," the third baseman was the "third base custodian."

For New South Wales, the highpoints of the game had to be getting Tom Daly in a rundown and catching Tris Speaker napping off base. For the Sox, the most exciting play was probably Buck Weaver's three-run inside-the-park home run in the second inning. The White Sox drubbed New South Wales 10–1. Klem and Sheridan shared umpiring duties, with Klem acting in his familiar role of announcer. As in the rest of the world, Klem drew high praise for the stentorian majesty of his voice.

With the natives disposed of, the White Sox and Giants played each other. The Aussies witnessed a very close game of baseball, the White Sox edging out the Giants 5–4. The contest inspired a blasé response from the *Herald*'s reporter.

> Not withstanding, there was nothing thrillingly spectacular, principally perhaps, because each combination was mechanically so efficient and executed plays as if they could not help it. Still many attractive features were produced that served to keep the onlookers continuously interested. There was plenty of hitting, smashing drives, lofty slogging, line hits, bunts, and infield smashes, all of which were cleverly handled whenever possible. The control of the pitchers, the pace of the base runners, and the speed and the accuracy of the throwing, the vigor and the impetus of the foot-sliding, and the wonderful work of the outfielders, all contributed to a brilliant exposition of baseball.[22]

The large crowd went home happy, or at least contented. The players checked into the Hotel Australia. The evening was spent in another whirlwind of entertainment. A lavish banquet, hosted by legendary Australian boxer and sports impresario Reginald "Snowy" Baker, was held at the hotel. Everyone appreciated the dinner not just for the food but also because, for a change, it was not stag. The touring American vocal group, the

Primrose Quartette, four obese men who billed themselves, appropriately, as "a thousand pounds of harmony," was the evening's main entertainment. The quartette sang racist "coon songs" and popular American tunes. The four were purportedly tearing up the Australian stage and drawing raves from the local press.

Germany and the "Sextette" sang "Shoenus" to close the banquet. After dessert, the men and women went their separate ways, with the men accompanying Baker to Snowy Baker Stadium to take in a boxing match. Appropriately, the gladiators for the main bout were an American versus an Australian.

Snowy Baker was the fight promoter without peer in Australia. The sport was under his almost dictatorial control. Baker had established worldwide links, exchanging boxers between six continents. He had brought Eddie McGoorty to Australia from Oshkosh, Wisconsin, in November 1913. Baker promised McGoorty $5,000 if he would come to Australia and fight, bulk up to the light heavyweight division, then return to the States to fight in the heavier class. McGoorty accompanied the players to Snowy Baker Stadium, where they watched Milburn Saylor of Indianapolis, Indiana, pummel Alf Mory in a lightweight division match lasting fourteen rounds. The women went to the Trivoli Theater for an evening of music and entertainment before all returned to the Hotel Australia and turned in.

The next morning was Sunday, 4 January 1914, allowing the tourists a Sabbath rest on dry land. The day was spent relaxing and visiting the sights. A motorcade brought the tourists to the harbor, where everyone was treated to a picnic lunch at the lush Clifton Gardens, Sydney's prime watering hole. The single men of the party were delighted, as there was a large gathering of Australian bathing beauties at the gardens. That evening, dinner was provided by the New South Wales Baseball Association with all of the usual pomp and circumstance.

Monday, 5 January 1914, dawned, and it was back to baseball for the tourists. The schedule would be similar to Saturday's doings. At 1:00 P.M. there would be a contest between a team of New South Wales amateurs and the Giants, followed by the Sox and Giants tearing into each other. After lunch, before New South Wales and the Giants took to the field, the tourists engaged in an impromptu cricket match. Aware of Jimmy Callahan's boast about trying to introduce cricket to America, the tourists decided to at least attempt the game.

The White Sox, led by Germany Schaefer, took aim at the wickets. The baseball players loved cricket bats. A Major Leaguer would kill to be allowed to wield a cricket bat at the plate. With a gripping end a little thicker than a broom handle and a broad, flat face, a cricket bat would make mincemeat of Major League pitching. So attractive were the hitting prospects that Charles Comiskey himself took a turn at bat. "I should think I ought to be able to knock the ball out of the lot with a paddle like that," he said as he strode toward the wicket.[23] Looking every inch the prosperous businessman he had become, the paunched Comiskey, in his dark suit, dug his white dress shoes into the ground and slugged the first ball bowled his way over the fence.

After his clout, the Old Roman was informed that his shot was worth six runs and that there was no need to run to the next wicket if you hit one out of the grounds. There is no wasted energy in cricket. All in all, however, the tourists were underwhelmed by cricket. Iva Thorpe, recalling the day's events in her diary, was certainly not the last person to comment on the slowness of cricket in comparison to baseball.

The first contest of the day was to be between the Giants and the New South Wales Blues. The Blues went with their own battery this time around, recruiting the Franks brothers, the best pitcher and catcher in the province. H. Franks made it through the first inning without allowing a run. Then the floodgates opened. The Giants outscored New South Wales 15–2. The game's most significant moment came in the top of the fourth inning when John McGraw inserted himself in relief of Hooks Wiltse. The Little Napoleon had not pitched anything other than batting practice since his first year in the minor leagues back in the 1880s, yet he turned in a creditable performance, retiring the side in order in the fourth and getting one strikeout. He also hit well off the Aussies, driving in a run. He pitched four innings; for reasons unknown (possibly for the sake of McGraw's vanity), the game was extended two innings beyond its scheduled five.

What the old man was doing on the mound became clear in the next day's edition of the *Sydney Morning Herald*. There, across the front page, above a Giants team photo, stood John McGraw in the batter's box, hand clenched around the handle of the bat, wrists at the ready. The Giants manager had outshone Comiskey again. Let Commy play cricket, at age forty Mugsy could still play baseball with the big boys.

The joust between the Sox and Giants was less a blowout than Saturday's contest, with the Sox topping the Giants again, this time by the score of 10–5. Bill Klem worked the game with a local umpire, allowing Jack Sheridan a rest and giving the Australian arbiter, one T. Proud, a chance to tutor under the best umpire on the planet. In the press box, Gus Axelson performed a similar task, sharing scoring duties with a member of the Australian press corps while educating him on the subtleties of scoring.

By 6:00 P.M. everyone was dining at a reception in the town hall. Lord Mayor Sir Richard Watkins Richards made presentations and saw the tourists off by train for Melbourne at 7:00 P.M. Displaying some of the paranoia about the press and public that would cost him dearly in later years, Comiskey chose to wait for the next train. He had no desire to deal with either interviews or the inquiring public. With his inner circle of trusted friends and relatives, Comiskey traveled separately to Melbourne. The Victoria Railroad took them south and west to Melbourne, the capital of Victoria, Australia's smallest province.

En route to Melbourne, the players read the following boast in a Melbourne newspaper: "The reception accorded the world's base ball tourists by the people of Melbourne is to be greater than that given to them by the population of Sydney." This prompted Germany Schaefer to retort, "We shall see."[24] Their train sped on through the Australian twilight and evening; it would not arrive at their destination until 11:00 A.M. on 5 January 1914. For the first time in a month the tourists would travel by rail. All slept fitfully, eagerly anticipating what sort of welcome Australia's capital city would provide.

Here is how the *Melbourne Argus* described the arrival of the tourists.

There was a large crowd at Spencer Street Station yesterday when the express train from Sydney arrived, and 35 motor-cars stood ready in the yard. As soon as the train had come to a standstill a pleasant-faced man, in cream flannels, stepped on the platform and someone called, "It's John McGraw." Not one member of the waiting party had ever seen him before but his features, which have been pictured so frequently in American papers for the last 15 years, were already familiar to everyone. There was a rush to shake the new arrival's hand, and then three loud cheers went up.

Mr. McGraw is the manager of the American Baseball team known as the "Giants," and the success of his team has made him famous wherever the national game of the United States is played. Behind Mr. McGraw were 20 young athletes, built on massive lines, to whom the title "Giants" was no misnomer. Mr. Callahan, manager of the Chicago Americans, better known as the "White Sox"—almost immediately afterwards descended from the special car, and his party was given an equally enthusiastic greeting. "Well I never realized that people could be so kind," said Mr. McGraw as he shook hands right and left. "Australia is all right."[25]

Huge bouquets were presented to every woman in the touring party by

J. S. Milford, president of the Victorian Baseball League. Following formal greetings from various dignitaries, the tourists piled into their motorcade of cars for the jaunt to the Oriental Hotel.

After checking into the hotel the tourists dressed for lunch. The lord mayor himself, Councilor D. V. Hennessy, would be hosting the tourists at a buffet lunch in city hall. Anyone who was anyone in Victoria was on hand to meet the tourists. Even a short list impresses. Among those present were Australia's minister of external affairs, the leader of the Federal opposition, the premier of Victoria, the U.S. consul, the president of the Melbourne Cricket Club, and the club's secretary.

John McGraw introduced each player to the lord mayor, who proposed a toast to "the King and to the President of the United States."[26] He followed this with essentially the same speech the tourists had heard in Melbourne, interchangeable platitudes.

Ted Sullivan, during his turn at the podium, put to rest any Australian fears about the purpose of the tour by broaching the subject head-on. "Wherever English people settle," he said, "they always brought with them a love of 'square' sport. The object of the present tour was not to supplant any national game but just to let other people see how Americans played their own great pastime."[27]

For all the tourists and Australians involved in the tour, the big event occurred later in the afternoon. At 4:00 P.M. the tourists, along with most of the participants in the buffet at city hall, were invited to tea at Government House hosted by the governor-general of Australia, Lord Thomas Denman, and his wife, Lady Denman. The reception was held in the state drawing room, which was decorated with bowls of blue and white agapanthus, the respective team colors. Because the weather was so beautiful, the tea itself was served outside on the veranda and in the garden surrounding the fountain court. Government House was the most spectacular mansion any of the tourists had ever seen. The gardens, beneath century-old trees, were the most fragrant and exotic they had encountered. Here they posed for group photos.

The governor-general was the first foreign head of state that the tourists met on their travels. The proximity to power and the perks of authority were quite heady. Lord Denman turned out to be a regular Joe. He had been a keen cricketer in his youth and was fascinated at the prospect of seeing a baseball game. He peppered McGraw with questions about baseball and its popularity in America. He also promised to throw out the first pitch for their game if "McGraw would call next morning and teach him how to pitch."[28]

The players were delighted to discover that the charming and breath-takingly beautiful Lady Denman was quite the athlete, too. At one point Lord Denman tossed his wife a baseball from a distance of fifty feet. The remarkable Lady Denman stepped up and caught it with her bare hands, then returned to her conversation without missing a beat.

After being wined and dined by Australia's ruler in the afternoon sun, the tourists' evening entertainment was an extended smoker at the Savage Club. A classic example of British imperialism in vogue in 1914, the Savage Club was truly something else. The club's walls were decorated floor to ceiling with trophies "of the bloodthirsty type and gathered in peace and war by its members. Zulu war clubs, boomerangs, javelins, spears, muskets, swords, billies, scalping knifes, and daggers from all parts of the world."[29]

The invitations that the Melbourne Savage Club sent the tourists are true artifacts of the time. A racist caricature cartoon of an African native in a baseball uniform throws the ball to another caricatured black squatting behind the plate. At bat, another cartoon African awaits, grinning broadly, wielding a giant war club in one hand and a Zulu shield in the other. In place of the umpire a cartoon shaman dances with arms akimbo. The "African" word "Kahbooka" is spelled out by the path of the ball, beneath which is inscribed "Show the New York Giants and the Chicago White Sox how."[30]

After a night of revelry and speeches, everyone returned to the hotel to prepare for the next day's activities. Attendance promised to be outstanding, as Lord Denman and Lord Mayor Hennessey declared a half holiday for the players' benefit. As had been the case in Sydney, the Giants were scheduled to start off the festivities by playing a local nine. The Victoria Baseball Club would be the opponent.

The morning of 7 January 1914 dawned beautifully; a warm morning was followed by a delightful afternoon breeze. Most of the tourists spent the early part of the day at the zoological gardens. Zoos were popular attractions for the tourists; they visited every one they could find since the tour began in Cincinnati. Other tourists went sightseeing. True to his promise, first thing in the morning McGraw made his way to Government House. There he spent the morning teaching the governor-general how to pitch. But whatever diversion a player chose for his morning, everyone was at the Melbourne Cricket Grounds by 1:00 P.M. for lunch.

At lunch, more doors opened to the tourists. Lord Denman presented the key to all Australia to the travelers, while the prime minister presented the key to New Zealand and Tasmania. The interest of so many politicians caught the players completely off guard. Every one of the politicos, it seemed, cornered a "baseballer" (as the Australians called them) and questioned them about the sport.

Victoria's cricketers were closely following the activities of the tourists. Baseball actually had a notable following in Melbourne, with the local league boasting of a fair number of members. Unlike virtually everywhere else on earth, quite a few cricketers in Australia also played baseball. Australian cricket clubs promoted baseball as a wintertime exercise for cricketers.

Australia was in the midst of the very same debate that had raged in the United States around 1870, "Baseball or cricket, which will it be?" Some Australians were convinced that baseball was destined to win out.

Certainly Australia's cricketers learned that good baseball ability translated to better cricket skills. The proof of that was none other than Frank Laver, president of the Victorian Baseball League. In 1897 Laver had toured the world as part of a baseball team. Perhaps no one whom the tourists had come in contact with had been as personally influenced by A. G. Spalding. Spalding's 1890 tour inspired Australian baseball players to take up a challenge laid at their feet by Spalding and take their own team to the world. The Australians' tour of the world was a disaster. The players ran out of money in the United States and had to wire their homeland for enough funds to return home.

Laver revolutionized cricket when he adopted the curve ball to cricket's stiff, side-arm delivery. He had spoken at the Savage Club, holding the baseball players in thrall as he described his adventures on the diamond and explained how baseball had improved his cricket ability at all levels. Laver had been instrumental in winning the Ashes (cricket's highest honor) from England twice. He was as popular as any sportsman in Australia, and his fondness for baseball helped to make the sport more acceptable to the general public.

Laver was prominently visible when the Giants took on the Victoria club at 3:00 P.M. A large crowd of about ten thousand turned out at the Melbourne Cricket Grounds for the spectacle. Once the game began it was clear that it would not be much of a contest; the Giants completely obliterated the Aussies 18–0.

The Australian media were not quite sure of what they had just witnessed. The *Melbourne Age* was especially colorful in describing the events of the day.

It was the novelty of the thing which chiefly appealed to the spectators.

To see an American base ball team taking the field is to be greatly impressed at the outset. There are nine men a side, and the New Yorkers, as they stepped on the ground, looked a formidable and rather fearsome contingent. In size they are above average; one or two of them would easily turn the scale at 14 stone, and they added to their bulky appearance by wearing loose and baggy garments, surmounted by white hats pulled down well over their eyes. It is hard to say which they more resemble—a band of Arctic explorers, braced for a march due South or a contingent of prize fighters getting ready for the ring. The man who acts as catcher—a position corresponding to that of wicket keeper at cricket—is fearfully and wonderfully arrayed against all possible mischances of the game. He carries a heavy glove in one hand, he has his legs incased in pads of considerable size and thickness, and he wears around his body the sort of leather buckler that would be a fair protection against a Macedonian phalanx. One would not be surprised to see him mount a charger and gallop three times around the ground, defying all and sundry to mortal combat. It is rather a disappointment to find that he intends to do nothing more than stand in the base immediately behind the striker and catch the occasional balls that come his way.[31]

Most of the crowd recognized the origins of the game they were witnessing. As the writer for the *Melbourne Age* pointed out, "To say that base ball is very much like rounders—that juvenile game that which the young Australian plays with his sister until he reaches a certain age—is to state an obvious truth."[32] Ironically, in the land of cricket, a game that can take three days to play, this writer complains that baseball is too slow. "But the game as a game, seems to lack tensity and continuous interest. It is rather suggestive of a large garden party. It reminds the Australian onlooker of his first open-air picnic. It is not to tell the truth, the kind of pastime over which a crowd, other than an American crowd would be expected to get excited. It is not calculated at this stage to supplant either cricket or foot ball as a means of making Melbourne holiday."[33]

The *Melbourne Argus* was also highly critical of Australia's native base-ballers. "The players representing this State in physique seemed almost like underdeveloped and weedy youths compared with the thick set, stocky athletes they were called upon to face. Even the well-known cricketer P. McAlister, who captained the side, looked thin and narrow-chested in such company. The visitors in their street clothes give an impression of massiveness, but when they put on their padded playing costumes, the word 'Giants' describes them well."[34]

The only problem the Giants encountered while dispatching Victoria was an injury to Mike Donlin. "Turkey" Mike severely wrenched his knee rounding first, leaving him unable to play in the later game against the White Sox. As in Sydney, Bill Klem umpired the game with a local umpire, one Mr. Westwood. The duo also worked the nightcap.

The preliminary game between Victoria and New York took fifty minutes, then it was time for the main event. At 4:00 sharp Governor-General Thomas Denman walked to the rubber to throw out the ceremonial first pitch. Frank McGlynn and Victor Miller had the cameras rolling. Lord Denman, despite John McGraw's tutelage, performed his duties like virtually every other politician in history, bouncing the ball well short of the plate. Afterward, all of the players signed the ball and presented it to Lord Denman.

While the Giants won the contest 12–8, both teams, with the exception of Jim Thorpe, played subpar baseball. The reason comes from the *Melbourne Argus*.

As one of the journalists traveling with the visitors stated at the official luncheon tendered by the Melbourne Cricket Club to the Americans, baseball games in the United States are never played just after the teams have been lavishly entertained. Most of the players after yesterday's games had concluded, recalled those remarks and said, "Here, here." They fully appreciated the honor done them by the premier sporting club of Australia, but they blamed the luncheon for "spoiling" their game. "We seemed dead," said one of the White Sox stars as he pulled off his uniform, "I have never seen the boys put less life into their work before." When the long, running catches, the sprints round the diamond and the dashing rushes after batted and thrown balls are recalled, it will be wondered what the players are like when they have not dined. There were one or two who modestly kept out of sight while the luncheon was in progress—among them "Jim" Thorpe, the Indian athlete, who won distinction at Stockholm at the Olympic games. Thorpe is only at the baseball learners stage at present but, Mr. McGraw, manager of the "Giants," expects to mould him into the greatest player in the world eventually. Meanwhile, he pays him a retainer of 1,300 per annum. Thorpe naturally takes baseball very seriously, and he is always in training. He wanted to make a show yesterday, and that is why he stayed away from lunch. His abstinence we rewarded during the afternoon, when he was constantly applauded for his work in the field, and few will forget his rush around the bases on two occasions, particularly when he made a home run.[35]

This game perhaps marked Jim Thorpe's finest single day's performance on the entire tour; at Melbourne he was spectacular. Thorpe clouted two long home runs and made some spectacular outfield grabs. Although Iva does not comment much about her husband's play in her journal, she takes great delight in his performance in Melbourne and mentions how proud she is of her "Snooks."

Aside from Thorpe's performance, the Australian press was impressed with Bill Klem. As in Japan and in the States, Klem's impressive vocal cords garnered superlatives from the press. From the *Melbourne Age*:

> The umpire, who stands behind the striker, combines the duties of judge and herald; everytime [*sic*] a player went to bat, the umpire turned to the crowd, and in strident tones, with a voice that could be heard all over the grounds, announced to the listening multitude who the distinguished batsman was. Thus, it was, "Ladies and gentlemen"—(cheers)—"the striker is Jim Thorpe"—(renewed cheers)—"the undoubted champion athlete of the world." (Tremendous cheering.) If the striker happened to be caught or otherwise disposed of, the umpire sang his dirges in this fashion: "He's out!" The umpire who acted as public announcer yesterday was Mr. Klem, and the deep, sepulchral tones of his voice were greatly admired.[36]

When the game concluded, the tourists visited Melbourne's legendary white beaches for a swim and some relaxation, the favorite point being an amusement park called Luna Park. Reminiscent of New York's Coney Island, the place was crammed with people. The ballplayers received a big hand from the crowd when they entered the park, and the band broke into "The Star-spangled Banner." After an evening frolic in the tropical sands, all returned to their hotel for the next day's activities.

The following morning, 8 January 1914, would be the tourists' last day in Australia's capital. The hosts of that morning's banquet were the trustees of the Melbourne Race Course. The trustees informed the stunned players, and an utterly appalled Comiskey, that to ward off corruption, all of the race courses and cricket pitches in the nation were owned and supervised by the Australian government.

After lunch the Giants, White Sox, and the Melbourne Base Ball Club watched two teams of local schoolboys put on an exhibition. At the conclusion of their exhibition, Charles Comiskey presented the youths with a gift. The Old Roman gave each of the teams brand new uniforms and gloves, delighting the boys. Equipment scarcities were another problem impeding the growth of baseball Down Under.

Baseball had been added to the public school athletic curriculum largely through the tireless influence of Frank Laver, who once again was a prominent name and face in the crowd. Comiskey's largesse was, as usual, self-serving. "If we get the boys interested in baseball they will have men rooting for them in no time and then will follow an adoption of the really red-blooded sport for the spectator and player," is how the Old Roman passed off the thanks showered upon him for the baseball outfits. "Those of us who have been living in the land of baseball and freedom are not a bit unselfish, and if we can help the rest of the world to a little pleasure, you can always call upon us."[37]

At 1:00 P.M. it was the White Sox's turn to demolish Victoria. The Australians put on a slightly better performance this time around, actually scoring runs. The final tally, White Sox 16, Victoria 3. The fact that Victoria was able to score at all was probably a direct result of the fact that Callahan saved his normal pitching rotation and sent Germany Schaefer to the mound. Schaefer's antics on the mound drew some laughter from the more than ten thousand fans in the audience. "The pitcher's exaggerated windup and his ludicrous antics with the ball kept the crowd in roars of laughter. His shammed indignation when Egan was sent in to pitch later added to the fun."[38]

The game between the Giants and White Sox on the eighth was everything the game on the seventh had not been, well played, exciting, and close. Red Faber and Joe Benz brought everything they had to the mound, each going the distance in an eleven-inning game won by the Giants 4–3. Hooks Wiltse, who played centerfield for the injured Mike Donlin, delivered the big hit of the game, a bottom-of-the-eleventh triple, which was followed by Lee Magee's game-winning single.

Immediately after the game the players hustled over to the Spencer Street station to catch the 5:30 special express to Adelaide. The station was crowded with well-wishers and echoed with shouts of gratitude and good-byes. Mugsy turned to the throng before boarding the train. "'We will come back,' said Mr. McGraw, 'I like Australia.' As the train drew out the Americans were cheered and they replied vigorously."[39]

The rest of the evening the tourists gazed in awe at the exotic and almost unreal landscape of Australia, blazing orange under the rays of the setting sun. Others busied themselves with cards, cigars, and assorted diversions.

When nightfall arrived, the train trek became like any road trip in the States. It felt good to sleep in a train again.

The tourists arrived in Adelaide at 11:00 A.M. on 9 January 1914. Nestled on the Gulf of Saint Vincent, the capital of South Australia was the Southern Hemisphere's gateway for shipping to India and the East Indies. Unfortunately, the tourists would not be able to get more than just an impression of the city; the time allotted them in Adelaide was a brief two hours, just enough time to shake hands with the lord mayor and greet the well-wishers at the terminal. Everyone would have to be at the docks at 1:00 P.M. Their ship, the R.M.S. *Orontes*, was scheduled to sail at precisely 2:00 in the afternoon.

Back in the States it was still 8 January 1914, a day when it seemed as if all the newspaper reporters in the country realized en mass that the Federal League was going to prove a formidable opponent to baseball's established order. Charles Weeghman's vision of a ballpark and team in Chicago was edging closer to reality with his acquisition of the necessary acreage on Chicago's North Side. Established players were skipping contracts, and James A. Gilmore's pockets looked mighty deep. It would be the last date that such a blurb as the following from page two of the *Chicago Daily News* would appear: "All quiet in the base ball war—the war being busy burning more or less merrily beneath the surface." All hell was about to break out as baseball's Cold War became a global conflagration.

TEN

Sir Thomas Lipton and the
Shadow of the Pyramids

Well, by gosh, Tom, you're all right. – Germany Schaefer to Sir Thomas Lipton

The R.M.S. *Orontes* was very much like the R.M.S. *Empress of Japan*. It was a huge, three-stacked vessel whose route ran from Melbourne through the great Australian Bight to Fremantle, then north and westward through the Indian Ocean to the British colony of Ceylon, and finally to the British protectorate of Egypt. Somewhat perversely, the ship was named after a companion of the mythical Aeneas who had drowned in a shipwreck.

The voyage from Australia to Ceylon would take nine days. Before the tourists reached their destination, however, they needed to sail around the southern reaches of Australia. For three days the *Orontes* sailed through choppy seas under windy but fair skies to Fremantle, on Australia's south-west coast, arriving at 11:00 A.M. on 13 January 1914.

After a week on terra firma, some of the tourists were briefly seasick when encountering the choppy seas, but all had settled down quickly. The tourists received word via the wireless that there would be no game in Fremantle. Local organizers had been unable to secure a ball field. A disappointed crowd of expatriate Americans and Australians welcomed the tourists to town anyway. The tourists toured the town and then motorcaded to Perth in a fleet of American-manufactured automobiles, the first motorcade from one town to another since their passage from Bisbee to Douglas, Arizona, back in November, half a world away.

Perth impressed the tourists for its beauty but not for its weather. Sam Crawford was heard to exclaim, "It's a beautiful town, if only it would snow once in a while."[1] Frank Farrell likened the breezes in Perth to a "blast furnace," an opinion seconded by Iva Thorpe. In climatic terms at least, the drives across the "Outbacks" of Arizona and Australia were very similar.

In Perth, capital of Western Australia, Comiskey had the ignominy of going broke. While Comiskey had a $121,000 credit line, the Old Roman tried to pay for his dinner with his last available cash, a $20 gold Double Eagle. Perth's merchants had never seen such a coin and would not accept it as legal tender. With no other funds on his person, a humiliated Comiskey made a dash across the street to a bank. The bankers recognized the coin and exchanged the White Sox owner's money, minus $1.40 for the bank's time and troubles. The brief financial crisis resolved, the tourists scrambled back to their automobiles for a return to Fremantle and the *Orontes*. At 6:30 P.M. the *Orontes* slipped its moorings, turned north by northwest, and set sail for Colombo, the capital city of Ceylon, Great Britain's tea plantation.

As the mass of Australia disappeared astern in the twilight, the tourists settled into life at sea for the nine-day sail. The tourists picked up right where they left off. The shuffleboard league resumed its schedule, with Steve Evans and Dick Egan taking the crown. Only a game behind the champions was the team of Jim Thorpe and Hooks Wiltse; in third place, the team of John McGraw and Germany Schaefer. As the competition closed and the champions were crowned, a long, sustained cheer went up from the rest of the tourists assembled for the finals.

With shuffleboard for blood at a close, the tourists set about to thinking up more diversions. On 16 January the Onion Club was born. Created by a committee self-dubbed the "Tango Four," bachelors Germany Schaefer, Buck Weaver, Fred Merkle, and Tris Speaker were put in charge of entertainment for the rest of the tourists. The Tango Four decided that what was needed was a record player. All the tourists pitched in some cash to buy the record player from the ship's stores. A drawing was then held to determine who would be the owner of the record player and be the "official music master" for the tour. Steve Evans won the lottery and was sworn in as president of the Onion Club. The club took its name from the many crates of American onions on-loaded at Fremantle. Every evening the president of the Onion Club would eat an onion, after which he would select the tunes to which all the tourists would tango.

The rituals of the Onion Club seem bizarre till one realizes that the Tango Four were parodying the club activities and rituals that were so much a part of male life in the United States. Elks, Masons, Order of the Redman, and a slew of forgotten clubs had membership halls or lodges in every city and village in America. The era marked the last great period of club participation for men. Almost every man of any class in America belonged to a club or society. Club activity crossed political and racial lines, with many white clubs having parallel programs for African Americans. The

Knights of Columbus was birthed in this time period so that Catholic men could join a club without risking papal censure for mixing with Freemasons and other secret societies. Tris Speaker was himself an ardent Freemason who in a few years would advance to the thirty-third degree.

So well attended were the Onion Club's meetings that the regular four-piece band was exiled to the second-class deck. Most of the tourists enjoyed dancing. Jim and Iva Thorpe were outstanding dancers. When it came to filling their dance cards, the bachelors had their pick of all the lovely unattached women on board. Many joyful hours passed to the recorded strains of tangos, fox-trots, and ragtime. Dancing had entered another one of its periodic worldwide crazes. Vernon and Irene Castle's international celebrity status had given dance an air of debonair sophistication. Newspapers in many cities included instructions for the latest dance steps in their daily editions. A dance could be created in London and three weeks later be all the rage in St. Louis. Along with the increased popularity of dancing came editorials in small town papers and dire warnings from the pulpit of the dangers and corrupting influences of public dancing. The popularity of dancing definitely had a generational component as well. Older members of the tour, such as umpires Jack Sheridan and Bill Klem, did not know how to dance. Neither Comiskey nor McGraw was ever seen out cutting the rug.

One of the more amusing pranks carried out on the *Orontes* occurred during the sail to Fremantle, on the twelfth day of January. Like schoolchildren, a group of tourists played follow the leader. Jim Thorpe was selected to lead this day's band of adventurers. He led the tourists, both male and female, all over the decks of the great ship. When he spied Charles Comiskey resting in a deck chair, the hero of Carlisle had an impish inspiration. Thorpe leaned over the Old Roman and kissed him. Everyone in line followed his lead. Comiskey did a slow burn; he didn't even like shaking hands with his own ballplayers! Thorpe's stunt was the perfect antidote to Comiskey's attitude.

After assaulting the White Sox's owner, the players really got carried away. Their next target was Mrs. Hugh Keough. The widow of Hugh Keough, late Chicago sportswriter and photographer, had gotten engaged (in her eyes at least) to Mike Donlin while on tour. Donlin, a true cad, though widowed himself for a little more than a year, was already engaged to one Rita Ross of Asbury Park, New Jersey. "Turkey" Mike, upon witnessing the mass kissing of Keough, feigned outrage and promptly broke the "engagement."

Unlike all the other ships upon which the tourists had sailed, the crew of the R.M.S. *Orontes* was entirely British. Before long the tourists were pining for an efficient Chinese crew; all of the previous vessels on which they had sailed had been staffed with a Chinese crew. Jimmy Callahan, livid with frustration, berated the service. "If they're pressing your suit, they forget to remove the iron. If they spill a plate of soup on your brand new Tux, if they step on your feet, if they overcharge in the buffet, if they forget to return your change, if they allow the juice of a stewed prune to light upon your last clean dress shirt; they're sorry, sir, so sorry. They say it so often it sounds like a Mohammedian chant."[2] It was almost enough to send the adamantly pro-Irish Callahan over the edge.

Most of the diversions aboard the *Orontes* matched those of the *St. Albans*; even deck cricket was available. Hans Lobert's performance with the cricket bat greatly impressed the citizens of England witnessing his performance, one of whom was heard to remark, "What a pity that that young man should devote his life to base ball when he could be such a marvelous figure in cricket."[3] Among the English passengers, Lord and Lady Hackett inspired a great deal of gossip. Lady Hackett, still in her teens, made every man's head turn and every jaw drop; her husband, Lord Hackett, was a doddering old man pushing seventy. Iva Thorpe, for one, was appalled at the relationship.

The tourists certainly were a mystical bunch, receiving visits from both Father Christmas and the lord of the deep himself, King Neptune. On 19 January 1914 King Neptune (looking suspiciously like Bill Klem) appeared on board with his court. A day's sail south of the equator, King Neptune and his secretary, Sinbad, announced that any who had not previously crossed the equator should prepare for initiation the next day into the Ancient Order of Salts. The king and his court then inspected all the liquid libations on board and disappeared.

The next day Neptune returned; this time his doctor and his barber were part of his court. At precisely 2:30 P.M. the festivities began. This ritual, or variations of it, have been a part of life on the seven seas since at least the days of Magellan. Frank McGlynn describes what transpired.

A great platform was erected near the stern of the ship, just above the steerage quarters. In front of this was a huge canvas tank filled with salt water. The victim who was taken by Neptune's police was tried for encroaching for the first time on equatorial waters. The usual penalty was that they be shorn and shaven, and immediately a white brush was dipped into lather (no one knows what it was made of) from a bucket, and spread over the entire visage and head of the unfortunate culprit. The barber then proceeded to shave him with a wooden razor two feet in length amid shrieks of laughter from the onlookers. The lather was finally removed after taking handcuffs from the prisoner's wrists and tossing him into the arms of sturdy men, who stood in the tank waiting to give him the dunking that through the afternoon was the fate of nearly every stoker, petty officer, and seaman on the ship.[4]

Also dunked were all male members of the touring party. After the baptism by Neptune, each participant received a "certificate of admittance." Lee Magee's read, "This is to certify that Lee Magee is hereby admitted to the FREEDOM OF THE SEAS, into the ANCIENT ORDER OF SALTS, he having been duly baptized in the presence of his most watery Majesty, King Neptune. Signed, Sinbad, his most watery Majesty's Secretary."[5]

Magee paid more attention to the contents of the lather he was smeared with. According to Magee, the lather consisted of "flour paste and axle grease." Before being lathered up, the initiates were anointed with a noxious mixture of "vitriol, soap, machine oil, and turpentine."[6] At 11 P.M. the *Orontes* crossed the equator, and Bill Klem, mysteriously absent during Neptune's visit, was once again sighted on deck.

That evening the tourists were entertained with performances by the stewards of the *Orontes*. One was an accomplished Cockney comedian who drew big laughs. Another steward was an amateur escape artist, aping Houdini with a pair of handcuffs. The showstopper, however, was a magician. A steward took Bunny Hearn's proffered gold pocket-watch. He then, apparently, smashed it to bits. Bunny Hearn was then presented with a loaf of bread, a knife, and instructions to cut the loaf in half. Sure enough, nestled within the loaf, Hearn's watch awaited discovery, unharmed and still ticking. While fairly mundane by our standards, the trick mesmerized the tourists. Even Frank McGlynn, who had seen Blackstone and Houdini, was awed.

The most significant event of the next day, Wednesday, 21 January, occurred in the form of a Marconigram that read, "Would be delighted if you lunch with me. Galle Face Hotel, Thursday, 1 o'clock. Kindly say how many. Lipton."[7] The Lipton whose name appeared at the bottom of the wireless message was none other than Sir Thomas Lipton, and he was inviting every member of the party to a reception and luncheon on the twenty-second at the Galle Face Hotel in Colombo. The tourists did not waste a second in replying in the affirmative. Arriving in Colombo at 9:00 A.M. on the following morning, the *Orontes* anchored deep in the harbor. The tourists piled in to a steam transport and arrived at the docks. Ceylon looked like paradise—brilliant white sand, stately palm trees, and a landscape studded with beautiful, exotic flowers. Singhalese men poled their catamarans over the water garbed only in long, beautiful sarongs, their shiny black hair fixed in place by ornate golden combs. A good portion of the natives went about naked or nearly so. The women's exotic beauty enthralled the men and irked the wives. Many of the natives chewed betel leaf, which in addition to its slight narcotic effect stains the teeth and gums a bright red. At first glance, the tourists thought that the islanders were wearing excessive amounts of lipstick or, worse, were suffering from the worst cases of bleeding gum disease in human history.

Their hotel, the Galle Face, sat right on the beautiful blue Indian Ocean. Four stories tall, the hotel lacked for nothing. Built in 1864, its simple yet elegant Victorian lines made it very popular with visitors. The location could not be beat; not only was it on the beach, but it was also downtown. The American consul's offices were an easy walk from the Galle Face. If one were disinclined to walk, rickshas were available. Those human-powered vehicles seemed to appear wherever the British held power.

Ceylon was known to the ancients as Taprobane (Greek for copper colored). When Muslim traders came across the island, they named it Serendip, which gives us our English word "serendipity," an accidental discovery. The island has entranced whole empires. India, Portugal, the Dutch, and the English had by turns controlled it. Since 1796 the British reigned supreme, with no Englishman wielding more power on the island than Sir Thomas Lipton.

Like a character out of the novels of Charles Dickens or Horatio Alger, Thomas Lipton was the epitome of a self-made man. Born in bitter poverty in Glasgow, Scotland, as a youth Lipton had made his way to the United States. In America, Lipton toiled at a variety of menial jobs—migrant farmworker, newspaper boy, deckhand. Upon returning to England, Lipton became a businessman, opening the world's first department store.

A genius at advertising, Lipton lured people into his store through all sorts of gimmicks. One of his favorite promotions for opening a store was to have a huge piece of cheese made with a gold coin inside. The cheese was then sliced and distributed for free. Crowds would turn out hoping to nab the golden slice. These same crowds would then spend far more in Lipton's stores than the cheese cost. The 150-pound fruitcake presented to the tourists in Seattle, which was now, like the players, circling the globe on its third ship, was inspired by Lipton's legendary store cheeses. Store ownership provided Lipton an entrée into the tea importation business, where he made his fortune. What Bill Gates would one day do for computer software, Thomas Lipton did for tea.

It could be rightfully said that Sir Thomas Lipton almost single-handedly changed how the British Empire took its tea. He revolutionized the industry, changing everything about it. How tea was shipped, how it was brewed, where and how it was grown, all were altered through Lipton's ingenuity. Now at the age of sixty-three, the man on the tea box held an impressive list of accomplishments, including a knighthood, innumerable yachting trophies, the creation of soccer's World Cup, worldwide recognition, and popular acclaim. Lipton was the richest man in all the British Empire and probably the richest man in all the world.

His experiences in the United States in the 1870s had turned Lipton into a complete American-phile. He had seen baseball at every level in America, from Major League games in America's most storied stadiums to the game at its most basic level of tenement streets and rural sandlots. He claimed to love baseball more than cricket. Since the entire American population of Colombo in 1914 was just five lonely souls, Lipton may very well have been the most knowledgeable baseball fan on the whole island. In 1912 Lipton had attended a World Series game at the Polo Grounds. Gus Axelson recorded Lipton's feelings toward baseball. " 'I hope,' he said to President Comiskey later, 'that you will be able to play in England. I want to see the game introduced in the British Isles. I like baseball myself, probably because I got used to it in the United States.' "[8]

Aside from his stores and beverages, Lipton was also familiar to many Americans as a yachtsman. Dubbed "the Loveable Loser" by the American press, Lipton was continually stymied in his quest for the one yachting trophy that had so far eluded him, the America's Cup. Three times the Scotsman had contested for the cup; each time his yachts, each one named *Shamrock*, reached the finals only to be trounced by the defending champion Americans. Undaunted, the *Shamrock IV* was at that moment being constructed in a boatyard near Chicago according to Lipton's specifications.

The Scotsman even had an impact in the worlds of fashion and botany. History records that Thomas Lipton was the first man to wear a colored necktie. Before Lipton scandalized London and appeared wearing a blue bow tie with white polka dots, men had exactly two choices, solid black or white. Every male neckwear trend since, from the bola with a rhinestone slide to hand-painted silk ties, wide or narrow neckties, those of rayon or leather, are the direct result of Lipton's foppishness.

Lipton's popularity inspired one gardener to name his hybrid white roses the Thomas Lipton. The hardy white roses were perfect for planting in colder northern climes. Like its namesake, the Thomas Lipton Rose is stocky, resilient, and perennial.

Lipton first hit Ceylon in 1889, just after Spalding's All-Stars had toured the island. Tea had become the main product of Ceylon decades earlier when a blight destroyed the island's coffee industry. Before Lipton, tea on the island was grown in scattered plantations, generally run by English settlers and landlords. Lipton spent lavishly, buying up as many tea plantations as he could, then consolidating his holdings. Now instead of relying on distant, often unreliable or low-quality sources from China and other parts of Asia, Lipton could control price and quality while shortening shipping routes considerably. Lipton's rule was absolute and his economic impact on the island enormous. Before Lipton's arrival, Ceylon was a sleepy, isolated possession, which Britain largely ignored. Now the island was an essential link in the British economy, with tens of thousands of people directly or indirectly dependant upon Ceylon's tea industry for their livelihoods. In Ceylon itself, Lipton employed thousands of Singhalese whom, depending upon which sources you believe, he ruled either as a grandfatherly, mostly benevolent dictator or as a cantankerous, pernicious slave master.

Sir Thomas Lipton met the tourists at the docks as they arrived at 9:00 A.M. For the entire day he served as escort and host. After everyone reached the Galle Face, Lipton led a sight-seeing motorcade about Colombo, even driving the lead car.

The history of the island's various occupations remained visible in its warring architectures. Portuguese boathouses, Dutch administration buildings, English banks and hotels, Hindu temples, all added to the exotic lure of the city.

The tour concluded just in time for lunch. The noon meal promised to be spectacular. It would be held in a huge conservatory that abutted the banquet hall of the Galle Face. Best of all, Sir Thomas Lipton would be footing the bill. It is not every day that the richest man in the world picks up your tab.

After freshening up and dressing for lunch, the tourists made their way to the conservatory where Lipton was holding court. Looking as dapper as ever, Lipton greeted the tourists in his trademark blue polka-dot tie, white slacks, and charcoal waistcoat and jacket. Later, when they ventured out-of-doors, Lipton topped off this ensemble with a white pith helmet.

Sir Thomas then opened the proceedings with the following announcement. "Ladies and Gentlemen, I want you to feel just as much at home as if you were in New York or Chicago."[9] A short time later Lipton was regaling the tourists gathered round his table with the story of his life (the Lipton authorized version of it, that is). While Lipton paused in midspeech, Germany Schaefer placed his hand on Lipton's shoulder and said, "Well, by gosh, Tom, you're all right." Lipton immediately sensed that Schaefer was making a sincere offer of friendship. After a pause lasting for only a few seconds, he extended his right hand and replied, "Schaef, old boy, put it there." The rest of the afternoon the two addressed each other as "Tom" and "Schaef," as though they had known each other their entire lives. Sometime later Jimmy Callahan confided in Frank McGlynn, "Nobody in the world but Germany Schaefer could have said what he said and had it so quickly understood and accepted."[10]

After lunch all the tourists and Lipton gathered on the wide lawn of the hotel for pictures. McGlynn and Miller pulled out their movie equipment, capturing some great candids of Lipton interacting with his guests. They also shot footage of a Tamil snake charmer who had been brought in to entertain the group. The tourists made a circle on the lawn about the Hindu snake charmer, with the Callahan children front and center. It was like watching a chapter out of Rudyard Kipling's *Jungle Book* come to life, minus the mongoose.

Lipton's love for children is obvious in the photographs taken on the lawn. Margaret Callahan, dressed in white, her straight black hair surmounted by an enormous white bow, got to sit on the millionaire's lap. For another photo, her brother, Danny, dressed in short pants and wearing a Buster Brown haircut that made him look very much like a smaller version of his sister, got to share his sibling's perch. Though Lipton had two children of his own, he was estranged from their mother even while she was pregnant with his second son. His first son died in childhood, and Lipton had no contact whatsoever with his only surviving heir. Such inconsistencies did not stop Lipton from adoring others' children.

With photography and motion picture taking concluded, the tourists began to get serious about what their tour was officially supposed to be about: playing baseball. The players hustled to the Victoria Gardens racetrack, where the game was scheduled to be played. At 3:30 P.M. all was ready for the first pitch. Despite the lateness of the start of the game, five thousand people turned out. The crowd was certainly not there because they were baseball fans. If Ceylon's citizens were familiar with any Western sport it was cricket. Cricket fields dotted Colombo's parks and plantations. The fact that the game was free, was well advertised, and that Sir Thomas Lipton would be in attendance were probably the reasons that so many turned out at the racetrack. This crowd was like no other the tourists had played before—Singhalese men in their sarongs with golden combs in their hair, turbans on Indian Brahmans, Englishmen in formal dress, England's Sikh police force with their silver daggers glistening in the sun, Tamils in their native dress.

Because the game got off to such a late start, the teams were able to play only five innings before twilight set in. The White Sox won the game 4–1. Mike Donlin was back in the Giants lineup, his knee having healed nicely on the voyage to Ceylon. The teams were having so much fun in Colombo that baseball became a definite afterthought. For the first time some of the ballplayers didn't even bother putting on their uniforms. Only Walter Leverenz of the Sox and the Giants' Bunny Hearn dressed for the game; the rest of the pitchers—Scott, Faber, and Wiltse—went shopping.

After the game Lipton hosted a ball for the players. He was a gracious host, autographing all of their menus, accepting a baseball signed by every member of the party, and inviting them all to visit him on his yacht when he challenged for the America's Cup later in the year. Lipton danced with all the women and often asked Germany Schaefer, "Schaef, will you join me?"[11]

Lipton told of his quest for the America's Cup. He recited anew one of his favorite jokes. "I drank my tea from a saucer for the reason that I could not lift the cup." His many near misses and the jovial attitude he maintained while coming so close to glory endeared him to the media and the public at large. After all, who couldn't identify with finishing second? One of his favorite tales involved his beloved yachts. When the first *Shamrock* was anchored off the coast of Tompkinsville, Germany, a local man was blessed with a son. In honor of the famous yacht's arrival, the German farmer gave his son the first and middle names of Thomas and Lipton. A few years later *Shamrock II* weighed anchor off Tompkinsville, and again the farmer's wife delivered a son. Sure enough when the *Shamrock III* arrived in Tompkinsville, so did another German baby boy. When Lipton heard of this amazing coincidence, he invited the couple to tour his yacht, and they in turn sincerely wished that he would win the cup.

Comiskey and McGraw thanked Lipton for his hospitality. The Giants' skipper concluded the speechmaking as diplomatically as possible. He said, "While I as an American, cannot say that I wish Sir Thomas would win the cup, I do hope that it will be a very close contest."[12]

The postgame ball went on until 11:00 at night. At that hour the tourists reboarded the tender and returned to the *Orontes*. The tourists had tried to talk Captain Staunton of the *Orontes* into staying at least one more day. Lipton had hoped to give them all an opportunity to see Kandy, summer capital of the island in its precolonial apex. However, Staunton had firm orders to be in Suez on the first day of February. Touring Kandy, with its wonderful history and fantastic art and temples, would require at least a two-day layover. Though Staunton was fond of the tourists, he was more attached to his own paycheck.

Sir Thomas Lipton accompanied the tourists on their return to the *Orontes*, where the party atmosphere continued. Revelries were not completed until 2:00 A.M., when Lipton went over the rail of the *Orontes*, boarded one of his own yachts in the harbor, and made his way home. At the same moment, two hours behind schedule, the *Orontes* slid out of Colombo's harbor and into a stone calm Indian Ocean.

After Lipton sailed off the tourists discovered that the Scotsman had one more surprise in store for them. He had hidden aboard the ship about four hundred pounds of his finest Ceylonese tea. Every tourist discovered handsomely made teak boxes, each inscribed with their name, containing their portion of tea.

The next morning Comiskey and McGraw sent a Marconigram to Lipton, thanking him for his hospitality and his generosity. The women wanted it to be made clear in the message how especially grateful they were for the tea. Every member of the touring party attached his or her name to the wireless message. Lipton responded to this note with humility. In closing, his final words to the tourists were, "I'll catch up to you in London."[13] Most of the tourists would recall their stay with Sir Thomas Lipton as the social highlight of the tour. His closing words made it tempting to steam ahead directly to England and skip the rest of the tour. But no one wanted to miss the Pyramids.

In Colombo, to their total delight, the world travelers discovered that American newspapers were available. The players greedily devoured every sports page they could get their hands on. The extent of the Federal League's challenge to the Majors became known to them for the first time. What the owners had considered a joke was getting the last laugh. Players were jumping their contracts with the established Major Leagues for much better offers from the upstart Federals. Everyone realized that they were worth a great deal more than they were being paid by Comiskey and McGraw.

They read of trade rumors involving Dick Egan and Mickey Doolan. For the first time they learned that Thomas Lynch had been replaced by Pennsylvania governor John K. Tener as president of the National League. Coincidently, Tener had visited Colombo as a member of Spalding's touring All-Stars. The players promptly drank a toast to the new president of the National League, wishing him good health and good fortune. He was definitely going to need it. Tener would continue in his duties as governor while presiding over the National League. At the same time, both he and the American League's Ban Johnson would be engaged in combat against the rival league in a battle that promised to get very messy very quickly.

The promise of fast cash with the Federal League inspired much conversation among the players. Right now, the money figures the players were throwing around amounted to just so much bull. They could not imagine life without the reserve clause, so the money that the papers claimed the Federal League was paying seemed unreal. None of them had any idea how soon and how temptingly real those Federal League offers would become.

There were more things to do than speculate about the Feds. The weather was spectacular, especially in the evenings. While the seas were a bit choppy, the ship made relatively good time, averaging 190 knots against a headwind on 23 January and 396 knots on the twenty-fourth. Late in the evening of the twenty-third, the *Orontes* entered the Arabian Sea. A huge albatross with a wingspan of between eight and ten feet immediately began to shadow the ship. The appearance of this apparition caused a great deal of conversation between Captain Staunton, his crew, and passengers. Normally, the limit to the albatross's range is some two hundred miles south. They rarely venture out of the South Pacific. For those on board who had read their Coleridge, the bird must have been an eerie sight indeed.

On the evening of the twenty-fifth, the *Orontes* Social Club hosted a formal ball. For the single men, this meant another opportunity to make mischief. With the assistance of movie director and former stage actor Frank McGlynn, several of the men set about to conspire to deceive. Utilizing McGlynn's expertise in makeup, Joe Benz, Fred Merkle, and Jack Bliss dressed as German counts, complete with neatly trimmed mustaches and goatees. Joe Farrell donned a stovepipe hat, false whiskers, and a wart to become Abraham Lincoln. The quartet then mingled with the partygoers. McGlynn played the part of the straight man.

To the bachelors' delight, no one recognized them under their disguises. For the rest of the evening the German "counts" conquered the *Orontes*. Merkle and Benz, who had both grown up in German American communities, mimicked the German accents they had heard all their lives, injecting enough real German to convince the English passengers that genuine Teutonic nobility was sharing their first-class accommodations.

The following morning the *Orontes* entered the Gulf of Aden. An unspoiled gulf in 1914, dolphins and flying fish abounded. For the first time since they had sailed the Pacific, whales were sighted close to the ship. This time it was grampus cavorting about the ship for nearly an hour before it entered the Red Sea. Grampus, which comes from the Greek for "one from hell," was an early name for the killer whale.

The pod of killer whales seemed to take delight in playing about the *Orontes*. One whale in particular shadowed the ship, swimming alongside and spouting constantly. The presence of the grampus caused the tourists to start a rhyming contest. Whoever could compose the best rhyme about the grampus would be the winner. Joe Benz put his punishing wit to work and composed this "winning" entry.

> The Blowing Grampus
> "Enough of this."
> Said Benz to Bliss,
> "Let's stop this young typhoon."
> "For aught we know,"
> Said Jack to Joe,
> "He'll think he's a simoon."[14]

For those reaching for your dictionaries, a "simoon" (also spelled "simoom") is a mythical creature residing in the winds of the Nile, which when roused causes sudden, deadly, and violent desert storms.

The albatross disappeared astern, and at last the tourists got a glimpse of the tour's fourth continent, Africa. The Somaliland coast appeared over the horizon, ancient mountains rising above an exotic and impossibly beautiful land. In rapid succession the *Orontes* rounded Cape Gwardafuy on the Somali coast, then passed Abyssinia (Ethiopia) and Eritrea before threading Bab el Mandeb, the inlet to the Red Sea. The inlet was called "the Gateway of Tears" with good reason; the tourists saw several recently wrecked ships dotting the coastline. Three lighthouses in close proximity offered silent testimony to the treacherous nature of the waters. One wreck was so recent that salvage operations were still going on. Those aboard the *Orontes* watched men offloading the large vessel's cargo into small boats. Many ancient boats plied these waters. The color, sounds, and smells were like nowhere else on earth, familiar as a Sunday school lesson yet as alien as the far side of the moon. The tourists were very much aware of the history and import of the lands through which they were traveling.

As the *Orontes* sailed passed Perim Island with the coast of Africa on the left and the Arab peninsula on the right, some of the more experienced English travelers and crew members told the tourists of the dangerous cannibals residing in Africa and of the fierce Arab war parties in the desert vastness. Though it existed mostly for show, the *Orontes* did carry a small cannon, which Captain Staunton was permitted to use. The cannon's sole use was to give the ship's passengers a sense of security. Truly determined pirates would not have been slowed in the least.

On 28 January, while sailing in the Red Sea, the *Orontes* passed close to the city of Mocha on the Arab peninsula. At the same time, Frank McGlynn enticed John McGraw to perform for the camera. What exactly he did for the film director is lost to history. The only reference to it comes from Lee Magee, who wrote cryptically that McGraw "does several mysterious stunts before the camera."[15] That evening everyone commenced to packing, three days ahead of time in preparation for offloading in Suez.

After two days of choppy seas, the *Orontes* neared the port of Suez. The highlight, however, was on the port side—Mount Sinai, which could be seen clearly even though it was seventy-five miles inland. Mount Sinai was where, according to Exodus, Moses received the Ten Commandments. For all of the tourists, seeing the mountain was a great privilege.

Word came down through the pursers that the tourists should be ready the next morning at 8:00 A.M. to disembark at Suez. This came as a shock to most of the tourists, who had expected to leave the *Orontes* when it reached Port Said on the Mediterranean. Rather than sail through the Suez Canal on board the *Orontes*, Comiskey and McGraw discovered that they could save seventeen hours by getting off at Suez and taking the train to Cairo.

On 31 January 1914, the evening before they arrived at Suez, the *Orontes* sailed close enough to shore that local peddlers in their humble watercraft could approach the great ship. Joe Farrell aptly coined these colorful but pesky vessels "bumboats." By now the tourists had encountered enough of these boats to know the ins and outs of haggling. The best bargainer on board was Buck Weaver, who was promptly assigned the task of purchasing all the souvenirs. The Arabian sea "bumboats" offered olive-wood carvings, seashells, bits of coral, ivory trinkets, and pieces of fabric.

Arriving at Suez promptly at 8:00 A.M., the tourists prepared for transit to shore. To accomplish this unscheduled task, a small tender hauling a leaky, rusting, ancient barge pulled alongside the *Orontes*. All of the tourists' luggage was unceremoniously dumped overboard into the waiting hands of Egyptian porters. Then a gangway was laid between the two vessels, and with the assistance of the porters, the tourists joined their luggage. It was the most unseaworthy vessel the tourists had ever set foot upon. The barge bobbed along behind the tender like a metal cork. The two-mile journey to shore seemed interminable. Aside from wobbling like a drunken seagull, the barge was so decrepit they could practically hear it rust. There were, of course, no seats, so the tourists made do with steamer trunks and suitcases. Compounding the misery, a cold front rolled in, bringing a chilling wind. The tourists were used to the tropical warmth of the Indian Ocean, and the northern winds felt much colder then they actually were. Worse, there was no way to get warm; all of their warm clothing was inaccessible, buried somewhere in whatever piles of luggage that weren't being used as furniture.

At last the barge made landfall. In their haste to reach their train, Suez passed as a blur. The players stayed just long enough for each one to buy a fez before passing through customs and making sure that all of their luggage was accounted for. Then, fezzes, tourists, and luggage disappeared into a specially chartered Egyptian State Railway train. The Egyptian rail service had been hard-pressed to provide a proper train at such short notice. Just two sleeper cars were the best they could do. One of the sleepers was turned over to the women of the party; the other became the stag center of the universe. Since there were more men in the party than women, there were barely enough bunks to go around. Owners, players, and fans wedged themselves into berths as the train began to roll. Despite, or perhaps because of, the early hour, the familiar hum of steel wheels on steel tracks soon had everyone nodding off to sleep. For the next twelve hours the Egyptian landscape passed as an impressionist image painted on a canvas of dreams.

The tourists reached Cairo on 1 February 1914. They arrived at 7:00 A.M., only to be ushered to another special train to Heliopolis, a Cairo suburb where the last khedive of Egypt, Abbas II, resided. The hotel to which they were assigned, the Heliopolis Palace Hotel, was probably the swankiest hotel in the world. In addition to having some of the best gourmet chefs, the hotel's interiors were straight out of tales of the Arabian nights.

Built to cater to the tastes and sensibilities of the English who controlled Egypt and the many thousands of tourists who made their way to the Pyramids, the hotel created a Middle Eastern fantasy for its guests. Even in 1913 thousands of tourists made their way to Giza. The hotel was originally envisioned as a Monte Carlo of the Middle East; however, its investors were never able to overcome the khedive's objections to legalized gambling. They still made out handsomely, however. Unlike today's travelers, there were no budget tours. Only the wealthy or those prepared to spend enormous sums could hope to visit the Land of the Pharaohs.

Wintering in Egypt was a rite of passage for children of the wealthy. English and European students from all of the elite schools made holiday in Egypt, Italy, and Greece, absorbing and reveling in the glories of the ancients. American millionaires made pilgrimages to the Pyramids just as often as their European cousins. The industrial age and the wealth it spawned gave more people access to travel than ever before, much to the chagrin of the silk-shirt set.

Mrs. George W. Holland, a banker's widow, aired her complaints to the *New York Times* on 7 December 1913. While the Giants and White Sox were limping into Japan, Holland was returning from her holiday in the Old World. "The whole of the Orient has become either Anglicized or Americanized," said Holland. "You don't see any kind of hotels but English or American, and the primitive accommodations which, in spite of the hardships they sometimes entailed, helped to make the journey interesting, have given way to comfort and luxury approaching that of New York."[16]

Reflecting on the rapid changes she had witnessed in twenty-five years of traveling, Holland stated,

> When I first went up the Nile to Assouan [sic] there was only one substantial building on the spot and two or three mud houses. Nowadays Assouan with its shops and motor cars has become a little London. Where formerly when you went out to the Tombs of the kings by donkey and made your way through long tunnels by the aid of a flickering candle light, and part of the time you had to crawl to get throught [sic] narrow places, you now ride out comfortably in sand carts to find the tombs lighted throughout by electricity and a million or so steps leading down through roomy passages. They wouldn't even keep those resting places of the ancient Pharaohs sacred from the invasion of modern improvements. The result is that nothing you see in the Near and Far East is anything like as interesting as it used to be.[17]

While Holland may not have been happy with Egypt's transformation, the Egyptians themselves were quite pleased. As the tourists were being escorted to the Heliopolis Palace Hotel, their guides were quick to point out proudly the power supply. As Lee Magee noted, "[The] electric lines to the Heliopolis Palace Hotel, claimed to be the most magnificent in the world."[18] Arriving at the hotel at 7:00 A.M., while the desert air still chilled, the tourists were treated to a lavish gourmet breakfast, which they hungrily devoured.

By 8:30 in the morning the tourists were on their way to the Gizeh Plain. All traveled by automobile, a method that Holland would no doubt disapprove of. Donkeys and camels awaited at the plains so that all of the tourists could ride to the Pyramids in comfort and pose for photographs astride a camel. The cameras came out, and everyone got their pictures taken on the back of a camel, Comiskey looking much like a Middle Eastern potentate atop his "ship of the desert." For the next three hours the ballplayers toured the Pyramids and the Sphinx. To the party's delight, the word "LIPTON" was inscribed above the entrance to the Great Pyramid. Their most recent host had paid an Egyptian to have the advertisement chiseled into the stone lintel of the landmark. One of the few times that Sir Thomas's genius for advertising got the better of him, his pyramid stunt provoked much anger among the Egyptians. The British authorities, for the most part, just snickered at the tea man's stunt.

In the afternoon the touring party returned to the Heliopolis Palace Hotel for a spectacular lunch and to prepare for the game. Baseball's first Egyptian exhibition in twenty-five years occurred at 2:30 in the afternoon of 1 February 1914 at the Heliopolis Sporting Club. Abbas II served as host along with U.S. ambassador Olney Arnold. Before the game the khedive held an audience with Comiskey, McGraw, Callahan, Thorpe, and their wives. A keen sportsman, the khedive had been educated in England, becoming an avid polo player. His English was perfect.

The khedives had ruled Egypt from the days of the Ottomans until Napoleon's conquest. When the English took Egypt from Napoleon, they restored the khedive as their puppet. While those in his country increasingly chafed under British rule, Abbas II had become in many respects as English as the English. Though the khedive was officially royalty, Gus Axelson pithily pegged the nature of his power. "[The khedive] holds what amounts to a little less than a second mortgage on the Land of the Pharoes."[19]

As the first royal they would meet, all of the tourists were unsure of what to expect. "There were no Royal robes on him. Members of the American party who had preceded him to the clubhouse had looked for a dazzling display of gold lace, but they saw a man of medium height, dressed in an afternoon costume familiar in America and Europe, the only change being a red fez."[20]

The khedive invited the players' wives to sit next to him as they all watched the baseball game. Axelson again, "Most of the members were not sure whether to stand up, sit down or act naturally. When it was discovered that his highness was just like any other mortal, that he talked good English and was apt at interrogating the Americans on the national pastime the tension was relieved, and from then until the end of the fourth inning, when he departed, there was a real fan talk in Cairo."[21]

The khedive and the wives had the best seats in the house, a balcony above the field. A diamond had been laid out on the field of pebbles and rocks, which was normally used for playing polo. Though the khedive was called away to attend to matters of state, his departure did little to stanch the enthusiasm of the crowd of two thousand assembled to watch the game. No one painted a better picture of the first baseball game played in Egypt in a quarter of a century than Gus Axelson, whose vivid description appeared in the *Chicago Record-Herald* of 27 February 1914.

There were probably 2,000 within the inclosure of the Sports Club's ground at the opening game. Many Americans were in the crowd. The majority were English, and there was a fair sprinkling of Germans, Frenchmen and persons of other nationalities, including a number of prominent Egyptians. On the outskirts were the Arab of the desert, while the lowly fellaheen crouched low among the ribbon of shrubbery in right field. In the distance could be seen the "ships of the desert" in long caravans ambling in from the wilderness beyond. The bright red uniforms of the British soldiers looked doubly scarlet against the dull shades of the sandy wastes back of Evans' and Magee's territory in left field.

It is unlikely that any ball game has ever been played before a greater mixture of races. Besides those mentioned there were Armenians, Turks, Greeks, Syrians, and Persians. There was hardly a country in Europe which did not have its representatives. Then there were the many tribes and races of Egypt itself, those descended from the Nubians, Copts, and Ethiopians. Most of these looked on with a critical eye, but with the interest with which the youngster regards the first circus. It was American to them, which goes as "Greek" with us.

There was nothing except a wire fence around the field, but few viewed the game who had not settled at the gate. The prices were on the sliding scale, the best seats being chairs placed outside a wire netting back of the diamond, costing 40 plaster, or $2.08. There was nothing cheap about Egypt.[22]

The rock-hard surface, which played like the cement under an Astroturf pad in one of today's multipurpose stadiums, was normally used for polo. The equine athletes probably felt as brutalized by the field as did the American athletes. Despite having the worst playing surface of any place on the planet, Cairo inspired some of the best play anywhere. The wretched playing field left everything to be desired, but if one looked beyond the plain wire fence one could find charm and exotica. Huge palm trees bounded the field, the clubhouse offered the best amenities, and the botanical gardens were visible in the background.

Competition between the two teams reached a fever pitch in Cairo. McGraw's Giants were only two games behind the Sox at this point, and Mugsy badly wanted to tie things up before the teams hit Europe. As in everything else in life, baseball's Little Napoleon hated to finish anywhere but first. Reduced to just three pitchers, journeyman Bunny Hearn, aging veteran Hooks Wiltse, and the borrowed and still green Red Faber, the Giants had struggled on the world stage.

McGraw played for blood in Cairo, pulling out all the stops. This first game ended after ten innings in a 3–3 tie. Called on account of darkness, the contest satisfied everyone present save the sullen Giants manager. Jim Thorpe's play that day was absolutely spectacular. Accounting for all of the Giants' runs, he led off the game with a solo home run, then followed this feat with two hits, each driving in runs.

After the game the teams returned to the Heliopolis Palace Hotel for a sumptuous dinner. At 7:00 in the evening everyone went on sight-seeing expeditions. The athletes toured Cairo in Model T's, experiencing the city by gaslight. The driving abilities of the Egyptian chauffeurs left much to be desired. Joe Benz, Fred Merkle, and Jack Bliss discovered just how far behind the curve local drivers were in comparison to hackers in the States. Frank McGlynn chronicles their misadventures.

> The machine in going across one of the principal thoroughfares collided with a carriage in which was seated a beautiful Egyptian lady and her escort. Screams rent the air. The driver of the team slashed the chauffeur with his whip. Arabic execrations were poured forth in abundance, but finally the tangle was straightened and the party proceeded. Going a little further on, the rise of the hill, the engine on, the antiquated machine went dead, and the boys thought the better thing to do was to climb the hill on foot. After taking a view of the city below them by moonlight they walked back to the car, which by this time showed signs of life, and skidded a tremendous looking grade to the level ground. A few blocks later the machine went dead again. The Arab guide, who spoke excellent English, said, "Come, gentlemen, we will get another machine;" so leaving the chocolate colored native to fathom the difficulty with his motor, he hailed another taxi, also guided by an Arab. In his haste to get his "fare" the latter failed to see a carriage which was crossing his beam, and a collision took place, which threw the horse vehicle about twenty feet against the curb. A sure enough fight began. What the outcome of this affair was the boys never knew, for the astute guide said; "Come along, this is none of our affair," and hailing an antiquated carriage drawn by two Arab steeds, who looked like candidates for the boneyard, he bade them jump aboard, and in Arabic told the Jehn to whip up for the Heliopolis Hotel. The two skates, despite their miserable looking condition, clattered over the roadway at a tremendous clip, and the

old rattletrap seemed in imminent danger of parting at any moment. However, after a drive of several miles at top speed the boys were landed in safety at the steps of the hotel.[23]

Perhaps even worse than the ride itself was paying as much for a taxi in Cairo as one would pay in New York City.

After their night of sightseeing and hair-raising close calls, the tourists spent the next morning, 2 February 1914, journeying to the serenity of the Alabaster Mosque. Readily apparent were the changes the modern age was having even on the sacred places of Islam. The mosque was entirely electrified. In accordance with Islamic custom, to enter the building the tourists either had to doff their shoes or don woolen booties over their shoes. All of the tourists opted for the booties. Posing for pictures, they wore both the footwear and broad smiles.

Within the expansive interior of the prayer hall, which rises to 170 feet, dangled many lightbulbs, including a massive chandelier. All of the tourists were impressed with the mosque. Both its architecture and history were awe inspiring. Built over the course of twenty-seven years for Muhammad Ali, pasha of Egypt, the Alabaster Mosque also houses his tomb. In 1811 Muhammad Ali had come close to winning complete independence for his country. His methods were brutal but effective. The badly beaten English were made examples. Casualties were beheaded; the survivors were then forced to carry the severed heads of their comrades before being sold into slavery. Even harsher retaliation awaited England's allies, the Mamelukes, whom the pasha had massacred. Despite his despotic tendencies, most Egyptians and historians view Muhammad Ali as beginning the modernization of Egypt. The English were eventually able to assert their authority, however. They gained control of the Land of the Nile in 1882 when one of the pasha's descendants gave England economic control of Egypt. Once the English held the economy, they essentially ran the nation.

Following the tour of the mosque, with its soaring twin minarets and breathtaking views of Cairo and the Pyramids, Frank McGlynn took charge of the party. After the players changed into their uniforms, the director filmed some of his key sequences in the Egyptian desert. He hired a team of camels and mules to ferry the players out to Gizeh. His reasons for taking his film crew through the desert were simple, atmosphere. As McGlynn himself writes, "By engaging Arabs to carry the apparatus into the desert, we were able to get motion pictures of the caravan as it moved across the plain, with the beautiful mosque for background."[24]

But even in the isolation of the desert the tourists could stumble into trouble and danger. Joe Benz immediately discovered that one could indeed become as seasick on a "ship of the desert" as one could on the regular kind. That was not, however, the worst event of the day. As Frank McGlynn noted,

An impromptu fight, which was not in the cards was engaged by a number of Arab drivers. What the trouble was none of us could discover, but it took the combined efforts of the Turkish Desert Police, a real genuine Arab Shiek [sic] and the dragonmen who were conducting the party to separate the belligerents. It was a lively "scrap" while it lasted, but none of the participants seemed to have suffered any physical punishment. As near as we could find out, the cause of the difficulty was the claim of one camel driver to a large size tip, given him by one of the boys, who thought that he was the native who had charge of the camel on which he had ridden.[25]

Twenty-five years earlier, Spalding's All-Stars posed for what is perhaps their most famous portrait, the players sprawled out upon the paws and legs of the Sphinx. Comiskey and McGraw, courtesy of McGlynn, were doing this one better; they were bringing motion pictures to the ancient monument. Mindful of Pathè's exclusive rights, the players were discouraged from bringing along their personal still cameras, but some players ignored the ban. The only formal record of the tourists visiting the Gizeh Plain in their uniforms has been lost along with McGlynn's film.

Perhaps the most significant, or at least the most visually interesting, event McGlynn and Miller recorded were the antics of Ivy Wingo and Steve Evans. The duo tossed a baseball over the Great Sphinx. McGlynn's own account of this stunt states, "Ivy Wingo, the catcher for the New Yorks, stood on an eminence 100 feet in front of the Sphinx, and threw the ball completely over its head, a distance of probably 300 feet, where it was caught by Steve Evans."[26]

The tourists were certainly kinder to the ancient monument then were Spalding and his men when they visited the Gizeh Plain in 1890. The All-Stars and White Stockings had a contest to see who could give the Sphinx a "black eye." They all took turns flinging a baseball at the face of the Sphinx in an attempt to hit its eye.

Before McGlynn could get his camera up and running, however, a small simoom stopped by. A sandstorm lasting for about fifteen minutes blew out of the Sahara and across the Gizeh Plain. Seeking refuge from the storm of stinging sand, the players huddled together at the base of the structure, nestled between its paws. In all of its years the Great Sphinx perhaps never nuzzled such a motley gathering of mortals.

McGlynn also had the men play a mock game before the Pyramids for his camera. There were the obligatory landscape shots, all tied together by some sort of narrative. With filming completed, the teams and their director packed up their equipment and returned to the Alabaster Mosque, boarded their waiting cars, and drove to the Heliopolis Palace Hotel. The athletes kept their uniforms on because after lunch it would be game time again. The second and final game played in Egypt was a real humdinger. Under a broiling sun, the White Sox and Giants played the most intensely fought game of the entire series.

John McGraw desperately wanted to win this game to salvage at least half of the Egyptian series. Attendance more than doubled for this second game; the word of mouth regarding baseball in Cairo must have been good. U.S. consul general Arnold and the vice deputy consul showed up with just about every staff member from the consulate. Much of the rest of the crowd was comprised of British and Egyptian soldiers. McGraw sent Red Faber to the slab and then watched, along with an audience of five thousand, as the Sox and Giants battled like scorpions on the hardpan.

This game was not played like anything even remotely resembling an "exhibition" game. Years later Buck Weaver would tell Hal Totten,

> We were playin' for keeps—ridin' each other and there was plenty of hard feelin's.
>
> Well, we hit Cairo, Egypt and things got so bad we almost had a free-for-all right there. We got to ridin' Fred Merkle and Fred Snodgrass and callin' 'em boneheads, and the whole National League got up in arms about it. Finally McGraw gets in his two bits' worth—and that's the start of my story.
>
> He started tellin' us off—and when McGraw told someone off, they usually stayed told. But not us.
>
> "Go-wan," I yelled to McGraw. "You got a powder-puff ball club. You're yellow. You ain't got the guts of a canary bird. I only hope we get you guys in the World Series. Then we'll show you what a real fightin' ball club is—you and your yellowbellies."
>
> Now, remember—I'm just 28 years old. And here I am pullin' this kind of stuff on McGraw. Well we ironed out that trouble. But none of us forgot about it. And you can bet McGraw didn't either.[27]

Although Weaver's recollection was a bit faulty—Fred Snodgrass was at that moment actually back home in Oxnard, California, playing semipro baseball—the Sox and Giants did ride each other throughout the tour. Snodgrass and Merkle heard "bonehead" from the opposition's side of the diamond many times. The desert sun probably shortened fuses on both sides, making the Cairo games even more confrontational than "normal."

Much to McGraw's displeasure, the Sox quickly built a six-run lead. The Giants chipped away at the Sox, thanks in no small part to Jim Thorpe, who seemed to play better the hotter the weather became. Thorpe put on an even more spectacular show on day two in Cairo than he had in the previous game, going four for four and driving in one run and scoring another.

In the bottom of the ninth, the Giants had a chance to tie it up. With no outs, the Giants had runners on first and second. Both Mickey Doolan, occupying second, and Fred Merkle, on first, possessed speed. "Laughing Larry" Doyle, the Giants team captain, strode to the plate and worked the count to three balls and two strikes. Doyle then blasted a screaming liner on the next pitch; both runners took off at the crack of the bat. The White Sox's Buck Weaver leaped into the brilliant blue Egyptian sky and snagged Doyle's liner on the fly, tagging out Doolan as he touched the ground; then, like a sleek desert cat, Weaver turned and threw the ball to Tommy Daly at first. Daly tagged the base before Merkle could get back to it. A triple play! Had Weaver had the presence of mind, he could have, in the opinion of several witnesses, turned the triple killing unassisted. The only triple play of the tour, the final outs of the game left McGraw livid.

When the Giants and White Sox met in the World Series three years later, both teams would recall this duel in the sun. McGraw, who could nurse a grudge better than few men in history, would come to view the 1917 World Series as his chance to exact "revenge" for Cairo. This February day burned deeply into McGraw's soul.

That evening the players put aside their differences and hit the dance floor. The dance floor in the Heliopolis Palace Hotel was under the rug in the ballroom. At night a phalanx of burly Egyptians would appear; roll up the mammoth, beautifully hand-stitched rug; then disappear with it for parts unknown as the band began tuning up. Cairo was crawling with tourists from all over the world, and the bachelors in the party easily filled their dance cards. Buck Weaver and Steve Evans tutored many of the tourists from around the world on the latest dances. The two were such good teachers that they received a round of applause from their students. The single men later visited three dance halls in Cairo. In Egypt's dance halls, the tourists heard again a joke about Americans that had been following them since Australia.

A Scotchman, while viewing the statue of George Washington, was approached by an interested American.

"I think you will agree with me sir," said the American, "that he was a great and good man; a lie never passed his lips."

"Weel," said the Scot, "I suppose he talked through his nose like the rest o' ye."[28]

While the single men hit the dance halls, the married tourists made other plans for the night. Seven married couples hired an Egyptian guide who took them to a French cabaret and then out to watch some Egyptian belly dancers. Iva Thorpe was appalled by both shows, punctuating her disgust in her journal with an exclamation point. It is not known how the husbands felt about the evening's entertainment.

The next day, 3 February 1914, would be the tourists' last full day in Cairo. No games were scheduled, so everyone made their way about the city, sightseeing, shopping, and nosing around the museums. The morning's excitement occurred back at the polo grounds. The hardpan, now shorn of its diamond, served as a landing strip for the man whom the *Sporting News* called "the Birdman from Khartoum," French aviator Mark Poupre. The French dominated aviation, laying claim to one record after another. Poupre's just-completed flight had taken him the entire length of the Nile from Khartoum in the Sudan, where the White and Blue Niles merge, to Cairo. The tourists stopped in at Poupre's improvised landing strip and delighted in the tale of his adventures. Poupre's arduous trek amazed the tourists. The technological limitations of airplanes in 1914 necessitated frequent stops, during which Poupre had to deal with hostile natives, insects, dust storms, dangerous improvised landing sites, and a myriad of technical problems. Many of the tourists sought to board Poupre's plane and shake the aviator's hand, congratulating him on his astounding feat.

At the Cairo State Museum, the athletes were sincerely impressed with the glories of ancient Egypt. They all agreed that the pharaohs were as advanced as the Americans themselves and could have done anything, including play baseball. Only Ted Sullivan would not agree that the Egyptians could have played baseball. Sullivan was about as repulsive a racist one could find in America at the time. During the heyday of his playing career, Sullivan was especially nauseating during exhibitions against African American teams. During these contests, Sullivan would smash watermelons with a sledgehammer along the baselines and hurl vile invectives at the opposing team. Those wondering how Comiskey came into his own racism should take a long look at his mentor and devoted friend.

After touring the museum most of the tourists visited Cairo's endless bazaars. They are reported to have purchased "slippers, beaded crocodiles, swords, whisk brooms, bronzes, etc."[29] To a considerable deficit to everyone's pocketbooks, Buck Weaver did not do any of the haggling, so all of the tourists paid far more than they could have for their doo-dads. Souvenirs were not cheap in Cairo. Scarab dealers were the most often encountered. They were everywhere—in the hotel, in the streets, even within the confines of the Alabaster Mosque itself. Prices for the imitation beetles ranged from a low of $12 to a high of $400. Supposedly "authentic" scarabs were sold for even higher prices to the truly naive. Good negotiating, on the other hand, could net you a $12 scarab for a mere $2. Most of the tourists were of the opinion that the elaborate provenances devised by the vendors about their worthless glass baubles were entertaining enough that they justified the prices charged.

The only really big event of the day was a 4:30 P.M. gathering at the consulate. U.S. counsel Arnold, along with his wife, held an informal reception. Every member of Cairo's high society turned out for the reception. Somehow, no matter how "informal" these receptions were, every man had to don a suit and tie.

Hobnobbing with the blue noses did not affect Joe Benz in the least. When asked to sign the guest register, the irrepressible butcher's son composed the following.

Cairo
There amid the bright effulgence
Gleams a solitary star,
While the crescent moon is rising
Like an Archer Avenue car.
There from many stately turrets
Comes the sweet, sonorous air,
Wafting words upon the desert.
"Baksheesh, baksheesh" It's a bear.[30]

About the same time as the reception, John McGraw was singing Jim Thorpe's praises to the media and to anyone else who would listen. Through Joe Farrell of the *Sporting News*, the Giants manager opined, "Jim Thorpe has developed into a corking player, both from a hitting standpoint and as a fielder."[31]

After the reception the tourists had one more night of luxury in the Heliopolis Palace Hotel. Come 9:00 A.M. on 4 February, all the tourists had to be on the train for Alexandria, Egypt, to catch the ship that would transport them across the Mediterranean Sea. The morning gathering of bleary-eyed ballplayers at the terminal was bittersweet; the tourists really had enjoyed Cairo more than any other place that they had visited so far. It would be hard to leave, but Europe awaited. The tourists did some last-minute bargaining, attended to their ever-growing mass of luggage, and said their final good-byes to the city that all of them had fallen in love with.

As the hands of the terminal's main clock sped toward the departure hour, it was discovered that Jack Sheridan was unaccounted for. A hasty search of all of the train's cars and berths failed to turn up the man in blue. He was not at the station either. At first the men made jokes, rejoicing that an umpire had finally been wished away. But as departure time moved inexorably nearer, mirth gave way to concern. At the appointed hour the tourists' train pulled out of Cairo. Delaying any time at all might have made them miss their ship. The schedule was tight in any case: arrive in Alexandria at 1:00 P.M. and at 2:00 P.M. board the S.S. *Prinz Heinrich*. There was no "wiggle room" to search for a wayward umpire.

The journey to Alexandria carried the tourists through the fertile Nile Valley, virtually unchanged since the days of Joseph and the patriarchs. The valley's residents wore traditional clothing while working their fields of grain and cotton. Seeing these ancient people work their ancient land using methods thousands of years old made a powerful impression on the mind.

The tourists swept through Alexandria as an hour-long spending juggernaut. Some of the tourists had discovered that the price for cigarettes in Alexandria was staggeringly low. The traveling party flung a hail of money from their pockets, purchasing and stockpiling enormous amounts of cigarettes. The packages of cigarettes soon ended up under the beds and in the cabinets of the staterooms all over the *Prinz Heinrich*, the fourth ship that the tourists would call home.

ELEVEN

Across a Storm-Tossed Europe

I am *not* an agent for the Federal League. –Tris Speaker, in Paris, defending himself against rumors to the opposite effect

The Hamburg-American Line's *Prinz Heinrich* ran regularly between Alexandria and Naples, following a course ancient as the Caesars'. When Mercator drew his first maps, one of his finely detailed compass roses traced the same path that the *Prinz Heinrich* always followed.

Captain Zander, smartly dressed in his liner uniform modeled after German imperial naval attire, commanded a German crew that prided itself on service and efficiency that rivaled that of the kaiser's fleet. The tourists delighted in this change of pace from the English crew of the *Orontes*. The service and the food were praised as the best of any ship on which they had sailed. There were no bizarre menu surprises like "Bubble and Squeak" or bland English "delicacies."

Day one at sea, 5 February, set the tone for the voyage. Skies were clear, but the Mediterranean Sea was choppy. The oldest sea is fickle, with ever-changing moods. Continual weather changes would be the hallmarks of the *Prinz Heinrich*'s trek. The tourists adjusted their routines to the snug existence of ship life once more.

Iva Thorpe took advantage of her free time to do some laundry. She washed all the items by hand and then hung them out to dry on a makeshift clothesline in her stateroom. Already looking ahead, the happy couple was studying French so that they could have even more fun in Paris.

Later that same evening came one of the scenic highlights of the entire tour: the midnight passage of the Strait of Messina, which divided the "toe" of Italy's boot from the island of Sicily. Crossing from the Ionian Sea to the Tyrrhenian Sea on an ocean as smooth as polished marble, the *Prinz Heinrich* sailed close enough to the island of Stromboli for the passengers to witness the eruption of its volcanic namesake, Mount Stromboli. The tourists had seen an eruption before, in the Aleutians back in November. There really was no comparison between the spectacles, however. Whereas the eruption in Alaska occurred during daylight from a fair distance away on rough seas, Mount Stromboli seemed close enough to touch, the entire crater being illuminated by fire, heat, and smoke. Awe inspiring, the volcano reminded all present of Pompeii's fate.

By 7:00 A.M. their ship was sailing past the island of Capri under absolutely perfect weather. The rest of the day saw the tourists engaging in last-minute packing, finalizing plans to disembark, and answering Marconigrams from the Naples welcoming committee. Duke D'Abruzzi, Count Filangeri, and seemingly every American in the city were anxiously awaiting the arrival of the tourists, sending them a wireless to that effect while the *Prinz Heinrich* was still seven hours out of port.

The tourists' 8:00 P.M. arrival time found Naples shrouded in fog and mist, entirely blocking out any view of the city. For the baseball party, Naples seemed much like any of the other ports that had greeted the tourists. Joe Farrell reports:

> Here again, as in all seaports visited, the novelty purveyor was on hand in the little rowboat bargaining while the boat pulled up to the dock. Youthful divers surrounded the Prince Heinrich, and dove in marvelous fashion for coins tossed into the water by the players. They never missed a coin. It was like a two-ring circus.
>
> High above the chatter of the beseeching divers could be heard the voices of male and female singers, who in small boats with specially constructed stage and mandolin accompaniment, garroted "Funicull Funicula," and "Ciribirlbin." But nothing distressed the hard hearted tourists now.
>
> Shrieks of silence greeted the demise of the above two, for which encore a setting of Italian Lyrics to "Everybody's Doin' It Now," fractured the dromedaries vertebra and drove the teams to the dining salon, where the medical investigator pronounced all free from measles and kindred ailments and granted shore leave.[1]

The official welcoming committee, while sizeable, was nothing like those in other parts of the world. Italy was virgin territory for baseball. While there were some Italian Americans playing baseball, most notably Ping Bodie, the game itself was essentially unknown in the Land of the Caesars. Their welcoming committee escorted the tourists to one of two hotels. Most went to the Hotel Bertolini, with the overflow housed at the Hotel Parker.

These hotels would house the tourists for the next three days. Both were beautiful, but the smaller Hotel Bertolini was especially opulent, possessing much Old World charm.

In twenty-five automobiles, the tourists made their way through the impossibly crowded streets of Naples, spiraling ever upward to the heights of the city. Horse carts and burros were everywhere. Cars, carriages, and delivery vans pushed their way through the streets, often two or three abreast. By far the most insane traffic patterns that they had yet encountered, the tourists watched slack-jawed as pedestrians with astounding regularity abandoned the sidewalks, darting in seemingly suicidal dashes across Naples's avenues and boulevards.

For most of the tourists, the treacherous route came to a blessed end at the Hotel Bertolini. The touring party lined up to sign the hotel's huge golden register. Just above the place where they were to sign, the tourists encountered the handwriting and remarks of Sir Thomas Henry Hall Caine, a current guest of the hotel. Caine, who lived from 1853 to 1931, was the best-selling and most highly paid novelist of the era. His novels and plays were enormously popular, averaging sales in the hundreds of thousands; some sold millions. Combining religious and emotional sentiment, his novels, by today's standards, read like ponderous, overwrought stuff. His 1913 novel, *The Woman Thou Gavest Me*, became something of a cause célèbre when it was banned in England and elsewhere. Caine visited Italy often. He had been the English poet and painter Dante Gabriel Rossetti's personal secretary until Rossetti's death. It is in that role that Caine is mostly remembered today. He is also recalled as the person to whom Bram Stoker dedicated his novel *Dracula*.

Caine's words in the register read, "At last we stood breathless with adoration on the balcony of Bertolini's Palace, Naples."[2] Steve Evans wasted no time in warping Caine's sentiment. After reading Caine's words, Evans said, "Admiration for the way everything alive and stationary avoided the hill climbing contestants."[3]

The desk clerk was effusive in his praise of his employer, proudly dropping names of those whom had previously occupied the athletes' rooms. "Emanuel III (current crown Prince of Italy), H.R.H. Prince Tommasso of Savoy, H.M. Elizabeth of Austria, the King and Queen of Sweden, The Grand Dukes of Russia, the Hon. Crispi Prince Bulow, Verdi, Carducci, Panzacchi D'Annunzio, Tolstoi, Zola, and others equally famous, but these travel-hardened ball players refused to be impressed and merely felt of the beds to see if they were soft."[4]

At the hotel, the mystery of Jack Sheridan's disappearance was at last solved. A telegram from the umpire awaited the tourists. It seems that Sheridan's off-season occupation got the better of him. The mortician had become so wrapped up in the mummies and their associated funerary relics at the Cairo State Museum that he lost track of time and missed the train.

It was first feared that Sheridan would be stranded in Egypt for two weeks, the time it took for the *Prinz Heinrich* to complete another round-trip to Alexandria. Sheridan had, in fact, several options. An Austrian-Lloyd mail steamer had left Alexandria shortly after the *Prinz Heinrich*. If Sheridan missed that ship as well, on the other end of the rail line a Peninsular and Oriental express would leave Port Said the next day. The Austrian ship offered the fastest route, as the Peninsular and Oriental express would be taking the Suez Canal.

While the tourists would spend three days in Naples, no games were scheduled. Comiskey and McGraw did try to schedule a game but ran into an irresolvable dilemma. Naples was so crowded that no suitable field could be found that was large enough. Without a game, tourism replaced athletics. The welcoming committee was severely disappointed, especially those in the American colony. Their disappointment was doubled by the fact that the weather in Naples turned out to be perfect for baseball. The Americans in Naples who had talked up the game incessantly for months, only to end up looking foolish, were especially perturbed.

The tourists, disappointed that they would not be putting on an exhibition, had the consolation of Naples's innumerable tourist attractions. News of earthquakes concurrent with the Mount Stromboli eruption resulted in some rather lurid and dire headlines in the local papers, causing a few in the party to rush back to the hotel and launch a campaign to abandon Naples and head directly to Rome. Cooler heads prevailed, and the sight-seeing adventures continued.

Following the stream of tourists throughout history, the company divided into groups, taking in the ruins of Pompeii and Herculaneum and the beaches of Capri. They climbed Mount Vesuvius and visited the aquarium, the museum, the castle La Mar, and other destinations. The three days were chock-full of events.

Sanctimonious Ted Sullivan believed it was his place to admonish the players, especially the bachelors. "Ted Sullivan tells us we should remember that we are now in a 'Christian country' and that we should begin to behave."[5]

Some of the bachelors Sullivan lectured—Tris Speaker, Steve Evans, and Fred Merkle—promptly sailed off to the island of Capri, Italy's island of sun and debauchery since before Caligula. As Joe Farrell so aptly put it, "It is hard for some of the boys to drop the abandon of the Orient, and still linger fond memories of the delights of—for instance—Cairo. It will be a long time before we forget that town."[6]

The Thorpes, like the rest of the party, had a blast. At the art museum, Jim Thorpe revealed an artistic eye, purchasing three reproductions of paintings for the walls of his apartment back in the States. The two also toured the gardens of Bertolini. Iva loved flowers, and the duo visited every botanical garden they could while on tour.

While it would be difficult to name the most significant event in Naples, the Sunday dinner would probably be it. On Sunday evening, 8 February 1914, Cavaliere F. Bertolini, hotel impresario, hosted a dinner for the baseball teams. The guest of honor and keynote speaker, fellow hotel guest Hall Caine. The English novelist presented two miniature bronze statues to the teams. The bronzes, gifts of Bertolini, were reproductions of famous Roman and Greek art. The Giants received a reproduction of *The Gladiator*, the original of which Comiskey had admired earlier in the Naples museum. The White Sox were recipients of *The Discus Thrower*, the original of which now resides in the Louvre in Paris. Each bronze was emblazoned with a quote written especially for the occasion by Hall Caine. The inscription on the Giants' statue read, "Baseball is the brother of war but its battles shed no blood.—Hall Caine." For the White Sox, Caine composed the following, "Sport is the uniter of nations and a strengthener and upbuilder of men.—Hall Caine."

What, if anything, Hall Caine knew about baseball is a complete mystery to this author. If he knew anything about the sport at all, it was an informal and passing knowledge. Certainly the sport never appeared in his novels, whose modern-day sections were set almost exclusively on the Isle of Man. Nonetheless, McGraw and Comiskey made generously appropriate speeches of acceptance. The evening dinner was enjoyed by all, with festivities continuing into the early morning hours.

While a game might have been played earlier in the day on Sunday if a field could have been found, the men went to play the ponies instead. Horse racing has attracted baseball players since before the days Philadelphia spelled its National League entry's name "Fillies." While some of the men did well, Bill Klem lost his shirt at the track. Normally quite adept at the ponies, Klem's nose for horses went dead in Naples, as he picked five straight losers. Not only was his reputation as a keen horseman tarnished, the plans he had made for the winnings were shot as well. Before the trip to the track,

Klem had stated that he planned to buy pearls for his wife and play the casinos in Monte Carlo with his winnings.

It is probably just as well that the teams could not find a field on which to play. Large numbers of Italian royalty attended the horse races. Even if the players could have found a venue, it is likely that nearly everyone who would have otherwise attended the game, aside from local Americans, would have preferred mingling with the blue bloods at the racetrack than attend an unknown, foreign sport.

In all ways save one, Naples was a delight. Some of the tourists visited a pasta factory. It was not a pleasant experience. Located in a run-down section of Naples, the factory, like the rest of Italy, desperately needed an infusion of American pure food laws. Gus Axelson noted, "It seems as if this toothsome dish originated along the dirtiest streets and in the most odiferous locality. Why the odor of a tannery should add to the flavor of the 'string' could not be fathomed by our most learned members, but tanneries and spaghetti factories seem to grow together. It is no secret that macaroni and spaghetti have been scratched off the bill of fare by some of our most renowned epicures."[7]

During their time in Naples, a trio of tourists, Frank McGlynn, Fred Merkle, and Mickey Doolan, took in *Madame Butterfly* at the St. Carlos Opera House. Not only was the building's classic baroque architecture impressive, but the music was spectacular. The glory of the music led Merkle to remark, "Why the orchestra alone is worth the price of admission; I have been watching these violins and it seemed as if twenty bows were moved by one hand."[8]

The three were equally intrigued by the prima donna, a fetchingly beautiful brunette soprano. Although the three tourists would later attend operas in Rome and London, they agreed that no performance equaled that of this one magical afternoon in Naples.

The women of the party did their utmost to enjoy the Italian city. Every woman in the group shopped to the extreme in Naples. Most shopped with particular items in mind, cameos, coral beads, pearls, and gloves. The men viewed the "bargain hunting," especially for gloves, with amusement. "Did not one of the women travelers buy ten pairs of gloves for $9, and while doing it run up $15 of automobile charges? The husband was the only one who could not figure out the bargain. Those who will be blessed with glove gifts on the return of the tourists will have to determine the value of the kids."[9] The best quote from Naples, and perhaps the entire tour, was uttered by Sam Crawford at the aquarium. The tourists gazed in fascination at the multitude of creatures from the briny deep, finally stopping in front of the glass-enclosed octopus tank. Seeing the creature, Crawford "called it the Federal League."[10]

Back in the States, James Gilmore, the cash behind the Federal League, had received his first death threat on 1 February 1914 in the form of an anonymous letter containing a life-size tracing of a black hand. The classic mob warning letter of the era, it was a none too subtle warning to back off organized baseball. Gilmore was not intimidated.

Monday morning meant catch-up time for those who were not already packed; everyone had to be at the Naples station by 12:30 to meet the 1:00 P.M. special for Rome. This send-off was more subdued than most; only a few members of the welcoming committee bothered to say good-bye. Under clear, cool, and beautiful skies, the tourists' special began its journey northward through the Italian foothills for Rome. All was calm on a beautiful Italian winter's day.

Shortly after the train passed Caserta, about thirty-two miles out of Rome, Charles Comiskey was struck with a frightening illness. The White Sox's president was seized by a sudden chill and shortness of breath, looking for all the world like he was having a heart attack. Panic quickly set in. By fortunate coincidence, Dr. John Edward Jones of Virginia, the American consul to Genoa, was aboard the same train. (Jones had been in Naples to conduct an inspection of the American consulate there.) Jones quickly determined that Comiskey was in no danger, diagnosing his sufferings as "an acute attack of indigestion with marked cardiac symptoms."[11] In other words, a really, really bad stomachache. The doctor stayed with the baseball magnate until Comiskey checked into his hotel room in Rome. By late in the evening of 9 February 1914 Comiskey was somewhat recovered and resting comfortably in his suite at the Bristol Hotel.

About the same time Comiskey saw his life pass before his eyes, the entire party almost met with disaster. The incident, which may have precipitated Comiskey's attack, occurred as the tourists neared the Volturno River. A twenty-foot section of track spanning the river had been removed for repair. For reasons unknown, the engineer of the train carrying the tourists missed the signals warning him off the tracks. A phalanx of uniformed railroad workers blaring away on trumpets and gesticulating wildly materialized along the tracks. Workers who lacked trumpets screamed their lungs out, trying to get the engineer's attention.

Fortunately, the railroad dervishes captured the engineer's attention. He stopped the train, put it into reverse, and pulled onto a parallel track before heading north again. The tourists shuddered as their train passed the detour point. Beneath the twenty-foot gaping maw of nothingness was a sixty-foot drop, a raging river, and hard, unforgiving rocks. It was not difficult for the tourists to imagine themselves the victims of a grisly train accident with no survivors.

Later in the day the tourists pushed the unpleasentries of Comiskey's illness and the near train wreck to the back of their minds as they got their first view of Rome. As twilight settled over the Eternal City, the tourists caught a glimpse of St. Peter's dome as they passed an ancient Roman aqueduct. After pulling into Rome's main station, the tourists immediately departed for the Bristol Hotel and settled in.

From the time of their arrival in Rome, Tris Speaker and Sam Crawford began receiving telegrams from Federal League agents, urging them not to sign new contracts until they had returned home and listened to the Federal League's offers first. In baseball's universe, things were coming to a head fast. On the surface, McGraw and Comiskey put up a blasé attitude. Through Comiskey's favorite reporter, Gus Axelson, the ailing baseball owner issued the following official spin.

> The Federal League hubbub in the States is not causing worry among the Sox-Giants world-touring party. The first batch of papers from home was received a couple of days ago, and since then the tourists have been sitting up nights absorbing the startling facts from the seat of war.
>
> Comiskey and McGraw have been discussing the matter since the papers arrived but there is no fear of trouble. After arriving from Naples today "The Old Roman" said he can see no reason why the Federal League cannot invade Chicago. He thinks the White Sox will continue to play as in years gone by. He is of the same attitude now as in the past whenever a third club for Chicago is discussed.
>
> Comiskey adds that organized baseball is prepared to combat the "outlaws." A war fund awaits just such an emergency. He refused to go into details because of his not being well enough informed of the situation.[12]

After a night of discussing issues such as the moral ambiguities of "jumping" for fast cash to the Federal League versus fulfilling one's contract and thus being paid far less than one was worth, the baseball players awoke on 10 February 1914 under overcast, misting skies, a damp chill in the air. Because Comiskey was just not physically up to the task, Ted Sullivan and John McGraw were sent on one of the more bizarre errands of the tour. In the same city that once held daily gladiatorial contests resulting in gore, dismemberment, and death, Roman authorities now would not permit baseball to be played unless it could be proven that the sport was not "brutal."

Baseball had never been played in Rome before. Spalding's tour visited Rome twenty-five years earlier, but Spalding had never actually gotten around to playing any baseball. In his typically understated manner, Spalding had tried to requisition the Colosseum for a game, only to encounter bitter opposition to the idea from Italian authorities. The Colosseum was completely unsuited for playing baseball anyway. Perhaps reports of Spalding's irresponsibility and long memories on the part of Roman politicos gave the city's leaders a false impression as to what baseball was all about. In any event, the two managers hustled over to Rome's administrative offices and made a sales pitch for America's pastime.

Rome's officials were not impressed. They "demanded that a net be placed in front of the spectators and that a few innings be played behind closed gates that they might be sure that no danger could fall."[13] Sullivan and McGraw agreed to put on just such a demonstration the very next morning.

While Sullivan and McGraw were talking themselves hoarse, Commy was undergoing a rigorous medical examination in his hotel room. Dr. Jones, who had not left Comiskey's side since the train ride from Naples, called in a specialist, Dr. Guiseppe Bastianelli. Bastianelli owned a reputation as a world-renowned diagnostician, an opinion cemented when J. P. Morgan came calling upon him for treatment. The good doctor thoroughly examined the White Sox's owner. Despite living the high life for so many years, Comiskey was not in that bad of shape. Perhaps predictably, Bastianelli's examination "found the internal organs in good condition with the exception of the stomach and the liver."[14] It is amazing that the hard-drinking Comiskey had any liver left at all.

Comiskey claimed to have suffered attacks similar to the one near Caserta, only not nearly so severe, on a regular basis. Bastianelli recommended that Comiskey undergo X-rays the next day as a precaution. Comiskey was amenable to this, so long as it did not conflict with the tourists' scheduled meeting with the pope. Bastianelli also put the White Sox's president on a strict diet. For the remainder of his stay in Rome, Comiskey would be permitted only condensed goat's milk.

The healthy tourists took Italian king Victor Emmanuel up on his amazingly generous invitation. The king had invited all of the tourists to visit his royal palace, the Palazzo Quirinal, only a short walk from the Bristol Hotel. The tourists were awed by the majesty of royal living. The king's gardens were as beautiful as the furnishings and the architecture.

Victor Emmanuel was too busy attending to the affairs of state to meet with the tourists, but for most, the privilege of ranging about his house was compensation enough. Iva Thorpe was so taken with the beauty of the king's gardens and with one flower in particular that she surreptitiously removed a blossom and preserved it in her journal, duly noting the plant's royal origins.

The urban citizens of New York and Chicago found the subterranean roadway beneath the Palazzo Quirinal absolutely astounding. Totally unlike the grungy subway systems of their home cities, this was a vibrant, colorful showplace. Running for four city blocks beneath the entire length of the Palazzo Quirinal, the walls of the subway were tiled in beautiful pastel colors.

The morning of 11 February 1914 dawned cold, gray, and wet. A steady morning rain altered everyone's plans for the day. It prevented the tourists from demonstrating the nonbrutal nature of their avocation. Rome would not get a chance to see baseball this day either. The tourists, however, did not mind missing baseball this day, no matter how cold and foreboding the weather; today everyone was going to meet the pope. It was as formal an event as the tourists were ever likely to attend. Despite the hour of their audience with Pope Pius X being 11:00 in the morning, all of the tourists wore formal evening clothes. The men wore morning coats and white vests with matching white bow ties. If they had a stovepipe hat, they wore one; others donned black bowlers. To conform to protocol the men were supposed to wear matching headgear, but apparently no two of them had the same taste in chapeaus off the diamond. Instead, most of the men greeted his holiness bareheaded. Others left their hats in the limousines that ferried them to the Vatican. According to Gus Axelson, a good portion of the men in the party had already shipped much of their wardrobe ahead to London, so tuxedos, though considered improper attire, would have to do.

For the women, only black and gray formal gowns were acceptable. Within the limited color range, the women had much more sartorial freedom than did the men; almost anything modest would be acceptable. The Callahan children were dressed almost as twins in white shoes, white stockings, and matching charcoal overcoats. Margaret Callahan wore a black bonnet, her mother a veil.

Nearly all of the tourists were Catholic, making this meeting one of the spiritual highlights of their lives. Even the Protestants in the group were awed. Before leaving the Bristol Hotel, the Reverend John McNamara had briefed everyone on proper etiquette and conduct while in the Vatican.

For the humble, baseball-loving priest from Baltimore, nothing could top this day. His friendship with McGraw had certainly provided the most unexpected of dividends. Serving as the tourists' guide and interpreter was Monsignor Charles A. O'Hearn, vice president of the American College at Rome. O'Hearn currently was also acting rector to the college. A Chicago native and huge baseball fan, the monsignor was as impressed with meeting the players as the players were impressed to be in the Vatican.

Actual admission to the Vatican required a ticket. These had been issued through Father McNamara. Though the pontiff's chamberlain looked askance at the men's attire, he duly admitted the sixty-five-member-strong party into the majesty of the Vatican. To get to the pope's reception room, the Hall of the Conclave, the tourists had to wind their way up a seemingly endless number of stairs of pure white Carrara marble. On all sides the beautiful, priceless, and historic artwork of the centuries lined the walls. When at last they reached the Hall of Conclave the tourists arranged themselves in a semicircle and awaited Pope Pius X in awed silence. One could almost hear the hearts beating. Every tourist, save Comiskey, whose illness forced him to sit, awaited the pope standing up. The wait would be short.

Gus Axelson describes what occurred next.

There was no announcement. There were no heralds announcing, "the King." No, not a sound. A pin dropped on the mammoth cardinal rug would have made a sound. Before reaching the threshold could be heard the shuffled walk of Pope Pius X, whose seventy-nine years undoubtedly hung heavy on his shoulders. This man, whom millions of devoted followers call "father," hesitated just for an instant as his kindly eyes roamed over the congregation in front. There were old and young, from white hair to curly locks. There were creeds represented not his own, but there were no exceptions made, and the apostolic benediction fell on all.

The pontiff had advanced toward the center of the room. Having given the benediction, he stopped for an instant, but there was no awkward pause. Monsignor O'Hearn immediately approached the holy father, and in Italian gave the pontiff the name of the party, the import of the visit to Rome, told how they had traveled two-thirds around the world.

There was no question about Pius X being interested. He listened intently to what Monsignor O'Hearn had to say, replied that he hoped for a safe journey home and that they would be victorious in their undertaking. He also announced that he would bless them individually and also their relatives and friends and any religious articles they had with them.

That he took more than an ordinary interest in the visitors could be seen from the animated manner in which he replied to Monsignor O'Hearn, but his effort was really more than a compliment to the Americans. It was apparent that he was a weary man, that the exacting and multitudinous duties are gradually sapping his strength where in years gone by he must have compared favorably to the athletes before him.

His cassock and cape still covered a seemingly sturdy body, but the deep lines in his face and the slight stoop to his bearing told of a gradually weakened constitution. Under his zucchetto, stray silver locks hung loosely toward his shoulders, adding to that patriarchal mien which was so noticeable when he entered. There was not one in the room who would not have liked to wish him a long and happy life, but etiquette forbade any outward manifestation, and slowly the successor to Saint Peter turned toward the exit.

As the pontiff reached the door leading into his private apartment he noticed the youngest members of the party for the first time, Margaret and Dan Callahan. Stopping directly in front of them he patted them on the heads, gave them his blessing and with a farewell nod, disappeared.[15]

The dignified bearing of the pope as well as the surroundings impressed all of the tourists. Both Sam Crawford and Tris Speaker, the two most prominent members of the small Protestant contingent, would in interviews over the next few months claim that the most impressive event of the tour was the audience with Pius X.

Once the pope took his leave, Monsignor O'Hearn led the group into an antechamber to meet Cardinal Merry del Val, papal secretary of state. The still fairly young cardinal was a Chicago native and a huge sports fan. The tourists took note of a photograph on the cardinal's desk; it showed a much younger Merry del Val in a baseball uniform. The cardinal had requested this meeting because of his admiration of the athletes. He kept up to date on all of the sports news from the United States, following pennant races a half a world away from his offices in the Vatican. The cardinal chatted up the group, singling out Jim Thorpe on his Olympic triumphs and shaking everyone's hand. Cardinal del Val's geographical distance and the resultant spotty coverage of the American sports scene had the effect of making him come across as a bit daft. He took one look at N. E. McBride and decided that the distinguished-looking man just had to be an umpire. McBride, who was actually an Illinois state representative, decided to take the cardinal's confused praise as a compliment. He set the cardinal straight, graciously thanking him in the process. (Begging the question of when a politician is confused with an umpire, which profession has greater cause to be upset?) At another point, the cardinal set eyes on the Sox's Sam Crawford and said, "These must all be Giants." Father McNamara diplomatically corrected him with, "Oh no, there are just as many White Sox." "Oh well, they look like Giants anyway," replied the cardinal.[16]

Most of the rest of the time the teams were in his office the cardinal talked baseball with Comiskey and McGraw. He wished them luck on the remainder of their voyage, hoped that the teams would get a chance to play if the gloomy Roman weather would depart, and wished both teams good luck and much success in the upcoming baseball season.

After chatting with Cardinal del Val, the tourists returned to the Bristol Hotel. Comiskey, however, was taken to a hospital by the ever-present Drs. Jones and Bastianelli, where he underwent extensive X-rays of his gastrointestinal tract and chest. The operator of the new-fangled X-ray machine was a professor named Ulderice de Luca. At the end of a long day of extensive, expensive, and embarrassing medical procedures, the triumvirate of medical practitioners came to the conclusion that Comiskey was suffering from nothing more exotic than a stomachache.

Iva Thorpe seemed to realize just how popular her "Snooks" was only after their meeting with Cardinal del Val. The fact that his fame had reached the Vatican had more impact than being asked to meet the khedive, front-page photographs in newspapers around the world, or the standing ovations across the United States. The explanation for her epiphany seems no more complicated than the fact that the Vatican was as far from the world of sports as one could get. For her husband to have fame among athletes and sports fans was not a surprise to Iva; after all, she had married "the big man on campus." For him to be famous in as unathletic and cerebral an environment as the Vatican gave Iva an entirely new perspective on her husband's fame.

Gus Axelson wrote an article, "Sox and Giants Find Thorpe World Famous," documenting Jim Thorpe's world-girdling fame. His words mirror those of Iva in her journal.

> Jim Thorpe, with the blood of Sacs and Foxes flowing in his veins, is apparently known wherever dwells people who can read.

At every place newspapermen, natives and others have assailed members of the party for diverse and sundry information regarding the personnel and incidents of the trip. Naturally, as some fame has accorded to Thorpe in the past, the one interrogated usually starts off with something about Thorpe. "Oh, yes, thank you, but we all know about Mr. Thorpe. What we want to know is something about the other members of your party."[17]

The rest of Axelson's article does not parallel Iva Thorpe's diary. It is, however, worth quoting because it provides invaluable insights into how the Thorpes were perceived in various nations as they made their way around the world.

Thorpe has, however, been a surprise in store for the majority of those who have a reading knowledge of Jim Thorpe, Indian. Up to date he has never been picked out first hand by visitors, either to the ship or on land. Most all have painted Jim in advance dark of skin. And as for his wife. It is with considerable credulity that the visitor accepts the statement that the light-complexioned, husky-looking athlete is Jim Thorpe, and that the pretty and vivacious girl is Mrs. Thorpe.

"Why, are not American Indians black?" is usually the cross query. At least they figure they must be of the copper hue of the story books. Who shall say that the romance is not all knocked out of the tradition of the "noble redman."

Once persuaded that Thorpe is Thorpe this great athlete soon becomes the attraction. He is pointed out in the hotels, on the fields and on the streets. Are they acquainted with his prowess on the athletic field? All that is necessary is to read the columns in native and English newspapers about the mighty deeds of James. His career is an open book in Japan, in the English possessions, and of course the Philippines. He is no stranger to China. That country in conjunction with the Philippines and Japan, now has an Olympic of its own.

ACTION CALLED UNJUST

On the baseball field his every move has been watched. His speed, both in the field and on the bases, has been marveled at and apparently he has lived up to the advance notices. His record in the Olympic games is well known to everybody in the least informed. In this connection it has been noticed that he has everywhere been sympathized with for the loss of the trophies so gallantly won at Stockholm. Although the Sox and Giants have visited countless countries where the spirit is high, the opinions have been unanimous that an injustice had been done to him.

The very fact that such an action had been taken has undoubtedly increased Thorpe's popularity. In practically every formal speech of welcome and at the many banquets and receptions any allusion to Thorpe's prowess has been received with cheers. By the same token there has never been a gathering where speeches have been made where some reference to the famous Indian has not been made.

Mrs. Thorpe Popular

This laudation almost around the world does not seem to have turned Thorpe's head. He has been one of the most unassuming on the trip, and without a doubt young Mrs. Thorpe has been one of the most popular. It is she who has carried a fascinating smile four-fifths around the world at this writing. It is not down by the daily journals that she has acted otherwise. The traditional austerity of the Indian is also due for a revision along with the color.[18]

While Rome was an adventure of the first order, there were some definite negatives about the city, the oppressively dank and drizzly weather being one. Many of the tourists, including the Thorpes, contracted colds in the miserable weather. The tourists also unhappily discovered that the Eternal City abounded in graft, corruption, and shady characters. One pearl vendor tried to sell his "authentic" wares to Nancy Comiskey. The Old Roman's wife was no fool. First offered for $120, the string of pearls soon dropped to $100; still no sale. In desperation, the smooth operator dropped the price to a rock bottom price of $20; still Nancy Comiskey passed.

Other costs could not be avoided so easily. Rome tapped the tourists' wallets more than any other city they had visited to this point. As the Joe Farrell writing for the *Sporting News* put it,

About the third day in Rome it was ascertained that the idea of the famous American bucket brigade used to such good advantage by our forefathers in extinguishing fires in rural towns was taken from the present system of tipping in the city that formerly ruled the world. Rome exists on tips. In this instance the chauffeurs, cab drivers, postcard boys, coral venders, hotel front door openers, rosary sellers, museum custodians, tramp guides, church entrance beggars, church exit beggars, elevator man that takes you up, elevator boy that takes you down, chambermaid that shakes the bed, chambermaid that makes the bed, the waiters in the dining hall, the clerk that hands you the key, the boy who takes your grip away, the maid that serves the tea, these and a thousand more constitute the tipping brigade. The traveler is the bucket.[19]

The depressing weather broke just once, briefly on the twelfth, while the teams were in Rome. By fortunate coincidence the sunshine came just as Frank McGlynn was filming more staged mayhem for the camera at ancient Rome's most famous sports venue. McGlynn directed Jim Thorpe and Fred Merkle as they engaged in a wrestling match on the floor of the Colosseum. The wrestling took on an authentic sheen, as Merkle had no desire to take a dive. Thorpe would often wrestle his teammates, a practice McGraw frowned upon. Thorpe was almost never the instigator of these matches. Because Thorpe did not at first glance appear to be any more imposing or powerful than themselves, many of his Giants' teammates thought that they could get the better of Carlisle's finest. Not one of them was ever proved right, however. Despite being challenged time and again (often without his consent), Thorpe won every match. This bout would prove no different. Thorpe out-muscled New York's big first baseman, placing his foot in the small of his vanquished foe's back, gladiator style. He turned his eyes toward the emperor's box where Steve Evans sat in for Caesar. Evans gave the thumbs up, and Thorpe released his defeated "foe."

The fleeting sun splash provided a spectacular view of the ancient stadium. The athletes would have gotten more out of their experience, however, if they had not, unfortunately, hired a tour guide who spoke only Italian. From McGlynn's account of the day: "He imagined the boys could understand him and proceeded somewhat as follows: 'Collosseo, Flavio, Multo, Antiquo, Arco, Di Constantino, Palacia, Caesari, Arco Di Tito, Forum Romanum (etc. etc.),' with liberal Italian descriptive adjectives. After listening attentively to the harangue, Steve Evans, pretending to understand perfectly, turned to the boys and said: 'You see fellows, I told you we did right to get an Italian guide, these English speaking guides wouldn't tell you all this.' "[20]

While touring the grand stadium, the ballplayers could not help but compare the gladiators' arena to their own ballparks. Just imagining a crowd of eighty-seven thousand (then the current estimate of the stadium's capacity) thrilled them. Imagining the Colosseum in its pristine state, however, made the players realize that it could never have been a suitable venue for baseball. "Every ball hit in the air would have been a home run; but still the players longed for one good game inside the walls, with a good, old-fashioned Roman mob in the bleachers with thumbs in working order.

It would have been a cinch for the home team, according to Tris Speaker and Mike Donlin, as no vestal virgins would ever have elevated their thumbs to save such a wretch as Bill Klem."[21]

The tourists enjoyed the other relics of Rome as well. At the Forum, Ted Sullivan pointed out the spot where Marc Antony stood weeping over Caesar. Utilizing all of his oratorical skills, Sullivan laid the sentiment on thick, nearly breaking into tears as his soliloquy reached its zenith. Puncturing Sullivan's ballooning pomposity, Germany Schaefer strode to the spot and issued the following "dire" warning, "Be wary before deserting Caesar and parlaying with the Federal League."[22]

The tourists' sojourn in Rome attracted two additional personalities. U.S. ambassador Nelson Page often dropped in on the tourists. Concerned about Comiskey's health, the ambassador seemed equally keen for a ball game to be played. The ambassador offered to throw out the first pitch when and if the tourists received permission to play.

Frank M. Ish, part owner of San Francisco's team in the Pacific Coast League and president of the Western League, toured the sights of Rome with the Giants and White Sox. Ish, in the midst of his own winter tour of Europe, had scheduled his tour of Italy to coincide with that of the Major Leaguers. His visit also gave him a chance to check up on Jack Bliss, who had played for Sacramento of the Pacific Coast League throughout the 1913 season.

Ish, as well as Comiskey, was wise to keep an eye on his employees. Back in the States, the "outlaw" Federals and organized baseball were on a collision course. Two significant events in the baseball war took place on 11 and 12 February 1914. First was the firing of Cubs manager Johnny Evers. The legendary second baseman, immortalized in the poem "Tinker to Evers to Chance," was wildly popular with fans and players alike. Without giving a reason, Cubs president Charles W. Murphy fired Evers on the eleventh, replacing him with ancient and crusty Hank O'Day. Reaction from all quarters was instantaneous, raucous, and angry. Cubs fans were livid, loudly venting their anger at both Murphy and his team.

The immediate winner of Murphy's ill-timed move was Chicago's Federal League team. As Irving Vaughn put it in the *Chicago Record-Herald*, "That the axe should fall at this particular time ranks as one of the biggest 'bone' plays of all time: Every fan who questioned Murphy's performance yesterday mentioned in the same breath the Federal League. It is evident that the Cub boss in one stroke has created more public sentiment toward the 'outlaws' than they themselves could have aroused with two or three seasons of the highest class of baseball."[23]

Joe Tinker, manager of Chicago's Federal League team, echoed what the Chicago fans were saying. Tinker had played at short for years next to Johnny Evers. His frustration at the reserve clause and martinet owners like Murphy had turned the once-contented Cubs' shortstop into a radical baseball labor organizer. Vaughn caught up to Tinker just before the latter left for a New York strategy session with Federal League officials.

The manager of the local "feds" argued that Murphy's loss will be Weeghman's gain. Tinker did not say that he would resign his post in favor of Evers if the third league could sign up the "canned" Cub leader.

"There is now an outward attitude of hostility toward Murphy," said Tinker. Recalling how Murphy had summarily dismissed Frank Chance, his former teammate, and first baseman on the last Cub team to win a World Series, Tinker continued.

"With Evers receiving the same treatment as did Chance only about a year ago, Murphy must expect a reaction. You can get away with things just so long, and regardless of what step the league takes to discipline the Cub boss for his apparently rash act there will be a falling off of attendance at the West Side park. We will benefit there from. We base our claims for recognition on the treatment we intend to give the ball player," continued Tinker. "Our success in landing players has been because of our cry against the reserve and the ten-day clause. The latter is stricken from most of our contracts that cover definite terms. The release of Evers carries out our contention that there is no equity in a baseball contract. Evers signs for five years, Murphy cancels the agreement without notice after a year has elapsed. Evers is now out as manager, but retained by the club and can not play elsewhere. There is no justice there. The majors could not have furnished a better example."[24]

News of the firing reached Europe the next day, 12 February 1914. At their hotel, the players discussed Murphy's action. There was unanimous support for the fired manager. Giants captain Larry Doyle was heard to opine that "Evers got a raw deal." Fred Merkle, who had been turned into a verb by Evers's actions in the infamous 1908 September game, supported the fired Cubs manager.

Even the ailing Comiskey, an ardent supporter of the reserve clause, thought that Murphy had made a tremendous mistake that would benefit the Feds. Offering his views on the matter to Gus Axelson, Commy said, "The owner of the Cubs, to my way of thinking, has made a mistake in dropping Evers under the existing conditions. Murphy is doing much to help the Federal League cause, for by disposing of Evers, especially the way he did, Murphy undoubtedly made enemies of hundreds of fans who patronized his club in past seasons."[25]

J. P. McEvoy, witticist for the *Chicago Record-Herald*, presented this doggerel about the controversy for his readers' amusement.

Refrain
"Whatever you say about Murphy is so,"
Says Tinker to Evers to Chance,
"And telling the truth is to libel him, bo,"
Says Tinker to Evers to Chance,
"Of serpentine ethics we've had more than enough;
We're through with his double-dyed, double-cross stuff—
And we'd like to say more, but we'd have to get rough,"
Says Tinker to Evers to Chance.[26]

The following day baseball compounded its reputation for stupidity by blacklisting the Federal League, issuing a formal statement to that effect. Somehow, the owners managed to get the Players Fraternity to rubber-stamp their blacklist proclamation. The machinations used by the owners to pull this off during their meeting at New York's Waldorf-Astoria Hotel were worthy of the most byzantine intrigues. Circumventing the players themselves, the owners got David Fultz, president and counsel for the Players Fraternity, to sign the agreement. Fultz's action essentially made the Players Fraternity agree to the legal validity of the reserve clause, the very beast that the fraternity had been organized to fight against in the first place.

The agreement decreed that any player who jumped to the Federal League would automatically forfeit his membership in the fraternity. Amnesty would be provided, however, for any player who had already signed a Federal League contract if they rejoined their original Major League club before opening day. Joe Tinker, naturally enough, was enraged. He called the owners' coup "Dave Fultz's backdown." If one imagines the players as a starving, captive tiger, then the owners had just insulted the tiger and stuck their very meaty arm between the bars of the cage.

On 12 February, while Frank McGlynn was filming in the Colosseum, Chicago fandom was exploding, and the first mortar rounds were landing in the baseball war, Charles Comiskey was preparing to leave Italy. Against his doctor's orders, Commy split off from the rest, leaving via private railcar to Paris to get some rest. If he didn't feel better after Paris, the Old Roman planned to drop out of the tour completely and head home to the States. Traveling with his wife, Nancy; her traveling companion, Mrs. Keough; and his life-long friend Ted Sullivan, Comiskey was physically separated even from them. Comiskey traveled in sequestered privacy, an entire railroad car to himself. From his luxurious suite in Paris, Comiskey would send daily updates on his condition, reassuring the two teams about his health.

Everyone else spent an additional day in Rome. Last-minute purchases, sightseeing, and relaxing filled the agenda. Once again rain prevented athletic endeavors. The tourists also heard from the missing Jack Sheridan once more. The umpire missed Rome entirely; now he sent word that he would not make Nice, France, either. Sheridan had indeed missed every other connection to Europe and had to await the return of the *Prinz Heinrich*. He planned to catch an express train for Paris as soon as setting foot in Naples in order to rejoin the teams and resume his officiating duties. For Bill Klem, this meant that he would be the sole umpire for any games the teams were able to play in Nice. This really was no hardship for Klem, as he had called perhaps hundreds of games from behind home plate without any assistance.

On 13 February 1913 at 6:30 P.M. under a steady drizzle, the White Sox and Giants left Rome for Nice, France, on the Riviera. A decidedly anticlimactic ending to their visit, the tourists made a muted exit from Rome. Disappointment hung about the air at the station, and rain seemed somehow appropriate for their departure. Everyone thought that they had missed something by not playing a game in Rome, an opportunity they would never get again.

Their trip to Nice took fifteen hours by rail, with the tourists arriving in Nice at 9:30 the following morning. As railroads go, it would be hard to think of a more scenic one to travel on than the tracks between Rome and Nice. The rails rolled along Italy's west coast, with spectacular views of the Tyrrhenian and Mediterranean Seas, then traced the arc of the Gulf of Genoa before finally scaling the Maritime Alps and entering France. Everything about the Mediterranean city was a joy. While much of the rest of France shivered under a blanket of snow, Nice was balmy and beautiful. Palm tress lined the city's wide streets, and, best of all, the city had become a twenty-four-hour party. As the players checked into their rooms at the Terminus Hotel, they were delighted to discover that the city was in the midst of its annual carnival.

The carnival was tempting, but beckoning even more loudly were the legal gambling halls of Monte Carlo. Monaco and its legendary casinos were a mere fifteen minutes away by rail. Virtually every member of the party climbed aboard the next train to experience the gambler's Mecca. The rest of that day, everyone tried to break the bank.

Monte Carlo was the kind of decadence you just could not find back home in the United States. In the States you could bet the ponies, period. Every other form of gambling was illegal. Lots of money changed hands at ballparks and boxing rings, but that was strictly under the table. America was a land without sweepstakes, without lotteries, without so much as a bingo hall. Organized crime ran the numbers rackets and had its talons all over organized sports. The idea of legal gambling, complete with casinos, would have brought on a fit of apoplexy in virtually every politician in America. They were elected to put a stop to such sinful activity as this.

Awesome as the place was, not even in Monte Carlo could Germany Schaefer suppress his prankster's heart. Schaefer was sometimes called "Prince" by his teammates. The sobriquet was generated purely out of affection, as everyone considered him a "prince of a fellow." Upon hearing him addressed as "Prince," word spread around the gambling hall that the baseball player was actually a visiting royal dignitary. Schaefer, naturally, allowed this supposition to stand. "Immediately there was a flurry of excitement, as Herman advanced to the table, but when he risked the fabulous sum of five francs on the red, his prestige as the scion of a royal house immediately vanished."[27]

Then as now, Monte Carlo was the place to mix and mingle with royalty, millionaires, actors, and celebrities from every corner of the globe. The single men in the party were severely disappointed to discover that most of the women gathered around the tables were middle-aged housewives.

None of the citizens of Monaco were present on the gambling floor. Ironically, it was illegal for Prince Charles's subjects to enter the gambling halls of their own principality. The trade-off was quite lucrative, however, as they lived comfortably off of the tax revenues foreigners paid to run and operate Monte Carlo.

No one did better than winning $500 at the gambling tables. Most broke even or pocketed $20 profit for their night of indulgence. Everyone reported having a good time except for a sullen John McGraw. The Giants' manager proclaimed the Monte Carlo casino was "one big joke." His opinion was probably tempered by bad luck. As *Sporting Life* said, "This may, however, be due to the fact that he was the heaviest, possibly the only loser of the base ball party which visited the famous Casino and took the chances all visitors are expected to take."[28]

Lee Magee had a bad night as well, dropping $500. Larry Doyle, on the other hand, was seen with "two hats full of Francs."[29] After a night of gambling and reveling in the casinos of Monte Carlo, the teams returned to the Terminus Hotel in Nice.

The following day, Sunday, 15 February 1914, turned out to be, perhaps, the most surreal day of the tour. The date corresponded with the apex of the Nice Mardi Gras. More than five thousand people wedged themselves into the streets to watch the parade. Another ten thousand actually paraded down the streets. The Nice carnival attracted participants from around the world. Many of the marching revelers wore huge costume heads, a tradition that did not fade away until the 1950s.

This was an opportunity the players simply could not pass up. Putting on their uniforms, the players commandeered several open carriages, added a few American and French flags, joined the parade, and blended right in. All along their route down the Avenue de la Gare the teams and their carriages were bombarded with confetti. Bushel baskets full of confetti fell all about them. The players scooped it up and tossed it back. Together, the players had purchased enough of their own confetti to fill each of their carriages knee deep with the stuff. The players tossed all of their confetti and had at least as much thrown back at them. Along Place Massena, Frank McGlynn and Victor Miller had the camera rolling, filming the procession as it passed. Some of the floats were quite spectacular, a favorite being a gigantic winged Pegasus, its mane some thirty feet above the street.

Good humor ruled the day. Even the one potential mishap became an opportunity for laughs. At one point in the parade route, a float directly in front of the tourists dislodged some bricks on an arch it passed through, littering the street with bricks and masonry. The shower of building materials prompted Steve Evans to remark, "Look out for the Irish confetti," a joke that his Irish partisan teammates found very amusing.[30]

After parading down the main avenues of Nice, the players made their way to the local football (soccer) stadium for their game. The field was surprisingly rocky and uneven. The diamond was improvised, and huge expanses of netting had been strung up to protect the fans. Twenty-five years earlier, A. G. Spalding's All-Stars debuted baseball in France on these same grounds to little popular acclaim or memory. The audience in Nice was almost exclusively vacationing American millionaires and wealthy Europeans. Ticket prices were adjusted accordingly. Seats in Nice were the highest of any place in the world, twenty francs, the equivalent of four U.S. dollars. Sadly, though probably not surprisingly, several of the millionaires tried to obtain free passes to watch the Sox and Giants square off in the Riviera sunshine.

One of the gate-crashers, unidentified in the press save as "one of the richest men in St. Louis," got nowhere with the man at the turnstiles, so he appealed to one of the players directly. The millionaire knew the player and managed to parlay that relationship into four free passes.

The game itself was a dandy one, with Chicago defeating New York 10–9. Diversions and sideshows nearly eclipsed the game. The French aviator Lacrouse displayed his monoplane before the game, then flew it over the field, boosting attendance. Once the crowd showed up, Lacrouse circled the field three times at tree-top level, yelled "Au revoir" to the crowd, then disappeared into the western sky.

As an interesting aside, the previous autumn, a pilot had sought permission to fly over the crowd at the Army-Navy game. His request was denied on the grounds that such a stunt was too dangerous. Lacrouse did not seek anyone's permission, nor would he have obeyed a flying ban. Part skilled pilot, part daredevil, Lacrouse confided to Comiskey before the game that he was after the transatlantic prize. Lacrouse, like apparently every great aviator, had an archrival, Mark Poupre, the flier whom the tourists had met in Cairo. In the span of a few weeks, the tourists had met two of the greatest living French pilots.

Before the game, Jim Thorpe gave in to the wishes of the large crowd and put on a display of his Olympic prowess, throwing the shot put and discus. He also played some nifty baseball. On the other end of the scale, Lee Magee played a "listless" game, distracted by his losses at the Monte Carlo tables on Saturday night.

The crowd was very much into the game, applauding and cheering at just the right moments. This should not be attributed to any Gaullist love of baseball but rather because of the sizable number of Americans in the stands. Those present were interested in having a good time above all else. Germany Schaefer, always at his best when he had an audience, was only too happy to provide the crowd with some laughs. Schaefer strode up to bat wearing one of the huge carnival masks. Schaefer's mask bore the visage of an old man with a long and flowing gray mustache. After striking out on three straight pitches, he turned to the crowd and said, "I am growing old." Schaefer then returned to his seat to the crowd's laughter.

Some baseball was played in France. Spalding funded a small league there for years. Most of the teams were in the northern part of the country around Paris. The sport had little appeal to the French, however. Bat-and-ball sports just did not seem to take hold in the country. Cricket had similarly failed to make any inroads. Both sports were played to limited appeal before the Great War. France had even sent a cricket team to the Olympic games of

1900 held in Paris. Little more than a dozen years on, however, the sport had faded from public view.

After the Great War, cricket would, for all intents and purposes, vanish from the French countryside. Baseball would hang on, just barely, largely due to the influence of American expatriates and American dollars. Despite Spalding's desire or that of W. H. Burgess, the president of the Vesinet, France, baseball club, the sport, to quote Burgess, would not "soon be a popular sport" in France.[31] This was evident even in how Frenchmen dressed for the sport. The French dressed like they were participating in a track meet, shorts and light clothing.

In Nice, the Federal League scored its first theft of a world tourist. Not simply content to send telegrams from Joe Tinker informing all readers that "we have more than doubled salaries," the Feds sent flesh-and-blood recruiters to Europe to sign up tourists before they got back to the United States. Mickey Doolan, Phillies shortstop and Giant for the duration of the tour, made no bones about where his allegiances were.

> "I will go to the Federals unless the Phillies meet my terms in a contract for 1914," said Doolan, "I had not signed for the coming season when I left the East last October, and have not heard from club officials. Before joining the world tourists I talked over my plans for 1914 with the Philadelphia management and announced my terms. I have not heard whether they have been accepted.
>
> "The Federals look like a good thing, and if players like Joe Tinker, Mordecai Brown, and Otto Knabe have lined up with the new organization they certainly must have been given better contracts than they ever held with clubs in the National League."[32]

Doolan even had a Federal League team picked out as his preference, Baltimore, so that the Philly native would not have to play too far from home. The Federals did not hide the fact that they were also after Sam Crawford and Tris Speaker. While McGraw and Callahan could exercise their influence to keep Federal agents out of the lobby of the Terminus Hotel, there was very little that they could do to keep the Feds from talking to the players in the street. The boldness of the Federals was sending shockwaves throughout organized baseball. The National Commission was beside itself in dealing with the Federal League threat. They were about to take more unprecedented action.

After the game, Nice's revelry continued. The parade route exploded in a riot of colored lights, fireworks, and lanterns of every description. The players, in order to stand out in the darkness, blew wads of money at local

merchants to procure masks, makeup, and costume finery. The partying
continued through the night. The next morning the tourists, hung over
and bleary-eyed, arose at the crack of dawn to catch the 8:30 A.M. *Riviera
Express* for Paris.

Those ballplayers who could stay awake were blessed with viewing some
of the most beautiful landscape anywhere. The 675-mile railroad journey
offered a one-day tour of France. Their route carried them through the
heart of France's wine country; its beautiful, tidy farms; and the charming
cities of Marseilles and Lyons. Every noted place in the guidebooks sped
past the *Riviera Express*. At 10:00 P.M. the train rumbled into a darkened,
rain-swept, cold but still intoxicating Paris. The baseball teams tumbled
out of their train and made their way to the St. James Hotel.

Charles Comiskey had been ensconced in his suite at the St. James for a
few days now and was much recovered. Everyone in the party was heartily
cheered at how much better the White Sox's master looked. Propped up
on his pillows in his suite in the St. James, the old man held court. The
time off from the heady pace of the tour had been exactly what he needed.
His thoughts of going on to the States alone for recuperation had largely
evaporated, though Comiskey was by his own admission quite homesick,
desperately wanting a view of downtown Chicago.

Jim Thorpe was the only tourist to have visited Paris previously. In 1912
the U.S. Olympic track team took advantage of some open days at the
conclusion of the games to visit Paris. Abel Kiviat, silver medallist in the
1,500 meters, described the wonder that Thorpe was in Paris.

> He was a hell of a nice gentleman, but he never had a nickel. When
> we'd buy a beer, he couldn't. He just didn't have anything. After the
> Games some of us went over to France. We figured we'd get a lot of
> free wine and stuff. The prizes were 12 quarts of champagne for first
> place, 6 for second, and 3 for third. But the American officials told
> us no because it would make us professionals. But they did say we
> could help ourselves to the punch bowl after the competition, which
> we did.
>
> During our three day stay in Paris someone discovered a chandelier
> that must have been 10 feet off the floor. We all put a dollar in the
> pot to see if anybody could touch it. Thorpe didn't have a buck, but
> we gave him credit. There were about 14 of us in the room. Everyone
> tried it. Alma Richards of Brigham Young, who won the high jump
> at six feet, four inches, tried, but he couldn't. But Jim Thorpe did,
> and he was about four inches shorter than Richards.[33]

Paris was, of course, more than ten-feet-high chandeliers, and the tourists wasted no time in exploring the charms of the City of Lights. Steve Evans and Germany Schaefer publicly declared that they intended to be "naughty." As soon as the two checked in, their personal restraint checked out.

> The party was no sooner housed in the St. James than the clerk and bellboys were eagerly questioned as to where to go first and last. A shrug of the shoulders and whispered "Montmarte" seemed to have the effect necessary, and it was an impatient gang which waited for the night lights.
>
> The players were told of the mysteries and frankness of the Moulin Rouge, the Bal Tabrin, the Rat Mort, and Monico's and were advised to see these places early. After describing the pleasures to be seen there it was suggested that the tourists conserve their energy in the early evening and wait for the risqué entertainments of Albert's Alley, which is shrouded in darkness until midnight and then does a flourishing business until dawn.[34]

Not all of the tourists so eagerly engaged in "dissipation," the current phrase to describe just such activities. The married couples spent their time at the Louvre, at the theaters, and at the opera. The Thorpes went to these places, as well as to the Moulin Rouge and other tourist destinations. But even the nondissipaters where overwhelmed by the nightlife of Paris. Like just about every other member of the tour, the Thorpes got virtually no sleep at all in Paris for the four days the two teams would spend there.

Certainly the sportswriters knew what was going on and who was doing what to whom in Paris, but the fourth estate was a different animal in 1914. The press was far more interested in titillation rather than actual scandal. An Edwardian moral code prevailed; a nod and a wink were fine, but a journalist would rarely offer more. Sports journalists held their subjects up as heroes and rarely pushed a star ballplayer off his pedestal. Grantland Rice, perhaps the greatest sport journalist of the era, offered a neat encapsulation and satire of the prevailing standard in a poem he penned about the tourists' antics in Paris.

In Gay Paree

They told us what happened in Tokio town
And the ways of the young Japanese;
They spieled about Pekin with more than a touch
Of chopsticks and laundries and fleas.
They told us of Melbourne and Sydney, Et. Al.

Of visiting ranches and such;
And eke of the Cairo-cooked roundup of food
That put Commy's stomach in Dutch.
They told us of Venice and Naples and Rome.
And the fanfest arranged with the Pope;
Of wonderful paintings they lamped on the way,
Attached to the usual dope.
They told us of London, of gulping down tea.
Of royalty there without stint:
They told us what happened in Paris as well—
But I'm not gonna put it in print.[35]

At least one tourist went to Paris as neither a dissipater nor a sightseer but as a student. Andy Slight, the Chicago youth from Logan Square and member of the White Sox for the duration of the tour, paid a visit on Sammy Strang at a Paris conservatory. "Singing" Sammy Strang, while playing Major League baseball with the New York Giants, began a life-long love affair with opera. When his ten-year-long playing career ended in 1908, he dedicated himself to opera. Now a singer of note, Strang was gaining more fame on the floorboards and in the limelight than he had achieved as a leather-chasing baseball player. He was spending the winter of 1914 in Paris, training his voice. As a player, one of Strang's nicknames had been "the Dixie Thrush"; now he was a full-time songbird. Through contacts Slight had made with the Giants, Strang invited Slight to visit him and even wrangled the young man an audition. The conservatory staff were bowled over by Slight's performance, imploring him to forget about athletics and concentrate his energies on opera.

In Nice there had been a few Federal agents lolling about, trying to recruit tourists. Paris, however, was crawling with Federal agents. There was absolutely no way that McGraw, Callahan, and Comiskey could keep an eye on their charges. Back home, organized baseball was paranoid that they would lose every significant tourist to the Feds even before the teams hit London. Tris Speaker had become so vocal in his support for the new league and its goals that Callahan accused him of being a Federal agent, a charge that Speaker vociferously denied. In an unprecedented action, the National Commission certified Comiskey, Callahan, and McGraw to act as agents for Major League Baseball. The three tour leaders would attempt not only to get their own players under contract but also to negotiate contracts on behalf of the Phillies, Red Sox, and Cardinals, the teams that had players on the tour. Such an arrangement violated the National Commission's own policies. Players were only supposed to be negotiating with one team's representatives at a time, and agents were only supposed to represent one team at a time, preventing one owner from gaining advantage over another and, more important, preventing players from obtaining any leverage in their negotiations. The reserve clause tied a player to a particular team for a fixed number of years; even if he wanted to negotiate with another team's agents, he could not. But as the hurricane force called the Federal League hit U.S. shores, organized baseball went to war, intending to win by any means necessary.

Outside the St. James, the heavens over Paris maintained a steady drizzle. Two horse-racing tracks had been set aside as venues for the baseball games in Paris, St. Cloud and Parc de Princes. Diamonds had been prepared, posters printed, and a word-of-mouth publicity campaign launched. Even though he was ill, Comiskey had spent much of his sickbed time working the phones drumming up support for the games. The weather did not appear to be at all promising, but Commy vowed that the teams would do their best to play anyway.

The morning of the seventeenth dawned. Paris was gray, wet, and cold, and the first game of the Paris series was canceled. With no athletics on the schedule, the players were free to visit the sights of Paris. Of course, not all the men were early risers; the previous evening's dissipations had resulted in many casualties.

Just about all of the tourists visited Napoleon's tomb. For Ted Sullivan, the tomb was an especially profound experience. Sullivan's book of the tour, *History of World's Tour, Chicago White Sox and New York Giants*, one of three published in 1914, is an odd read. Identities are hidden behind aliases such as "Mrs. Highbrow" and "Spotlight man." Sullivan talks a great deal about himself and Commy but very little about anyone else on the tour. In a writing style that apparently dates from the Cretaceous period, Sullivan's narrative of Paris stops dead at Napoleon's tomb. For the next twenty pages, the reader is treated to a history of Napoleon's entire career from birth to Waterloo (perhaps the longest digression in the history of American sportswriting). It is as if Sullivan latched onto the tour for the sole purpose of communing with Napoleon's ghost.

After taking in the sights, the tourists enjoyed their most memorable dinner of the entire tour. U.S. ambassador Myron T. Herrick, George Kessler, and his business partner, Sam Elizas, manufacturers of White Seal Champagne, hosted the most opulent dinner any of the tourists had ever attended. Every member of the touring party turned out for the dinner. Present were not only the ambassador and the multimillionaire businessmen but a cross section of high-ranking officials of the French Republic. Elizas had actually been traveling with the tourists for a week. After attaching himself to the tour in Rome, he spent most of his time schmoozing with the players. Leaping at the chance to show off the benefits of capitalism, this dinner was something else, with gold plates, crystal wine glasses, gold utensils, silk napkins, delicacies by the score, and an endless stream of the world's finest wines and champagne. In the corner, a quartet played mood music on antique instruments.

Three thousand miles away, Phillies owner William F. Baker was having a day that was much less fun. Angered at Mickey Doolan's defection to the Feds, he announced to the press that his club "has taken all the steps necessary" to retain Doolan. Court action loomed. "Doolan," he said, "took the trip around the world with the consent of the Philadelphia club officials, and he is insured in favor of the local club on his return to this country."[36]

The Boston Red Sox contacted Jimmy Callahan, authorizing him to offer whatever money was necessary to land Tris Speaker. Despite some very hard negotiations, Callahan could not get Speaker's John Hancock on a contract. In the end, monetary offers had less effect on bringing Speaker back into organized baseball's fold than did Callahan's appealing to Speaker's sense of honor. Callahan got Speaker to pledge upon his word of honor that he would not sign with the Feds until he gave the Red Sox a chance to match any Federal offer. Speaker sincerely doubted that the Red Sox could match the kind of money the Feds were whispering about, but his word was his bond.

Rain fell on each of the next four days. The weather was not as bad, however, as what the tourists had played in back in the States. Cold, raw, and chilly with a steady rain, it was nonetheless better than what the tourists had endured in Medford, Oregon. The lack of athletic activity led some French papers to accuse the tourists of shirking. The press did not hesitate to remind Comiskey of his promise that the teams would do their best to play despite the weather. Gus Axelson wrote about just how unpopular the American baseball teams became in Paris. "The globe girdlers were lucky to get out of Paris with a whole scalp. The French citizens, police, and high officials were considerably wrought up because no game was staged after lots of money had been spent in preparations. They did not figure, as did the tourists, that it was impossible to stage a contest with rain falling all the time. Some of the promoters threaten to take the matter up with Ambassador Herrick, and it is just possible that it may develop into a diplomatic incident of some note."[37]

The charges of shirking may have had some validity. Paris certainly had more distractions than the average city. Few places in the world have such an intersection of culture, vice, fashion, society, and gastronomy—all the seven deadly sins in one place, often just blocks from each other. The Paris winter turned even the most parsimonious tourist into a money sieve. The wives and widows bought gowns and hats by the armful. Then, as now, owning a "Paris original" was a female badge of honor. And then, just as now, the prices for a Paris original were better in the French capital than in London, New York, or Chicago. All of the men became clotheshorses on the tour. Although the men would do most of their buying in London, the haberdashers of Paris could loosen their wallets just as easily as those on Bond Street. Even glum Bill Klem succumbed to the fashion craze, buying a mustard yellow jacket to go with the mahogany walking stick presented him in Shanghai.

At 9:15 A.M. on 22 February the very weary tourists snuck out of a very disappointed and angry Paris for Calais. The party boarded a Channel steamer, and just sixty-six minutes later they were in Dover, England. The first exposure to sea travel in weeks was a dreaded thing, especially for the tourists who had stuffed themselves to the gills with Paris's finest foods. The fears proved unfounded, as the Channel was in good humor that day, with barely a ripple on the water. Not one tourist became seasick during the crossing, a first for the tour. By 5:30 P.M. the tourists were in their rooms at the Cecil Hotel. American and British cultures were about to collide.

TWELVE

Baseball Fit for a King

The impudence of the Yankee knows no limits; and their baseball visit here has afforded another opportunity for the display of it. – *London Sketch*, February 1914

England's famously gray, rainy weather, along with T. S. Eliot's notorious yellow fog, rolled in as soon as the players crossed the threshold of the Cecil Hotel. It appeared that Grantland Rice's prophesy from October 1913 would prove true: "The keen-eyed expert who arranged the Giants–White Sox tour was a wonderful student of nature, climate, atmosphere and foreign lands. For example, he has the two clubs booked for London around mid-February. Now we are far from being endowed with a gambling disposition, but any citizen who wishes to wager that the Giants will be able to edge in one-third (1–3) of their February London schedule will be accommodated up to our ultimate kopeck."[1]

The tourists would garner more interest from the press and general public in England than in any other place, save perhaps Australia. Interest in these games had been brewing for months. The huge number of American expatriates and steady stream of tourists in London and all of the United Kingdom had over the years fueled a genuine curiosity about the sport. Baseball was played in most of the British colonies with varying degrees of passion. If one looked hard enough, one could find baseball teams scattered about the isles, even some small-time league action.

Britons who traveled were often quite taken with the game. Sir Arthur Conan Doyle, the creator of Sherlock Holmes and a complete American-phile, loved baseball. He found it much more exciting than cricket. When playing baseball, Doyle's preferred position was shortstop. Baseball also had developed some following among Britain's seafarers. The tourists met one such fan in the form of Captain Dixon-Hopcraft, but he was not alone in his passion for the game. A United Fruit steamer, the *Tivives*, had a team in the Caribbean League. An entirely British vessel, the baseball team was composed from its officers and crew. Authentic terrors of the Caribbean League, the steamer's team went undefeated through most of its 1913 season.[2]

A large contingent of fans met the two teams as their train pulled into the station. Seemingly every American in London was present, as were large delegations from the British press and representatives from English club teams. While everyone else made ready to meet the assembled crowd, Jimmy Callahan did not even stick his head out of the train. The Sox manager continued northward, apart from the teams. Callahan was bound for Ireland to look up relatives and enjoy the beauty of the Emerald Isle. He promised to return in time to manage the Sox for their big game, however.

The trek across the Channel saw a more somber group of baseball players than those who had dined with Sir Thomas Lipton only a few weeks before. Gone was much of the enthusiasm for the tour and each other. Weather, travel, and homesickness played a part, but baseball politics was the biggest factor in altering the players' mood. Even the nature of the players' conversations had changed. Players and management tried not to mention the powerful words "Federal League" in the presence of each other, as it generally deteriorated into shouting matches and hurt feelings.

About the only baseball issue left to discuss was Charles W. Murphy's departure as president and owner of the Cubs. Baseball's ownership cabal decreed that Murphy simply had to go. Governor Tener's first act as president of the National League was to order Murphy to sell the Cubs. On 21 February 1914 Charles P. Taft of Cincinnati became the new president and owner of the Cubs. Not one owner or player in baseball lamented Murphy's demise. For alienating his fan base though his crass stupidity in the handling of Evers and Chance, Murphy had to forfeit his professional life. Even with Taft on board, the Cubs would play second fiddle to the Chi-Feds for all of the 1914 season. With Chicago being the largest city in organized baseball to have a Federal League franchise, success there would only embolden the "outlaws" and encourage the players' brotherhood. For the owners, this scenario heralded Armageddon.

The Federals were making inroad after inroad on the tourists. The baseball players who had stayed stateside were just as much fair game as those in Europe. The new league signed Arthur Fromme on 18 January, and now they were closing in on Matty as well. While the tourists were roaming London, Matty was receiving visitors from the Federal League in Pasadena, California. The Brooklyn Tip-Tops offered Mathewson his dream job, that of manager. Matty went on record stating, "I have received the Federals' offer and I will give it careful and serious consideration."[3]

Matty's remuneration would surely be astronomical, as league president James Gilmore told Matty that "he could name his own terms" to manage for the Feds.[4] The Giants' front office had really let things slide while McGraw was out of the country. The team's only dealings with Matty were to send him an unsigned contract for the 1914 season. No cover letter, no incentives, just sign this contract and return it to New York please. Mathewson decided that he would do nothing until he talked the situation over with McGraw upon McGraw's return to the States. Matty would report to Marlin, Texas, with an unsigned Giants contract in his pocket and a thousand questions for his good friend John McGraw.

Reporting to Marlin in an identical predicament was Jeff Tesreau. Offered a lucrative Fed contract, Tesreau bluntly told anyone who would listen that he intended to take up the Feds on their offer unless the Giants matched it. It looked very likely that when McGraw returned to America, his Giants would be in disarray.

This would be the first year that the Giants would go to spring training without McGraw. Likewise, the White Sox had never before departed for spring training without Comiskey. The Giants headed for familiar Marlin, Texas; the Sox were experimenting with a new locale, Paso Robles, California. The White Sox would be under the charge of Kid Gleason, who would manage the team until Jimmy Callahan returned to the States.

The tourists were still without Bill Sheridan, although he was expected any day. Sheridan had somehow managed to miss all of the connections on his journey from Alexandria, Egypt. Side bets were accumulating as to whether the umpire would make it to England in time to catch the *Lusitania*, let alone work a game. Sheridan still had three days in which to make it to London before any games were scheduled. Even if the tourists had wanted to play, fog, rain, and wind made any game impossible. London delivered its most Dickensian pea-soup fog from 23 through 25 February, reminding one and all that it was indeed wintertime in England.

The tourists spent those days shopping and sightseeing. The men cruised the haberdasheries of Soho with the same ferocity that the women had shown at the dress shops of Paris. Comiskey and McGraw also made good use of their time speaking to the press. Comiskey spouted platitudes, while McGraw's earthiness was captured in all its raw beauty by Britain's scribes. On 24 February 1914 the two men held court, and McGraw's comments nearly destroyed either team's opportunity even to play a game in England. When interviewed by the *Pall Mall Gazette*, McGraw let loose with "American soldiers are superior to the British because of the athletic discipline in the United States and because every American soldier has learned to play baseball and through that game has benefited his mind as well as his body."[5]

The *Pall Mall Gazette* fired back with a blistering editorial the next day. The paper labeled McGraw as "impertinent" and stated that "[McGraw] possibly was not in a position to criticize either the English or American soldiers."[6] The *Pall Mall Gazette* and a few other English newspapers called for a boycott of the game to protest McGraw's statements.

The writer for the *London Sketch* was positively livid. "The impudence of the Yankee knows no limits; and their baseball visit here has afforded another opportunity for the display of it. John J. McGraw, manager of the Giants, says that baseball is a much better game than cricket, and he also offers testimony that England is losing her snap and vigor." The writer continued his screed:

> No more than my readers do I like the indiscriminant use of stale expletives but—his impudence—yes, that is the very least I can say.
>
> We are losing our vigor, are we? It's none of his business; but how does he come to that conclusion? It is because a few scaremongers lamented with indecent sobs our failure to win certain fantastic trials of skill! *** anyhow let me tell him that we do not in the least desire the sham vigor of the Yankee—that hysterical hustle WHICH ACHIEVES NOTHING BUT RAGTIME, REVUES, POLITICAL CORRUPTION AND DYSPEPSIA. We do not believe that breakneck speed and solid vigor are the same thing. The less we yield to the Yankee fever, the stronger we shall be.[7]

So great were the fireworks that even McGraw concluded that he was "talking too much."[8] For much of the rest of their stay in London, the Giants manager would be most unusually silent.

Charles Comiskey said much the same thing as McGraw without igniting a powder keg under himself. Comiskey, raised around political machines his whole life, understood proper public discourse. He managed to come across as a refined gentleman, again proving that it is not what you say but how you say it. "Our tour has been a happy one in all respects. It has been not only an exhibition of swift and thrilling sport, but an exhibition of American manhood which ought to enhance our prestige among the nations. Our men made a fine impression, not only by their physical prowess, but by their friendliness and good manners."[9]

The White Sox chief did have his worries in London. On 25 February

1914, while the Sox back in the States were still trying to find their way to Paso Robles, Comiskey dispatched some of the most Irish members of his Royal Rooters out on a seek-and-recover mission. Norris "Tip" O'Neal, Jim Mullen, and a few others were sent off to County Kilkenny to try and ferret out Jimmy Callahan. The Sox manager had not been seen since his departure on the twenty-second for Ireland, and with the big game in London scheduled for the twenty-sixth, the boss was getting nervous.

Both McGraw and Comiskey were having health troubles, which were only exacerbated by England's notorious weather. Comiskey's stomach problems reemerged, and McGraw was confined to his hotel room with a bad cold on what he claimed were doctor's orders. Mugsy had caught a cold in the damp of Paris. Cavalier about his health, McGraw ignored his illnesses until they became too obvious to ignore. He complained also that the yellow coal smoke enveloping the city would bring on pneumonia. It is just as possible, however, that the Giants manager inflated his illness so that he could duck out of that evening's speaking event. McGraw did not want to give the British press another chance to allow him to make a fool out of himself.

For a time it looked as though none of the tour's principals would be in attendance at the lavish banquet being thrown at the Savoy. Planned months in advance, the dinner was the brainchild of American actors who worked the British stage. The thespians, along with other American notables, would host the baseball teams at London's finest establishment. Fortunately, one-third of the tour's leading triumvirate, Jimmy Callahan, arrived back in London just in time to attend the banquet and relay McGraw's and Comiskey's regrets.

The sumptuous dinner featured Lord Desborough, one of King George V's closest friends, offering the following pronouncements: "[He] spoke glowingly on the athletic relations of England and America. He advanced the opinion that the white races of the earth have completely demonstrated their superiority in every athletic enterprise and he praised base ball as an invigorating, health-building and morally clean sport."[10] The British lord prattled on, oblivious to the presence of Jim Thorpe, whose athleticism had so recently deflated just such pretensions.

Lord Desborough had toured America extensively in his youth, hiking the Rockies and swimming the Niagara River, among other prodigious feats. Now a noted boxing promoter in his native land, Lord Desborough promised to do his utmost to get King George V to attend the Americans' baseball game at Chelsea Football Stadium.

Harry Gordon Selfridge, an American who had gone to England and made his fortune with a London department store, spoke on behalf of all American expatriates. Selfridge had been pining for a real baseball game almost from the moment he had taken up residence in London.

In addition to the banquet, the American actors had also seen to it that free passes to all of London's theaters were presented to the tourists. These passes were eagerly snapped up by the tourists, all of whom managed to see at least one play while in the city.

As everywhere else the tourists went, the Thorpes were the center of attention. The two drew crowds everywhere in London. Thorpe's success in the Olympic games had not gone unnoticed in Britain; neither did his racial identity. England had a fixation with the myths of the American West. Buffalo Bill and his western shows always did tremendous business in the United Kingdom. In Thorpe, England had a "genuine Red Indian" to fawn over. Even at the theater where the Thorpes went to take in *Broadway Jones and the Melting Pot*, among other shows, the couple was immediately mobbed. If Jim Thorpe disappointed the British in any way, it was in not meeting their expectations as to what a "wild" American Indian should look like. The British had honestly expected him to be wearing feathers and scalps.[11]

The twenty-sixth day of February 1914 dawned cool and clear for what proved to be the single most anticipated game of the entire tour. Lord Desborough successfully prevailed upon his friend the king to attend the game. The Giants and White Sox ended up putting a tasty dish before the king, playing what was arguably the best game of the entire tour.

While unquestionably the greatest attendance of any game of the tour, actual numbers are hard to verify. The British press unanimously gave a figure of twenty thousand to twenty-five thousand, while the American press gave estimates of between thirty thousand and thirty-five thousand. Certainly one can say that there were at least twenty thousand spectators at the event. Both the American and British press likely printed numbers that confirmed their own presumptions as to the popularity of the sport in England.

Even the preliminaries brought out excitement. The players paraded from their hotel to the game in full uniform, inspiring much curiosity, many comments, and last-minute walk-up purchases of tickets. A personal box for the king was set up behind home plate. Luxuriously appointed with purple and gold satin lining, the box featured a stone staircase and a narrow flower garden with potted flowers, including hyacinths in full bloom. The lavish spectacle inspired Jimmy Callahan, fresh with Irish pride from his tour of the homeland, to remark that some holes should be cut in the safety netting to send a message to the king. By extreme good fortune, Callahan's Irish nationalism sentiments were not overheard by London's scribes.

To many English reporters, the transformations made to the Stamford Bridge Grounds for baseball came as a shock. The reporter for the *Manchester Mirror* wrote:

> Sporting London, or some 20,000 of it extended a very hearty welcome to the American "ball" players at Stamford Bridge yesterday. Those present were privileged to witness the cream of the baseball talent. It revealed, as was fairly well understood, an up-to-date version of the old English game of "rounders." The Chelsea football ground presented a very unfamiliar spectacle, with the line of stands covered from roof to ground with a wealth of wire netting. What with the tenantless goals, a disused cinder-path, and the glint of a purple and gold impromptu Royal box usurping the customary directors' stand, the place was unrecognizable but for its peculiar environment.[12]

That the king had promised to put in an appearance already made the day significant. Never before as king had George V entered Chelsea stadium. He and the rest of Britain had no idea what to expect from the game, but that was not the case for the thousands of Americans in London for business, school, or pleasure. Gus Axelson and U.S. ambassador Walter Hines Page offered to explain the finer points of the game to George V. Once the game started, the king would be seated between Ambassador Page and Irwin H. Laughlin, the ambassador's personal secretary.

Until the king arrived, the Giants and White Sox engaged in a preliminary game of shadow ball. As everywhere else the teams had launched the stunt, the London edition of shadow ball was a huge success, evoking as much laughter in England as it had in California. The shadow ball game also helped both sides loosen up. Having not played for two weeks, everyone was rusty. The practice also made the teams aware of the only potential handicap for the day, the February weather had left the soccer grounds slick and a bit soggy.

This report from the *Manchester Mirror* gives a sense of the electricity apparent from the crowd awaiting their sovereign.

> His Majesty's coming was impatiently awaited by a company comprising many people of the highest rank and most nationalities. At the announcement of his arrival the baseball teams lined up below the Royal box. With the assembled thousands on their feet and the air re-echoing with the cheering in response to a call of "Three cheers for

the King," the Royal party received an especially warm greeting from the players. The leading spirits of the display, in Messrs. Comiskey, Callahan, and McGraw, having been presented to His Majesty, the crowd settled down to watch the game amidst unceasing calls of Play ball![13]

When introduced to the managers and Comiskey, the king, nattily attired in a dark suit and black derby, shook their hands and remarked, "I am delighted to see you gentlemen here with your ball teams."[14] The baseball teams offered three cheers to His Majesty in response. After cheering the king, the game ball made its way from Ambassador Page to the king and from the king to Jimmy Callahan and then in turn to Bill Klem, who tossed it to Jim Scott, the White Sox starting pitcher. Scott, who relied on the spitter, promptly expectorated all over the baseball. Frank McGlynn and Victor Miller dutifully recorded all of this activity with their camera. The game ball lasted one pitch, being tossed to the first batter, Mike Donlin, for a strike before being retired from play. After the game McGraw and Callahan would present the ball, dyed a hideous brown by Scott's tobacco-laden saliva, to Comiskey as a souvenir.

As in every other corner of the globe, Bill Klem's vocal majesty impressed everyone. The fact that he could be heard in all parts of the stadium without any problem amazed those gathered for the game. As he had everywhere else, Klem provided elaborate introductions for each player as they stepped up to the plate. Once again he had a partner; Jack Sheridan had at last returned from his sojourn in Egypt.

The reporter from Manchester struggled to describe baseball. "It was for all the world like our cricketers 'having a few down at the nets' before the match starts. Physically, a finer collection of athletes could not well be found. Their catching and throwing were up to the highest standard known in this country. The powerful strokes of the batsman volleyed the ball to prodigious heights, and on occasions to such extreme lengths as half way up on the big bank on the western side of the ground."[15]

Seeking cricket metaphors that would help his audience understand the action, the same reporter wrote, "These 'ball' players also indulge in fancy catching and tossing of the ball from one to another known to the cricket field. They are far away twin brothers, these men in the coloured flannel loose-fitting knickerbockers suits, to our cricketing fraternity. The whole of them would, apparently, qualify for the onerous post of 'cover point.' "[16]

The White Sox and Giants responded with a terrific game, one that captured the foreign audience completely. Scoreless for the first two and a half innings, the White Sox brought in two runs in the bottom of the third, to which the Giants immediately responded by tying up the game in the top of the fourth. The game remained tied until the tenth inning, when both teams plated two runs, leaving the game deadlocked. In the top of the eleventh, Tom Daly, life-long journeyman, had his most memorable day in baseball, hitting a home run into the deepest part of the stadium to win the game. The final score read 5–4 in favor of the White Sox. Appropriately, Daly, a Canadian, was the only member of the world tour who really was a royal subject. Red Faber went all eleven innings in a losing effort, while Joe Benz, who relieved Jim Scott after six innings, earned the win.

Both teams went into a win-at-all-costs mode, producing high tensions as each side fought for the win. A game marked with sparkling plays by both the defense and the offense, the contest brought out the best in the athletes. Tris Speaker hit what could easily have been the game's fourth home run, but Lee Magee, "sprinting as he had never done before made a leap in the air and speared the ball with one hand. Disgusted, Speaker yelled: 'Yes, you lucky stiff. You tried that grand stand play eleven times on this trip without making it and now you pulled it off before the king.'"[17]

As for the king, he enjoyed the game greatly. George V became completely enrapt in the ball game, not even noticing when a foul ball smashed some glass above the royal box. While others nearby dived for cover, the king's attention never wavered from the baseball game. Photographers captured the king with a broad smile upon his face. "His Majesty told Ambassador Page that he had never enjoyed an afternoon more."[18] When the game concluded, he stood and cheered and sent the following message to be delivered to the teams. "Tell Mr. McGraw and Mr. Comiskey that I have enjoyed the game enormously."[19]

Like other audiences familiar with cricket, the American pitchers' velocity and ability with a baseball awed the spectators. Pitching was praised as both the sport's greatest asset and the hardest thing to follow about the game. The *Manchester Mirror* again:

If there is one drawback about baseball (to the English eye) it is the apparent hopelessness of anyone ever being able to make any score worth mention against such scientifically skillful pitching (it is really throwing, pure and simple), and so tight a field. The alertness, fine judgment, and precise throwing of the ball about the playing field seem to form an impossible bar to the batsman ever reaching that difficult first base, let alone the other three points, or bases, set out on the parallelogram. All are guarded by zealous, sure-handed basemen.

But now and again, mostly when the least expected, the defense is pierced. Generally it is a ground stroke that enables some true-eyed batter to overcome the unmistakable superiority owned by the fielding side, which likes nothing better than the soaring flights of the white covered and easily sighted ball. The stroke par excellence, however, is the one "over the fence," that is a drive right over the boundary. We saw two such yesterday afternoon.[20]

The British press itself held widely varying but mostly negative opinions of the sport they had just witnessed. The *Chicago Evening Post* published a collection of opinions from the various British newspapers. Here is a sampling of that paper's excerpts.

"Baseball is just rounders, played hard."

"We who had awaited the exhibition with a keen desire to understand and admire were a little dashed at its transparency *** it is rounders."

"Even rounders on the village green would have more excitement."

"Their faces are all curiously alike—big and square."

"The crowd laughed when a Chicago man got a hard crack on the ankle and limped across the ground in pain. Also it cheered when a Chicago man drove the ball by chance out of play and into one of the Chelsea goal nets. A section of it seemed to find this convincing, but asked whether the Sox hadn't won by a goal to nil."

"His club *** rather like a thin Indian club."

"A cricketer would find it hard to hit a ball."

"A poor game."

"This exciting game."

"The word 'rounders' annoyed the Americans, but there is no essential difference."[21]

After the game Jimmy Callahan was a changed man. Completely won over by the king's enthusiasm, the Irish rebel had been converted into a loyal subject. Upon his return home he offered the following pronouncement: "We played to the biggest crowd of the trip in London, and there was no more enthusiastic rooter than King George. He must have been coached on the game, for after the second inning he showed familiarity with the plays and actually kept detailed score. The King made a big hit with the players. He is most democratic, and acted just like an ordinary fan."[22]

With the conclusion of the game, the teams took advantage of their London play passes and shopped and toured the city some more. At midnight all the men of the party gathered for an all-night smoker and beefsteak feast at Murray's Club. The following morning, 27 February 1914, produced another thick fog, confining the tourists to the theaters or last-minute bargain hunting. That evening the tourists packed up everything they had accumulated on their tour. More than one tourist had to purchase an extra suitcase or two. Some of the more enterprising tourists had already shipped much of their accumulated loot home via the mails.

At 9:15 A.M. on the last day of February 1914 the tourists shipped out by train for Liverpool where the luxury liner, the *Lusitania*, awaited their arrival. Liverpool's docks were a beehive of activity. England's main shipping port never ran at less than full tilt. The tourists had less than an hour from the time they arrived at 1:45 in the afternoon until the ship sailed at 2:30 to have their bags loaded and to check themselves into their staterooms. They were an excited bunch. The tour had been wonderful, but there was not a soul among them who was not homesick. Everyone would have time to reflect on the tour during the six-day cruise to New York.

The *Lusitania*, still one of the fastest and grandest ships afloat, had set the transatlantic speed record in 1907, a year after its first voyage. Elegance on the sea, the *Lusitania* remained the pride of the Cunard Line. The picture of wealthy Americans and Brits mingling amid the dinning rooms and deckchairs of ships like the *Lusitania* is an iconic image of the world before the Great War. The tourists enjoyed the luxury of this great ship to the fullest. Although cold weather usually confined activities below deck, the baseball teams greatly enjoyed their passage, by far the smoothest of any the tourists had experienced. Storms delayed their arrival in New York for one day, but so serenely did the *Lusitania* sail that not one tourist became seasick.

Four days into their voyage the tourists put on a show. On 3 March the *Lusitania* held a benefit for the Mariners Charity, an aid organization for disabled sailors and the survivors of sailors killed in service to the Crown. The benefit brought the tourists together for the final time. Germany Schaefer played his tune "Shoenus," the "Sextette" reassembled for the final time, and the women in the group entertained on their musical instruments. The benefit would mark the last harmonious notes of the tour.

The next day, back home in Chicago, more than four thousand people gathered to watch the groundbreaking for Weeghman Park, home to the Federal League's Chicago Whales. In less than a month the Chi-Feds would complete the prettiest baseball palace in Chicago. (This jewel is still with us. It is now known as Wrigley Field.) With the new stadium and their seemingly unlimited bank accounts, no one in baseball could ignore the upstarts any longer.

On Friday, 6 March 1914, a cold, raw day with steady snow falling, the *Lusitania* arrived in New York. The unsigned tourists were floored to discover just how valued they were by the Federal League. The upstarts sought to rent their own vessel to greet the *Lusitania* as it arrived in New York harbor. What *Sporting Life* described as "the Player Melee" and others called the "Battle of the Dock" ensued.

The *New York Morning Telegraph* described the pandemonium of the tourists' return:

> Greeted by one of the noisiest ovations ever witnessed in New York City, the world tourist Giants and the White Sox returned to this city on the *Lusitania* yesterday morning, after an absence of nearly six months on foreign shores.
>
> Magnates and baseball fans crowded the dock and tested the stability of the heavy structure, until the planking beneath thousands of feet groaned in protest. Uproarious welcome-home and joyous salutations were hurled at the incoming players almost before they were within hearing distance, and the men climbed upon each other's shoulders in their enthusiastic efforts to catch a first glimpse of their heroes of the diamond.
>
> The players were met by tugs loaded with magnates and fans and upon landing were whisked into automobiles and driven up Broadway to the Imperial Hotel. Their upward journey was in the nature of a triumphal parade, and no conquering warrior of the old days was ever accorded a more genuinely enthusiastic greeting upon his return from great achievements than were the globetrotting baseball players yesterday morning.[23]

James Gilmore rented two ships. He hoped to use one vessel to pull alongside the *Lusitania* and offer Fed contracts to the returning heroes. Gilmore, however, did not anticipate the craftiness of his rivals. Eighty of Comiskey's cronies, including Ban Johnson, president of the American League, rented the steamship *Niagara* to sail out and greet the *Lusitania* even before it docked, thus beating Gilmore to the punch. Organized baseball used some rather ham-handed intimidation tactics to foil the Federal League at every turn. A band of gunmen from the East Side, Tammany Hall's army of strong-arm enforcers, patrolled the streets leading to the waterfront with orders to "intercept" the representatives of the Federal League. Mordecai "Three Finger" Brown and James Gilmore's Federal League agents successfully made their way to the waterfront by keeping a sharp lookout for, and making some mad dashes to avoid, the Tammany Hall thugs. Having failed to keep them away from the waterfront, the

Major Leagues switched gears. James Gaffney, owner of the Boston Braves and member of the Tammany Hall political machine, used his influence to get the Federal League's ships locked in quarantine.

With their ships unavailable, James Gilmore and the rest of the Federal League agents once more changed tactics. The group obtained passes to greet the players at the dock as they stepped off the *Lusitania*. There were six thousand folks out in the snow to welcome the players back to the United States. Many of them, including a delegation some five hundred strong from Chicago, wore purple ribbons emblazoned with the gold lettering of the official welcoming committee. Working anonymously among this throng, the Feds recruited defectors from organized baseball. While the players shook hands with well-wishers, the Federal League agents slipped them business cards signed by every Federal League manager inviting them to their headquarters at the Knickerbocker Hotel.

Grantland Rice, commenting on this incredible reception wrote, "There are moments in our imagination when we had dreams of taking a trip around the world. But not in the wildest or most piercing phantasmagora [sic] of our mental make-up have we been able to dream of such a tour coming to an end at dockside with three rival establishments pleading with us to accept all the bullion we could take away on a truck."[24]

The scene at the Knickerbocker Hotel was surreal. George Ward of Brooklyn's Tip-Top Bakery and James Gilmore of the Indianapolis Feds opened the money tap. Obscene offers spilled out all over the Knickerbocker. Walter Fritsch, part of the St. Louis Feds' front office, told *Sporting Life*,

> Two hours after the *Lusitania* docked, Lee Magee, Steve Evans, Tris Speaker, and Mike Doolan were at our headquarters. I rented a fourth room so that "Brownie" could confer with Magee. The first thing Magee said was "Fellows, I'm for the Federal League, heart and soul, but I'm pretty certain of being traded to New York, and if I get a chance to play in the World's Series I will value that pretty highly. McGraw is after me, and promised to put through a trade for me if I do not jump." Well, some interesting things happened in our headquarters. I saw Tris Speaker fingering a certified check for $18,000, with the two $500 bills, which was the Brooklyn Federals' first offer. Speaker finally handed back Ward's money saying "For God's sake, men, take this money away or I'll fall. I promised on my word of honor that I would give Lannin a chance before I signed up."[25]

To retain their most valuable box office attraction, Red Sox president Joseph

J. Lannin was forced to match the Federal League offer. Speaker received a contract for at least $16,000 a year for three years and a $5,000 signing bonus, an almost incomprehensible salary for a professional athlete. One statistician was so struck with the amount that he went to the trouble to figure out Speaker's hourly remuneration. The figure he came up with, "Speaker will get $58.44 an hour or $116.88 a game."[26]

Nearly all of the tourists improved their situation financially. The Feds were disappointed that they did not land more of the tourists. Stealing the world travelers from organized baseball would have been quite a feather in their caps. The Feds were only able to sign Mickey Doolan, who joined the Baltimore Terrapins, and Steve Evans. Evans's salary with the Brooklyn Tip-Tops remained undisclosed, but he was seen that night in Manhattan flashing three $1,000 bills.

Germany Schaefer came very close to jumping to the new league. Speculation in the press had it that the jokester had already leaped. He claimed that he "wanted to go to the club that appreciated a joke by showing something more negotiable than a smile." And "You can't pay for one joke with another."[27] In the end, Schaefer returned to the Senators for another year.

After dodging the crush of fans, reporters, and Federal League conspirators, Comiskey and McGraw set about the final business of the tour, two mammoth banquets in New York and Chicago. Both owners also went to great lengths to explain that despite playing to in excess of an estimated one hundred thousand fans around the world, their tour had in fact made no money. *Sporting Life* determined, however, that "the games in the United States brought in almost $100,000 at the gate. A few days ago announcement was made that the receipts were almost $75,000 over expenses. At any rate, the tour made money."[28]

The two banquets featured everything—celebrities, booze, and dancing. The gargantuan fruitcake that the teams had dragged with them since Seattle, miraculously vermin free, was sliced right down the middle. The half featuring John McGraw's visage would be consumed at the party for the Giants at the Biltmore Hotel on Saturday, 7 March 1914. Comiskey and Callahan would be consumed at the Chicago Home Coming Banquet held at the Congress Hotel three days later.

As soon as he set his feet back upon terra firma, Ted Sullivan was loudly proclaiming a White Sox plan for a tour of South America after the 1914 season, an idea hatched when the teams were sailing through the Coral Sea on the *Orontes*. The only continent not visited by the tourists on their round-the-world tour made the next logical conquest. Sullivan could hardly wait to get this venture rolling.

The Biltmore dinner was the more sedate of the two. Six hundred friends of the Giants and Major League Baseball were seated in groups of six at tables filling the Biltmore's grand ballroom. Live flowers covered the tables along with cards, fancy menus, and offbeat party favors. Every guest received a "pocket electric lamp and a large wax doll attired in a baseball uniform."[29]

Aside from expounding more on the idea of taking two baseball teams on a South American tour, Ted Sullivan gave one of his usual long-winded speeches at the Biltmore banquet. The verbal fireworks of the evening were delivered by Ban Johnson, who issued a death warrant for the Feds. "I am not now in favor of peace-making methods. There is no need of dealing with these 'pirates.' The American League doesn't favor this silly stuff. There will be peace when the Federal League is exterminated. We have come to greet the world's tourists and we will refuse to have any conference with the representatives of this 'joke' league."[30]

"Dav's Day Dreams," a column in the *Chicago American*, put Johnson's worries in simple verse.

> "The Feds are harmless," the magnate said.
> "They won't injure us a bit."
> Then he wandered into his office
> And threw a conniption fit.[31]

Ban Johnson's rage brought swift reaction from Federal League president James Gilmore. "Is this the same Johnson who encouraged contract jumping when he was making his league leap to the front as president of the struggling American League? I think Ban Johnson is a trifle bit peeved because he has recently discerned that we have more financial backing than the American and National Leagues put together."[32]

The ugliest incident of the New York banquet was a shouting match between Mickey Doolan and William F. Baker, president of the Philadelphia Phillies. Doolan's jump to the Baltimore Terrapins enraged Baker, who felt sure that he possessed a valid contract for the second baseman. Baker took Doolan's defection as a personal affront and reacted by insulting Doolan's manhood. The matter would end up in court, but no judge would prevent Doolan from playing for the Terrapins.

Even before the Chicago banquet, the tourists were breaking up. Jim Scott and Joe Benz were the first to leave. Scott's departure was by far the saddest. While partying at the Biltmore, Scott received the news that his brother had passed away in Landers, Wyoming. He departed immediately for home.

Joe Benz did not hang around for either party. Spurred on, no doubt, by the awful Pacific crossing and by the example of all the happy honeymooners on the world tour, Benz made his way to Chicago on the first available train. He planned to wed immediately; nothing would be allowed to get in his way. The *Chicago Inter-Ocean* had a reporter waiting for the butcher's boy. Here is his account of Joe Benz's return to Chicago.

> As soon as Joe stepped off the train he stuck out his head and said, "Aint I the kid?"
>
> "You bet you are," replied Miss Alicia Leddy of 4924 Indiana Avenue and planted a smacking kiss upon Joe's map right before everyone in the depot. Joe couldn't stop long enough to tell of his trip, because he said he had to make arrangements for his marriage which is scheduled to take place on Tuesday.[33]

Before departing to make wedding plans, Benz did opine about meeting George V, and Thorpe, the tour's greatest attraction. "'I shook hands with the King of England,' exclaimed Benz, producing his mit [*sic*] for inspection, as if the touch of royalty still lingered on the calloused palm. 'We all did. He's a good fellow, and said something nice to all of us as we went along. Thorpe improved 100 per cent on the trip, and he'll be a regular before too long.'"[34]

The Tour to End All Tours closed with a bang in the Gold Room of the Congress Hotel in Chicago on 10 March 1914. *Sporting Life* accurately called the gala "A Tribute to Comiskey." If there was one thing Charles Comiskey knew how to celebrate, it was himself. The Woodland Bards Association pulled out all the stops, turning the welcome-home banquet into a celebration of Comiskey and all things Irish.

Even the party favors at this event favored Comiskey. Each man as he entered was randomly assigned a white cap emblazoned with either "White Sox" or "Giants." Adorning each table were menu cards and paper baseballs bearing photographs of Jimmy Callahan and Charles Comiskey. There was, however, one truly wonderful souvenir. All attendees received a souvenir book entitled *The Home Coming*, written and compiled by Ed Heeman and Ring Lardner. This little item, now quite rare, has the distinction of being Lardner's first published book. Lavishly illustrated with cartoons, quips, and farcical retellings of the tour around the world, the book complemented the evening's atmosphere brilliantly.

Neither John McGraw nor any of his Giants would be present for

Commy's shindig. After the party at the Biltmore, McGraw made his way directly to Marlin, Texas, to take over spring training, his players following close upon his heels. McGraw sent a letter of regret to the Chicago banquet, while team captain Larry Doyle sent a letter on behalf of his teammates. Affixed next to Doyle's signature were those of Jim Thorpe, Hooks Wiltse, Mike Donlin, and Bunny Hearn.

Joe Benz's absence was explained by his marriage that morning. He did, however, send the best telegram of the night. "No place like home. Have just started one of my own."[35] Seated off to one side near the speaker's table were the remaining White Sox who had circled the globe—Germany Schaefer, Buck Weaver, Steve Evans, Andy Slight, Jack Bliss, Walter Leverenz, Tris Speaker, Dick Egan, and a still-grieving Jim Scott. Germany Schafer stood up as part of the preliminaries and led the boys in "Shoenus," which he also called "Schnitzelbaum." The comic rendition of lines such as "Oh, du shoenus, oh magnolious," had the crowd in hysterics.

After that, things turned maudlin. "Smiley" Mike Corbett, over whose booze the world tour had begun, came out and croaked his original composition, "The Old Home Plate." The rest of the night it was Irish standards and lots of beer. One of the evening's highlights, however, would come in the form of a spectacular grand entrance. Beautiful (and quite probably scantily dressed) Doris Reber was carried through the assembly on a platform astride a giant albino stag that had been shot by Comiskey himself. The singer's platform was deposited at the front of the ballroom. From her perch, she led the assembled crowd of seven hundred in singing "The Star-spangled Banner."

Ban Johnson, Ted Sullivan, and all the rest of Charles Comiskey's sycophantic devotees made speeches, each more pompous than the last. Governor Tener, president of the National League who had toured the world with A. G. Spalding, got to deliver the keynote address. The following day Ban Johnson would accompany the Old Roman to his retreat in Wisconsin. Commy needed rest, as his stomach continued to bother him.

Weeks later, as opening day 1914 approached, the Old Roman paid the ultimate homage to John McGraw, a man whom once the entire American League had despised as a turncoat and a traitor. Although they would always address each other as "Mr. McGraw" and "Mr. Comiskey," an unquestioned deep respect had developed between the two men. Comiskey's respect for his former rival was so great that he remarked: "I do not think that Mr. McGraw received full credit for what he did on the memorable trip of the Giants and White Sox around the world. Could I have a year to pick a partner for the journey of the kind we just finished I could not possibly find a better one than John J. McGraw."[36]

Comiskey closed the interview with some of the highest praise he ever gave anyone. "If I should ever make another trip I could ask for no greater favor than to have John J. McGraw as a partner."[37]

Afterword

1924

A decade after Comiskey's and McGraw's triumphant world tour, the event had already been lost in obscurity. The rise and demise of the Federal League, the Great War, and Prohibition had driven the few memorials of the tour to the back pages of the nation's sports sections.

Comiskey and McGraw decided to memorialize their triumph and restore it to public consciousness by going on tour again. The 1924 tour possessed a far less ambitious itinerary; the two teams planned to go only as far as Europe. Ireland, Scotland, England, France, Belgium, Germany, and Italy were the scheduled destinations. Sportswriters used the same language of a decade before. *Time* magazine referred to the teams as "missionaries," then continued the analogy, "Instead of Bibles and hymn-books, these missionaries will carry with them balls, bats, mits [*sic*]. Instead of love and light, these missionaries will shed baseball fanaticism all over Europe."[1] This tour, however, never caught on, either with the public or the athletes themselves. Poorly financed and ill-timed, the tour got only as far as Paris before being summarily abandoned. As *Time* put it in its follow-up coverage, "They came, they saw, they gave it up."[2]

Neither Comiskey, McGraw, the White Sox, the Giants, nor the world was the same. The decade had been especially hard on Comiskey. After the pinnacle of a World Series Championship in 1917 against McGraw's Giants and a return to the Series after the Great War in 1919 came the "Black Sox" scandal. The ugly truth that some of the Sox had conspired to give the Series to the Reds at the behest of gamblers broke late in the 1920 season, with the White Sox locked in a tight pennant race.

Commy tried to hold his championship team together even as his empire collapsed around him. Alternating between support and condemnation for his players, Comiskey turned to memories of the world tour for solace. "I would rather close my ball park than send nine men to the field with one of them holding a dishonest thought toward clean baseball—the game John McGraw and I went around the world with to show people on the other side."[3]

By 1924 Charles Comiskey had been permanently marked by the scandal. His Sox were perennial troglodytes, incompetently managed and in financial disarray. Commy's men wielded a solid brass touch when it came to signing talent. Good money followed bad, as Commy threw cash at one worthless prospect after another.

This was not how Comiskey wanted to be remembered. It could all have turned out so differently. On 26 October 1931 Comiskey passed away in his paneled estate in Eagle River, Wisconsin, a tired, broken man with a shattered heart and a million-dollar estate.

Lou Comiskey, who had honeymooned on the world tour, took over the Sox upon his father's death. Far more a fair dealer than his old man and possessing a better eye for talent, Lou had begun to reverse the White Sox's long slide. Then, during the dark days of the Great Depression, he, too, passed away, far too young at just fifty-four years old.

John McGraw had a wonderful year in 1924. His Giants returned to the World Series, where they were beaten by Walter Johnson and the Washington Senators in seven games. The Giants were still the kings of New York, but McGraw saw the future of baseball just across the borough line in the Bronx, and he wasn't happy about it. Babe Ruth, who had hit his first professional home run in North Carolina on 7 March 1914 (ironically, in the same ballpark where Jim Thorpe hit his first home run), the same day that the tourists were celebrating their return to New York, was revolutionizing baseball. The Yankees had begun to eclipse the Giants both on the field and at the gate. After decades as top dog, Mugsy was starting to know what second place felt like. Never again would he be on top either in baseball or in the Big Apple. He would manage the Giants until 1932, but never again would he fly a pennant from the roof of the Polo Grounds.

After returning home in March 1914, Jimmy Callahan resumed his leadership of the Sox. But the team came out of the gate flat, quickly disappearing to the second division. Two weeks before New Year's Day 1915, Jimmy Callahan was terminated as White Sox manager. Offered other managerial positions, Callahan could never restore luster to his managerial reputation. During the post-tour years he and Josephine were blessed with another son. Always active in scouting and other baseball-related activities, Callahan traveled widely and wove a large circle of friendships about himself composed of folks from all areas of life. In 1934, while in Boston paying his good friend James M. Cohan a visit, Callahan suffered a massive heart attack and passed away at sixty years of age. Most of his obituaries noted his status as one of the original White Sox of 1901 or his role as team manger, slighting his contributions to the world tour.

By 1924 Germany Schaefer was dead. He died in 1919 of a hemorrhage in Saranac Lake, New York, while on a scouting assignment for the Giants. The first tourist to die, Schaefer was only forty-two years old. It is said that John McGraw wept for the only time in public at Germany Schaefer's funeral. Christy Mathewson was dying in 1924. America's first sports idol had signed up too late to fight in the Great War. Reaching Europe in 1918 after action was essentially over, Mathewson joined the Chemical Corps. He, along with Ty Cobb, was inadvertently gassed during a training exercise. The gas weakened the Big Six's lungs, and he contracted tuberculosis. Never the same afterward, he endured a long, painful convalescence. The weakened Matty managed the Reds and later assumed the presidency of the Boston Braves. In 1924 he suffered a relapse. After rallying for a time, Mathewson sought treatment at a sanitarium in Saranac Lake, New York. On 7 October 1925 Christy Mathewson passed away at the very same sanitarium where Germany Schaefer breathed his last breath.

Frank McGlynn struck out as a director in Hollywood. Although he had been quite successful in his work for Thomas Edison, he was unable to compete with talents like D. W. Griffith. He turned to his first love, acting. Between 1919 when he first assumed the role as the lead in *Abraham Lincoln* on Broadway until the rise of Raymond Massey, McGlynn was Hollywood's preferred choice to portray the sixteenth president. In seven films from 1924 to 1939 McGlynn portrayed Abraham Lincoln. No other actor has portrayed the Great Emancipator as many times on the silver screen.

Mike Donlin's return to Australia as a baseball player in the planned new professional league was prevented by the Great War. Like Frank McGlynn, he turned to acting for his livelihood. After the 1914 season Donlin relocated to California, where he had a steady but by no means significant film career. Usually cast as a heavy, he took occasional turns at comedy. He rarely looked back upon his baseball career. For Donlin, the Giants were really only the Giants when Matty was on the mound and when cheers for "Turkey" Mike reverberated about the Polo Grounds.

By 1924 Victor Miller had established himself as one of the best cinematographers in Hollywood. Shortly after the completion of the world tour, Miller changed his last name to Milner and went on to become a legend at Paramount Studios. Miller's ability with a camera would ultimately be rewarded with an Academy Award for cinematography in 1934 for *Cleopatra*.

Steve Evans discovered that his flashy jump to the Feds would not go unpunished. After two stellar years with the Brooklyn Tip-Tops and the Baltimore Terrapins, Evans found himself unable to secure work in the Majors. His prankster personality had at last worn out its welcome, leaving Evans as one of the few league-jumpers for whom the Majors' black list became permanent.

Bill Klem insisted that he never made a mistake behind the plate. His umpiring skills would one day result in his being enshrined in Cooperstown, but John McGraw never appreciated his talents. Klem's parting shot to McGraw was to throw him out of his final game as manager of the Giants.

Buck Weaver was on a different sort of black list in 1924. Although some researchers have claimed that Buck may have tried to warn Comiskey that the fix was in for the 1919 World Series, he was ignored. Weaver never took a dime from the gamblers. He wanted no part of the fix, and he played his heart out in the Series. His reward for having "guilty knowledge" of the fix was a lifetime ban from baseball. Despite several appeals to Commissioner Landis, the ban was upheld. Weaver's case stands as a monument to Judge Landis's egomania. Of the eight "Black Sox," Buck Weaver remains the only one about whom not a hint of scandal has ever been produced, yet he remains ineligible for admission to the Hall of Fame.

Jim Thorpe's Major League career was at an end in 1924. He would continue to play minor league ball until he was past forty, however. The star of Carlisle never quite fit into the Giants mix. Perhaps out of jealousy over Thorpe's fame or disappointment that the Native American was not a baseball superman, McGraw poisoned the well. Though the Giants manager claimed again and again that Thorpe could not hit the fastball, any serious assessment of the record shows that this claim is false. During his last season in the Majors, 1919, he hit .333 with the Boston Braves. The highlight of his career, however, may have occurred in 1917 as a member of the Cincinnati Reds. On 2 May 1917 Arky "Hippo" Vaughn and Fred Toney pitched no-hitters against each other. Incredibly, each pitcher carried his no-hitter into the tenth inning. In the top of the tenth Thorpe drove in the Reds' only run to win the game. Thorpe's hit ended what was probably the greatest one-day combined pitching performance in history.

By 1924 Jim Thorpe's main interest, however, was not baseball but football. The first president of what would become the National Football League brought the professional game the respectability and the audience it needed to survive. It really is no exaggeration to state that without Jim Thorpe there would be no such thing as the National Football League today.

Thorpe's personal life never matched his on-field glories, however. Always a hard drinker, he turned to the bottle even more after the death of his son, Jim Jr., during the influenza epidemic of 1919. His personal life and his marriage never recovered from this blow. Eventually, Iva and Jim divorced. So bitter was the separation that Iva cut Jim's face out of virtually every photograph in the house and refused to talk about him for years. Yet in spite of the rage she felt toward the man whom she had once called "my Snooks," Iva retained the diary that she had kept during the tour, the treasured relic of a love and of an age and of places irretrievably lost.

Coda

The tourists' adventures inspired praise and verse from America's sportswriters and cartoonists as had no other previous sporting event. Surely most did not envision a day when the tour would all but vanish from memory. Grantland Rice perhaps captured the tone best. Contrasting the tour to the ephemera of current culture, such as Eva Tanguay's "acting," the tourists appeared almost as Odysseus returned. Unlike Tanguay, who sat beneath the floodlights and smiled fetchingly, building an entire career out of the line "I don't care," the world tour was seen as a heroic venture deserving its own epic of the sort that Grantland Rice was only to happy to provide.

> The Return
> The Long Sleep is over—the Nation is waking;
> The Dread Epoch fades and the live one is back;
> The old earth rebounds with a quiver and quaking,
> And high flies the mush as they whirl down the track;
> The atmosphere reels—and it isn't the Comet—
> There is a whirr with the stir of the day.
> And Federal leaguers and other intriguers
> Are reeling along with the kale they will pay.
>
> CHORUS
>
> For Commy and Cal, and McGraw again
> Are back to the umpires law again,
> Back to the old fatigue;
> To the land of the brave and the poor white slave,
> To the Income Tax and the Mexican rave,
> And eke to the Federal league.

The dead year is past and the live one beginning
As on to the frolic we move in a stream;
For now comes the revelry back to its inning,
Where pallid existence moves out from its dream;
The kale laden bustle—the rustle and Hustle—
The Fed's ringing chorus of "Lay on, McDuff!"
The clash at the dock where the dough Leads the tussle
And damned be any magnate who first cries "Enough!"

CHORUS

For Commy and Cal and McGraw again
Are back to the wild March thaw again,
Back to the old intrigue;
To the wear and tear of the Grizzly Bear,
To the Eva Tanguayan "I don't care"—
And eke to the Federal league.[1]

Notes

1. A Tour Is Born

1. Timothy Paul Sullivan, *History of World's Tour, Chicago White Sox and New York Giants* (Chicago: M. A. Donohue, 1914), 9–10.

2. Sullivan, *History of World's Tour*, 10.

3. Christy Mathewson, *Pitching in a Pinch: Or Baseball from the Inside* (Lincoln: University of Nebraska Press, 1994), 166.

2. Filling Out the Lineup

1. "World Tour of the Chicago White Sox and New York Giants," *Base Ball Magazine*, February 1914, 47–48.

2. "World Tour."

3. "World Tour."

4. "The Tour of the World," *Sporting Life*, 1 November 1913, 7.

5. G. W. Axelson, *"Commy": The Life Story of Charles A. Comiskey* (Chicago: Reilly & Lea, 1919), 221.

6. Sullivan, *History of the World's Tour*, 10.

7. "Game Was a Winner," *Blue Rapids Times*, 27 October 1913.

8. "Game Was a Winner."

9. William B. Meade and Paul Dickson, *Baseball: The President's Game* (Washington DC: Farragut, 1993), 95, 100.

10. David Osinski, "Baseball in the Olympics," in *Total Baseball*, ed. Jim Thomas and Peter Palmer, 4th ed. (New York: Warner Books, 1995), 582.

11. "Thorpe in Baseball," *Literary Digest*, 15 February 1913, 363.

12. "Thorpe in Baseball."

13. Robert W. Wheeler, *Jim Thorpe: World's Greatest Athlete*, (Norman: University of Oklahoma Press, 1979), 156.

14. "News Items Gathered from All Quarters," *Sporting Life*, 20 September 1913, 15.

15. Axelson, *"Commy,"* 234.

16. Clark Griffith, "Twenty-Five Years of Big League Baseball," *Outing* (April 1914), 42.

17. Lawrence Ritter, *The Glory of Their Times: The Story of the Early Days of Baseball Told by the Men Who Played It* (New York: Vantage Books, 1985), 35.

18. Ritter, *Glory of Their Times*, 35–36.

19. *New York Times*, 24 September 1908.

20. Harry Grayson, *They Played the Game* (New York: A. S. Barnes, 1945), 89.

21. Robert L. Davis, "Stealing First Twice," *The National Pastime: A Review of Baseball History* 21, 16.

22. Ritter, *Glory of Their Times*, 189.

23. At the time, sportswriters referred to any player who plunged into matrimony as a "benedict," a traitor to bachelor pride and honor.

3. Base Paths a Continent Wide

1. "Federal Leaguers Talk War," *Chicago Daily Tribune*, 15 October 1913.

2. "Giants Off on Tour of the World," *New York Herald*, 18 October 1913.

3. "Giants Off on Tour."

4. "Giants Off on Tour."

5. "Cubs Out Today for Revenge on City Champions," *Chicago Inter-Ocean*, 17 October 1913.

6. Jack Ryder, "Notes of the Game," *Cincinnati Enquirer*, 19 October 1913.

7. Jack Ryder, "Giants Start the Tour Right," *Cincinnati Enquirer*, 19 October 1913.

8. W. A. Phelon, "White Sox and Giants Perform in Punk Game," *Chicago Inter-Ocean*, 19 October 1913.

9. Phelon, "White Sox and Giants."

10. Bill Bailey, "Weaver Pulls a Clever Little Trick on Matty," *Chicago American*, 28 October 1913.

11. *Chicago Daily Tribune*, 22 October 1913.

12. "Spalding Goes Abroad," *New York Telegraph*, 22 October 1913.

13. "M'Graw Presents Ball to Aged Fan," *Ottumwa Daily Courier*, 23 October 1913.

14. "Fans, Overjoyed, Lavish Favors on Big Ball Players," *Sioux City Tribune*, 23 October 1913.

15. Axelson, *"Commy,"* 229.

16. *Blue Rapids Times*, 20 October 1913.

17. "Long Hits by Sox Beat Giants, 8–5," *Chicago Daily Tribune*, 25 October 1913.

18. "Fans in Kansas See Giants Lose," *New York Herald*, 25 October 1913.

19. George E. Phair, "Gatling Gloom Chasers," *San Francisco Examiner*, 2 November 1913.

20. "West Eager to See Giants," *New York Herald*, 2 November 1913.

21. "Sox Beat Giants," *Joplin Daily Globe*, 25 October 1913.

22. "Mrs. M'Graw Not a Fan," *New York Morning Telegraph*, 25 October 1913.

23. "King Walter Meets the Boys," *Joplin Daily Globe*, 21 October 1913.

24. "King Walter."

25. "King Walter."

26. "King Walter."

27. *Joplin Daily Globe*, 26 October 1913.

28. "Finally See Johnson Pitch," *Joplin Daily Globe*, 28 October 1913.

29. "One Man Killed, Fifty Hurt, When Stands Collapse," *(Oklahoma City) Daily Oklahoman*, 29 October 1913.

30. G. W. Axelson, "Russell Loses Game in Old Home Town," *Dallas Morning News*, 31 October 1913.

31. G. W. Axelson, "Giants Defeat Sox in Game at Beaumont," *Dallas Morning News*, 1 November 1913.

32. "Federals to Wage General Warfare," *Dallas Morning News*, 2 November 1913.

33. "John McGraw Expresses Doubt; Donlen [*sic*]-Klem Feud Breaks Out," *Houston Chronicle*, 3 November 1913.

34. "John McGraw Expresses Doubt."

35. "John McGraw Expresses Doubt."

36. "Matty Won't Play Sunday but He Will Shoot Ducks," *Houston Chronicle*, 4 November 1913.

37. G. W. Axelson, "Reports of Tour Being Postponed Denied by M'Graw," *Chicago Record-Herald*, 4 November 1913.

38. Axelson, "Reports of Tour."

39. "Ball Players on Westward," *Abilene Daily Record*, 5 November 1913.

40. "Ball Players on Westward."

41. G. W. Axelson, "Crowd and Heat Greet Tourists as Texas Fades," *Chicago Record-Herald*, 6 November 1913.

42. G. W. Axelson, "Rarified Air Hampers Pitchers at Douglas," *Chicago Record-Herald*, 7 November 1913.

43. "Douglas Game Pleases Fans," *Bisbee Daily Review*, 7 November 1913.

44. "Giants Trim White Sox and Furnish Fandom with Local Ball Fest," *Bisbee Daily Review*, 8 November 1913.

4. Pacific Dreams

1. Harry A. Williams, "Mathewson Defeated by Chicago White Sox," *Los Angeles Sunday Times*, 9 November 1913.

2. Williams, "Mathewson Defeated."

3. Williams, "Mathewson Defeated."

4. Harry A. Williams, "Sox and Giants Tie in Weird Exhibition," *Los Angeles Times*, 10 November 1913.

5. "Meyers Hero of the Game," *San Diego Sun*, 11 November 1913.

6. Ritter, *Glory of Their Times*, 195.

7. Frank McGlynn, "Striking Scenes from the Tour Around the World," pt. 1, *Base Ball Magazine*, August 1914, 61.

8. Ritter, *Glory of Their Times*, 196

9. Harry A. Williams, "White Sox Had Grudge against C. Mathewson," *Los Angeles Times*, 12 November 1913.

10. Williams, "White Sox Had Grudge."

11. Ritter, *Glory of Their Times*, 196.

12. McGlynn, "Striking Scenes," pt. 1, 62.

13. "World's Tour Success John McGraw Satisfied," *Sacramento Bee*, 13 November 1913.

14. Harry B. Smith, "More Rain Will Mean the Players Will Have a Layoff," *San Francisco Chronicle*, 13 November 1913.

15. Paul J. Zingg and D. Medeiros, *Runs Hits and an Era: The Pacific Coast League 1903–58* (Urbana: University of Illinois Press, 1994), 31.

16. G. W. Axelson, "Sox Support Russell and Win Handily," *Chicago Record-Herald*, 14 November 1913.

17. Douglas Erskine, "Fiery M'Graw Fired from First Game," *San Francisco Examiner*, 14 November 1913.

18. "Baseball Notes," *San Francisco Examiner*, 14 November 1913.

19. Leon Wing, "Matty Licks White Sox with Ease," *San Francisco Examiner*, 16 November 1913.

20. "Giants-Sox Pickups," *San Francisco Examiner*, 16 November 1913.

21. "Gleason's Motion Picture Stunt Worked in This City," *San Francisco Chronicle*, 16 November 1913.

22. Leon Wing, "Call Out the Oaks," *San Francisco Examiner*, 17 November 1913.

23. Handy Andy, "Bodie Slips Away; Stage Loses Him," *Chicago Tribune*, 16 October 1913.

24. Grantland Rice, "Playing the Game," *Chicago Evening Post*, 7 March 1914.

25. Bob Chieger, *Voices of Baseball: Quotations on the Summer Game* (New York: Signet Books, New American Library, 1984), 141.

26. "Apple Day Is Generally Observed Throughout State," *Medford Mail Tribune*, 18 November 1913.

27. "Diamond Stars Come Here by Train Load," *Portland Evening Telegram*, 18 November 1913.

28. "Diamond Stars Come Here."

29. "Diamond Stars Come Here."

30. "Diamond Stars Come Here."

31. "Salem Man Gets Valued Trophy," *Portland Evening Telegram*, 20 November 1913.

32. "Boosters Banquet Enjoyable Feast," *Portland Evening Telegram*, 19 November 1913.

5. ACROSS A RESTLESS SEA

1. Portus Baxter, "Big Leaguers Disappoint Fans," *Seattle Post Intelligencer*, 19 October 1913.

2. Baxter, "Big Leaguers."

3. Baxter, "Big Leaguers."

4. Ray Robinson, *Matty: An American Hero Christy Mathewson of the New York Giants* (New York: Oxford University Press, 1993), 159.

5. "Germany Schaefer Loose Again," *San Francisco Chronicle*, 24 November 1913.

6. Ring Lardner, "The Busher Beats It Hence," in *You Know Me Al* (Urbana: University of Illinois Press, 1992), 236.

7. *The World Almanac and Encyclopedia, 1915* (New York: Press Publishing Company, 1914), 368.

8. "The White Sox Triumph," *Sporting Life*, 18 October 1913, 3.

9. Charles C. Spink, " 'Commy' Relates His Experiences," in *The Homecoming*, by Ring Lardner and Edward Heeman (Chicago: Edward Heeman, 1914), 26.

10. John O. Says, "Aboard the Good Ship *Empress of Japan*," in Lardner and Heeman, *Homecoming*, 32.

11. Joe Farrell, "World's Tourists' Rough Voyage Across Pacific Ocean," *Sporting News*, 1 January 1914, 1.

12. Farrell, "World's Tourists' Rough Voyage."

13. Ring Larder, "Chicago's Beau Mond," in *Collected in Some Champions: Sketches and Fiction*, ed. Matthew J. Bruccoi (New York: Charles Scribner's Sons, 1976), 41.

14. McGlynn, "Striking Scenes," pt. 1, 64.

15. Frank Farrell, M. Dick Bunnell, and Lee Magee, "Diary of the World Tour," in *World Tour National and American League Base Ball Teams October 1913 March 1914: The Triumph of Organized Base Ball* (Chicago: S. Blake Willsden, 1914), 1.

16. McGlynn, "Striking Scenes," pt. 1, 65.

6. THE LAND OF THE RISING SUN

1. *(Tokyo) Jiji Shimpo*, 7 December 1913.

2. *(Tokyo) Jiji Shimpo*, 7 December 1913.

3. *(Tokyo) Jiji Shimpo*, 7 December 1913.

4. Bill Bailey, "Fear of Seasickness Keeps Tourists at Home," *Chicago American*, 20 November 1913.

5. (*Tokyo*) *Jiji Shimpo*, 7 December 1913.

6. Farrell, "World's Tourists' Rough Voyage."

7. Farrell, "World's Tourists' Rough Voyage."

8. Irving Vaughn, "Favors All-Star Series at Frisco in Fall of 1915," *Chicago Record-Herald*, 28 December 1913.

9. Farrell, "World's Tourists' Rough Voyage."

10. G. W. Axelson, "Japanese Quick to Adopt Big League Ways," *Chicago Record-Herald*, 30 December 1913.

11. "How Press of Japan Viewed Invasion of World Tourists," *Sporting News*, 8 January 1914, 3.

12. "How Press of Japan Viewed Invasion."

13. "How Press of Japan Viewed Invasion."

14. Frank McGlynn, "Striking Scenes from the Tour Around the World," pt. 2, *Base Ball Magazine*, September 1914, 70.

15. McGlynn, "Striking Scenes," pt. 2, 71.

7. China and Points East

1. Joe Farrell, "Players Arrange Own Diamond," *Sporting News*, 22 January 1914, 5.

2. G. W. Axelson, "Chinese Fail to Show Interest in Baseball Game," *Chicago Record-Herald*, 14 January 1914.

3. Axelson, "Chinese Fail."

4. Axelson, "Chinese Fail."

5. Farrell, "Players Arrange Own Diamond."

6. H. P. Burchell, writing as John McGraw, "Chinese Greet Clubs," *Chicago Daily News*, 17 January 1914.

7. "Sidelights on Sporting Men and Incidents," *Chicago Daily News*, 17 January 1914.

8. G. W. Axelson, "U.S. 'Jackies' Carry Baseball to World Ports," *Chicago Record-Herald*, 25 January 1914.

8. Uncle Sam's Tropical Playground

1. Joe Farrell, "Girdlers Are Lionized at Manila," *Sporting News*, 5 February 1914, 3.

2. Farrell, "Girdlers Are Lionized."

3. McGlynn, "Striking Scenes," pt. 2, 76.

4. Grayson, *They Played the Game*, 70.

5. Farrell, "Girdlers Are Lionized."

6. Farrell, "Girdlers Are Lionized."

7. Farrell, "Girdlers Are Lionized."

8. McGlynn, "Striking Scenes, pt. 2, 76.

9. Baseball Down Under

1. Joe Farrell, "Australia Warm in Its Welcome," *Sporting News*, 12 February 1914, 3.

2. Farrell, "Australia."

3. G. W. Axelson, "St. Nick Arrayed in Pongee 'Togs' at Equator," *Chicago Record-Herald*, 26 February 1914.

4. Axelson, "St. Nick."

5. Farrell, "Australia."

6. McGlynn, "Striking Scenes," pt. 2, 77.

7. Farrell, "Australia."

8. Axelson, "St. Nick."

9. Axelson, "St. Nick."

10. "Australia Is Due," *Sporting News*, 9 January 1914, 5.

11. "Australia Is Due."

12. G. W. Axelson, "Brisbane 'Fans' Crowd Park to See Tourists Perform," *Chicago Record-Herald*, 9 February 1914.

13. G. W. Axelson, "Baseball Threatens to Eclipse Cricket in Australia," *Chicago Record-Herald*, 10 February 1914.

14. Farrell, "Australia."

15. "The Baseballers Arrive," *Sydney Morning Herald*, 4 January 1914.

16. "Baseballers Arrive."

17. "Baseballers Arrive."

18. "Baseballers Arrive."

19. "Australia Has Arrived," *Sporting Life*, 13 September 1913, 9.

20. "Baseballers Arrive."

21. "Baseballers Arrive."

22. "Baseballers Arrive."

23. Axelson, *"Commy,"* 253.

24. "Hear Yankee Airs at Sydney," *Sporting News*, 12 February 1914, 3.

25. "Baseball Teams—Americans Arrive," *Melbourne Argus*, 16 January 1914.

26. "Baseball Teams."

27. "Baseball Teams."

28. Joe Farrell, "A Great Welcome from Melbourne," *Sporting News*, 19 February 1914, 8.

29. Farrell, "Great Welcome."

30. Invitation reproduced in Farrell, Bunnell, and Magee, *World Tour*.

31. "American Baseballers," *Melbourne Age*, 8 January 1914.

32. "American Baseballers."

33. "American Baseballers."

34. "Baseball Exhibition," *Melbourne Argus*, 8 January 1914.

35. "Baseball Exhibition."

36. "American Baseballers."

37. G. W. Axelson, "Comiskey Equips Melbourne Boys for Ball Games," *Chicago Record-Herald*, 9 January 1914.

38. "American Baseballers."

39. "American Baseballers."

10. Sir Thomas Lipton and the Shadow of the Pyramids

1. Joe Farrell, "Sir Thomas Lipton Feasts World Tourists at Columbo," *Sporting News*, 26 February 1914, 7.

2. Farrell, "Sir Thomas Lipton."

3. Farrell, "Sir Thomas Lipton."

4. Frank McGlynn, "Striking Scenes from the Tour Around the World," pt. 3, *Base Ball Magazine*, October 1914, 66.

5. Farrell, Bunnell, and Magee, "Diary."

6. Farrell, Bunnell, and Magee, "Diary."

7. G. W. Axelson, "Tourists Entertained Royally by Lipton," *Chicago Record-Herald*, 23 February 1914.

8. Axelson, "Tourists Entertained."

9. McGlynn, "Striking Scenes," pt. 3, 67.

10. McGlynn, "Striking Scenes," pt. 3, 68

11. Farrell, "Sir Thomas Lipton."

12. McGlynn, "Striking Scenes," pt. 3, 68.

13. Axelson, "Tourists Entertained."

14. Farrell, "Sir Thomas Lipton."

15. Farrell, Bunnell, and Magee, "Diary."

16. *New York Times*, 7 December 1913.

17. *New York Times*, 7 December 1913.

18. *New York Times*, 7 December 1913.

19. G. W. Axelson, "Tourists Find Worlds Scarce—King Sees London Game," *Chicago Record-Herald*, 27 February 1914.

20. Axelson, "Tourists Find Worlds Scarce."

21. Axelson, "Tourists Find Worlds Scarce."

22. Axelson, "Tourists Find Worlds Scarce."

23. McGlynn, "Striking Scenes," pt. 3, 71.

24. McGlynn, "Striking Scenes," pt. 3, 70.

25. McGlynn, "Striking Scenes," pt. 3, 70.

26. McGlynn, "Striking Scenes," pt. 3, 71.

27. Buck Weaver quoted in Hal Totten, *The Armchair Book of Baseball* (New York: Simon and Schuster, 1968), 489.

28. Joe Farrell, "They May Be Christians but Differ Little from Heathens," *Sporting News*, 5 March 1914, 5.

29. Farrell, "They May Be Christians."

30. Farrell, "They May Be Christians."

31. Farrell, "They May Be Christians."

11. Across a Storm-Tossed Europe

1. Farrell, "They May Be Christians."

2. Farrell, "They May Be Christians."

3. Farrell, "They May Be Christians."

4. Farrell, "They May Be Christians."

5. Farrell, "They May Be Christians."

6. Farrell, "They May Be Christians."

7. G. W. Axelson, "Pompeian Ruins Seen on Tour," *Chicago Record-Herald*, 28 February 1914, 9.

8. McGlynn, "Striking Scenes," pt. 3, 72.

9. Axelson, "Pompeian Ruins."

10. Farrell, "They May Be Christians."

11. G. W. Axelson, "Sudden Illness Grips Comiskey on Way to Rome," *Chicago Record-Herald*, 10 February 1914.

12. Axelson, "Sudden Illness."

13. G. W. Axelson, "Comiskey Rallies and Allays Fears," *Chicago Record-Herald*, 11 February 1914.

14. Axelson, "Comiskey Rallies."

15. G. W. Axelson, "Pope's Audience Brings Tourists Delight of Trip," *Chicago Record-Herald*, 1 March 1914.

16. Axelson, "Pope's Audience."

17. G. W. Axelson, "Sox and Giants Find Thorpe World Famous," *Chicago Record Herald*, 25 February 1914.

18. Axelson, "Sox and Giants Find Thorpe World Famous."

19. Joe Farrell, "Lose Interest in Old World Sights," *Sporting News*, 12 March 1914, 5.

20. Frank McGlynn, "Striking Scenes from the Tour Around the World," pt. 4, *Base Ball Magazine*, November 1914, 78.

21. G. W. Axelson, "World Tourists Fail to Enlighten Rome," *Chicago Record-Herald*, 4 March 1914.

22. Farrell, "Lose Interest."

23. Irving Vaughn, "Murphy's Act a Great Boost, Claim Federals," *Chicago Record-Herald*, 12 February 1914.

24. Vaughn, "Murphy's Act."

25. G. W. Axelson, "Comiskey Terms Ousting of Evers a Serious Mistake," *Chicago Record-Herald*, 13 February 1914.

26. J. P. McEvoy, "The Gist and Jest of It," *Chicago Record-Herald*, 12 February 1914.

27. McGlynn, "Striking Scenes," pt. 4, 78.

28. "McGraw Talks of Monte Carlo," *Sporting Life*, 7 March 1914, 13.

29. G. W. Axelson, "Enthused Crowd Sees White Sox Win at Nice," *Chicago Record-Herald*, 17 February 1914.

30. McGlynn, "Striking Scenes," pt. 4, 79.

31. "France Takes to Base Ball," *Chicago Record-Herald*, 16 March 1914.

32. G. W. Axelson, "Feds Approach Star on World Ball Tour," *Chicago Record-Herald*, 16 February 1914.

33. Lewis H. Carlson and John J. Fogarty, eds., *Tales of Gold* (Chicago: Contemporary Books, 1987), 9.

34. G. W. Axelson, "World Touring Party Rejoins 'Old Roman,'" *Chicago Record-Herald*, 18 February 1914.

35. Grantland Rice, "Baseball By-Plays," *Sporting News*, 19 March 1914, 4.

36. "Take Steps to Hold Doolan," *Chicago Record-Herald*, 8 February 1914.

37. G. W. Axelson, "World Tourists Reach London Ready to Play," *Chicago Record-Herald*, 24 February 1914.

12. Baseball Fit for a King

1. Grantland Rice, "Playing the Game," *Chicago Evening Post*, 27 October 1913.

2. "British Team Arrives Here," *Chicago American*, 7 November 1913.

3. "'Matty' Considering 'Fed' League Offer," *Chicago Record-Herald*, 24 February 1914.

4. "'Matty' Considering 'Fed' League Offer."

5. *Pall Mall Gazette* quoted in G. W. Axelson, "M'Graw Stirs English by Boosting Yankees," *Chicago Record-Herald*, 25 February 1914.

6. Axelson, "M'Graw Stirs English."

7. *London Sketch* quoted by Grantland Rice in *Chicago Evening Post*, 12 March 1914.

8. G. W. Axelson, "Monarch of England to See Baseball Game," *Chicago Record-Herald*, 26 February 1914.

9. "Comiskey Pines for Home," *Sporting Life*, 7 March 1914, 13.

10. "Nobles Honor the World Tourists," *Sporting Life*, 7 March 1914, 10.

11. *Chicago Evening Post*, 7 March 1914.

12. "Baseball Match," *Manchester Mirror*, 27 February 1914.

13. "Baseball Match."

14. Frank McGlynn, "Striking Scenes from the Tour Around the World," pt. 5, *Base Ball Magazine*, December 1914, 86.

15. "Baseball Match."

16. "Baseball Match."

17. Axelson, *"Commy,"* 259–60.

18. Axelson, *"Commy,"* 260.

19. G. W. Axelson, "Enlightening the World with Baseball," *Harper's Weekly*, 4 April 1914, 24.

20. "Baseball Match."

21. "Bally Well Put, Ol' Top," *Chicago Evening Post*, 7 March 1914.

22. "Welcome for Tourists," *Sporting Life*, 14 March 1914, 10.

23. Frank McGlynn, "Baseball Tourists Are Given Royal Welcome," *New York Morning Telegraph*, 7 March 1914.

24. Grantland Rice, "Playing the Game," *Chicago Evening Post*, 7 March 1914.

25. "World Tour Echoes," *Sporting Life*, 14 March 1914, 3.

26. "Sporting Notes and Gossip," *Chicago Evening Post*, 12 March 1914.

27. "Welcome and War Mixed," *Sporting Life*, 14 March 1914, 11.

28. "A Review of the Tour," *Sporting Life*, 7 March 1914, 14.

29. "Welcome and War Mixed," 10.

30. "Welcome and War Mixed," 9.

31. "Dav's Day Dreams," *Chicago American*, 15 January 1914.

32. "Welcome and War Mixed," 9.

33. "Benz Gets Home Ahead of Tourists," *Chicago Inter-Ocean*, 8 March 1914.

34. "Benz Gets Home."

35. "A Tribute to Comiskey," *Sporting Life*, 21 March 1914, 15.

36. "Are Good Friends Now," *Sporting Life*, 28 March 1914, 13.

37. "Are Good Friends Now."

AFTERWORD

1. *Time*, 22 September 1924, 30.

2. *Time*, 24 November 1924, 28.

3. Irving M. Stein, *The Ginger Kid: The Buck Weaver Story* (Dubuque, Iowa: Elysian Fields Press, 1992), 238.

CODA

1. Grantland Rice, "Playing the Game," *Chicago Evening Post*, March 1914.

Bibliographic Essay

Surprisingly little has been written about the 1913–1914 world tour of the New York Giants and the Chicago White Sox. My primary sources date almost exclusively from 1913–1914. Three books were published about the tour in 1914: Ted Sullivan's self-published opus, *History of World's Tour, Chicago White Sox and New York Giants* (Chicago: Sullivan, 1914); Ring Lardner and Edward Heeman's *Homecoming* (Chicago: Edward G. Heeman, 1914); and *World Tour National and American League Base Ball Teams October 1913 March 1914: The Triumph of Organized Base Ball* (Chicago: S. Blake Willsden, 1914) by Frank Farrell, M. Dick Bunnell, and Lee Magee. Each has its merits and faults, with Sullivan's tome having the least interest to researchers.

Chicago's newspapers gave much better coverage to the tour than did the New York papers. The *New York Herald*, the *New York Times*, and the *New York Tribune* did some great reporting of the tour. However, I found that the sportswriting in Chicago tended to be better than that found in New York. Gus Axelson wrote more about the tour than any other person, and his modern style would not look that out of place in today's newspapers. I have relied a great deal on Axelson's daily columns in the *Chicago Record-Herald* and other articles that he wrote for *Collier's* and *Harper's* magazines. Axelson's often fawning biography Charles Comiskey, *"Commy": The Life Story of Charles A. Comiskey* (Chicago: Reilly & Lee, 1919), has several chapters devoted to the world tour.

I found something of value in just about every Chicago newspaper. In addition to the *Record-Herald*, I enjoyed Bill Bailey's columns in the *Chicago American*. Bill Bailey was actually Bill Veeck Sr., whose son would send a midget up to bat and would go on to own the White Sox. The *Chicago Daily Journal* provided insight into the Chicago's tabloid culture, and the *Chicago Evening Post*, which published columns by both Ring Lardner and Grantland Rice, deserves some hosannas.

Sporting Life, the "other" baseball newspaper of the day, apparently had a fly on the wall for every important baseball event of 1913 and 1914. Whereas

J. Taylor Spink of the *Sporting News* made a deliberate decision to ignore and slant his paper's coverage of the upstart Federal League, *Sporting Life* held no such compunctions. Grantland Rice and others could get stories about the Feds published in Philadelphia that the St. Louis paper would not touch. One really can't study the Feds objectively unless one reads both.

Joe Farrell, who was primarily a songwriter and sheet music salesman, wrote some of the chattiest and most insightful stories of the entire tour. I found his columns for the *Sporting News* and a handful of the Chicago papers to be some of the best reporting on the tour, period. His status as a fan accompanying his beloved Sox around the world made his reporting especially keen.

Frank McGlynn, the world tour movie director, had an eye for detail and a nose for adventure. His five-part serial on the world tour in the *Base Ball Magazine* remains a classic. Little read, mostly because the *Base Ball Magazine* has not yet been microfilmed, his reporting on the tour was my primary window on this fascinating tale. McGlynn's film has been lost to history, but because of his detailed writing, I was able to reconstruct much of what he filmed. His footage, if it is ever recovered, would prove a gold mine for researchers. For example, no film exists of Jim Thorpe, the greatest athlete of the first half of the twentieth century, doing anything athletic. McGlynn's film was taken when Thorpe was at his prime. It really is a shame that we don't even have any idea how Thorpe moved. The closest we may come to judging how graceful Thorpe was on the athletic field is a scene in the classic film *King Kong*. Thorpe plays one of the native dancers. He is spectacularly easy to pick out, even under the makeup, because he is the best, most graceful dancer of the bunch.

Lawrence Ritter's classic *The Glory of Their Times: The Story of the Early Days of Baseball Told by the Men Who Played It* (New York: Vantage, 1985) remains the baseball book by which all others should be judged. Ritter's book made some stories of the tour, such as Hans Lobert's mad dash around the bases against a horse, famous. When comparing Ritter's recorded conversations of these great men with contemporary press accounts, it is astounding to see how well men like Lobert could recall even some of the smallest details forty or more years onward.

Richard C. Lindberg wrote the massive and invaluable *The White Sox Encyclopedia* (Philadelphia: Temple University Press, 1997). It was a reference source I turned to time and again. Perhaps someday an equally daring soul will compile a similar work about the Giants.

John Thorn's *Total Baseball*, 5th ed. (New York: Viking, 1997), provided most of the player statistics.

New York reporter Harry Grayson's forgotten and long out-of-print classic *They Played the Game* (New York: A. S. Barnes, 1945) provided information about Mike Donlin, Fred Merkle, and others that simply cannot be found anywhere else.

I used daily newspapers from approximately forty cities to complete this book. Often, the only way to find "new" information is by diving into old microfilm. The San Francisco and Los Angeles papers, especially, were full of enlightening details. I knew that this story could only be told through the daily papers of the towns the tourists visited. I was able to obtain at least one newspaper from virtually every city that the athletes passed through. I was unsuccessful for a handful of cities. In some cases, like Douglas, Arizona, no copies of the daily papers from 1913 remain in existence. Other places, such as Oxnard, California, apparently believe their microfilm is gold plated and cannot be loaned to anyone. It these cases, I used newspapers in nearby cities that sent reporters to the game or relied upon the observations of wire reports.

Index

Abbas II, 185, 187–88
Abe, Isoo, 112
Abilene TX, 66, 67–69
Abilene Daily Record, 68–69
Adelaide, Australia, 157, 170
Agua Prieta, Mexico, 70
Aguinaldo, Emilio, 137
Alabaster Mosque, 190–91, 195
Alaska, 98
Albee, Harry Russell, 92
Alexandra, 123–24, 127, 128
Alexandria, Egypt, 195–96, 197, 229
Ali, Muhammad, 190
All Stars (also called the All-Americans), 181
All-Stars, and world tour of 1889–1890, 5, 8, 21, 113, 177–78, 191, 218
America's Cup, 177, 180
Arizona, 1, 33, 69
Arnold, Olney, 187, 192, 195
The Ashes, 165
Association Park (Kansas City MO), 53
Astor House Hotel (Shanghai, China), 124–25, 127–28
Atkin, Jack, 81
Atlantic City NJ, 65, 66
Athletic Park (San Diego CA), 76–77
Australia, 5, 11, 112, 146, 147, 150, 158–60, 171; history of baseball in 152, 158, 159
Axelson, G. W. "Gus," xvii, 15, 29, 42, 61, 68–69, 83, 112, 115, 125, 133, 154, 161, 177,

187–88, 202, 204, 206, 207–8, 209–11, 225

Bailey, Bill, 15, 29, 108–9
Baker, Reginald F. "Snowy," 159–60
Baker, William F., 225, 241
Bakie, Captain, 145, 147, 148, 149
Ballingall Hotel, 46, 66
Baltimore Orioles, 3
Baltimore Terrapins, 220, 240, 241
Barron Falls (Cairns, Queensland Australia), 151–52
Base Ball Magazine, 1, 10, 11
Bastianelli, Guiseppe, 205, 209
Beaumont TX, 61–62
Bell, Gen. Franklin, 138, 140, 141, 143
Benz, Joe "Blitzen," xvii, 28, 38, 55, 61–62, 66, 80, 102, 117–18, 132, 136, 151, 154, 182, 183, 189, 191, 195, 235, 241–42, 243
Berger, Joe "Fats," 26
Berkeley, Busby, 23
Bertolini, Cavaliere F., 201
Bilibid Prison (Manila, Philippines), 143
Biltmore Hotel (New York), 240, 241
Bird Island (Australia), 147
Birdman from Khartoum (Mark Poupre), 194
Bisbee AZ, 69, 71–72, 171
Bisbee Daily Review, 70–71
Black Sox Scandal, 25–26, 245

Blake, Helena Elizabeth (Mrs. Jeff Tesreau), 35
Blavatsky, Madame, 6
Bliss, Jack, xvii, 26, 51–52, 81, 182, 183, 189, 213, 243
Blue Rapids KS, 14, 48–52
Blue Rapids Times, 14, 26
Bodie, Ping, 86, 87–88, 198
Bonham TX, 59–60
Boston Braves, 238–39, 247
Boston Red Sox, 223, 225
Boxer Rebellion, 123
Bridwell, Al, 30, 60
Brisbane, Australia, 152–54, 157
Brisbane Cricket Grounds, 153–54
Bristol Hotel (Rome, Italy), 203, 204, 206
Brooklyn Tip-Tops, 228, 239
Brown, Mordecai "Three Finger," 220, 238
Bruce, John E., 8
Brundage, Avery, 17, 18
Brush, John, 24
Buffalo NY, 62
Buhl, William, xvii, 102
Bund (Hong Kong), 134
Bunnell, Dick, 14
Burchell, H. P., xvii, 103, 104, 127
Burger, Joe "Fats," 52
Burns, John, 110
Burton-Harrison, Governor General, 139
"The Busher Beats It Hence," 97

Caine, Sir Thomas Henry Hall (Hall Caine), 199, 201
Cairns, Queensland, Australia, 145, 150–52
Cairo, Egypt, 185–95, 201
Cairo State Museum, 194, 201
Callahan, Danny, xvii, 38, 100, 147–48, 179, 208
Callahan, Jimmy "Nixie," xvii, 12, 22, 23, 27, 28, 38, 41, 42, 44, 45, 56, 61, 76, 81, 82, 83, 87, 96, 101, 109, 110, 117, 153, 157, 160, 169, 174, 187, 220, 223, 225, 228, 229, 231, 232, 234, 236, 242, 246–47; as manager, 22; and relationship with Comiskey, 12, 22

Callahan, Josephine, xvii, 147–48, 246
Callahan, Margaret, xvii, 100, 147–48, 179, 206, 208
Canadian Pacific Railroad, 98, 104; and shipping line, 97; and use of the wireless, 103–14
Capri, Italy, 198, 200–201
Cardiff Giant, 6–7
Carlisle Indian School, 16
Carslake, Brownie, 152
Castle, Vernon and Irene, 113, 173
Cecil Hotel (London), 226, 227
Celebes, 147
Ceylon, 5, 112, 171, 172, 175, 177–78; history of, 175, 178
Chance, Frank, 30, 76, 78, 213–14, 228
Chaplin, Charlie, 23, 86
Charleston, Oscar, 140–41
Chase, Hal "Prince," 25–26, 53, 54, 68, 75, 82, 91, 96
Chataqua, 14, 49
Chelsea Football Stadium. *See* Stamford Bridge Grounds
Chicago, 40–41, 55
Chicago American, 35, 108, 241
Chicago City Series, 35–36, 98
Chicago Cubs, 30–31, 35–36, 42, 213–14, 228
Chicago Daily News, 99, 127, 170
Chicago Daily Tribune, 49, 88
Chicago Evening Post, 88, 236
Chicago Inter-Ocean, 36, 39, 242
Chicago Record Herald, 42, 110, 187–88, 213, 215
Chicago Whales, 228, 214, 237
Chicago White Sox, 2, 5, 15, 35–36, 151, 229, 245
Chicago White Stockings, 6, 9, 191
Chi-Feds. *See* Chicago Whales
China, 9, 11
Cincinnati OH, 33, 35, 37–40, 41
Cincinnati Enquirer, 38, 39
Cincinnati Reds, 27, 54, 247
Clifton Gardens (Sydney, Australia), 160

Cobb, Tyrus "Ty," 19, 21, 22, 38, 41, 44, 247

Cobbs, Thomas F., 125

Cochrane, Mickey, 17

Cohan, George M., 156, 247

Cohan, Josephine, 156

Colombo, Ceylon, 172, 175, 178, 181

Colosseum (Rome, Italy), 205, 212–13, 215

Comiskey, Charles A., xvii, 2–3, 7–9, 10, 11–12, 13, 14–16, 19, 21, 22, 23, 25, 26, 27, 28, 33, 34–35, 38, 40, 42–44, 49, 70, 81, 83, 84, 92–93, 96, 97–100, 109, 118, 122, 126, 128, 148, 149, 152, 153, 154, 157, 161, 162, 168–69, 172, 173, 180, 181, 184, 186, 187, 194, 201, 203–4, 205, 209, 213–16, 221, 223, 224, 225, 229, 230–31, 234, 240, 242, 243, 245–46; childhood of, 4–5; as owner, 15, 26, 28, 245–46; as player, 5

Comiskey, Grace (wife of Louis), xvii, 149

Comiskey, J. Louis "Lou," xvii, 28, 130, 152, 246

Comiskey, Nancy (wife of Charles), xvii, 22, 147, 211, 215

Comiskey Park, 36, 87–88, 96, 150

Congress Hotel (Chicago), 240, 242

Conner Hotel (Joplin MO), 54, 56

Cook, Joseph, 156, 157

Cooper, James Fenimore, 6–7

Copper Queen Hotel (Bisbee AZ), 71

Coral Sea, 150

Corbett, Mike "Smiley," 2, 16, 243

Corran, Alexander, 149–50

Crawford, Sam, xvii, 22, 36, 42, 44, 48, 61, 63, 72, 76, 80, 86, 91, 92, 98, 114, 145, 148, 174, 202–3, 204, 208, 220

cricket, 152, 160–61, 179, 219–20; compared to baseball, 234. See also deck cricket

Crows, Jack, 91–92

Cruse, Lee, 57

Cuba, 98, 137

Dallas TX, 60–61

Daly, Tom, xvii, 26, 51, 75, 159, 193, 235

Davs Dream, 5, 241

deck cricket, 145–46, 174

Delmarva Star, 17

Demaree, Al, 29

Denison TX, 60

Denman, Lord Thomas, 163–64

Desborough, Lord, 231, 232

Des Moines IA, 102

Dixon-Hopcraft, W., 101, 104, 105, 106, 129, 130, 134, 227, 234, 243

Dixon IN, 43

Dominican Republic, 137

Donlin, Mike "Turkey," xvii–xviii, 31, 44, 45, 64, 81, 83, 85, 86, 101, 114, 116, 120, 143, 146, 157, 169, 173, 180, 213, 247

Doolan, Mickey, xviii, 32, 42, 55, 64, 83, 114, 115, 154, 181, 193, 202, 220, 225, 239, 240, 241

Doubleday Myth, 6–7

Douglas AZ, 69–70, 71, 171

Douglas Field (Douglas AZ), 70

Dover, England, 226

Dover Senators, 17

Doyle, A. Conan, 227

Doyle Edith, 35, 57, 91, 128

Doyle, Jimmy, 36

Doyle, Larry "Laughing," xviii, 29, 35, 41, 58, 62, 70, 72, 91, 114, 118, 193, 214, 217–18, 242–43

Dugdale, Daniel, 95–96

Dugdale Park (Seattle WA), 95

Dunne, Edward, 41

Duvall, Clarence, 6

Eager, F. Z., 153

Eagle River WI, 42, 243, 245

Edison, Thomas, 2, 55, 247

Egan, Dick, xviii, 27, 54, 86, 127, 169, 172, 181, 243

Egypt, 11, 33, 112, 234, 200

Eisenhower, Dwight David, 18

El Paso TX, 52, 68–69

Emmanuel, Victor, 205–6

Empress of Japan, 97, 100, 101, 103–7, 109, 110, 114, 116–17, 118, 120, 121, 122, 123, 128, 129–30, 135–36, 171

Evans, Steve, xviii, 27, 53, 65, 81, 110, 239, 240, 102–3, 141, 146, 172, 191, 199, 200, 212, 218, 222

Evers, Johnny, 30–31, 36, 213–14, 228

Ewing Field (Oakland CA), 82

Faber, Urban "Red," xviii, 19, 28, 38, 54, 61, 66, 82, 87, 101, 110, 180, 189, 192

Farrell, Frank, xviii, 171

Farrell, Joe, xviii, 94, 102, 110, 123, 126, 129, 135, 148–49, 152, 157, 182, 184, 195, 198, 201, 211–12

Federal League, 62, 181, 182, 203, 204, 228–29, 213–15, 220, 222, 228, 238, 240

Field of Dreams, 48

Finlay, Frank, xviii

Finlayson, William, 154

Formosa, 129

Fort Bliss TX, 69

Fort Root AR, 70

Fort Smith AR, 43

France, 11, 112

Franks, H., 161

Fremantle, Australia, 171, 173

Fritsch, Walter, 239

Fromme, Arthur, 29, 32, 34, 41, 58, 63, 82, 84, 92, 228

Fultz, Dave, 215–16

Gadsen Hotel (Douglas AZ), 71

Galle Face Hotel (Colombo, Ceylon), 175–176, 178

Gaston Park (Dallas TX), 60

Gehrig, Lou, 17

George V (King of England), 231, 233–34, 235, 236, 242

Gilmore, James, 170, 203, 238–39

The Girl and the Pennant, 46–47

Gleason, John, xviii, 75

Gleason, Kid, 229

Glendora CA, 78

The Glory of Their Times, 24, 47, 78

Gordon & Koppel Field (Kansas City MO), 53

Grand Hotel (Tokyo, Japan), 110, 114, 117

Great Barrier Reef, 150

Great Britain, 113, 232

Great Pyramid, 186–87

Griffith, Clark, 15, 23, 42

Griffith, D. W., 247

Hanlin Hotel (Cincinnati OH), 39–40

Hanlon, Ed, 138–39

Happy Valley Athletic Club (Hong Kong), 131–33

Hartford Courant, 17

Hawaii, 5, 113

Hearn, Bunn "Bunny," xviii, 29, 32, 87, 132, 141–42, 175, 180, 243

Heeman Ed, 242

Helena, 124

Heliopolis Palace Hotel (Cairo, Egypt), 185, 186, 187, 189, 192, 193

Heliopolis Sporting Club, 187

Herrick, Myron T., 224, 225

Herrmann, August, 8, 40, 57, 242

Hewitt, George, 52

Hideyoshi, Toyotomi, 119

History of Worlds Tour, Chicago White Sox and New York Giants, 2, 24

Hite, Mabel, 31

Holland, Mrs. George W., 185–86

Hong Kong, 126, 128–34

Hong Kong Hotel, 130

Hotel Australia (Sydney, Australia), 159, 160

Hotel Bertolini (Naples, Italy), 198–99

Hotel Jefferson (Peoria IL), 42

Hotel Parker (Naples, Italy), 198

Houdini, Harry, 2, 175

Houston TX, 62, 65–66

Houston Chronicle, 63, 64

Hubbard TX, 61, 66

Huerta, Victoriano General, 69

I.I.I. League Park (also known as Three Eye or League Park) (Springfield IL), 41

Imperial Hotel (Tokyo, Japan), 117

India, 11
Indianapolis IN, 160
Indianapolis ABC's, 140
Indianapolis Feds, 239
International League, 31, 62
International Olympic Committee, 18, 19
Isbell, Frank, xviii, 28, 61, 62–63, 68, 76
Ish, Frank M., 213
Italy, 11, 112, 185, 197–216

Japan, 9, 11, 153
Japan Advertiser (Tokyo, Japan), 117
Japanese Exclusion Act, 117
Jennings, Hughey, 139
Jiji Shimpo (Tokyo, Japan), 108, 113
Johnson, Ban, 8, 40, 63, 182, 238, 241, 243
Johnson, Walter "The Big Train," 28, 41,
    42–43, 54–55, 56–58
Jones, Davy, 23
Jones, Fielder, 92
Joplin MO, 41, 54–56
Joplin Daily Globe, 51, 55–56

Kamada, 112
Kansas City MO, 53–54
Kansas City Packers, 53
Kansas City Star, 13, 24
Keefe, Jack, 87, 97
Keihin Press, 108, 109
Keough, Mrs. Hugh, xviii, 173, 216
Keiō Base Ball Association (Tokyo, Japan),
    111
Keiō University (Tokyo, Japan), 108, 110,
    111, 112, 113, 114–15, 116
Kilgore, W. H., 89–90
Kimishima, T., 111
Kinney, Arthur T., xviii
Kinsella, Dick, 66
Kinsella, W. P., 48
Kiviat, Abel, 221
Klem, Maria, 68, 147
Klem, William "Bill," xviii, 8–9, 15, 16, 21,
    63–64, 67–68, 69, 74, 76, 77, 80, 83, 84,
    85–86, 90, 91–92, 101, 112–13, 114, 132,

133, 147, 159, 161, 168, 173, 174, 201–2,
    213, 215, 226, 234, 248
Knabe, Otto, 220
Kōbe, Japan, 110, 118–19, 120
Koombana, 150

Lajoie, Napoleon, 21–22
Lakewood NJ, 92
Landis, Judge Kenesaw Mountain, 141, 248
Lardner, Ring, 10, 15, 29, 73, 86, 87
Laver, Frank, 165
League Park (also known as Three Eye or
    I.I.I. League Park) (Springfield IL), 41
Leverenz, Walter, xix, 27, 42, 53, 60, 70,
    84, 144, 145, 158, 180, 243
Lipton, Sir Thomas, 171, 175, 176–81, 186–
    87, 228
Los Angeles CA, 73–76, 78
Los Angeles Times, 74, 76, 79–80
Lobert, Hans, xix, 32–33, 38, 61, 78–79,
    80–81, 98, 114, 127, 136, 174
Lobert, Rea, xix, 57
London Sketch, 228, 230
Louvre, 222
Lusitania, 229, 237, 238, 239
Lynch, Thomas (tourist), xix, 102, 130
Lynch, Thomas (National League presi-
    dent), 8, 181
Lyric Theater, 46

Mack, Connie, 14, 15, 19, 27, 34
Madame Butterfly, 202
Magee, Lee, 32, 76, 96, 114, 115, 133, 175,
    184, 186, 217, 235, 239
Mall, Ben, 51–52
Manchester Mirror, 233–34, 235–36
Manila, Philippines, 139, 147
Manila Hotel, 139–40, 142, 229
Manila League, 140, 143
Manning, George Jeremiah, 138
Marion Hotel (Salem OR), 92
Marlin TX, 65–66, 229
Martin Hotel (Sioux City IA), 48
Mathewson, Christy "Matty," 29, 38–39,
    53, 54, 56–58, 60–61, 63, 64–65, 68, 73,

Mathewson, Christy (*cont.*)
  78, 79–80, 81, 82, 83, 84, 85, 96, 108–9,
  228–29, 247
Mathewson, Christy Jr. "Matty Jr.," 68
Mathewson, Jane, 68, 82, 96–97
Mattick, Walter "Wally," 26–27, 52–53
Mayes, C. T., 114–15
McAleer, James A., xix, 23, 45, 100, 148
McBride, George, 42–43
McBride, N. E., xix, 209
McCain, Colonel, 138, 143
McCormick, "Moose," 30–31
McGlynn, Frank, xix, 75, 79, 80–81, 86,
  105–6, 115, 120, 130–31, 136, 144, 148–49,
  155, 167, 174–75, 179, 182, 184, 189–92,
  202, 212, 215, 218, 234, 247
McGoorty, Eddie, 156, 160
McGraw, Blanche, xvii, 52–53, 66, 88–89,
  93
McGraw, John, xvii, 2–9, 10, 11, 12–13,
  14–15, 19–20, 28–29, 31, 34–35, 38, 39–
  40, 41, 43, 48, 54, 56, 61, 63, 65–66, 67,
  68, 70, 74, 75, 80, 81, 82, 83, 84, 88–89,
  90–91, 93, 96, 98, 101, 108, 109, 116, 117,
  118, 119, 121, 126, 128, 136, 137, 142, 144,
  150, 151, 153, 157, 161, 162, 167, 169, 172,
  173, 180, 181, 184, 187, 188–89, 192–93,
  195, 201, 204–5, 207, 209, 217, 220, 223,
  229, 230, 231, 243, 245; as manager, 246;
  childhood of, 4
McGraw, Minnie, 88
McNamara, Reverend John, xix, 206–7,
  209
Medford OR, 89–90, 94, 126, 225
Medford Hotel (Medford OR), 89, 90
Melbourne, Australia, 162–69
Melbourne Age, 145, 165–66, 168
Melbourne Argus, 162, 167–68
Melbourne Cricket Grounds, 163
Melbourne Race Track, 168–69
Melkle, Willard, 127
Merkle, Fred, xix, 29, 30–31, 60, 68, 81, 86,
  101, 102, 114, 115, 120, 126, 127–28, 172,
  182, 189, 193, 200, 202, 212, 214

Meyers, John "Chief," 29–30, 58–59, 76,
  77–78, 82, 85, 87
Miller, Victor, 75, 105–6, 115, 130, 155, 167,
  191, 218, 234, 246–47
Miller, Ward, 43
Milwaukee WI, 42, 68
Miners Park (Joplin MO), 51
Minneapolis Messenger, 48
Minnett, Alf, 160
Miyake, Daisuke, 115
Monaco, 216–18
Monte Carlo, 202, 216–18
"Monty Python," 90
Morgan, Sir Arthur, 154
Mori, Shigeki, 115
Mory, Alf, 160
Moulin Rouge, 222
Mount Fuji, 107
Mount Stromboli, 197–98
Mullen, James, 102, 110
Multnomah Hotel (Portland OR), 91, 92
Murao, Jiro, 112
Murphy, Charles W., 213–14, 228
Murphy, John S., 43
Muskogee OK, 58
Myrtle Street Grounds (Ottumwa IA), 45

Nagasaki, Japan, 119–21
Naples, Italy, 197–203
National Commission, 8, 11, 15, 17, 21, 220,
  223–24
National Hockey Association, 19
New Mexico, 1
New South Wales Base Ball Association,
  154, 156, 158–59, 160–61
New York Giants, 2, 16, 19–20, 55, 65, 127,
  229, 246
New York Herald, 49–51
New York Morning Telegraph, 43, 52, 238
New York Times, 31, 103, 127, 185–86
New York Yankees, 246
New Zealand, 5, 112, 146, 164
Niblio, Fred, 156
Nice, France, 216–20

Nicholson, Admiral Reginald F., 140
Northern Pacific Railroad, 93, 96

Oakland CA, 81, 82, 83, 86–87, 116
Oakland Oaks, 87
Oaks Park (Oakland CA), 82
O'Brien, Mrs. Joe, 52
O'Day, Hank, 31, 213
O'Hearn, Charles A., 207–8
Oklahoma, 56–58
Oldfield, Barney, 76
Oliver, C. N. J., 156–57
O'Neil, Norris. L. "Tip," xix, 13, 25, 231
The Onion Club, 172–73
Opium Wars, 130
Oregon, 89–93
Oregon Hotel (Portland OR), 91, 92
Oriental Hotel (Melbourne, Australia), 163
Orontes, 170, 171, 172, 173–74, 175, 180, 182–84, 240
Oroville CA, 83
Osaka, Japan, 110, 116–17, 118, 120
Osaka Daily News, 118
O'Sullivan, Thomas, 154
Ottumwa IA, 44–45, 55, 73
Ottumwa Daily Courier, 45–46
Oxnard CA, 26, 578–79, 192, 234

Pacific Coast League, 26, 52, 82
Page, Ambassador Nelson, 213, 234
Palace Hotel (San Francisco), 81
Pall Mall Gazette, 229–30
Palmer, Will, 77
Panama Pacific Exposition of 1915, 85
Paris, France, 36, 197, 221–26, 231
Pasadena CA, 96, 228
Paso Robles CA, 231
The Peak (Hong Kong), 131
Peoria IL, 42
Pershing, Gen. John "Blackjack," 70
Perth, Australia, 157, 171–72
Phair, George E., 49
Phelon, William, 39
Philadelphia A's, 14, 19, 34, 54, 88

Philadelphia Phillies, 32, 55, 127, 223
Philippines, 12, 126, 134–44
Phillips Dodge Corporation, 69
Pittsburgh Pirates, 22, 173
Plank, Eddie, 19
Players Brotherhood, 29
Players League, 9, 15, 29
Polo Grounds, 30, 96, 116, 177, 246, 247
Pond, Arlington (Arlie) "Duck," 138–40, 142–44
Pope Pius X, 206–8
Portland OR, 13, 90
Portland Evening Telegram, 92
Portland Morning Oregonian, 92
Portland Oregonian, 34
Poupre, Mark (the Birdman from Khartoum), 194
Prince Rupert, 97, 100
Prinz Heinrich, 196–98, 200
Pulliam, Harry, 31
Pyramids, 185, 186, 190, 192

Quiros, 124

Rader, Don, 89
Rath, Morris "Morrie," 26, 52, 83, 96
Reach All-Americans, 113
Reach Sporting Goods, 113, 132
Reber, Doris, 243
Recreation Park (San Francisco CA), 84, 85
Recreation Park (Portland OR), 92
Redland Field (Cincinnati OH), 33, 37–38, 40
Reese, A. B., 55, 56
Rice, Grantland, 222–23, 227, 239, 251–52
Rice Hotel (Houston TX), 62
Richards, Lord Mayor Sir Richard, 162
Ritter, Lawrence, 24, 78
Robinson, Wilbert, 138–39
Rocky Mount Railroaders, 17
Rome, Italy, 33, 203
Rossetti, Daniel Gabriel, 199
Rowe, Charles, 78
Royal Rooters. *See* Woodlands Bards Association

Russell, Lefty "Reb," 36, 40, 45, 49, 58, 59–60, 62, 63, 64, 75, 82, 87
Ruth, George Herman "Babe," 88, 246
Ryder, Jack, 38

Sacramento CA, 81
Sacramento Senators, 52, 81, 213
Salts, Samuel, 45–46
Sammons, Thomas, 108, 110, 112
San Diego CA, 76–77, 96
San Diego Sun, 77
San Francisco CA, 9, 14, 35, 82–88, 116
San Francisco Chronicle, 82, 86
San Francisco Examiner, 49, 83, 84, 86
San Francisco Seals, 82
San Jose CA, 96
Savage Club (Melbourne, Australia), 164
Saylor, Milburn, 160
Schacht, Al, 40
Schaefer Herman "Germany," xix, 23–25, 27, 44–45, 46–49, 53, 65, 69, 81, 86, 89, 100, 101, 102, 103, 109, 120–21, 129, 131, 141, 144, 145, 160, 162, 169, 171, 172, 178–79, 180, 213, 217, 219, 222, 240, 243, 247
Scott, James "Death Valley Jim," xix, 27–28, 41, 54, 58, 68, 70, 77, 92, 101, 102, 114, 115–16, 141, 180, 234, 241
Schalk, Ray, 26, 51, 76, 82, 84, 85–86, 92–93, 96
Seattle WA, 14, 82, 94–95, 120, 176
Seattle Giants, 95
Seattle Post-Intelligencer, 94–95
Selfridge, Harry Gordon, 231–32
Seys, John O., 99–100
shadow ball, 74, 84
Shafer, Arthur "Tillie," 113
Shamrock II, 180
Shamrock III, 180
Shamrock IV, 177
Shanghai, China, 121, 122–29, 130, 132, 142
Shanghai Amateur Base Ball League, 125, 126
Shanghai Race Club, 125, 128
Sheridan, Jack, xix, 8–9, 16–17, 36, 98, 103, 112, 115, 132, 133, 159, 161, 173, 196, 199–200, 229, 234

Shoeless Joe, 48
Sindall, Joan W., 65–66
Sioux City IA, 46–48, 53, 57
Sioux City Tribune, 47–48
Slight, Andrew "Andy," xix, 26, 51, 55, 84, 86, 102, 223
smallpox, 71, 129
Smith, Harry B., 82
Snodgrass, Fred, 29–30, 59–60, 79, 82, 85–86, 192
South Bend IN, 43
South Main Street Park (Tulsa OK), 57
Southwestern League, 70
Spalding, A. G., 5–6, 9–12, 18–19, 21, 36, 41, 43–44, 112, 113, 152, 157, 191, 205, 219, 243
Spalding's World Tour of 1889–1890, 5–6, 18, 36, 41, 112, 191, 205, 218
Spanish American War, 137, 139
Sparrow, Harry, 62, 64
Speaker, Tristam "Tris," 19, 22–23, 38, 44–46, 58, 61, 66, 71, 82, 83, 89, 98, 100, 112, 114, 115, 116, 118, 126, 133, 146, 147, 153, 159, 172, 197, 200, 204, 208, 220, 223, 225, 235, 239–41, 243
Sphinx, 186, 191–92
Spink, Charles C., 99
Sporting Life, 11, 21, 22, 41–42, 158, 217, 238, 239, 240, 242
The Sporting News, 11, 22, 99, 102, 122, 148, 152, 194, 195
Springfield IL, 41–42
St. Albans, 130, 134, 135–36, 137, 142, 143, 144, 145–48, 150, 152–53, 154, 155–56, 174
St. Carlos Opera House (Naples, Italy), 202
St. Francis Hotel (San Francisco CA), 81
St. James Hotel (Paris, France), 221, 222, 224
St. Joseph MO, 53
St. Louis Browns (American Association), 5
St. Louis Browns (American League), 19–20, 27, 53, 73

St. Louis Cardinals, 26, 27, 52, 53, 65, 223
St. Louis Terriers, 34
St. Nicholas Hotel (Springfield IL), 41
Stamford Bridge Grounds, 231, 233, 236
Staunton, Captain, 180, 181, 182, 183
Steinfeldt, Harry, 30
Steininger, Edward, 34
Stovall, George, 53
Strait of Messina, 197
Suez, Egypt, 184
Sugase, Kazuma, 112, 115
Sullivan, Ted, xix, 3–4, 10, 13, 16, 25–26, 30, 31, 34, 58–59, 98, 148, 154, 163, 194, 200, 204–5, 213, 215, 224, 240, 241
Sullivan Sleepers, 16
Sydney, Australia, 147, 150, 154–162
Sydney Cricket Grounds, 156, 158
Sydney Morning Herald, 156, 158, 159, 161

Tacoma WA, 94–95
Taft, Charles P., 228
Taft, William Howard, 32
Takahama, 115
Take Me Out to the Ball Game (movie), 23
"Take Me Out to the Ball Game" (song), 155
Tammany Hall, 239
Tasmania, 164
Taylor, Private Chester, 57
Tener, James K., 181, 228, 243
Terminus Hotel (Nice, France), 220
Tesreau, Jeff, 29, 32, 33, 35, 45, 52, 59–60, 66, 82, 83, 87, 96, 109, 228
Texas, 58–69
Texas League, 59
Texas State Fair, 60
Time, 245
Tivives, 228
Thompson, Tommy, 113
Thorpe, Iva, xix, 39, 78, 91, 111, 114, 120, 168, 171, 173, 174, 197, 206, 209, 211, 222, 249
Thorpe, Jim, xix, 16–21, 29–30, 33, 38–39, 42, 46, 47, 48, 49, 57, 58, 64, 68,

72, 76, 77, 78, 82, 83, 85–86, 91, 111, 118, 120, 124, 128, 146, 167–68, 172, 173, 187, 189, 192, 195, 197, 208, 209–12, 219, 221–22, 232, 242, 243, 246, 248–49; and Olympics of 1912, 16–19, 38, 31, 36; salary of, 19; signing with the New York Giants, 19–20
Three Eye League Park (also known as I.I.I. or League Park) (Springfield MO), 41
Thursday Island (Australia), 149–50
Tinker, Joe, 214, 215, 220
Torres Strait, 147
Torres Straits Pilot (Thursday Island, Australia), 150
Tokyo, Japan, 101, 108–18, 120, 131
Tokyo Times, 117
Trotten, Hal, 192
Tulsa OK, 55, 56–58
Tyler, E. A., 154–55, 157

United States Olympic Committee, 17, 18, 33, 35, 37
University of Washington, 111
U.S. Grand Hotel (San Diego), 77, 78
USS *Saratoga*, 139
USS *Wilmington*, 133–34

Vancouver, British Columbia, 66, 94
Vatican, The, 206–8
Vaughn, Irving, 213
Veeck, Bill, Sr., 15, 29, 108–9
Victoria, British Columbia, 94
Victoria, Hong Kong, 129–30
Victoria Base Ball League, 169
Victoria Gardens Racetrack (Colombo, Ceylon), 179–80
Von Der Ahe, Chris, 3

Wagner, Honus, 22, 32–33
Ward, George, 239
Warren Park (Bisbee AZ), 70, 71
Waseda University (Tokyo Japan), 111, 114–15

Washington (State), 93–96

Washington Hotel (Seattle WA), 95

Washington Park (Los Angeles CA), 74, 76, 77

Washington Senators, 42, 54, 98

Weaver, George "Buck," xx, 25, 39–40, 49, 53, 75, 76, 82, 86, 102, 114, 136, 145, 151–52, 154, 159, 172, 184, 192–93, 195, 248

Weeghman, Charles, 170, 237

Weeghman Park (Wrigley Field), 237

West End Park (Houston TX), 63–64

White, "Doc," 27, 53–54

Willets, Mr., 104, 130

Williams, Harry, 74, 75–76, 79, 80

Wilson, Horace, 111

Wiltse, Della, 68, 149

Wiltse, George "Hooks," xx, 29, 32, 42, 58, 70, 83, 104, 129, 139, 144, 147, 154, 161, 172, 180, 189, 243

Wing, Leon, 85, 87

Wingo, Ivy, xx, 32, 114, 118, 191

Wisconsin, 35

Woodlands Bards Association, 15, 29, 40, 231, 242

World Series, 34, 35, 55

The World Tour Giants and White Sox, 75

Wright, George, 18

Wright, Harry, 18

Yangtze River, 123–24

"Yankee Doodle," 154

Yokahama Gazette, 117

Yokohama Harbor, 107

Yongala, 150

Young, Rida Johnson, 46–47

Zander, Captain, 197